The Brazilian Workers' ABC

for Christy Wines,
with our appreciation
for a wonderful intellect
+ great personality — a great
teacher + worthy representative
of the best of the United State,
Good luck in your new
adventure with Neil.
we'll miss you
John Iny
Jan French

The Brazilian Workers' ABC

Class Conflict and Alliances in Modern

São Paulo • **John D. French**

The University of North Carolina Press

Chapel Hill and London

© 1992 The University of North Carolina Press
All rights reserved
Manufactured in the United States of America

The paper in this book meets the guidelines for permanence
and durability of the Committee on Production Guidelines for
Book Longevity of the Council on Library Resources.

96 95 94 93 92   5 4 3 2 1

Library of Congress Cataloging-in-Publication Data
French, John D.
    The Brazilian workers' ABC : class conflict and alliances in
modern São Paulo / by John D. French.
        p. cm.
    Includes bibliographical references (p.   ) and index.
    ISBN 0-8078-2029-6. — ISBN 0-8078-4368-7 (pbk.)
    1. Trade-unions—Brazil—São Paulo Suburban Area—History—20th
century.   2. Labor movement—Brazil—São Paulo Suburban Area—
History—20th century.   3. Labor policy—Brazil—History—20th
century.   I. Title.
HD6615.S33F74   1992
322′.2′098161—dc20   91-50936
                                                            CIP

Portions of this work appeared earlier, in somewhat different
form, in "Industrial Workers and the Birth of the Populist Republic in Brazil, 1945–1946," *Latin American Perspectives* 16
(Fall 1989): 5–27, and "Workers and the Rise of Adhemarista
Populism in São Paulo, Brazil 1945–1947," *Hispanic American Historical Review* 86 (February 1988): 11–43, and are
reproduced here by permission of the journals.

To Jan Hoffman French,

Dr. J. Bruce French and Helen Harquail French,

and Marcos Andreotti (1910–1984)

Contents

A map of the ABC region will be found on page 69, and a
section of illustrations will be found following page 151.

Acknowledgments

This book is a personal and collective product involving the contributions, large and small, of hundreds of institutions and individuals. In 1980 a grant from the Yale Council on Latin American Studies permitted an exploratory trip to Brazil, while the generous support of the Fulbright-Hays Commission, the Social Science Research Council, and the Inter-American Foundation allowed me to spend a fruitful sixteen months in the field in 1981 and 1982.

The success of any historical research depends, of course, on the preservation and accessibility of relevant primary material. For all the Brazilian decrying of the national neglect of history, my experience has left me with nothing but praise for the public servants responsible for the working archives of the many Brazilian institutions where I worked. My largest research debt is owed, without a doubt, to the Tribunal Regional Eleitoral de São Paulo and its personnel. The TRE's well-preserved archives are a neglected national treasure whose use, in the future, will reshape our ideas about modern Brazilian politics.

Special thanks are due to the director of the TRE's Subsecretaria Judiciária, Dr. José Eduardo da Costa Manso, who enabled me to examine the TRE's judicial records. I must also acknowledge the invaluable assistance of my good friend Geraldo de Souza Machado, at that time chief of the Serviço de Informática. Over the course of many months, Geraldo provided ample evidence of his genuine enthusiasm for my work and his willingness to share the knowledge he had gained in years of employment at the TRE. Similar hospitality was shown by the employees of the Santo André *cartório eleitoral* that covered what used to be the 156° Zona Eleitoral.

The highly professional personnel of the Fundação SEADE (Sistema Estadual de Análise de Dados) and the Arquivo do Estado de São Paulo were of great assistance. I also owe special thanks to Paulo Sérgio Pinheiro, my advisor in Brazil, and to Marco Aurélio Garcia, then director of the Arquivo Edgard Leuenroth at the Universidade de Campinas.

During my research in ABC, I accumulated a special debt to my fellow researchers of ABC's history who actively collaborated with and supported my project, including the acknowledged pioneer, Dr. Octaviano Gaiarsa. I owe special thanks to my colleague and friend Ademir Médici, himself a published researcher, who has always been of great help to me in my research. My good personal friend Valdenizio Petrolli did far more than I had the right to expect. A journalist, politician, historian, and preservationist of enormous energy, Valdenizio gladly joined me in the quest for yet more sources and archives, pleased at finding someone who shared his enthusiasm for ABC's past.

From the beginning of my research in Santo André, I received a warm reception from the president and employees of the Câmara Municipal, including Deize Ramos Fini, then Chefe da Divisão Administrativa. A similar hospitality was shown by the staff at the Câmaras and Prefeituras of São Caetano and São Bernardo do Campo. For help in carrying out research in the Prefeitura Municipal de Santo André, I owe a vote of thanks to a supportive Rodolpho Mansueto Dini, then coordinator of the Assessoria Técnica do Gabinete, and to then-Prefeito Lincoln Grillo. Dr. José Carlos Picolli, of the planning sector, was also most helpful in grounding me in the urban development of the *município*. The employees of the Arquivo Morto and Secção de Estatística helped make my work there a pleasant and fulfilling experience. Valdenizio Petrolli expedited the microfilming of relevant materials at the prefeitura after my departure.

My friend Salvador dos Santos Filho, at that time head of Santo André's Biblioteca Municipal, helped me in using both library and nonlibrary facilities. I was also graciously assisted by my friend Nilza Barbosa do N. Saiki, the then head of the library's periodicals section.

For assistance in carrying out marriage samples in Santo André, I owe special thanks to Octavio de Oliveira, of the 4° Cartório de Notas e Oficio de Justiça, and to Judge Luiz Antônio Garrido de Paula. As president of the Associação Comercial e Industrial de Santo André, Fausto Polesi authorized my research in their archives, in which I was greatly aided by Francisco Canassa, ACISA's Gerente Administrativo. The employees of the archive of the *Diário do Grande ABC* were also of great help in my work, especially Airton Rezende, along with Antônio Manieri of the *Fôlha do ABC* and Alécio Strabeli of the *Jornal de São Caetano*.

In understanding the realities of working-class life and struggles in

ABC, I owe a great deal to my more than fifty hours of interviews conducted with Marcos Andreotti, a lifelong union militant and Communist in Santo André who died in late 1984. Over four months of interviews, I came to understand the admiration felt by the thousands of ABC workers who, whatever their politics, had repeatedly elected Andreotti to union and political office since the 1930s. A man of great personal courage and dedication, Andreotti had done much, since the age of fifteen, to bring a better life to the workers of Brazil. I would also like to thank Philadelpho Braz, retired leader of the metalworkers' union, for deepening my understanding of the 1940s in our recent interviews.

A book marks an important transition which reflects a much longer intellectual evolution. My parents, Dr. J. Bruce French and Helen Harquail French, helped me find my way toward the study of humankind's history, as did Martin Swenson, my junior high school English teacher—a choice that was stimulated by the personal example, while I was still in high school, of the outstanding social historian Herbert Gutman at the University of Rochester.

A history major from my first week at Amherst College, I learned much about my future craft from Professors Andrew Lees, Frederic L. Cheyette, and John Petropulous. Historian Bruce Laurie of the University of Massachusetts provided me with my first introduction to the study of labor history, while sociologist Steve Buff guided me in my undergraduate honors essay on U.S. labor. As an apprentice in an artisanal occupation, I owe a great debt to my graduate teachers at the University of Pittsburgh: Harold Sims, Magnus Mörner, and Murdo Macleod. At both Pittsburgh and Yale, David Montgomery gave generously of his time to this project and inspired me by his personal example, intellectual engagement, and encyclopedic knowledge.

I had my first professional exposure to Latin America, as an undergraduate, with Emília Viotti da Costa, an outstanding teacher with whom I took my first course in Latin American history in 1974. As my dissertation director at Yale University, Emília was generous in sharing her vast knowledge of Brazil and the craft of history. With little tolerance for fuzzy thinking, her challenges to easy assumptions and accepted wisdom have sharpened my skills and immeasurably improved this book at every stage. I am glad to have shared this experience with my friend and colleague Iver Bernstein.

While teaching at Utah State University, I received additional support from the History Department and the Women and Gender Research Institute. Since 1988, the College of Arts and Sciences, the Latin American and Caribbean Center, and the Department of History of Florida International University have been generous in providing needed assistance. I am especially appreciative of the FIU Summer Mini-Semester A Research Appointment that I was awarded in 1988.

The present book has been greatly improved as a result of the contributions of my many friends and colleagues who participate in the annual Conferences on Latin American Labor History that have been held since 1984. I have also benefited from the feedback received during the dozen conference presentations I have given since 1985. In particular, I would like to acknowledge the useful comments and support of Robert Alexander, Charles Bergquist, Daniel James, and Hobart Spalding.

In its various forms, this book has benefited from the careful editing of my friend Barbara Armentrout. I am further indebted to Simon Collier, Barbara Weinstein, Reid Andrews, and Steve Ellner, who provided detailed readings of the book in its final manuscript form. I would also like to thank David Perry, Ron Maner, Julia A. McVaugh, and the rest of the staff at the University of North Carolina Press for bringing the book to fruition. And I am grateful to Alexandra Gomez, who has made precious time available to me over the last three years to finish this project.

Finally, I would like to thank my *companheira* and wife, Jan Hoffman French. Since 1976, Jan and I have shared in the many adventures that have brought us to this point. Giving fully of her energy and intelligence from the beginning, Jan's many contributions have made this book as much a collective project as our children Paul Joseph and Elizabeth Nora.

Abbreviations

ABC   One administrative unit until 1945, the ABC region encom-
         passes today's *municípios* of Santo André, São Bernardo do
         Campo, São Caetano do Sul, Diadema, Mauá, Ribeirão Pires,
         and Rio Grande da Serra.

ACISA   Associação Comercial e Industrial de Santo André (Commer-
         cial and Industrial Association of Santo André)

ANL   Aliança Nacional Libertadora (National Liberating Alliance)

CDP   In 1917, the Comitê de Defesa Proletária (Proletarian De-
         fense Committee) formed to negotiate an end to the São
         Paulo general strike. In 1945, the Comitês Democráticos Pro-
         gressistas (Democratic Progressive Committees), which were
         neighborhood associations, formed at the initiative of the
         PCB.

CGTB   Confederação Geral dos Trabalhadores do Brasil (General
         Confederation of Brazilian Workers), national trade union
         federation founded in September 1946 and outlawed in May
         1947

CIESP   Centro de Indústrias do Estado de São Paulo (Center of In-
         dustries of the State of São Paulo)

CIFTSP   Centro dos Industriais de Fiação e Tecelagem de São Paulo
         (Center of Weaving and Spinning Industrialists of São Paulo)

CLT   *Consolidação das Leis do Trabalho (Consolidation of Labor
         Laws)*

CMSA   Câmara Municipal de Santo André

CMSBC   Câmara Municipal de São Bernardo do Campo

CNTI   Confederação Nacional dos Trabalhadores na Indústria (National Confederation of Industrial Workers), founded in 1946

COSA   Círculo Operário de Santo André (Workers' Circle of Santo André)

CSP   Coligação dos Sindicatos Proletários (Coalition of Proletarian Unions), founded in 1933

DEE   Departamento Estadual de Estatística (State Statistical Department)

DET   Departamento Estadual de Trabalho (State Department of Labor)

DGABC   Diário do Grande ABC

DOPS   Departamento de Ordem Política Social (Social and Political Order Department), a police agency founded in 1924

DRT   Delegacia Regional do Trabalho (Regional Labor Delegacy), subordinate organ of the Federal Labor Ministry

DSP   Diário de São Paulo

ESP   Estado de São Paulo

FIESP   Federação das Indústrias do Estado de São Paulo (Federation of Industries of the State of São Paulo)

FOSP   Federação Operária de São Paulo (Workers' Federation of São Paulo), initially founded in 1905

IAPI   Instituto de Aposentadorias e Pensões dos Industriários (Industrial Employees' Pension and Retirement Institute)

LSN   Lei de Segurança Nacional (National Security Law)

MUSA   Museu de Santo André

MUT   Movimento Unificador dos Trabalhadores (Unifying Movement of Workers), founded in 1945

PCB   Partido Comunista do Brasil (Communist Party of Brazil), founded in 1922

PDC   Partido Democrata Cristão (Christian Democratic Party)

PMSA   Prefeitura Municipal de Santo André

PMSBC   Prefeitura Municipal de São Bernardo do Campo

PPP   Partido Popular Progressista (Popular Progressive Party)

PR   Partido Republicano (Republican Party)

PRP   Partido Republicano Paulista (Paulista Republican Party), the party that dominated São Paulo politics during the First Republic

PSB   Partido Socialista Brasileiro (Brazilian Socialist Party), founded in 1947; a party of the same name existed from 1932 to 1935 in São Paulo

PSD   Partido Social Democrático (Social Democratic Party), a conservative party founded in 1945 that nominated Eurico Dutra

PSP   Partido Social Progressista (Social Progressive Party), the party of Adhemar de Barros, founded in 1946

PST   Partido Social Trabalhista (Social Labor Party), founded in 1946

PT   Partido dos Trabalhadores (Workers' Party), founded in 1979 by Luis Inácio ("Lula") da Silva

PTB   Partido Trabalhista Brasileiro (Brazilian Labor Party), founded in 1945 by Getúlio Vargas

PTN   Partido Trabalhista Nacional (National Labor Party), founded in 1946

SESI   Serviço Social da Indústria (Social Service of Industry), founded in 1946

SP   The state of São Paulo

TRE   Tribunal Regional Eleitoral (Regional Electoral Court)

TSE   Tribunal Superior Eleitoral (Supreme Electoral Court)

TSN   Tribunal de Segurança Nacional (National Security Court)

UDN   União Democrática Nacional (National Democratic Union),
         founded in 1945

UOFT   União dos Operários em Fábricas de Tecidos (Union of Work-
         ers in Textile Factories)

USDS   United States Department of State

USNA   United States National Archives

The Brazilian Workers' ABC

Introduction • Workers

and Populism • Past and Present

in the Brazilian Labor Movement

Brazilian union leaders have only now learned, declared the charismatic head of São Paulo's most important autoworkers' union, that workers must fight their own battles and that trade unions must "become independent, once and for all." Speaking in 1978 on the heels of the first mass strikes since the military coup of 1964, the president of the metalworkers' union of São Bernardo do Campo and Diadema exuded a new confidence that workers could in fact win without outside aid or intervention. Luis Inácio da Silva ("Lula") drew a stark contrast with the populist era before 1964, when labor movements "were started for partisan [political] reasons . . . for the benefit of those in power or for those who were not in power but who desired to be."[1]

Quickly attracting national attention, the May 1978 strikes that catapulted Lula into national and international prominence originated in the suburban industrial region of metropolitan São Paulo known as ABC (after the *municípios* of Santo André, São Bernardo do Campo, and São Caetano do Sul).[2] Over the following four months, the strikes quickly spread to encompass between 300,000 and 400,000 workers throughout the state of São Paulo. For many observers, the down-to-earth Lula personified the emergence of a new, more independent Brazilian working class characterized by a form of militant unionism that was thought to have been absent since the rise to power of Getúlio Vargas in 1930.

Moreover, Lula openly criticized the state-sponsored union structures that were established in the 1930s and systematized in Getúlio Vargas's 1943 labor code, the famous *Consolidação das Leis do Trabalho* (*CLT*).

Lula attacked the *CLT* for castrating the unions and ridiculed the notion that this archaic industrial-relations structure, "constructed when there were hardly any workers in Brazil," was relevant to the "developed Brazil [of the 1970s] with a city like São Bernardo do Campo."[3]

Hailing the "greater class consciousness" of contemporary workers, Lula argued that they were no longer paralyzed by governmental paternalism. Today's workers, he asserted, had finally "ceased to believe in many things that had deceived them for a long time . . . [especially, the belief, due to] the pseudo-benevolences of Getúlio Vargas, . . . that governments could do many things for the working class." For too long, the worker's sense of being "impotent, weak, poor, and miserable" had conditioned him to "look to someone at the top, . . . [to] the people with power, . . . to do everything for him." For too long, the Brazilian worker had been exploited by elite politicians, who were pursuing interests that "were in fact far removed" from those of working people.[4]

Lula went even further and criticized the democratically elected presidents between 1946 and 1964 for having done little for workers. Speaking during a period of negotiated transition from military rule toward democracy, he also expressed skepticism about the opposition's calls for a Constituent Assembly. Such an initiative, he concluded, might repeat "the history of the Constituent Assembly of 1946 . . . [when the workers were] submitted to a constitution made by [and for] the elites" despite all the politicians' rhetoric about freedom and the working class.[5]

The thirty-two-year-old union leader spoke on the eve of an era of widespread industrial militancy that would reach millions in 1979. He used such historical contrasts to make sense of contemporary events that seemed, to most observers, to be without precedent. A striking historical personality, Lula heightened the effect of his carefully calculated naiveté and seeming guilelessness by consciously eschewing a leftist, populist, or nationalist rhetoric that could easily be associated with the past.

Lula's critical and iconoclastic stance highlighted the weaknesses of the legal trade unionism of the restrictive years that had followed the 1964 military coup in Brazil. Although quick to admit his lack of historical knowledge or of any personal experience with unionism prior to 1969,[6] Lula found that his struggle was best served by dramatic emphasis on the total distinctiveness of the "new" or "authentic" unionism of the late 1970s. Indeed, the discovery of the worker as a social force to be reckoned with was, in many ways, the most striking feature of the Brazilian transition toward democracy in the late 1970s and early 1980s.

Brazilian and foreign observers, whether scholars, journalists, employers, or government officials, interpreted the labor militancy of 1978–79 as a break with the whole of Brazil's past, and not with just the dictatorial period after 1964. We are witnessing, sociologist José Álvaro Moisés argued in 1982, the "end of an old cycle and the opening of another, entirely new cycle in the history of Brazilian trade unionism." British scholar John Humphrey also detected, among São Bernardo's autoworkers, "a decisive break with the [older] populist style of mobilization and activity" before 1964.[7]

Such assessments quickly found their way into the scholarly mainstream. Discussing regime transitions in 1985, North American political scientist Alfred Stepan could confidently assert that Lula's "new brand of unionism" stood in marked contrast to the past, when unions were "encapsulated in state-crafted corporatist structures, which reduced the autonomy of worker organizations." The working class, a Brazilian political scientist wrote in 1985, had finally "become organized and imposed its presence" on national life through a "strong, democratic and effective grassroots popular movement."[8]

The innovative "new unionism" also produced what came to be seen as its necessary political by-product in 1979 when Lula founded the Workers' Party (Partido dos Trabalhadores, or PT). Thus, the prevailing scholarly consensus on labor was broadened from the industrial relations sphere to politics; the creation of the PT was widely interpreted as marking a breakdown of entrenched patterns of elite political dominance in Brazil. According to enthusiasts such as Michael Löwy, Lula's Workers' Party marked the appearance "for the first time [in Brazilian history of] a mass party that is the authentic expression of the workers themselves."[9]

The PT, as seen by supporters like Löwy, marked a radical break with the "weighty heritage" of past popular and radical politics, which had been characterized by "rank-and-file passivity and demobilization, maneuvers at the top, and bureaucratic structures." Even North American political scientists have emphasized the PT's novelty as Brazil's first effort to establish working-class-based political organization under trade union leadership. The PT and the "increasingly independent and combative labor movement" that spawned the party, Margaret Keck argued in 1986, were historically unique in bringing "class-specific demands" into a political system where they "had not been important issues."[10]

We thus find a remarkable congruence between the self-perception of a contemporary participant like Lula and our current scholarly understanding of Brazilian labor history. Indeed, the events of the late 1970s seemed to provide the definitive proof that confirmed the scholarly consensus on workers, populism, and the Left that had emerged since the 1960s.

Labor, Populism, and the Left: The Corporatist Consensus

Populism was a form of nationalist, cross-class reformist politics that came to regional prominence during the 1930s and 1940s. As twentieth-century Latin America's most original political creation, populist politics shaped the entire era of development that finally came to an abrupt end with the military coups of the 1960s and 1970s.

Populism is usually defined as a nationalist and multiclass movement, typically urban in nature, that is characterized by an eclectic ideology, a clientelistic mass following, and a charismatic or redemption-oriented leader. Populism emerged during the crisis of oligarchic parliamentarianism and the region's search for alternatives to its traditional export-oriented economic strategies. Integrationist in orientation, populism has been widely viewed as the natural political complement to the era of import-substitution industrialization after 1930.[11]

Under leaders such as Brazil's Getúlio Vargas and Argentina's Juan Perón, populism was also responsible for the transformation of the region's labor movement by linking the trade unions directly to the state. In this way, populists fostered a form of interest representation that is generally characterized as corporatist in nature. Within the broader regional context, the Brazilian example of state intervention in industrial and labor relations has long been viewed as the paradigmatic example of corporatism in which "the state plays a major role in structuring, supporting, and regulating interest groups with the object of controlling their internal affairs and relationships between them."[12]

The capstone of the whole populist structure in Brazil, according to the most authoritative recent exponents of this view of workers' struggles before 1964, lay in the subordination of the trade unions to the state. Labor leaders, it is said, had compromised themselves by accepting the fascistic, corporatist union structures established during the Estado Novo dictatorship (1937–45). They thus adapted themselves to an extremely rigid and overly bureaucratized system designed to inhibit the mobilization of workers. Built from the top down and from the state outwards, official trade unionism derived its strength not from its membership but from its relationship to the elites holding state power.[13]

Unions in the populist era depended upon a strategy of political pressure and bargaining with the state that oriented their activities away from the factories and the rank and file. Subject to strict governmental control, the labor movement had only a limited ability to represent its members' interests within a system of state tutelage characterized not by free collective bargaining but by labor court litigation and governmental wage setting.[14] Acceptance of the law's definition of unions as "collaborating organs of the state" led labor's leadership to emphasize the unions' legally defined role as providers of medical, dental, and legal assistance to individual workers (*assistencialismo*).

Trade union leaders, it is said, discouraged actions that went beyond the demobilizing strictures of Brazil's consolidation of labor laws enacted in 1943, the *Consolidação das Leis do Trabalho*. In establishing what were and what were not legally valid grievances, the intricately detailed *CLT* served as a straitjacket that excluded workplace complaints and emphasized state regulation of employment conditions. Yet populist unionism, it is argued, also failed to effectively represent the workers' interests in the regulatory field because union leaders preferred to rely on the good will of the state. Labor leaders routinely paid more attention to the electoral success of various non-working-class politicians and to the shifting factional alignments within the Labor Ministry than to conditions at the point of production.[15]

Leaders were freed from the pressures of accountability to their membership because they were legally guaranteed the right to represent all the workers employed in a given industry within a certain geographic radius. Organized on a município-wide level, the unions made no effort to achieve a foothold within the factories through union delegates or factory commissions. The system of union financing based on an involuntary, government-collected union tax (*impôsto sindical*) received from all workers, whether union members or not, created further disincentives to mass membership.[16]

The unions did at times attain a numerically significant membership, but they continued to be characterized by a top-heavy bureaucratic structure and to lack real representativeness. Rank-and-file workers were not encouraged to participate in establishing the leadership or direction of their institutions. This demobilizing populist style of organization did,

however, preserve the positions and petty privileges of each union's bureaucratized leadership and prevented problems that might disturb its
non-working-class allies. Not surprisingly, the result was the phenomenon
of trade union *peleguismo* (derived from the word for saddle blanket)—a
bureaucratic and progovernment tendency that thrived, given labor's sym-
biotic relationship with the state.[17] Although strikes were by no means
unknown, populist unionism was incapable of organizing the laboring
masses for ongoing struggles. Rather than developing from within the
factories, the sporadic strike movements of that era were marked by dif-
fuseness, spontaneity, and lack of effective leadership. Indeed, union leaders on the whole shied away from militant strike actions that might invite
repression by the state.[18]

Brazil's populist unionism before 1964 thus failed to effectively represent
the workers' economic interests and workplace grievances. Can the excessive politicization of the unions in this period, the critics ask, be defended
in terms of a conscious trade-off between piecemeal economic gains and
concrete political advances? The populist era was, after all, a time of great
nationalist enthusiasm and of much-acclaimed programs of fundamental
social reforms. Yet the consensus view emphasizes that workers in fact
gained very little in the political arena during this period of cross-class
nationalist alliances symbolized by the amorphous *trabalhismo* (laborism)
founded by Getúlio Vargas. Firm positions could hardly be expected from
the "bag of cats" (*saco de gatos*) that was Vargas's Partido Trabalhista
Brasileiro (PTB), but the other so-called popular parties and opportunistic
populist politicians like Adhemar de Barros and Jânio Quadros were even
less interested in real change to benefit the workers than was the PTB.
Despite all the political hoopla and populist rhetoric, workers remained
dependents of the state, serving as a mass base for maneuvers by elements
of the dominant classes. The populist experience, in this sense, represented no break with the Brazilian tradition of political subordination of the
popular classes.[19]

Critics have also vigorously criticized the strategy adopted by the Left of
participating in this amorphous populist alliance, saying that it further
weakened the struggles of the popular classes before 1964. Despite its
claim of being the vanguard of the working class, the relatively strong
Communist Party (Partido Comunista do Brasil, or PCB), led by Luis
Carlos Prestes, followed policies defined not by workers' needs but by nationalist mystifications, statist infatuations, and Soviet foreign policy. The
Communists were characterized by their top-down approach and were

consistently opportunistic in both the trade union and the political-electoral arenas.[20]

Communist unionists contented themselves with penetrating union leadership bodies at any price because they were eager to exploit the petty advantages of the corporatist labor structure. The "parallel organizations" that grouped unions horizontally outside of the law, the Left's greatest innovation, were little more than bureaucratic organisms of a leadership distant from the rank and file. Dedicated to infiltrating the state labor apparatus, the Communists forsook the option of independently mobilizing workers on behalf of their own interests. The actions of the PCB reinforced the state-sponsored labor system it criticized rhetorically, making these structures a more effective fetter on working-class advances.[21]

Sharing Brazilian statist ideology, the Communist Party subordinated class and democratic demands to general political questions of national development. As leaders of the only significant radical group with a popular base, they placed their following in tow behind a mythological "progressive national bourgeoisie." Opportunistic to the core, their electoral strategy became captive to the passing needs of so-called populists like Adhemar de Barros or Jango Goulart.[22]

The dramatic mass strikes of 1978–79 seemed to confirm this already widely accepted view of the fatal weaknesses of earlier working-class and leftist movements. Moreover, the underdeveloped state of Brazilian labor historiography encouraged the teleological temptation of seeing past errors as leading inexorably to the "new unionism" and the PT. Much scholarly research took place during the 1970s, but it tended to focus almost exclusively on events during the First Republic (1889–1930); there were no empirically based studies of the workers' movement after 1930. When works on this period began to appear in the late 1970s, each established the falsity of one or another aspect of the established consensus—yet none challenged the total logic of this remarkably convincing corporatist synthesis of unionism, the state, radical movements, and conventional electoral politics.[23]

Populism's Lasting Legacy: A Flawed Vision of Brazilian Labor History

This book is the outcome of an investigation that began in 1979 with the realization that the established wisdom about workers and populism in

Brazil was historically questionable and conceptually flawed. The opening of Brazil's Nova República in 1985 can help us to achieve historical perspective on the nation's last extended period of electoral democracy, the Populist Republic of 1946–64. As the books are closed on twenty-one years of military rule, the existing historiography can now be seen as the final by-product of the populist era itself. Although advanced as a conscious revolt against the populist heritage, the current corporatist consensus was still decisively shaped by the intellectual effort to come to terms with the radical disappointments of the populist past. To arrive at a new interpretation, we must grasp the intellectual trajectory of this antipopulist synthesis.

Brazilian intellectuals and leftists in the mid-1960s were anguished by the ease with which the Right's revolution triumphed in 1964. They were stunned as they witnessed the collapse of their hopes for imminent radical reform, if not revolution. Although the labor movement was widely believed to be the nation's "fourth power" in the early 1960s, the truth was dramatically revealed on 31 March 1964, when, as Francisco Weffort has put it, both the government and the labor movement that supported it fell "practically without struggle, . . . [collapsing] like a house of cards."[24] Whatever their individual political perspectives, the losers of 1964 went through a wrenching reevaluation of the past in an effort to make sense of this unexpected reversal. This reevaluation was especially difficult because so many had shared the optimistic postulates of the reformist ferment and the developmental nationalism of the populist era. Indeed, the general certainty of forward movement toward a better, more just, and more humane society in Latin America underlay the first serious effort to come to terms with populism in the early 1960s.

In his classic 1965 essay, Torcuato Di Tella concluded that populism, for all its limitations, was still Latin America's best hope for meaningful reform. He described populist movements as garnering mass popular support with an anti–status quo message that crossed class lines. He argued that populism did "not result from the autonomous organizational power" of the popular classes, but he did not see populism's admittedly non-working-class leadership as an inherently negative feature.[25]

The reformist optimism reflected in Di Tella's essay soon gave way, however, to a more radical rethinking of the course of Latin American development. Over the next ten years, it became clear that Brazil's right-wing military coup was not an exception, but a portent of things to come. As disillusionment spread and deepened, Latin American intellectuals and foreign Latin Americanists were torn between their conviction that change was essential and their despair about the military coups that had so soon followed a more hopeful time. In this frustrating context, the one thing that Left-leaning scholars could do was to revolutionize their own ideas through a wholesale rejection of the past. The more optimistic (if mechanistic) modernization theory was now replaced with the more pessimistic and critical dependency perspective. Many broke dramatically with their earlier belief in a "progressive national bourgeoisie" or in the democratic mission of the middle classes. Spurred by the Cuban Revolution, many became convinced that only a more radical and revolutionary course could alter the historical scenario in which cross-class nationalist alliances, as in Brazil, seemed to produce defeat rather than advances for the popular classes.

As the first of the new wave of military interventions, the 1964 Brazilian coup was viewed as marking the end of a whole historical era. Many concluded bitterly that the time had arrived for an intellectual autopsy of what Kenneth Erickson, writing about Brazil, called "the corpse of populism." Burying his own earlier hopes and illusions, Erickson criticized even the term *populist* for its "misleading implications" and argued that populism's "apparently antiestablishment policies" merely masked "the fact that political elites from the ruling class lead and control populist movements." Others, like Brazilian sociologist Florestan Fernandes, denied that there had ever really been an authentically populist or popular movement in Brazil before 1964 and claimed that there had been only "a '*trabalhista*' manipulation of the masses, described with greater precision by the term demagoguery."[26]

The new corporatist synthesis presented populism as primarily a form of social control that, "despite rhetoric to the contrary," served "the class aims [not of workers but of] . . . politicians from the ruling class or petty bourgeoisie." By preventing "workers from building autonomous organizations," the movement channeled popular energies in directions that did "not challenge the existing class structure." Denying any but transitory gains for workers, Erickson, Hobart Spalding, and other scholars emphasized that advances "received as favors granted by populist politicians" crippled and weakened the labor movement and left the popular masses without "the collective strength to defend their gains" against reactionary attack.[27] Criticism was directed against leftist political and trade union leaders who had allowed their movements to remain weak and subordinate in the populist era. These scholars were especially critical of the existing left, particularly the Communist parties, who had forsaken socialist revolution for ambiguous theories of national democratic revolution by stages based on multi-class alliances against imperialism. It had taken the military coup of 1964, Francisco Weffort argued, to unmask the previously dominant concept of "bourgeois-democratic revolution through populism and nationalism."[28]

Yet even those who elaborated these new views of populism were aware, on some level, that the intellectual clarity of the revisionist postmortem was achieved at the expense of an understanding of the relationship between populism and the working class. Their confident judgments left unresolved the troubling question that had long bedeviled the Left: "Why did workers succumb to the blandishments of populist politicians," Erickson asked, "if the latter did not move the locus of political *power* down the social pyramid?"[29] If populism, as Weffort insisted, was indeed a "betrayal" of the popular masses, why did working people willingly "serve as a support for a [populist] regime in which they were dominated?"[30]

In answering these questions, the revisionists built upon a small but important body of empirical sociological research on migration, urbanization, and industrialization begun in the late 1950s and early 1960s.[31] Looking back with the advantage of hindsight, the disillusioned analysts initially made these sociological observations about rural-urban migration the key to understanding mass support for populism. Populism, for these authors, was closely related to the massive postwar industrial expansion in Brazil and elsewhere that had brought millions of migrants from rural or semirural backgrounds to burgeoning cities such as São Paulo to serve as unskilled factory workers.

The explanation of mass support for populism could thus be found, pioneering scholars like Francisco Weffort argued, in the absence of a developed sense of class consciousness on the part of a working class suffering from "premature massification." Brazil's rapid urbanization had created a mass society, without class cohesion, whose individual members were in a state of "political availability." Weffort went further in a polemical 1965 essay that categorized populism as typical of a situation where "the working class assumes the behavior of the masses," that is, of the "petty bourgeoisie." Brazil's atomized working class in the populist era, Weffort argued, lacked the distinct sense of class identity or "strong internal solidarity" characteristic of workers in nineteenth-century Europe.[32]

Experiencing the move to the city as a step upwards, the migrants' individual revolution disposed them to support the status quo. These rural migrants were illiterate, inexperienced in political or associative life, and lacking in proletarian traditions. They were therefore thought to have exhibited traditional attitudes that inhibited a class perception of the world.[33] Seeking paternalistic relations similar to those in their areas of origin, these "available urban masses" responded readily to populist politicians who manipulated them for their own interests in both the labor and political arenas. The success of demagogic populists such as Getúlio Vargas and Adhemar de Barros is thus thought not only to reflect an absence of class consciousness, but at the same time to have inhibited its formation.

The conservatizing political impact of rural migration in the populist era also gained credibility through a contrast with the independent militancy of the anarchist-led workers' movement before 1930, based among European immigrants. Possessing traditions of working-class militancy, the immigrant working class of the First Republic was thought more capable of class-conscious behavior than the native-born workers of rural origin who predominated after the Revolution of 1930 that brought Getúlio Vargas to power.[34]

As conceived by these analysts in the 1960s, the early workers' movement seemed, above all, an idealistic crusade in a nation where the social question was still treated as a matter for the police. Moreover, the dominant radical tradition of the First Republic, anarchism, was untainted by association with the failed legacy of communism, while its antistatist rhetoric had great appeal to scholars and activists living under a repressive military regime.

Thus by the end of the decade, Latin American intellectuals had arrived at an apparently satisfactory analysis of the politically challenging problem of populism. Yet these initial generalizations themselves soon came under attack from a number of angles in the 1970s. In Brazil, the development of a new line of historically oriented research into the workers' and radical movements during the First Republic invalidated the only substantive historical comparison underlying these views. Originating in an effort to identify the "elements of the genesis of populist mechanisms in Brazil," empirically based studies by Azis Simão, Paula Beiguelman, Sheldon Maram, Boris Fausto, Michael Hall, and Paulo Sérgio Pinheiro all highlighted the weaknesses of the early labor movement.[35] Sheldon Maram, among others, emphasized the ephemeral and ineffective nature of the anarchist-led workers' movement, which was crippled by ethnic tensions and the fundamental class ambivalence of the average immigrant. Michael Hall argued that although it was politically convenient as "a way of criticizing the developments of the populist period," the "legend of immigrant radicalism . . . [marked by] exemplary class consciousness and militancy . . . did little justice to historical reality . . . [and had for too] long distorted perceptions of Brazilian labor history."[36]

These studies undermined the stark contrast drawn earlier between an autonomous immigrant workers' movement before 1930, based on the violent rejection of capitalism, and a later domesticated movement, based on Brazilian-born rural migrants, that succumbed to populism. Moreover, scholars discovered that the co-optation and manipulation of workers and their organizations by politicians and the state were not unique to Getúlio Vargas and the populists. Although the new research did not cover events beyond 1930, it certainly suggested that scholars were still far from making sense of the actual historical experience of Brazilian workers.[37]

At the same time, historically oriented research in Argentina and Brazil on the period immediately after World War II challenged the implicitly reductionist portrayal of the weak class-consciousness of Latin American workers of rural origin. A short essay by Argentine scholars Miguel Murmis and Juan Carlos Portantiero decisively rejected Gino Germani's rural migration hypothesis as an explanation for Perón's mass following in 1946. The initial triumph of the Argentine populist was better explained, they argued, as a rational effort by organized labor to enhance its leverage within the Argentine political system.[38]

Breaking with elements of his earlier beliefs, the Brazilian scholar Francisco Weffort joined the attack by denying that the composition or outlook of the masses was responsible for popular failures before 1964. In his imaginative and forceful polemics of 1973 and 1974, he declared that such explanations were only the latest manifestation of the Brazilian elite's traditional belief in the inherent backwardness of the popular classes (*ideologia de atraso*). The blame for labor's repeated defeats, he argued, lay with the fatal and destructive misleadership offered to workers by their supposed leaders and self-proclaimed vanguards long before 1964.[39]

Weffort based his conclusions on a historical foundation that was firmer than that of earlier sociological studies. He was also the first scholar to stress the crucial nature of the post–World War II transition in Brazil. Following the pioneering labor analyst Evaristo de Moraes Filho, Weffort emphasized the postwar survival of the corporatist labor legislation established by Vargas under the dictatorial Estado Novo regime of 1937–45.

Weffort contrasted the statist straitjacket of trade union *unicidade* (rejection of union pluralism) and state tutelage of civil society with the democratic pluralism and the free play of conflicting forces that should have characterized the newly established liberal democratic order.[40]

Weffort's essays originated the current orthodoxy on the nature of what he called "populist unionism" after 1945. He was unequivocal in his condemnation of the policies of the Communist Party during its period of strength after World War II. By failing to break with the unions' dependence on the state, the PCB had condemned the working class to economic and political impotence. Reflecting a scholarly discourse increasingly based on a posited polarization between the "State" and "Civil Society," Weffort's persuasive antistatist stance also helped decisively to shift scholarly views of Getúlio Vargas, who had been looked upon with some sympathy in earlier debates.

As the man who had contributed more than any other to the consolidation of the centralized state, Brazil's preeminent populist leader Getúlio Vargas was now viewed more cynically.[41] The reformist and nationalist claims of trabalhismo were now taken at less than face value. After decades of propaganda about Vargas's gifts to the workers, populism was now presented, without ambiguity, as a form of political and economic control of the working class by the state.[42] Working-class support for populists could now be seen, in the words of Weffort's colleague José Álvaro Moisés, as a "spontaneous reaction" of a working class "unable to go beyond its instinctive reactions" due to the absence of correct revolutionary leadership.[43]

Weffort's imaginative reconstruction of the history of the Brazilian working-class movement was not without its critics. Even in 1973, Carlos Estevan Martins and Maria Hermínia Tavares de Almeida had challenged the logic of Weffort's critique of the Left in 1945. In 1979 Ricardo Maranhão's brief book, *Sindicatos e Democratização*, disputed the empirical foundation of Weffort's characterization of the postwar conjuncture. Yet these critiques lacked the compelling force of Weffort's reconceptualization of the sweep of Brazilian labor history.[44]

For his readers, Weffort's essays were a radical rupture with past understandings, and his work had an extraordinary impact on Brazilian intellectual life and the Latin American debate on the nature of populism. Weffort's rejection of structural determinism seemed to offer a way out of the fatalistic notion that things had to turn out as they did. It also allowed a hopeful rediscovery of the working class as a historical actor capable of its own choices. Workers were no longer to be presented as the passive product of a given social process or historical experience, but as a group capable of self-directed action, if led properly.[45]

Weffort's essays appeared in Brazil at the moment of the apparently definitive consolidation of an all-powerful military state. Writing at the height of the regime's much-touted "economic miracle," Weffort spoke to the feelings of political inefficacy that gripped an oppositional intelligentsia who had witnessed the collapse of the mass student movements and the armed opposition of the late 1960s. Yet his analysis was marked by an attractive optimism that held that, under the surface, something new was being born. Moreover, his discussion of the Brazilian Osasco and Contagem strikes of 1968 seemed to provide proof that the populist-communist-nationalist past was being overcome and replaced by a new radical thrust in the workers' movement.[46]

The views of Weffort, which reflected the evolving ideas of a significant group of intellectuals, received empirical validation during the labor agitation of 1978–79, and Weffort went on to become secretary general of the newly established Workers' Party. But although he claimed to have rejected the notion of working-class weakness and backwardness, he had not in fact resolved the populist conundrum that had been answered in more pessimistic ways by previous observers of the working-class majority. In a voluntaristic fashion, Weffort and his followers merely counterposed a hidden or misled, yet inherently revolutionary, working class to the historical realities of the past.

While exalting the working-class-in-the-abstract, Weffort and many later scholars rejected everything that the working class and its leaders, whether Communists, *trabalhistas*, or independents, had done or stood for before 1964. Based on still shaky empirical foundations, the intellectually forceful arguments of these scholars did not represent any real coming to terms with a contradictory and complicated past. In finding the answer to the paradox of populism in wrong leadership by the Left, they merely reformulated the key question on a different plane: Why did the workers follow leaders whose policies not only failed to defend their interests effectively but also perpetuated their domination by employers and the state?

When the present research project began in 1979, it was already clear that the existing generalizations about workers, populists, and the Left in

Latin America were wildly speculative in nature.[47] In 1985, the year that my dissertation was completed, historian John J. Johnson noted the absence of "studies at the national and local levels that [would] provide a solid historiographical base [for] generalization about Latin American labor." And that uniquely Latin American phenomenon "commonly labelled populism," he went on, had been studied to date almost entirely on the national and elite levels. We know far too little, he suggested, about the meaning of populism or populist ideology for workers and other members of the popular classes.[48]

Influenced by my extensive background in European and North American labor history, I realized in 1979 that only an empirically based grassroots study could provide new answers to replace the frustrating abstractions of the accepted historiography. A convincing refutation of the corporatist synthesis, I concluded, could be achieved only by approaching the problem of workers and populism from the bottom up—by moving from the specific to the general, from the local to the national, and not the reverse. Thus this book examines labor, industrial relations, and the political history of the suburban industrial region of Greater São Paulo known as ABC. As Brazil's fourth-largest industrial center since the 1930s, the ABC region was a natural choice for study, given its homogeneous industrial working-class composition and its wide spectrum of large-scale manufacturing enterprises. Moreover, labor militancy and working-class radicalism had characterized ABC long before the dramatic autoworkers' strikes of 1978–80 that produced Lula, the "new unionism," and the Workers' Party.

This book starts with the establishment of the first factories in ABC at the turn of the century, and it ends at mid-century with the consolidation of the Populist Republic that would endure until the military coup of 1964. *The Brazilian Workers' ABC* is not, however, a community study in the conventional sense. Rather, I place local developments firmly within their broader regional and national context in order to advance new causal explanations about the origin of the Brazilian industrial and labor relations system and the nature of urban electoral politics in the populist era.

My study of this important industrial region reveals a reality radically different from what we have been led to expect. While I expound on the fundamentals, the ABCs of working-class life and politics, I demonstrate the central importance of the clash of class interests between industrial workers and their employers. At the same time, I argue that a purely conflictual model cannot explain the outcome of these struggles, which are determined, above all, by the central importance of the workers' alliances with other social classes, groups, and individuals. Thus, the book provides a new approach to the classic question of workers and populists while shedding light on the nature of the populist politics identified with the figures of Getúlio Vargas and Adhemar de Barros.

Part One • Industrialization and

the Crisis of the Old Order, 1900–1945

One • The Rise and Decline of Revolutionary Unionism, 1906–1933

hen the São Paulo Railway was inaugurated in 1867, the profitable coffee railroad cut its way through the sprawling and sparsely settled parish of what was then called São Bernardo, today's ABC. The residents of this vast region practiced subsistence agriculture and provided services to travelers on the road from São Paulo to Santos. The English-owned São Paulo Railway quickly became the focus of the local economy, and the two railroad stations closest to São Paulo became the future industrial districts of Santo André and São Caetano.[1]

Significant industrial development did not occur in ABC until the turn of the century, when two substantial textile factories were opened in Santo André. By 1907, the textile factories and other, smaller enterprises in ABC were already employing at least 1,000 workers in a local population of 10,000, thus guaranteeing ABC's status as the preeminent industrial suburb of São Paulo. As in São Paulo, ABC's workers were recruited from the large body of European immigrant workers who flocked to the state of São Paulo.[2]

The earliest labor militancy in ABC occurred in the region's largest, most modern, and most mechanized manufacturing establishments. The first major work stoppage occurred in 1906 at ABC's largest factory, the Ipiranguinha textile plant in Santo André, which employed 500 workers.[3] The Ipiranguinha stoppage typified the wave of strikes that occurred in greater São Paulo after 1901. This generalized labor ferment coincided with the birth of an incipient urban labor movement, which held its first national and statewide meetings in mid-1906.

Although few in number, the 20,000 or so workers who labored in the state of São Paulo's large and small manufacturing establishments were the most singular by-product of an economic boom that irrevocably altered the Paulista economy and labor force between 1890 and 1900.[4] Increased urbanization and incipient industrialization had produced an occupational diversity that created new possibilities for modern forms of labor struggle. In a society where few had industrial training or experience, the rapid expansion of industry had created a strong demand for skilled labor. Yet large employers increasingly sought after 1901 to use their growing economic, technological, and political power to undermine the bargaining leverage of their skilled employees.[5] The workers affected by this increased employer belligerence moved from a belief in "natural" opportunity for those with skill to a belief in collective struggle.

The Ipiranguinha strike that began on 23 February 1906 was very consciously a skilled workers' job action undertaken by the factory's 150 weavers, who were angered by the failure of management to repeal its latest reduction in the higher-than-average piece rates they had been paid in the past. The weavers' month-long stay-at-home strike demonstrated the cohesion of these skilled workers and their certainty that they were indispensable; the weavers did not object when the owner reopened the factory's spinning section, because they did "not consider [the reopening] harmful to their cause."[6]

A smaller textile industrialist might soon have settled the strike on terms at least partly, if not fully, favorable to the demands of its prized weavers— but the large and wealthy Silva, Seabra & Cia. had the resources and connections to turn events to its favor. The Ipiranguinha began by cutting off the strikers' access to the company-owned store, while successfully requesting the dispatch of a state militia unit to Santo André. The company's resident owner, Agenor de Camargo, had been displeased by the initial response of local police authorities, who failed to treat the peaceful stoppage as an ipso facto violation of public order to be immediately and vigorously repressed.

The militia unit was initially withdrawn after a group of weavers, discouraged by three weeks of hunger and privation, returned to work. But this handful of fainthearted workers quit again after only a day back on the job. The management thereupon announced the firing of all the striking weavers, again laid off the workers in the spinning department, and declared an indefinite lockout. The militia then returned to Santo André, where the accompanying high-ranking police official was lodged in the home of factory-owner Camargo—an indication of favoritism that did not evoke comment in a society rigidly divided between the subordinate classes and the wealthy and powerful.

The determined managers of the Ipiranguinha had still further means to defend the company's interests. During what would be the last days of the stoppage, the strikers were arrested and beaten by militiamen, and their access to local merchants, from whom they had been buying food with contributions raised in ABC and São Paulo, was blocked. The final straw for the strikers, however, came when the company announced that weavers would be brought from Tatuí, São Paulo, to reopen the factory.

The spontaneous struggles of skilled workers like the Ipiranguinha's weavers coincided with efforts by several small groups of radicals to build an organized workers' movement in São Paulo. Although attacked for introducing the pernicious idea of class conflict to Brazil, the propaganda, celebrations, and polemics of these largely foreign-born anarchist and socialist intellectuals had been largely divorced from the lives and troubles of the state's working people in the 1890s. Yet the radicals had gained the allegiance of a number of practically oriented worker-intellectuals eager to bring the gospel of labor struggle to the masses. The most important recruit was Edgard Leuenroth, a printer who became the most outstanding labor leader in São Paulo throughout the First Republic.

The self-educated son of a German pharmacist, Leuenroth had joined the Socialist Circle of São Paulo in 1903, converted to anarchism in 1904, and in 1905 founded the first of a succession of labor papers, *A Terra Livre* (*A Free Land*).[7] Leuenroth's newspaper sought, above all, to "take an active part in the workers' movement." In its first issue, it attacked those who preached a sterile "isolation" from an insufficiently radical labor movement. The effect of such isolationism, it said, would be to "reduce anarchism to a simple political movement of the extreme liberal, to a philosophical tournament of dilettantes strolling through the florid fields of theory." As part of their commitment, Leuenroth and his fellow radicals established the Federação Operária de São Paulo (FOSP) in 1905 to prepare a conference of these new labor activists in the state.[8]

A Terra Livre embraced the Ipiranguinha strike as an encouraging sign of resistance against a large and powerful employer. Although lacking advance knowledge of or involvement with the striking weavers, the editors of *A Terra Livre* did not allow their own more ambitious agenda to prevent them from doing everything possible to aid the strikers. Strike support funds were raised in São Paulo, and most top FOSP leaders, including Leuenroth, traveled to Santo André on numerous occasions to offer their solidarity in local strike rallies—a "foreign influence" soon criticized by local authorities.

As activists, these labor militants sought to learn lessons for the future from the success and failure of different tactics and forms of struggle. Indeed, the issues raised by the Ipiranguinha strike were debated by the forty-three delegates to the First Brazilian Workers' Congress, held in Rio de Janeiro less than a month later. Exclusive craft unionism, the gathering concluded, was not the most effective form of organization for an industrial setting, and they recommended, instead, organization of a single industrial union that would include all workers.[9]

The congress participants sought to establish the proper guidelines for collective action by a social class that was only then emerging, even in developed regions like São Paulo. In building the labor movement, they faced a formidable barrier in the widespread blurring of the distinction between wage earners and other social groups, such as small manufacturers and merchants. Indeed, the majority of urban working people in São Paulo did not accept the notion of a horizontal division of society between employers and wage earners, which forms the basis of any coherent workers' movement. When the first factories were established in ABC at the turn of the century, the economy was family based and the majority of the region's population made their living through subsistence agricultural production, extractive activities, and employment in the region's small charcoal works, sawmills, and pottery works. For these working people, the idea of organized, collective struggle by labor was meaningless. Even as more and more workers fell into dependent status, large numbers were still bound to their employers through a common immigrant status and a shared ideology of hard work and thrift.[10]

Thus there were profound cultural, social, and political barriers to working-class organization in a world where a mix of laboring and petty entrepreneurial activities made the population's "definition as characteristically working class more difficult."[11] The earliest labor militancy in ABC originated in large textile factories precisely because the separation of owners and employees had gone the furthest in that industry. Yet even there, weavers were still tied to an ideology of unlimited opportunity—even though the employers were violating it in their drive to establish a modern and more truly capitalist manufacturing industry.

The fifty labor delegates who gathered in late 1906 for the First Workers' Conference of the state of São Paulo also debated the best and most useful "method of association" for workers and the "practical means" to better the wage earners' "economic and moral conditions."[12] At the same time, the São Paulo conference was not a gathering of trade unions in the modern sense but rather an undifferentiated labor and radical movement where leagues, centers, the radical labor press, and educational circles far outnumbered the few organized skilled trades, such as the printers or masons. Although exhilarated by their involvement in the epoch-making strike against Paulista Railroad six months earlier, the state's labor activists were chastened by the strike's defeat at the hands of a repressive state government.[13]

The Paulista working class as such is not, it is clear, to be equated with this tiny minority of organized workers and their leaders. Yet the existence and initiatives of this minority of labor activists can by no means be dismissed as irrelevant to the mass mood of the state's urban workers. Indeed, the central demand advanced by the delegates—the eight-hour day— would become the unifying demand of a broad movement of perhaps 10,000 workers in São Paulo and ABC in May 1907.[14] The eight-hour strike movement was joined by the employees of ABC's second-largest textile factory, Bergman, Kowarick & Cia., along with workers of other smaller local shops, who were undeterred by the Ipiranguinha defeat the previous year. Once again, the weavers were in the vanguard, and the FOSP hailed ABC's participation as "the beginning of an awakening in the interior."[15]

The 1907 eight-hour movement was an unpleasant surprise for São Paulo's ruling elites, and its outcome illuminates the political circumstances and constraints under which labor relations developed in São Paulo during the First Republic. The eight-hour strike spurred the state's thirteen leading textile manufacturers to form the Center of Weaving and Spinning Industrialists of São Paulo (Centro dos Industriais de Fiação e Tecelagem de São Paulo, or CIFTSP), whose founders included Frederico Kowarick and Justiniano José Seabra, owners of ABC's two largest factories. Eager to make the state authorities aware of their needs, the new group requested police intervention to help keep their factories open during the strike.[16]

To win state support, the newly organized industrialists had to appeal to a highly centralized state government that was responsive primarily to the coffee planters and allied commercial interests who dominated São Paulo's economic and political life. Although industry was as yet accorded only secondary importance by the government, the textile industrialists could depend upon the authoritarian mentality of Paulista plantation owners, who still enjoyed absolute authority on their own estates less than twenty years after the abolition of slavery.[17]

The maintenance of authority in the face of a disruptive threat from below was a principle easily grasped by the Paulista ruling groups, and they responded to the eight-hour strike with unrestrained hostility. The headquarters of the FOSP was raided on 14 May 1907, and its leaders were among those sentenced to prison in the strike's aftermath. In his annual message, state president Jorge Tibiriçá proudly reported the prompt repression of the disorder and the jailing of its instigators. In the federal congress, São Paulo's deputies led a successful drive for a deportation law aimed at foreign-born "threats to the public order," which was named the "Adolpho Gordo Law" after its Paulista author.[18]

The ruling Partido Republicano Paulista (PRP) found easy answers to the labor problem in the dogmas of classic nineteenth-century liberalism. After urging the use of a "strong hand" to deal with the eight-hour strike, the party's state newspaper argued, in classical laissez-faire terms, that the contractual relations between employer and employee were strictly private and individual in nature. Governmental intervention was justifiable—in fact, obligatory—only when necessary to guarantee freedom to work during a strike for all those who wished to.[19]

The solidity of São Paulo's oligarchical system of one-party rule contributed to the PRP's adoption of a purely repressive policy toward labor. Under this prevailing system of unrestrained boss rule (*coronelismo*), less than 2 or 3 percent of the total population voted, and the more-difficult-to-control urban voters were an insignificant minority of the state electorate. Under these conditions, the state's politicians were incapable of conceiving of a popular politics based on appeals to an urban constituency that included workers. Throughout the First Republic, the preferred strategy of the state's industrialists and government officials was repression, not dialogue: the social question was indeed a matter for the police.[20]

Yet strikes and labor organization were not viewed exclusively as law-enforcement problems everywhere in Brazil. The federal district of Rio de Janeiro provides a particularly clear example of the enormous impact that political factors could have upon an emerging labor movement. There was no controlled rural vote in Brazil's largest city, and political convenience had enfranchised all government employees, including some working-class groups, such as railroad workers. As a result, the city was the center of the "yellow," or noncombative, labor unions, often formed with the sponsorship of local politicians, who far outnumbered the Left-led unions of the city.[21]

This type of moderate, or politically minded, unionism was not feasible in São Paulo, where the oligarchy saw working-class efforts to alter the terms of the sale of their labor as violations of the public order. The state's repressive response thus reinforced the prestige of radical ideologies and leadership among the state's workers and added cogency to anarchist arguments that "capitalism and the state, boss and government, are allies for life and for death."[22]

Yet the accepted characterization of the Paulista labor movement before 1930 as anarchist or anarchist-led has blinded many historians to the movement's quite distinct phases of political development.[23] The anarchists' hegemonic role in São Paulo after 1917 was not, in fact, characteristic of the first phase of activism through 1908. Anarchists did not, for example, unquestionably dominate the Second Workers' Congress of the State of São Paulo held in April 1908. Like earlier national efforts, this gathering of delegates from twenty-one organizations included many moderate nonanarchists, among whom were the representatives of ABC's weavers and furniture makers. At the outset, a Socialist leader criticized the FOSP for taking on an "anarchist character" that violated the ideas of many workers. Seconding these complaints, a weaver from ABC also vocally opposed anarchist positions on several counts.[24]

Although such political differences created tension in 1908, they did not lead to hard-and-fast divisions, because hostility to employers and to the state served to unite workers with diverse political and occupational positions. São Paulo, unlike Rio de Janeiro, had no political interlocutor open to dialogue with the workers and willing to shelter their organizations.[25] Instead, the lack of any positive inducement by the state led to the workers' toleration for the aggressive revolutionary rhetoric of the anarchists.

Anarchists and Stonecutters

São Paulo's incipient labor movement had advanced rapidly between 1906 and 1908, but the dozens of newly established organizations, including the FOSP, disintegrated during the economic downswing between 1909 and 1912. The dispersal of labor's tiny vanguard demonstrates the fragile and seemingly ephemeral nature of labor organization. Yet these struggles had taught labor activists like Leuenroth important lessons that were carried over to labor's brief revival in 1913–14 and to its high point between 1917 and 1919.

The brief resurgence of labor in 1913 was marked in ABC by a dramatic strike of skilled stonecutters (*canteiros*) in the sparsely settled mountainous district of ABC known as Ribeirão Pires. Organized in 1908, the anarchist-led International Union of Ribeirão Pires Stonecutters sustained the highest level of continuous struggle of any group of ABC's workers in the First Republic. Their story highlights the economic advantages that allowed some nonfactory artisans to maintain organization and thus to disproportionately shape anarchist ideals and labor's tactics.

The hundred stonecutters who worked the quarries of Ribeirão Pires produced the curb- and paving-stone required by the enormous expansion of the city of São Paulo since the late nineteenth century. The 1913–14 strike grew out of a dispute over past-due wages, which led eighty stonecutters to strike the Duarte e Aranha quarry. The administrator called for police aid, and a detachment of two hundred soldiers from the state militia were sent to occupy the district. Despite the soldiers' intimidating presence, the stonecutters stayed out on strike for months, and the community divided into "anarchists" and "sheep," the name given to workers who refused to join the strike.[26]

Events took a dramatic turn when a group of forty or so soldiers "struck" as well, with complaints about poor food and having to sleep in the quarries. When a second detachment arrived, fighting broke out between the two groups of soldiers and the strike was then put down with vigor. The arrested soldiers and stonecutters, including women and children, were marched to São Bernardo between two rows of soldiers, and the union's leaders were indicted in São Paulo on charges of propagandizing anarchism.

The bitter defeat did not, however, still the stonecutters of Ribeirão Pires indefinitely. In 1917, they struck twice, first for a salary increase and later in solidarity with the São Paulo general strike. They struck once in 1918, three times in 1919—in May in solidarity with the general strike, in August over a salary reduction, and in November for an increase—and again in 1920, 1922, and 1923.[27] In none of these strikes did the contractors of Ribeirão Pires again resort to the repressive measures used in 1913, because they had learned that soldiers could not cut stone nor force a determined body of strikers to do so.

The stonecutters' bargaining strength is illustrated by the 1922 agreement that ended a "very cohesive" strike in Ribeirão Pires. The employers pledged to pay the union's strike expenses, to readmit all strikers, and to end their effort to appoint an administrator whom the stonecutters rejected. Moreover, the contract specified that new men could not be hired for thirty days, in order to allow the return of any stonecutters who had left during the strike.[28]

The market conditions governing the sale of the labor of the Ribeirão Pires stonecutters provided a firm foundation for their sustained militancy, relative economic success, and direct ties to anarchism and the organized workers' movement. The stonecutters' union was the only group from ABC represented at the 1913 and 1920 national workers' congresses. They were also the only local group that participated actively in the affairs of the national Brazilian Workers' Confederation (Confederação Operária Brasileira, or COB) in 1913–14. Represented at the 1914 state anarchist conference, they were the only ABC sponsor of a 1919 anarchist May Day rally in São Paulo that hailed the coming of communism.[29]

Anarchism captured important aspects of the lives and aspirations of these skilled artisans. The anarchist vision of a society of freely cooperating workers' federations must have seemed natural to the stonecutters, given the irrelevance of the employer to the process of production.[30] Working by task, the stonecutters were paid upon delivery of the slabs to the contractor, who then shipped them by rail to São Paulo; the contractor's only contribution was to provide the workers with the coal needed to prepare their tools. The existence of competing quarries in greater São Paulo heightened the pressure that the workers could bring to bear on the contractors through a strike or slowdown. The leverage enjoyed by local stonecutters also guaranteed the survival of an ongoing, recognized anarchist leadership that both reflected and strengthened the cohesion of this small occupational community.[31]

The strengths enjoyed by the stonecutters stand in marked contrast to the organizing prospects of the factory proletariat, who possessed little or no leverage to counter employer pressures, blacklisting, or state repression. The fact that even skilled weavers were unable to prevail over their employers suggests the major disadvantages of workers in large-scale industry. Would-be organizers of ABC's factory hands thus faced far greater difficulties in organizing, and the survival of such leaders and their ties to both the workers and the labor movement were necessarily more tenuous than in Ribeirão Pires.

Sheldon Maram was the first to alert historians to the objective economic realities that influenced prospects for organization by workers in different occupations and industries.[32] Yet he failed to explore the profound impact of these differential success rates on the composition of the workers' movement throughout the First Republic. Factory workers were a majority of the working class, but they made up only an infinitesimal portion of the labor movement despite their greater tendency to strike (almost always unsuccessfully).[33] Stable, skilled artisanal groups in nonfactory settings, by contrast, had a disproportionate impact in terms of both the composition and the outlook of the labor movement itself. Thus the First Republic's organized workers' movement was composed preponderantly of skilled nonfactory workers, whether artisans or not, while the majority of the unorganized labor force was employed in large factories.

Although formed in opposition to the ideology of upward mobility spawned by petty industry and artisanry, the emerging labor movement could not help but be disproportionately shaped by the militant dimensions of the same world of small enterprise. Indeed, ABC's stonecutters personified the strategy of "direct action" that the anarchists preached as the favored method of "proletarian rebellion." Only strikes, demonstrations, boycotts, and sabotage, the anarchists declared, could win the emancipation of the working class. Direct action against the employers, they argued, was the workers' only certain means to achieve real gains; moreover, direct action was also the people's only means to defend or enforce the rights to which they were entitled.[34]

The anarchists believed that direct action advanced both the proletariat's immediate material needs and their long-range revolutionary interests. They spurned intermediaries outside the realm of employer-employee relations, and they deemed talk of laws, governmental regulation, political parties, or elections—indirect action, in a word—as futile and even harmful to the workers' cause.[35] The anarchist ideal required that each and every worker display equal initiative, courage, and decision. In essence, the anarchists preached a form of working-class self-reliance that was especially appropriate for the stonecutters, who did indeed "unite themselves" to "live in struggle."[36]

Yet the vast majority of the working class, especially factory workers, neither belonged to nor understood even the more modest immediate aims of unionism—as Paulista labor leaders frankly admitted. To persevere in the face of these discouraging realities, anarchist labor militants had to reject the argument that labor struggle was useless without majority support. Herein lay the origin of the unionism of militant minorities that marked the labor movement of the First Republic. In a 1908 article, "Let Us Be Frank," the FOSP openly declared that they did not wish to make their "societies a complex of unconscious workers," "an amalgam of individuals without . . . a spirit of struggle." Rather, they favored a union composed of the minority of militant activists, the "flower of the workers' energies," who provided the movement with its essential "impulse, force, and solidity."[37]

Hence, the militants counseled against the closed shop—a factory or other enterprise where union membership is required for employment—and voted down the proposal for strike-relief funds supported by Santo André weaver Valentino Rossi at the Second Workers' Congress of 1908. To provide strike relief, they argued, would attract "unconscious workers" who lacked the necessary spirit of self-sacrifice and who would return to work once the funds were exhausted.[38] It was not that the radical labor intelligentsia failed to realize that "the larger the number of unionized workers, the greater the [union's] activity and energy";[39] rather, it was that in practice only a few groups, such as the stonecutters, even came close to achieving an unbreakable unity of purpose—facilitated, in good part, because they were so few in number.

The organizational model of early Paulista anarchists—an extreme federalism based upon the rejection of delegated authority—was better suited to the small-scale world of tens or hundreds, as in Ribeirão Pires, than it was to the thousands or tens of thousands involved in large-scale industrial manufacturing. As Azis Simão has noted, the union in these small production units functioned as a primary group based upon informal relations between individuals who knew one another well. Bureaucracy and hierarchy were anathema to this world, which tended to reject even formal distinctions between the rank-and-file and leaders.[40]

Important aspects of the theory and practice of São Paulo's early anarchist-led workers' movement, it is clear, were inappropriate for the new world of the industrial proletariat. Yet it would be wrong to dismiss these early anarchists as an atavistic expression of an insignificant minority of the working class. Although reduced to a handful of individuals at times, they worked tenaciously to achieve a strategic breakthrough by organizing the growing factory proletariat. The key to success, they were convinced, lay in finding the appropriate strategy and tactics. After all, the relative weakness of labor organization among industrial wage earners did not mean that their discontent had disappeared, but only that the weapons used in the past were ineffective.

As anarchist labor activists drew lessons from earlier defeats, they reaffirmed their earlier judgment about the impotence of exclusive craft unionism in textile manufacture, which employed 40 percent of the state's industrial workers.[41] At the same time, the difficulty of establishing trade unions in most industrial occupations led Paulista militants to modify their thinking about the organization of "workers' leagues" or "unions" on a geographic basis. During the heady days prior to 1909, labor's leaders had preferred separate organizations by craft or industry to leagues or unions of mixed occupations; by the World War I era, however, the neighborhood workers' league was given new emphasis as the appropriate mechanism for organizing industrial workers.[42]

Labor's leaders also concluded that a passive withdrawal of labor power or a dependence upon labor-market strengths alone could no longer win victories. The solution, they believed, was direct action on a mass scale through an offensive strategy of mass mobilization designed to guarantee the striking workers' cohesion while discouraging the weaker members of the class from strikebreaking. However, the success of this tactic was dependent upon a spontaneous mass militancy, which did not occur until the later years of the First World War.

The São Paulo General Strike of 1917

Although generals without an army, Leuenroth and his associates were well prepared when the economic difficulties of World War I finally provided them with a mass constituency responsive to their message of class struggle and working-class organization. By May 1917, the movement in São Paulo was in a period of unqualified revival, with renewed public agitation and the onset of strikes in the textile industry. On 9 June, Leuenroth launched a new anarchist labor newspaper, the famous *A Plebe*, which served as the guiding force in labor's rebirth over the following years. Increased popular suffering and discontent resulted in the intensification of protest actions in the city in early July, including the looting of food warehouses.[43]

The police and soldiers patrolling the streets increasingly clashed with strikers and demonstrators, leaving many workers hurt and arrested. The subsequent shooting death of a twenty-one-year-old Spanish-born shoemaker on 10 July led to the proclamation of the first general strike in Brazilian history. Tens of thousands of workers closed down the city of São Paulo. Within days, the strike extended to São Caetano, São Bernardo, and Ribeirão Pires as well as to cities in the interior of the state. On 17 July, even the railroad workers of Paranapiacaba in ABC joined in this massive outpouring of anger and solidarity.[44]

The vigor and extent of the 1917 labor rebellion revealed the depth of discontent among Paulista workers and took industrial employers and the state government by surprise. Although the government's repressive response recalled the events of 1907, labor's leadership conducted the strike on a far more centralized basis than the eight-hour movement of ten years before. In 1907, preexisting unions had conducted the factory-by-factory negotiations that ended the strike, and the FOSP had played an inspirational rather than an active leadership role. In 1917, by contrast, the city's various radical newspapers, workers' leagues, and political-social associations created a Comitê de Defesa Proletária (CDP) that drafted demands for the whole movement and oversaw negotiations with employers and the state. Indeed, some doctrinaire anarchists questioned the degree of centralism implied by the creation of the CDP.[45]

Not only was the 9 July formation of the CDP a new departure for Paulista labor, but its 12 July list of fifteen demands marked an important change in emphasis for the Paulista workers' movement. In framing a platform of struggle, the CDP consciously reflected the grievances of the unskilled factory workers who were numerically predominant in the strike. The demands for an end to child labor under the age of fourteen and a ban on night labor for women and for youth under eighteen were especially relevant to the textile industry.[46]

Other CDP demands addressed general working-class concerns, such as the need for a wage increase of 25 to 35 percent, prompt payment of salaries every two weeks, an eight-hour day, job security, and a 50 percent increase in the overtime differential. A third category of demands spoke to the defense of the new labor movement, including freedom for arrested workers, respect for the right of association, and no reprisals against active strikers. A final category of demands reflected the widespread urban discontent with shortages, high prices, and black marketeering: although such matters fell outside the realm of strictly employer-employee relations, the CDP demanded steps to lower the prices of essential foodstuffs, curb speculation, halt adulteration, end evictions, and reduce urban rents.

Yet the most noteworthy change in the views of the anarchist-led workers' movement was left unstated for reasons of theory: the nation's most intense and extensive display of direct working-class action would be used to wrest concessions from the state as well as from employers. It is not, as is often argued, that the CDP's anarchist leaders were contradicting their "antipolitical" stance by "formulating demands to the Brazilian state."[47] In fact, the antistatism of the anarchists in São Paulo has long been misunderstood; anarchist theory had always recognized a valid role for "political struggle," especially the "fight for the rights of economic association" and in defense of the people's legal rights of free association and expression.[48] The CDP's demands for the release of strikers and for the right to organize were consistent with the traditional anarchist stance toward the state: leave us alone to pursue our conflicts with employers.

Faced with a hostile state, the anarchist-led labor movement had demanded governmental nonintervention because they were confident that, barring repression by the state, the workers would be able to defend themselves through "direct economic action, pressure, and resistance." The outstanding innovation of 1917, however, was the prominence given to demands that required positive action by the state, and not simply governmental neutrality in labor conflicts. Indeed, the victorious end of the strike was reached not only by employer concessions but also by written pledges by the São Paulo state government to implement existing regulations on these matters and to seek further social legislation.

The possibility of resolving working-class grievances through other means, such as state action, had long been hotly debated by the labor movement. Prior to 1917, anarchist labor activists had categorically rejected the passage of proworker laws as useless and harmful. They justified their position by citing the proven ability of certain groups of workers, usually skilled, to win gains through their own strength. Thus they had presented direct action by conscious and "strongly organized" workers as a panacea for all, despite its limitations for unskilled industrial workers.[49]

The implicit recognition of a new, positive role for the state in 1917 marked these leaders' first admission of the limits of an exclusive emphasis on the tactics of self-reliance and direct economic action. They had come to realize that the means of struggle that produced solid results for the stonecutters of Ribeirão Pires were not equally relevant to all workers. Reflecting the difficulties of organizing the industrial working-class majority, a step had been taken toward adding forms of "indirect" action to labor's repertoire.

The rush to organization in August and September 1917 was not restricted to the traditional skilled mainstays of the Paulista labor movement. Although for *A Plebe* the Ribeirão Pires stonecutters would remain a model to be emulated by other groups of workers and even other stonecutters, the locus of organizational dynamism was in the geographic workers' leagues. As such leagues gained strength, they sought to organize unions in the largest occupations represented among their local memberships.[50] For the first time, cohesive organizations began to be built among the railroad workers of metropolitan São Paulo, including those employed in the mountainous ABC district of Paranapiacaba.[51] The upsurge of 1917 also saw the establishment for the first time of effective union organization among São Paulo's textile workers—an effort led by José Righetti, who remained the outstanding leader of the *categoria* (branch of industry) through the 1930s. A weaver who was an enthusiastic anarchist, Righetti led the União dos Operários em Fábricas de Tecidos (UOFT), founded in June 1917, which achieved bargaining rights for the first time in several of the city's textile plants by 1919.[52]

The anarchists' efforts to give coherent form to this unprecedented working-class militancy led to the refounding of the Workers' Federation of São Paulo (FOSP) on 24 August 1917. The platform adopted by the new FOSP reveals the two-sided evolution undergone by the Paulista labor movement since 1908. On the one hand, the platform reflected the influence of the unskilled industrial working class in its shift away from an *exclusively* economic form of organization and struggle—a step away from the more dogmatic forms of anarchist theory. On the other hand, this same shift in composition also facilitated the radicalization of the avowed goals of a labor movement freed from the constraints of the moderate and often economistic mentality of the skilled. The declining importance of these skilled groups after 1909 and the heady experience of mass action by the unskilled majority in 1917 opened the way for the anarchists' ultimate goal of an openly avowed revolutionary unionism based on direct action. Warning that all gains short of a revolution were relative, null, or deceptive, the FOSP's 1917 platform committed the union federation, first and foremost, to the "fall of the dominant social regime, [the] cause of the tyranny and exploitation to which the working class" was subject.[53]

The radical tenor of the refounded FOSP was shaped by labor's astounding success between São Paulo's first and second general strikes in 1917 and 1919. After rising to positions of unprecedented influence and visibility, however, Paulista labor radicals discovered that in the end even direct action on a previously unimaginable scale was incapable of defeating a vigorous counterattack by Paulista employers and the state government. By 1920, labor's organizations had been destroyed, mass involvement had declined, and it appeared as if little had been gained despite the energy and effort expended. The Brazilian anarchist and workers' movement splintered in the aftermath of defeat, as revolutionaries devoted their energies to bitter polemics—not against the enemy, but against one another.

Of the defeats suffered by labor in all of Brazil, one of the most thorough was that in São Paulo, where the subsequent decade of "labor peace" was guaranteed by heightened employer vigilance and systematic state repression. A decided labor revival in São Paulo occurred only after 1930, by which time the anarchists are incorrectly believed to have been reduced to irrelevance. In fact, São Paulo's anarchists remained the decisive force and the dominant ideological influence in the surviving labor movement well into the early 1930s. When the First Republic was finally overthrown in October 1930, only the anarchists, although weakened, had the forces to initiate a reorganization of the Paulista labor movement. In mid-March 1931, they organized the Third São Paulo Workers' Conference and once more refounded the explicitly anarchist FOSP—an organization whose representative nature was recognized by even its Communist rivals.[54]

Unfortunately, excessive attention to the ideological polemics between anarchists and their Marxist rivals had long obscured the extent to which all of São Paulo's labor movement—whether anarchist, Communist, Trotskyist, or socialist—was influenced by a shared anarchist heritage. It was not explicit adherence to anarchist theory that united Paulista labor, but rather a common form of trade union practice that had grown out of the state's difficult organizing conditions.[55] This shared theory and practice of "revolutionary unionism" saw the trade union as an institution of "conscious" minorities, which were distinguished from the "unconscious" mass of the working class. Trade unions were to be restricted to the most committed workers in order to avoid the domestication of the revolutionary spirit of the workers' institutions. Aware that such militancy was far from typical of the rank-and-file majority, labor activists embraced the theory of militant minorities, which both explained a discouraging reality and provided the strength to struggle onward.

Radicalized by their experiences, the determined activists who made up the Paulista workers' movement in 1930 still saw trade unions both as vehicles to gain material betterment and as the means for the revolutionary overthrow of the existing social order. Emphasis on the latter goal necessarily placed greater value on the resolute minority than on the vacillating majority, who were less able to grasp the broader goal of working-class liberation. Yet it was precisely this fusion of the workers' bread-and-butter concerns and the working class's revolutionary mission that exposed leftist Paulista labor leaders to potential disaster when the regime of Getúlio Vargas introduced new labor policies after 1930.

The Revolution of 1930

The meaning of the Revolution of 1930 for workers was unclear, but there was no doubt that it was *not* the start of the social revolution preached by Brazil's anarchists and Communists. Although the new revolutionary establishment was determined to follow more conciliatory tactics toward urban workers and their problems, it had not given up the repression of labor militants despite its propaganda, and occasional employer charges, to the contrary.[56] Rather, the scope of the state's repressive role was now limited by the definition of an area of legitimate union activity that was no longer subject to automatic police action.

The new government's famous Unionization Law of 19 March 1931, Decree 19,770, broke sharply with the negative and repressive policies of the past by according trade unions a clearly defined legal status as "consultative organs" of the state. Although São Paulo's conservative classes saw such innovations as dangerous and demagogic incitements, government officials like Labor Minister Lindolfo Collor saw sound conservative reasons for the new unionization law: banning "all propaganda of sectarian ideologies" within the legal labor movement, Decree 19,770 also provided for state tutelage of the unions. The Revolution, Collor declared, would put an end, once and for all, to "the old and negative concept of class struggle."[57]

Yet such governmental talk of class collaboration seemed blatant nonsense to the radical activists who had sustained the Paulista labor movement through the difficult decade of the twenties. They correctly perceived that the new unionization law was not meant to ratify the autonomous initiatives of radical labor. Rather, the government proposed to create cooperative legal unions, which, once officially recognized, would receive the state's support—to the detriment of radical-led organizations.[58]

The unionization law was denounced by anarchist and Communist union militants as an effort to divide and demoralize the working class, to destroy trade union freedoms, and to establish a fascist-style unionism as Mussolini had done in Italy. The real purpose, a São Paulo utility workers' union quite rightly observed in 1934, was to "impede the development of the revolutionary organizations."[59] Indeed, the new government's tactics eliminated, in theory at least, the confusion created by the previous regime's failure to separate the suppression of revolutionaries from the repression of "legitimate" labor organizations.

In according the state the right to recognize and regulate trade unions, the new unionization law injected the Revolution of 1930 and its many factions directly into the workers' movement as contending forces. Under these conditions, the traditional minoritarian approach of São Paulo's labor Left was potentially fatal. As a competing organizer of the workers, the state outflanked the Left by exploiting the gap between the radicalism of the activist core that made up most unions, and the more modest and immediate agendas of the masses of workers. After all, the radicals' hegemony within the São Paulo labor movement before 1930 had been due in large part to the high personal cost of union militancy, which radicalized many activists while discouraging sustained participation by workers who had no overarching sense of mission. By lessening the costs of union activity, legal unionism created the basis for political pluralism within the labor movement and consciously fostered the emergence of new, more moderate, labor leaders.

The Revolution's labor initiatives would have been less threatening if São Paulo's small but hardy band of radical labor activists had been leaders of a mass-based trade union movement deeply rooted among the workers of São Paulo's industrial park. Yet the common mistake in the literature has been to confuse the moral righteousness, working-class authenticity, and spirit of self-sacrifice of these activists with the notion that they "represented" or "spoke for" the Paulista working class.[60]

The shift in the state's role was irksome for radicals because it occurred precisely at a moment when the general political upheaval caused by the Revolution had created new possibilities for labor mobilization. Indeed, the confusion and frustration of many of São Paulo's radical activists would have been minimized if the government of Vargas had in fact been pursuing an antilabor policy, as they charged. Instead, the government's tactics disoriented leftist labor activists, who had for thirty years denounced the government for handling the workers with the policeman's club.[61] By ending the state's open identification with the industrialists, the new regime made the work of radical labor militants more difficult and forced them to redefine their strategy of revolutionary unionism if they were not to be swept aside.

By mid-1933, the growing state labor movement had largely accepted the new legal trade unionism, whether grudgingly or with enthusiasm. Anarchist and Communist arguments against participation had lost cogency as labor discovered the advantages offered by the new legal structures—much like the pattern in Rio de Janeiro during the First Republic. Governmental recognition, it was clear, did not necessarily mean government's enslavement of the workers or its contention of their demands and struggles.

In any test of size, membership, or influence, the legal trade union movement far outweighed both the anarchist FOSP and the Communist Frente Sindical Regional. In August 1933, this new reality received formal expression with the foundation of the Coalition of Proletarian Unions (Coligação dos Sindicatos Proletários, or CSP) at the initiative of the capital's union of bank employees.[62] With the support of all but the far Left, the coalition represented the solidification of a non-Communist and nonanarchist, but by no means subservient, leadership within the Paulista labor movement.[63] Although the CSP's power and cohesiveness should not be overestimated, it did introduce a new labor stance on the controversial issue of politics. "The unions," the CSP said, "have the defense of their categorias as their only and exclusive end and are completely distant from any and all movements of a political character."[64]

The coalition's stance reflected the differing ideological positions of member organizations, as well as a new conception of the relationship among working-class leaders (the "militant minorities" of past theory), the mass institutions of the working class, such as unions, and politics. The coalition had discovered the advantages of differentiating the economic— as represented by the trade union—and political—as represented by the party—aspects of working-class struggle, which had been fused in revolutionary unionism.

Anarchist critics, of course, rejected the CSP's nonpolitical claims; and politics had not, of course, disappeared from São Paulo's trade union movement.[65] Indeed, a completely nonpolitical stance would have been surprising, given the new legal trade unions' linkage to the government. Because the state was itself the object of political pressures that directly affected labor, the CSP would have to act politically in order to pursue even strictly trade union goals. Moreover, the consistent application of a truly nonpolitical position would have isolated the CSP from potential allies outside the arena of industrial relations who could influence the state.

By 1934, CSP leaders officially joined a newly formed non-Communist Coalition of the Lefts, organized to contest the planned 14 October state elections. Yet even as the CSP violated its own nonpolitical rhetoric, it still refused to pledge the trade union organizations *as such* to a given political trend.[66] Unlike the anarchists, the more radical elements of the CSP had found a new mechanism for the pursuit of the political goals important to the workers' movement: the political party and the electoral alliance.

These innovations in labor strategy have a direct bearing on the decline in anarchist influence in São Paulo after 1931. From the outset, the anarchist FOSP had steadily lost ground because of its principled refusal to accept the regime's unionization law, which had helped create the CSP. In a self-fulfilling prophecy, the FOSP's secretary general, the baker Natalino Rodrigues, had declared in 1931 that the anarchists preferred the "disorganization" of their unions to any compliance with the law. Three years later, another FOSP affiliate declared that "the disappearance of all union organizations" was "a thousand times to be preferred" to submission to Decree 19,770, an "unacceptable monstrosity."[67]

The suicidal nature of the anarchists' resistance to the changes of the early thirties has often been noted, but not the origin of their dilemma. Anarchist theory held that the trade unions were schools of anarchism through which the workers would be educated about their mission to overthrow capitalism. The new, legal unionism represented an invasion of their only means of revolutionary action because they rejected the party as a mechanism to pursue their revolutionary goal. An intensified purism and sectarianism marked the anarchists' inability to adjust, and they were further disillusioned by the receptiveness of workers and labor unionists to the new politics of the period.[68] The revolutionary class par excellence, it seemed, was happy to be invaded by the impurities and influences of other classes and the state. To remain true to their beliefs, anarchists isolated themselves from other union activists and, more importantly, from the masses of workers. Organized anarchism thus condemned itself to extinction within the working-class movement it had done so much to build in the previous thirty years.

As a minority even of the Left, the Communists had faced a similar dilemma in São Paulo between 1930 and 1933 because they too had frontally rejected the new legal unionism and the resulting political pluralism symbolized by the CSP. Yet unlike the anarchist FOSP, the Communists would go on to become a leading trade union current in São Paulo by 1935. The PCB's success reflected in part their greater tactical flexibility in the face of the government's new tactics. Although opposing governmental recognition of unions on any but the workers' terms, the PCB was still realistic enough to recognize as early as 1931 that the law provided "possibilities" that could be exploited by the workers in their struggles; a realization that, combined with grassroots pressure, eventually led to a reversal of the Communists' initial uncompromising opposition to the new legal unionism.[69]

The final element of the relative Communist success in São Paulo in 1934–35 can be found in the answers that Communists provided to the minority of revolutionary-minded workers faced with the state's transformation of the union structure. If the goal of overthrowing capitalism was not to be lost, the Communists argued, then revolutionaries needed an organization—a revolutionary party—separate from the mass institutions of the working class such as trade unions. To continue to be revolutionary, radical activists would have to become political, and the party's prestige and credibility were enormously enhanced when it was announced in 1934 that the legendary *tenentista* hero Luis Carlos Prestes had joined the PCB.

To the conscious minority of radical workers, the Communists in 1934 and 1935 offered a new conception of the militants' role. Rather than being abstract embodiments of their class, labor activists would be the leaders of a working class that, despite varying levels of militancy, would move toward greater class consciousness through struggle, led by their "vanguard," the Communist Party.

Unions would remain schools for revolution, and a "conscious minority" the teachers, but revolutionary propaganda would be of less importance to the learning process than conflict with the employers and the state. In this conception, it was essential that the primary goal be mass membership for the trade unions under Communist control—even if this involved significant sacrifices of revolutionary purity. These changes implied, above all else, a new relationship between the leadership and each categoria as a whole. It was essential that the unions' "conscious minority" begin to conceive of their role as leaders of the majority of the work force, whether union members or not. It was no longer possible to simply substitute themselves for the working class, as had been the tendency in so much left-wing rhetoric.

Although shaped by new state initiatives, the vibrant labor movement that emerged in the early 1930s in São Paulo was not produced by the laws written by bureaucrats and lawyers in Rio de Janeiro. Confronted with new challenges, labor responded creatively by exploiting the advantages offered by the new laws while striving to circumvent their disadvantages. To do so, they had to forsake the revolutionary unionism of the past and move from a trade unionism of "conscious minorities" to one of potential majorities. The increased politicization of labor's struggle led the nonanarchist factions of the state trade union movement, whether revolutionary or not, toward an increased interest in labor-oriented political parties and electoral politics. Labor's growing interest in indirect action, its acceptance of legal trade unionism, and its abandonment of revolutionary unionism changed the forms of working-class activism and radicalism in São Paulo but left the movement's goals of working-class emancipation unchanged.

Two • Workers and the Search

for Allies, 1917–1935 • Union

Legalization and the Politics of Labor

he citywide general strike of mid-1917 in greater São Paulo, the first in Brazilian history, was followed later in the year by equally impressive stoppages in Rio de Janeiro, Bahia, and Rio Grande do Sul. The workers, the Paulista anarchists wrote, had awoken from a state of "enervating apathy" with a spontaneity that fueled a "strike movement that touched the roots of revolt." And the distant news in late 1917 of the victory of a group of Russian anarchists and maximalists led by one Vladimir Illyich Lenin added to the radical activists' growing conviction that the moment of revolutionary reckoning was rapidly approaching.[1]

Yet experienced labor militants like Edgard Leuenroth had few illusions about the workers' strength or their enemies' determination. Preaching the unity of Brazil's "social vanguard," *A Plebe* in late 1917 emphasized the need for vigorous organizing while working-class enthusiasm was still high.[2] Anarchist activists like weaver José Righetti, leader of São Paulo's textile workers, were indefatigable as they spread the gospel of working-class strength through organization and struggle. In 1918, Righetti helped found a Workers' Union (*União Operária*) in neighboring Santo André, where he had relatives, and the new organization quickly gained the support of workers in many of the district's largest factories, especially in textiles.[3]

The rise and fall of labor organization in Santo André in 1918–19 illustrates the enormous obstacles facing São Paulo's industrial proletariat. Santo André provides a particularly compelling example because the district's industrial work force was already concentrated in unusually large units of production; whereas the state averaged 20 workers per industrial establishment in 1920, Santo André employed 49 per unit as a result of several major factories, such as the Ipiranguinha textile plant, that employed hundreds of workers.[4]

Although the wartime labor unrest had caught the employers and the oligarchy by surprise, the concessions made in 1917 did not mean that they accepted the aggressive new labor movement as an enduring reality. Within two months of the negotiated settlement in 1917, the state government began a vigorous repression of labor organizations with raids on union headquarters, attacks on demonstrations, and the jailing of CDP leaders, including Leuenroth.[5] As labor militancy continued, São Paulo's industrialists planned a counteroffensive. By May 1919, the employers in São Paulo felt confident enough to provoke a strike by dismissing their employees who were most directly involved with trade unions. Parallel actions occurred in Santo André, where the dismissal of activist workers at the Ipiranguinha plant led to a strike by the firm's five hundred employees on 1 May 1919. In São Paulo, the first clashes between strikers and the soldiers of the cavalry began on 2 May. By the next day, bands of workers were traveling to "proclaim" the strike in the factories of São Caetano and elsewhere.[6]

In Santo André, the leaders of the Workers' Union resolved to broaden the struggle by seeking support from the local populace and the workers in other factories. A march was planned for 5 May to start from the Ipiranguinha's workers' villa and to proceed through the streets of Santo André, seeking contributions and calling out the workers of other factories. The march was composed primarily of women—evidence of the mass involvement of unskilled workers—and the crowd carried the union's banner as it paraded peacefully through the streets, cheering the strike.

When the crowd approached the furniture factory of Streif & Cia., it was met by a militia sergeant and a soldier stationed there at the owners' request to prevent a strike. When the two tried to force the crowd back, a tumult ensued. Union leader Constantino Castellani, an eighteen-year-old weaver, protested loudly against the soldiers' actions, "receiving a rifle shot as a reply." The horrified crowd, including Castellani's sister, immediately seized the body while the two soldiers retreated.[7] The police and soldiers withdrew from the streets of Santo André in the next days, leaving the workers to their grief. A public wake attended by thousands of local residents was followed by a mass funeral procession escorting the body to the local cemetery of Vila Assunção. Within days, the union had gathered enough contributions to erect a gravestone to honor Castellani's memory.

In São Paulo, however, the soldiers of the state government were increasing their energetic intervention against strikers' protests. In the working-class neighborhood of Brás, they fought with the crowds that sought to disrupt the trolleys and dispersed a protest demonstration of men, women, and children in the Largo de Concórdia. In the port of Santos, the dockworkers joined the general strike, and by 6 May the movement was spreading throughout the interior of the state, reaching Campinas and Jundiaí.

Protest meetings and strikes were held in the textile-factory town of Sorocaba and among the stonecutters of Ribeirão Pires. In São Caetano, police and soldiers clashed violently with strikers, and members of the local strike commission were arrested and beaten and then transferred to jail in São Paulo. São Caetano's police *subdelegado* allegedly told policemen guarding a group of arrested strikers, "Shoot them if they try to escape, since killing a striker is no crime! They're enemies of order."[8]

Unlike that of two years earlier, the 1919 strike movement was vigorously repressed by the state and employers. In June 1919, for example, the prominent industrialist Antônio Pereira Ignacio, who owned a factory in ABC, not only provided the local police with the names of union leaders to be arrested but also enclosed a list of the workers he had dismissed from his factory. He even noted which of his ex-employees were the "most disorderly" and which merely showed a tendency to follow the troublemakers.[9] Throughout ABC the police closed union offices, and some of the arrested labor leaders were deported to the notorious Amazonian prison settlements of Ilha Grande and Ilha das Cobras. As the factories began to operate again, dozens of strikers learned of their dismissal. Labor's nucleus of union activists and supporters was uprooted and its members dispersed—some in flight, others in jail, and many more forced to move elsewhere to try to find employment to support their families.

Yet repression was not the sole explanation for the collapse of ABC's vibrant union movement after May 1919: equally important was the workers' loss of faith in their own ability to change things. Workers later recalled that the killing of Castellani fell "like a shower of cold water on the enthusiasm of the working class." The few strikes that did occur in ABC through 1920 lacked organization and coordination and were not successful.[10]

Workers' defeats, an economic downturn, and intimate police-employer cooperation combined to produce the calm that characterized labor relations in the early 1920s. The decline in industrial production and the new economic difficulties made the workers aware, employers said, that even a long strike in pursuit of their "eternal demands" would not have the results that it would have had in a time of normal production. The secretary general of São Paulo's textile industrialists' center (CIFTSP), Otávio Pupo Nogueira, devoted his considerable energies in early 1920 to initiating a centralized system of blacklisting designed to guarantee that "undesirable elements," "thieves," and "professional agitators" would be purged from the factories and kept out in the future.[11]

Police officials at all levels had full authority to act promptly at the behest of industrialists against the "agitators" of the working class. When a strike broke out at ABC's Fábrica de Tecidos São Bernardo in 1921, the CIFTSP's secretary general went to the scene in the company of the police. "With the instigators removed," Pupo Nogueira wrote, "work returned to normal."[12]

Labor and the Tenentes

The heights of mobilization achieved between 1917 and 1919 would not be surpassed for many years. Unprecedented general strikes had swept the nation's three largest cities, and the dominant classes were shaken by even the temporary paralysis of activities in the urban nerve centers of this still fundamentally agricultural nation. The "social question," as it came to be known, would henceforth be guaranteed a place in the debates of the elites, even as killings, beatings, police raids, mass arrests, firings, and deportations snuffed out the flames of resistance.

Having bested the unarmed workers, Brazil's dominant oligarchies could confidently return to their normal pursuit of regional and economic advantage within an elitist and fraudulent political and electoral system. Their peace, however, was short-lived. The rivalries of the 1922 presidential campaign and military discontent spawned a movement of dissident military youth, the *tenentes*, who rose in heroic if bungled rebellion in Rio de Janeiro on 5 July 1922.[13]

Voicing the grievances of the urban middle classes discontented with the patronage system, the *tenentista* movement served as a mirror in which all those who were disgruntled with the existing order were invited to see their own image. For the workers' movement, the armed movement of military youth seemed to offer a possible alliance that could alter the balance of power that had condemned their past struggles to defeat. By 1923, labor's various factions had been drawn into the military conspiracies that led to the successful tenentista seizure of the capital of São Paulo on 5 July 1924.

Yet the initiative clearly lay with the rebellious military men who, while welcoming support, viewed the unarmed and greatly weakened labor movement as fundamentally secondary to their plans. During their three-week occupation of downtown São Paulo, the revolutionaries distanced themselves from their former coconspirators and were unwilling to work closely with working-class radicals. Not only were ties to São Paulo's organized workers' movement tenuous, but there is little evidence that working-class support for the revolt went beyond passive sympathy.[14]

The tenentes, after all, had set out to overthrow the political establishment—not to make the social revolution sought by anarchists, Communists, and other labor leaders. The 1924 rebel manifestos in São Paulo failed to even mention the special needs and grievances of the growing working class. Not surprisingly, the workers' movement in the city did not rush into public manifestations of solidarity with the rebels until after government forces on 12 July began indiscriminately to bombard rebel-held facilities located in the heavily populated working-class and industrial neighborhoods of Brás, Moóca, and Cambuci. The government's decision, despite its growing military strength and unlimited supplies, resulted in hundreds of civilian casualties and mass panic.

Meeting in the headquarters of the printers' union, twenty-six "militants of the working classes" issued a manifesto three days after the artillery began to pound workers' neighborhoods. The "Motion of the Workers to the Committee of the Revolutionary Forces," drafted by an anarchist, was published in Leuenroth's newspaper, *A Plebe*, and contained the names and occupations of its twenty-six signatories. The group's membership was representative of the existing labor movement, if not of the working class: only four were industrial workers, and all were anarchists or anarchist sympathizers. The motion called upon the revolt's leaders to open a dialogue with the workers and to take action to meet the pressing demands of the working class.[15]

A symbolic step for the workers' movement, the motion reflected an important lesson learned from the struggles of 1917 to 1919. Stable progress, labor activists realized, could not be achieved solely through direct action restricted to the economic arena of struggle. Increasingly convinced of the need to overthrow the oligarchical state, they concluded that a political revolution was necessary to establish the minimal conditions of freedom required by the working class. Since 275,000 urban workers by themselves could not revolutionize a nation of thirty million, they increasingly sought potential allies among other social classes. Thus, the outlook of all factions of the Brazilian labor movement after 1919 began, as José Albertino Rodrigues has noted, to take on "an accentuated political character."[16]

The trajectory of anarchist weaver José Righetti provides the best example of the crisis of anarchism occasioned by this shift in emphasis. As the only signer of the 1924 workers' motion with a significant industrial working-class constituency, Righetti was more sensitive than others to the political preconditions necessary for even minimal organizing success. He had seen his organization, the União dos Operários em Fábricas de Tecidos (UOFT), destroyed in the early 1920s; from 1924 on, he fought hard for the success of the tenentistas' revolution, which promised a more supportive state. By the early 1930s, he was São Paulo's most prominent tenentista labor leader, closely identified with the architect of the São Paulo revolt, Miguel Costa.[17]

Although not central to the revolt, the workers' movement felt the brunt of the repression that followed the withdrawal of rebel forces from the city. In the ensuing months, many existing labor organizations were wiped out, Leuenroth's newspaper was suppressed (not to reappear until 1927), and many of the signatories of the workers' motion were arrested—at least four being deported to penal colonies, where two died. The freedoms of speech, press, and assembly were even more severely restricted after 1924, under the terms of the state of siege that had begun in 1922 and would last until 1927.[18]

The 1924 revolt also prompted the state government to establish a centralized political-social police agency, the Departamento de Ordem Política Social (DOPS), that specialized in labor and radical affairs. Working closely with the industrialists, the DOPS prepared for future interventions in labor disputes by compiling a "Recenseamento Operário" of São Paulo in 1927, which listed the total work force and other relevant information for each individual factory. The DOPS quickly proved a qualitative advance in both the sophistication and efficacy with which it carried out its antilabor mission.[19]

Thus an already weak labor movement in São Paulo was even further decimated in the mid-1920s, reduced to a handful of activists who were only weakly organized, if at all. And yet, although they were easily dismissed for their lack of influence, these militants began to rebuild the labor movement during the new phase of Paulista labor history that began with the economic upswing of 1927–28 and ended with the repression of 1935.

Labor's Revival in ABC

Although ABC's employers were able to reestablish their unchallenged authority after 1919, the sources of working-class discontent had not been resolved—which guaranteed that, sooner or later, the region's factory workers would again find the means to organize themselves. By the late 1920s, expanding industrial production had created favorable local labor market conditions that produced the first signs of renewed ferment. In 1927, for example, ABC's Prefeito Saladino Cardoso Franco called in a special DOPS detachment paid for out of municipal funds. "For fifteen days," ABC's police *delegado* reported, the political-social police inspectors worked "maintaining order unchanged, in a period of intense worker agitation."[20]

The following year a handful of Santo André workers led by an eighteen-year-old textile worker, Marcos Andreotti, founded a local Workers' Union modeled after the 1919 organization of similar name. Although lacking mass influence at the outset, this tiny nucleus of activists played the leading role in resurrecting the local labor movement in the early 1930s. And for its key organizer, Marcos Andreotti (1910–84), the Workers' Union was the beginning of a five-decade-long career as the ABC region's most important and talented trade union leader prior to Lula in the 1970s.[21]

Marcos Andreotti was born to Italian immigrant parents who worked on the coffee plantations in the interior of São Paulo. The Andreotti family moved to the capital in 1920, where Marcos first entered into contact with the labor movement. While working as an elevator operator in downtown São Paulo, Andreotti often listened to the speeches and heated discussions held by his fellow workers, many of them anarchists, in São Paulo's central square, the Praça da Sé—convinced that only good could come from such talk on the workers' behalf.[22] At home, Andreotti was given the responsibility of reading the anarchist *A Plebe* out loud for his father and other trusted neighbors.

As a resident of the historic working-class neighborhoods of downtown São Paulo, the young Andreotti personally witnessed clashes between workers and São Paulo's notorious mounted cavalry. In 1982, he still recalled with zest the time the workers had strung piano wire across the street, attracted the cavalry's attention, and then watched the galloping soldiers being unceremoniously dismounted. He remembered workers in 1924 rolling a giant cheese down the street away from a food warehouse looted in the first days of the tenentista revolt. It was also in São Paulo that the teenage Andreotti paid his first dues to the Partido Comunista do Brasil (PCB), even though he had no opportunity to become directly involved with a functioning Communist cell.

The Andreotti family moved to Santo André in 1925 to work in the booming Ipiranguinha textile factory, which then employed nine hundred workers. Andreotti, who had worked since the age of ten, began as a weaver's helper at the plant and then became an electrician's helper, the first step toward becoming a skilled electrician. Eager to learn more about the dramatic events of 1919, the rebellious teenager quietly sought out his fellow textile workers who remembered the murdered weaver Castellani.

In 1928, Andreotti discovered two weavers, Olivério Botani and Jorge Pellozo, who shared his curiosity and enthusiasm. Together these young "Communists" began to talk of resurrecting the organization destroyed in 1919. Taking the earlier anarcho-syndicalist organization as a model, they sought to unite the wage earners of various categorias into a new Workers' Union of Santo André. This combination of anarcho-syndicalist practice and PCB membership was by no means exceptional; these young working-class activists were drawn to what they perceived to be a common message of struggle and to a proven organizational form that reflected the prevailing philosophy of revolutionary unionism.

Santo André's new Workers' Union began as a sort of discussion group that met informally in a public square near the Ipiranguinha factory. Gradually the circle drew in activist weavers, metalworkers, chemical workers, and stonecutters. These militants, including several veterans of 1919, shared a common conviction that something had to be done to better the workers' conditions. Growing only by word of mouth, the union was largely restricted to the district of Santo André.

The Workers' Union was not an actual trade union, but rather an expression of the determination of a minority of activist-minded male workers to organize. Their disposition to struggle made a collision with the employers inevitable at some point, but the terms of this confrontation would be determined by the economic and political conditions after 1930, which were quite different from those of 1919. Politically, Andreotti's generation faced a regime at the state and federal levels determined to follow more conciliatory tactics toward workers and their problems. Indeed, the new Vargas regime issued close to fifty decrees between December 1930 and the end of 1934 that, among other things, legalized unions, restricted the employment of foreign nationals (the "two-thirds decree"), established mandatory working papers (*carteiras profissionais*), set maximum hours of labor, regulated the employment of women and children, mandated paid vacations, instituted labor courts, and organized pension funds.[23]

These initiatives undertaken by the government of Getúlio Vargas gave birth, in the late 1930s, to the regime's central labor mythology: that the social and labor laws enacted after 1930 were "an initiative of the state, a generous *outorga* [derived from *outorgar*, meaning 'to grant, confer, award, or bestow'] by political leaders and not a conquest realized by our laboring masses."[24] Later scholars have rightly rejected this paternalistic statist judgment but have unwittingly adopted an equally erroneous thesis: that the state's initiatives after 1930 were primarily an imposition on the working class and its vanguards.[25]

Such judgments obscure the continuities and discontinuities that link the workers' movement and the state before and after the Revolution of 1930. While failing to distinguish between quite discrete forms of state action, the external imposition model makes unrealistic assumptions about the strength of the workers' movement and thus distorts our understanding of the decisions made by working-class leaders. To make sense of the state's new role, we must not substitute a moralistic or wishful assessment of working-class strength for hardheaded empirical judgments about the actual level of class consciousness and cohesion in Brazil. Nor should we exaggerate the extent and nature of working-class organization or its degree of class-embeddedness, especially in São Paulo.[26]

The fundamental truth is that the least organized and least powerful working-class group in 1930 was the factory proletariat, which made up the majority of the urban working class. Moreover, it was precisely this fully proletarianized group working in large-scale industry that needed organization the most. Yet unlike certain artisanal or craft groups, the industrial workers had few advantages of skill or market position that would allow them to organize and to achieve recognition of their demands solely on their own initiative. Thus, to fulfill its pressing class demands, the industrial working class and its activist minority welcomed state action *in practice* (though often not in theory) as a potential counterbalancing force outside the private employer-employee nexus.

This tendency is illustrated by the experience of Santo André's Marcos

Andreotti. Although he did not view the Revolution of 1930 as *his* revolution, the young Communist was sympathetic to those who had ousted the hated old regime. As experienced by Andreotti, however, the immediate impact of the Revolution of 1930 had less to do with any positive governmental action on behalf of workers than with the lack of immediate governmental repression of open public discussion of workers' problems. Having legalized trade union activity, the government could hardly repress workers for organizing public meetings and activities to this end. Andreotti and the Workers' Union were quick to exploit these possibilities of escaping from a phase of virtually clandestine activity. A small office was soon opened and the union began to hold regular public meetings.[27]

The resulting labor revival in 1931 was felt throughout the ABC region, which had attracted many of the most modern establishments in the newer branches of industry established in São Paulo since World War I. Industrial employment in ABC had grown from 4,316 workers in 1920 to 6,409 in 1930 (a figure that was lower than the heights reached during the industrial boom of 1928–29). Forty percent of ABC's industrial work force in 1930 was employed in the then-depressed textile and clothing industries (2,235), followed by metalworking (1,217), the chemical industries (1,005), furniture making (885), and the ceramics and construction materials industries (597).[28]

Like Andreotti's Workers' Union, the handcraftsmen of São Bernardo's furniture industry were also quick to see the advantages of the legal trade unionism established by the new government's Decree 19,770. In 1931, the furniture workers of São Bernardo filed an application with the Labor Ministry for recognition as the Union of Furniture Makers, Carpenters, and Related Classes of São Bernardo. Granted legal status in 1933, their trade union was quickly accepted by local employers.[29] At the outset, at least, this woodworkers' union was not the expression of a radicalized working-class constituency. Rather, the union attached great value to its status as a respectable force in the local community, and its members' collaborationist bent led them to identify with the most progovernment trade union figures in São Paulo.[30]

The São Bernardo union was thus untainted by the sort of radicalism found among union militants like Andreotti in ABC's factory districts. With an established position of respect and influence, the furniture makers sought to pursue a sober trade unionism with governmental support that would bring them economic results even without more ambitious changes in Brazilian society.

Union militants in ABC's factory districts, by contrast, faced more formidable obstacles to their efforts to organize the region's large-scale manufacturing establishments. Ironically enough, these repressive conditions made the government's 1931 unionization Decree 19,770 of even greater importance to this group of radicals, despite their distrust of its motives. The young Communist leaders of the Workers' Union quickly realized that legal status might serve as a shield, however inadequate, against the employer repression that stymied their organizing efforts. Thus Santo André's union activists petitioned the Labor Ministry in 1931 for recognition as a Union of Various Occupations.[31] This union form reflected labor's anarchist heritage and embodied the militants' notion of class solidarity and the identity of interests of all workers. While complying with the letter of the law, they sought to maintain the organizational form that reflected their own class-conscious and antiparticularist views.[32]

The union's initial plans were frustrated, however, by the Labor Ministry's denial of their application for recognition in 1932. Yet this governmental decision, based upon the bureaucracy's notions of rationality and its suspicions of radicalism, in fact had a positive impact on the emerging labor movement: the activist minority was forced to move from abstraction toward the specific concerns of the workers in each categoria. The decision would force them to move away from this generic class unionism toward a form of organization that more closely reflected the particularist interests of rank-and-file workers primarily concerned with the wages, conditions, and needs of their own categorias.

After their first rebuff, union activists resubmitted documents in 1932 requesting recognition for separate unions covering the two industries where they had the largest number of activists and contacts: metalworking and textiles. The new applications, conforming to the strictures of the law, were approved in 1933 and opened a new era in the history of the workers' movement in Santo André.

Thus the new legal unions did not mark an abrupt transition from "independent" and radical unionism to a moderate and dependent unionism harnessed to the state. In applying for legal recognition, the leaders of the Workers' Union were not announcing their conversion to the theories of class peace and harmony of interests contained in the preamble of Decree 19,770. Rather, a compliance with the law's outward requirements was used simply as a legal cover to facilitate the goal they had pursued since 1928: the organization of workers to fight the employers. In fact, the "legalization" of the labor movement—whatever the motives of its architects—

increased the workers' room to maneuver and led to the consolidation of working-class activism within government-recognized trade unions by 1933. Far from being a product of the laws, the new legal labor movement flowed from the decisions made by working-class activists, many of them formed during the 1920s, who established legal unions that were largely outside of effective state control.[33]

The link to the state was only a limited constraint on the activists' actions in the early thirties because the government lacked the means, even in many capital cities, to monitor, much less control, the new unions. The formal abolition of the Workers' Union, for example, did not end cooperation among categorias. The local labor movement continued to function as one big union family despite the boundaries established by law. Textile and metalworker unionists continued to meet jointly, though separate minutes were drawn up, and unorganized groups like the chemical workers continued to find shelter within Santo André's metalworkers' union.[34]

The new, legally sanctioned unionism did, however, imply compromises that effectively ended the radicals' unchallenged sway within labor. In lessening the costs of union activity, legal unionism created the basis for political pluralism within the labor movement by creating space for the emergence of nonradical labor leaders. In some cities, company unionism was one result of the new system; ABC, however, saw the emergence of legitimate new leaders who, although they did not share the long-range goals of their more radical contemporaries, were sincerely concerned with bettering the workers' lot. The secretary of the Santo André metalworkers' union in 1934, Luiz Salvi Palmieri, was a good example of this new breed of union leadership.

Palmieri, a Pirelli employee, was hired by the government in 1932 to staff the newly opened local office of the National Labor Department. As the Labor Ministry's sole employee in ABC, he was responsible for issuing the government's new labor identification cards and for expediting grievances of individual workers where possible. Palmieri was a firm believer in the Revolution of 1930, a conspicuously progovernment stance that would have been unusual for a unionist in ABC during the First Republic.[35]

Palmieri had not been a member of the Workers' Union founded in 1928, nor had he been a founder of the metalworkers' union in 1932; yet this did not prevent his close cooperation with Andreotti and other radical workers. Indeed, Palmieri's office became the regular meeting place for the workers of Santo André in 1933 and 1934—known, in a calculated confusion of functions, as "the union." In mid-1934, his political connections in São Paulo were even useful in getting the money from the municipal administration to allow the metal and textile unions to reopen their own offices in Santo André.[36]

These labor developments occurred within a turbulent political context in the early thirties. To understand the labor politics of this period it is important to grasp the motivation behind the Vargas regime's initial opening to urban labor, which was far from being a disinterested *outorga*. The national government's initiatives toward workers after 1930 coincided with intense regionalist rivalries that pitted the regime against the interests of São Paulo's cohesive upper class of capitalist planters, industrialists, and their solidly structured mass base within the state. If workers needed and could use the state, the same need was also felt by important components of the new regime, which was, at best, a shifting and divided coalition of conflicting social forces and class factions that circled around Getúlio Vargas. Having seized control of the weak central state, various revolutionary factions consciously fostered the organization and structuring of the urban working class in an effort both to increase their own strength and to vanquish their powerful and by no means resigned or defeated enemies.

Thus, even the identification of moderate labor activists like Palmieri with Getúlio Vargas gave trade unionism an oppositional tint within the state. This political tie to Rio, in turn, provided Palmieri—who was fired by Pirelli—with some protection, since the federal government, although unable to force his rehiring, did appoint him as the Labor Ministry's representative in Santo André—in which capacity, as we have seen, he provided decisive aid to the emerging union movement in the district.

This alliance with Rio did not, it is clear, necessarily imply subordination or submission by the workers' movement to capitalist control. Indeed, the workers' immediate enemy—São Paulo's powerful industrial bourgeoisie—had been among the most prominent adherents of the anti-Getulista Constitutionalist Revolt in São Paulo from July to October 1932.[37] The Paulista working class's notorious apathy toward the sacred Paulista cause during this costly military conflict reflected a quite reasonable and widespread belief that favorable changes for workers were best guaranteed by the victory of the October Revolution led by Vargas. Moreover, the decisive military defeat of São Paulo's conservative classes in 1932 opened further space for labor's activities in the state. Experiencing rapid growth, the state labor movement saw its acceptance of the new legal form of trade unionism as validated by the opposition of the managers and owners of industrial enterprises in ABC toward any trade unions, whether government-linked or not.[38]

For rank-and-file Communist militants like Andreotti, employer resistance provided convincing proof that they were not betraying their goals by entering the legal unions, even though this strategy was explicitly opposed by the PCB's state and national leadership in the early 1930s. Andreotti must have felt some personal satisfaction when party policy on legal unionism finally changed—and in fact, his legally recognized metalworkers' union of Santo André was the *only* significant affiliate of the Communist Party's tiny state trade union grouping as late as 1934.[39]

Thus the regime's labor initiatives of 1930–33 were aimed, above all, at São Paulo, and they aided the Paulista labor movement in gaining a toehold in the antilabor industrial heartland. By 1933, however, the Vargas regime found that labor and certain radical middle-class minorities in São Paulo were too powerless to serve as a regional base for the regime's power. Vargas's subsequent turn toward conciliation with the Paulista oligarchy provides a decisive test of the meaning of the legalization of trade union organization.

Labor's response can be measured by the wary attitudes toward the federal government adopted in 1933 by the non-Communist, nonanarchist Coligação dos Sindicatos Proletários (CSP), the federation with which São Bernardo's Furniture Workers' Union was affiliated. The CSP admitted both legal and unrecognized unions and was formed without the prior approval of the Labor Ministry, which it criticized as a profoundly disorganizing factor in the union movement. This surprisingly critical attitude was a direct response to the Vargas regime's shift toward accommodation with the Paulista elites who had swept the May 1933 elections for the national Constituent Assembly.[40]

In its effort to neutralize the Paulista threat the Vargas regime, it became clear, was prepared to betray its local allies, including labor. In 1934, control of the state was turned over to Armando de Salles Oliveira, who served as the direct representative of the then-dominant faction of the Paulista oligarchy, especially the industrialists. Thus the decisive years from 1933 to 1935 were marked by increasing conflict between São Paulo's trade union movement and both the state and national governments. It is important to emphasize that only a tiny and insignificant group within São Paulo's legal trade union movement responded in the servile manner that might befit workers' leaders who have been previously labeled as *pelegos*—

that is, sell-outs who were more likely to represent the interests of government than those of their own members.

Employer defiance of the laws, and nonenforcement by the government, also encouraged the unions in ABC and elsewhere toward an increasing use of the strike weapon, labor's one means of direct pressure on both employers and the state. The strikes that marked 1934 and 1935 would reveal a definite increase in working-class strength, whether judged in terms of the number of organizations, their representativeness, or their ability to carry out collective action.

As the legal unions moved toward direct action in 1934, they benefited from a favorable but unintended side effect of the regime's labor initiatives. The revolution may have challenged the radicals' predominance within union leadership, but it also facilitated their organizing efforts among the mass of workers. Although legal status did not guarantee support from the majority of workers, it did increase the likelihood of establishing more-representative trade unions. Despite employer intimidation, more workers were willing to become active in the new unions because they believed the government's claim that it was their ally. The lessening of fear and passivity thus created broader-based union membership, which, in turn, strengthened the unity so essential to serious resistance to the employers—especially in the case of strike action, which demanded majority support in order to be effective.

Direct Action: The Strikes of 1934

There had been few strikes in ABC in the early thirties because of the general industrial depression and high levels of unemployment. Yet those difficult years had seen increasingly successful organizational efforts, which combined in 1934 with the marked revival of industry to produce important local strikes by both furniture workers and metalworkers.[41] Although both were led by legal trade unions, the two strikes were radically different in nature and outcome—proving, once again, that working-class praxis can never be derived solely from the institutional and juridical norms of labor legislation.

Furniture making in ABC was still predominantly a handicraft industry. It employed 14 percent of the region's total work force, primarily in the small furniture-making shops of the isolated district of São Bernardo. Metalworking, by contrast, was one of the most modern branches of Brazilian industrial manufacturing, employing 20 percent of ABC's workers. Whereas 57 percent of ABC's woodworkers were employed in factories of *under* 100 employees, only 10 percent of ABC's metalworkers worked in enterprises that small.[42]

The settings and work forces of the two industries also differed. Isolated from the railroad, the village of São Bernardo was a small, closely knit, and relatively homogeneous community still marked by a traditionalism inherited from the nonindustrial past. Workers and employers shared a background rooted in the subsistence agricultural and extractive industries of earlier decades. The ABC factory districts of Santo André and São Caetano, by contrast, were already large-scale urban settlements populated by outsiders drawn by the prospects of work. And the employers of the majority of ABC's metalworkers were among the wealthiest and most powerful foreign and domestic capitalist enterprises, such as General Motors and Pirelli, quite unlike the modest owners of São Bernardo's small furniture shops.

The first dramatic test of labor's newfound determination came in August 1934, when São Bernardo's furniture makers' union launched the longest, largest, and most successful strike of the thirties in ABC. Growing discontent burst forth in strike action on the morning of 22 August, when a local factory manager proposed unilaterally to lower the rate paid the workers for certain pieces of work. The strike quickly received the support of all of the industry's work force of over 1,000, including furniture makers, machinists, carpenters, and contracted and monthly workers.[43]

The union's main demand was for increases of 10 to 30 percent in current piece rates and wages. A week after the strike began, the employers made their first counterproposal through the local police delegado: they ignored the demand for an across-the-board increase but offered an additional 20 percent for the hour-and-a-half worked beyond the legal eight-hour day.[44] An assembly of strikers on 30 August rejected the employers' offer. They argued that the eight-hour day, already mandated by law, should simply be enforced by the government and not be the subject of negotiations with employers.

As the strike entered its second week, the furniture makers were sustained both by the solidarity received from São Paulo unions and by the garden plots maintained by many workers and family members. The employers, by contrast, felt growing economic pressure because most of them lacked the resources to resist a long strike. For them, each additional day without production meant the loss of more orders to competing producers in São Paulo.[45] The employers' frustration and uncertainty began to surface as they realized that they lacked the weapons to force the workers back to work on their terms. José Pelosini, owner of São Bernardo's second-largest factory, which had 137 workers, violently denounced the "Communist" strikers and publicly threatened to send thugs to burn down the union headquarters.[46] Yet Pelosini's bravado could not mask the emptiness of his threat: São Bernardo's furniture workers did not face the open hostility and repressive zeal of the local or state police, as might have occurred in the First Republic. Indeed, the furniture workers' union had nothing but praise for the conciliatory role played by the police.[47]

The very "correct" behavior of state and local politicians and policemen reflected a desire to avoid the electoral damage that might be caused by any repressive action. Not only did the strike occur two months before the state's hotly contested gubernatorial election, but the furniture makers also represented a large share of the total São Bernardo electorate. Under these conditions, the employers' refusal to negotiate could not continue indefinitely. Within four days of his violent outburst, José Pelosini began to show a willingness to negotiate. The union, although publicly skeptical of "illusory promises," responded with a more modest negotiating proposal that won the support of the hard-pressed smaller employers.[48] After this sign of "good will," the small employers signed a one-year labor contract with the union on 21 September 1934, and the rest soon followed.[49]

For the first time in ABC's history, a large body of workers had struck and won an all-round victory in a month-long strike. Yet the favorable outcome of ABC's longest and most successful work stoppage of the thirties should not blind us to the unique features of that strike movement. The lines that cut across São Bernardo during the strike were not solely those of class against class. Even the employers' camp was split, as most smaller employers sided with the strikers against their haughty and arrogant larger rivals, who were amassing an ever-greater share of production.[50]

The unskilled factory workers of ABC, by contrast, lacked virtually all of the elements that made for victory in São Bernardo. The restricted possibilities of the factory proletariat are most clearly revealed by the unsuccessful postelection strike that took place among the 500 workers employed at the Pirelli plant in Santo André. The strike at the Italian-owned plant, ABC's second-largest employer of metalworkers, dramatically illustrated the conditions in the most modern sectors of large-scale industrial production.

Although the majority of the founders and leaders of the local metalworkers' union, including its president, Marcos Andreotti, worked at Pirelli—and despite employer charges to the contrary—the work stoppage was spontaneous and surprised the union. Once the strike began on 27 October 1934, however, the plant's union militants devoted their energy to giving organized shape to the movement.[51]

At the outset, the strikers expected a rapid resolution of their grievances. When a meeting with management was announced for the second day of the strike, the workers were so sure of a favorable result that they returned to work on the following day. When their hopes were dashed, the Pirelli workers struck once again. Pirelli's managers responded by threatening to "lock out" their employees. Blaming third parties, a company director denounced strikes as a form of "indiscipline that generates anarchy."[52]

The strike mobilized all the union activists in Santo André as they sought to convert this act of protest into an organized effort. The metalworkers' union helped formulate the seven strike demands, which included, as top priority, a request for a 30 percent wage increase. The second key demand was for an eight-hour workday—because, despite governmental decrees and pledges, a ten-hour day, six days a week, was still the norm at Pirelli. A shorter workday, the workers argued, was especially important because of the plant's unhealthy conditions and the noxious chemicals with which they labored. The workers also sought an end to company violations of the government's law on industrial accidents.

The list of workers' demands included several noneconomic points that referred to the authoritarian and degrading treatment they received at the hands of foreign-born foremen and supervisors—a problem not shared by São Bernardo's furniture makers, who did not work under close supervision. To resolve these problems, the Pirelli strikers asked for the abolition of the fines deducted from their wages and demanded "complete respect" from their supervisors.[53]

The strikers' final two demands sought to guarantee the durability of the settlement they hoped to reach with the company. They demanded company recognition of the unionization of the plant, and thus the right to an organized say in their wage bargain. To avoid company persecution of their leaders, they also sought explicit guarantees against retaliatory firings of strikers.

Since the October 1934 elections were already over, municipal and state authorities, unconstrained by considerations of electoral advantage, were vigorously repressive in dealing with the Pirelli strikers (most of whom did not vote, in any case). The same police delegado who had showed such caution with the furniture makers was soon being denounced for his use of the police to protect the minority of workers who failed to heed the strike call.[54] The state political-social police agency, DOPS, assumed an even more explicit strikebreaking role: specialized DOPS agents were sent to Santo André, where they proceeded to intimidate the strikers, especially teenagers, and disperse those who gathered near the Pirelli factory to discourage strikebreakers. Police pressure and the workers' need for their wages brought the Pirelli strike to an end after six days without any substantive victories. Although the workers gained some increase in wages, they soon saw their leaders, including Andreotti, placed on the street and blacklisted by Pirelli and other local manufacturers.[55]

The majority of the workers, one discharged Pirelli worker lamented, did not in the end understand the "saintly mission that this strike strove for." In his letter to a local newspaper, Amadeu Nogueira Netto blamed the DOPS for forcing the workers back to work despite the justice of their cause. The employers' victory, he went on, was achieved only by using "terrorist" practices that were not, "it seems to me, permitted by our laws."[56] This comment reveals an important new aspect of working-class discourse during the thirties. The defeated striker did not denounce the regime's labor legislation and sympathetic rhetoric as a fraud; rather, he claimed the law for the side of the workers. He did not do so, however, because of any naive faith in the government. In fact, this generation of labor leaders had been quickly disabused of any illusion that state action alone could be depended upon to turn laws into realities. But if the laws did not equal realities, they at least defined the parameters of new rights that could be invoked to justify and advance working-class struggle.

The Pirelli case clearly reveals the weakness of the prevailing consensus that incorrectly argues, as did the Vargas regime as well, that the government's new labor legislation necessarily had a soporific effect on the working class. This interpretation could have been true only if the social and labor legislation of these years had in fact been observed by employers and enforced by the government. If that had been the case, the result might perhaps have been a passive and quiescent working class whose demands were being met without the necessity of open class struggle. The reality in the mid-1930s, however, was of consistent noncompliance with the law by employers and lackadaisical enforcement by the state. Although industrialists were unable to win revocation of the new laws, they could and did resort to passive resistance, and their obstructionist tactics were effective because there was not an adequate governmental enforcement apparatus. This gap between promise and reality underlay the radicalization of even the politically moderate leaders of São Paulo's legal labor movement. As Henrique Sabatini, president of the São Bernardo furniture workers' union, said in 1934, the Labor Ministry's laws remained "a dead letter within the walls" of local factories.[57]

For the anarchists, this reality of broken promises confirmed their conviction that no real benefits were ever won through such political intermediaries; only direct action guaranteed results. But though phrased in radical terms, this defeatist message of disillusionment did not fall on receptive ears, because forms of indirect action had by no means lost their compelling rationale and potential importance for the factory workers of ABC.

Ironically, the top manager of the Pirelli factory provided the clearest and bluntest explanation of the logic of indirect action as a labor strategy. The workers complained about wages, he correctly remarked, yet there were many other workers in ABC who earned far less than they did. As for claims of unsafe work, he asked whether there were not, in fact, other even more dangerous industries in Brazil. "Why," he asked, "demand from Pirelli that which is not demanded from other industries?"[58] An alliance with government, however uncertain, offered even skeptical labor leaders the tantalizing possibility of being able to impose certain basic uniformities in wages and conditions upon all employers.

From a theoretical point of view, the best solution to the problem raised by Pirelli's manager would have been the organization of all metalworkers into a powerful trade union at the local, state, and national levels. In this way, labor would establish the most certain means of pressuring the employers. Unfortunately, this solution required a degree of across-the-board solidarity and cohesion within the working class that did not in fact exist in the 1930s. The reality was that struggle developed unevenly from one factory to another, from one categoria to another, and from one region or city to another. Even under a militant and class-conscious, even radical, leadership, as in Santo André, the progress of organization was slow and the results were modest. Indeed, the defeat of the Pirelli strike wiped out the only real pocket of labor strength within the local metalworking industry.[59]

If workers were not to wait indefinitely to achieve their goals, they would have to develop a strategy based on these hard-and-fast truths. The anarchists' veiled acceptance of governmental action on behalf of workers in 1917 had reflected the realities of industrial working-class life. During the two decades that followed, industrialization intensified in São Paulo, with an enormous expansion in the number of industrial workers and in the size of the manufacturing plants in which they labored. In the broadest sense, the ensuing labor market shifts can be directly associated with the transformation of the labor movement's practice, its chosen weapons, and its politics.

Discussing early Latin American workers' movements, Adolf Sturmthal and David Felix observed in 1960 that "as long as the trade unions were limited in the main to such skilled groups, they had a relatively strong position in the labor market and consequently rejected governmental intervention in labor-management relations. This was characteristic of the period of anarcho-syndicalist influence." Yet "the progress of modern industry and the growth of unions to include semiskilled and unskilled workers," they went on, changed the status of unions in the labor market and led to "the close alliance between labor and government" that characterized later decades. Their simply stated thesis aptly characterizes an important dimension of labor's long-term transformation: the increasing acceptance of forms of indirect action, such as governmental labor regulations, as a means of advancing working-class interests.[60]

By 1935, however, this alliance-in-the-making between organized labor and the Vargas government was on very shaky ground. Contrary to the *outorga* thesis, the workers had received few actual benefits through state action during the transitional years of the early 1930s, at least in São Paulo.[61] Although it marked an important innovation in political rhetoric and governmental policy making, the avalanche of paper decrees on labor had little direct impact upon workers' lives or struggles. Indeed, the absence of state structures capable of enforcing these measures against powerful and recalcitrant industrial employers severely limited the impact of positive state action on the politics of labor during these years.

Rather, the workers' key gain after 1930 had been the *legalization* of trade union organization, which, it must be recognized, did not originate with the industrial bourgeoisie.[62] And in judging the state's new role in industrial relations after 1930, the crucial issue is whether such legislation, and the political initiatives behind it, created space for the strengthening of working-class power and organization.

Labor Politics and the Aliança Nacional Libertadora

The labor movement in ABC pursued a dual strategy in 1934–35 based upon use of the workers' economic and political weapons—namely, direct action through strikes, and indirect action through increased political involvement. On the political front, the new trade union movement faced a difficult challenge: winning the enforcement of the laws governing minimum wages, maximum hours, industrial safety, and vacations. The answer could come only through a more serious concern with politics, through the search for more dependable allies outside the arena of direct employer-employee relations.

Labor's shared sense of disappointment and increasing difficulties with the government facilitated the establishment of a common front between the CSP unions, such as the São Bernardo furniture workers, and more radical groups, such as the Santo André metalworkers. Spurred by the failure of the earlier alliance to yield the expected results, even the leaders of previously more moderate unions, such as the São Bernardo furniture makers, became more militant and politically radicalized, a process that led to their eventual support of the leftist Aliança Nacional Libertadora in 1935.

In mid-1934, the furniture workers of São Bernardo do Campo initiated local labor's first experiment in electoral politics by running their union president as the Socialist Party candidate for the state assembly in the October 1934 elections. The fact that Claudinor de Azevedo Marques became the first worker to run for office in ABC is not surprising, given that the furniture workers were the only important group of working-class voters in the region.[63] Nevertheless, his candidacy was unsuccessful. São Paulo's traditional oligarchical factions again swept the 1934 elections, demonstrating that there was as yet little basis for a left-wing electoral project in the state.

By early 1935, however, Paulista socialists, tenentes, Trotskyists, anarchists, and Communists had all united in the exhilarating if short-lived revolutionary adventure of the Aliança Nacional Libertadora (ANL, or Aliança).[64] Founded by disgruntled tenentes in March 1935 in Rio de Janeiro, the Aliança grew at a phenomenal rate for four months, until it was banned by the government of Getúlio Vargas. A broad popular front embracing all shades of leftist public opinion, the ANL promised the imminent replacement of the established order with a "popular government" that would oppose fascism, imperialism, and the large landowners. On the anniversary of the 1922 and 1924 revolts, legendary tenentista "cavalier of hope" Luis Carlos Prestes released a revolutionary manifesto that called for "All Power to the ANL!"

Although Prestes was unable to appear publicly, he and his mythology were of fundamental importance to the Aliança Nacional Libertadora. The genuine mass appeal of this thirty-seven-year-old revolutionary dated from the mid-1920s, when he had led a rebel detachment that kept the spirit of revolt alive after the failure of the 1924 tenentista revolt in São Paulo. The exploits of the Prestes Column, which covered 20,000 kilometers and survived several years of governmental extermination campaigns, had made the young revolutionary famous. But, unlike his fellow tenentes, Prestes chose a more perilous path when he opposed the Revolution of 1930 as insufficiently radical. By the mid-thirties, he had brought his name and popular appeal to the small, factionalized Communist Party, which he would lead, as secretary general, from 1934 until 1980.[65]

The Aliança appealed above all to the radicalized middle-class elements, who provided the defining themes and dominant leadership of the movement. Like Prestes, none of the ANL's national founders were workers, and the ANL's provisional state *diretório* in heavily industrialized São Paulo was composed of three attorneys, one professor, one doctor, and one military man.[66] Consciously multiclass in character, the ANL strove to harmonize the interests of different social classes through the unifying concept of the nation and the theme of national emancipation. If successful, the Aliança's attempted synthesis of national and class struggles would provide the workers a revolutionary government responsive to their needs. The Prestes nine-point manifesto of 5 July 1935, which became the Aliança's de facto new platform, pledged that the ANL's "popular government" would guarantee workers an eight-hour day, salary increases, and equal pay for equal work, as well as legislation enacting a minimum wage, social security, and pensions.[67]

As a broad insurgent alliance, the ANL complemented labor's own independent initiatives in a period of rising militancy. On 28 April 1935, four hundred delegates from eleven states gathered in Rio de Janeiro for the first truly national labor congress since 1920. Demanding passage of new prolabor laws and strict enforcement of those already on the books, the Communist leaders of the short-lived Confederação Sindical Unitária do Brasil placed their hopes on a revolutionary victory of the ANL's antiimperialist alliance of the "oppressed classes."[68]

The Aliancista fever reached the ABC region less than three months after the founding manifesto of 1 March 1935. In the seven weeks between 30 May and 17 July, local ANL diretórios organized at least three major meetings in Santo André, four rallies and marches in São Caetano, and two meetings in the district of São Bernardo. The ANL's mobilizations in ABC were unexpectedly large, with a combined attendance of approximately three thousand people. By the second week of June, ANL public headquarters were in operation in both Santo André and São Caetano. But the Aliança was far from being a project of the local labor movement in Santo André and São Caetano: unrepresented in the ANL's local leadership, the presidents of the local metalworkers' and textile workers' unions were not invited to address Aliança meetings.[69] Only the São Bernardo Aliança was marked by significant union participation in leadership, as a result of the furniture workers and their politically active leadership.

Although the Aliancista agitation in ABC was not oriented primarily toward the concerns of industrial workers, its non-working-class leaders solicited and received working-class participation.[70] Whatever the priorities of nonworker Aliancistas, ABC's leading labor activists saw the ANL as a movement that made a place for labor's struggle. For Communist labor activists, such as Andreotti, the ANL promised, at best, revolution—or, at the least, a few new allies for the workers' struggle against the employers. Personally acquainted with São Paulo ANL activist Augusto Pinto (who was later martyred), Andreotti attended all the ANL events in Santo André and served as the local representative of the Communist-ANL coalition newspaper in São Paulo, *A Platéia*. Feeling no slight at being ignored, the metalworkers' union adopted a unanimous resolution in which they formally joined the ANL.[71]

The scope and intensity of the Aliancista mobilization between March and June 1935 had few, if any, precedents in Brazilian history. By July, the ANL could claim hundreds of thousands of members throughout Brazil, and a thousand in Santo André alone. Yet the Aliancista constituency was unprepared for the raids and arrests of key ANL leaders that began after 11 July. The lack of the expected response from patriotic soldiers encouraged mass passivity and acquiescence, because the movement's civilian supporters lacked the resources to mount an effective resistance. The only militant local response to the outlawing of the ANL took place in the densely settled ABC factory district of São Caetano. On 13 July two thousand people rallied against this "fascist coup" of the government, and some five hundred workers soon went on strike at the Companhia Brasileira de

Mineração e Metalúrgica. While the strike's motivation is unclear, the state militia was quickly dispatched to São Caetano, where, on 16 July, they confronted a march of eight hundred workers from local factories. After arresting twenty or thirty workers, the soldiers were finally forced by the crowd to release their prisoners.[72]

Having placed great hopes in the ANL less than a month earlier, ABC's labor activists now realized that their middle-class allies were far less consistent and powerful than they had believed. This disappointing outcome did, however, demonstrate an unexpected advantage of labor's low visibility in the Aliança: ABC's legal trade unions simply continued their activities as if nothing had happened. With the state affiliate of the national trade union federation declared illegal, independent union representatives quickly formed a new federation to coordinate their activities.

In August 1935, ABC's labor organizations concentrated on choosing delegate electors from their unions to attend the state meeting that would elect class representatives to serve in the newly elected state assembly of São Paulo. A corporatist scheme dear to the tenentes, class representation of both workers and industrialists had guaranteed the Vargas regime crucial votes in the earlier national assembly. Unlike the government-manipulated process in previous years, however, São Paulo's trade unions were now well enough organized to try to convert the class-representation elections into a real expression of their point of view. The Santo André metalworkers' union sent Communist Marcos Andreotti as its delegate elector, and the São Bernardo furniture workers' union sent its Socialist president, Claudinor de Azevedo Marques. In October 1935, ABC representatives publicly protested the manipulation by the State Labor Department (Departamento Estadual de Trabalho, or DET) of the class elections to guarantee "a slate of unconscious workers" and "sell-outs" who would vote for "oppressive laws" in the state assembly.[73]

The vitality of trade unionism's institutional activities in ABC after the outlawing of the ANL reflected the continuing militancy of the local work force during a period of economic growth. In São Bernardo, the labor turmoil that began in mid-July 1935 led to a second major furniture workers' strike in September 1935. The workers' anger was directed against the village's three largest furniture factories, which were still using various subterfuges to avoid the 1932 eight-hour law. Under threat of dismissal, the workers at the furniture factories of José Pelosini, Narciso Pelosini, and Irmãos Corazza were being coerced into signing "voluntary" contracts to work nine-hour days. The employers were exploiting a major loophole written into the law that permitted a ten-hour day and a sixty-hour week if there was a signed agreement between the employer and his workers.[74]

For local unionists, this perversion of the government's labor legislation reflected the effort of "a group of industrialists with a retrograde mentality" who sought to "take from the proletariat the small conquests that have benefited" it in recent years. The São Bernardo furniture workers' union demanded that the DET outlaw this practice. The unionists were disgusted by the response of DET officials; as one worker said, they claimed "that the law is the law . . . [while leaving] us at the mercy of our exploiters." In these circumstances, the furniture workers turned once again to direct action as the means of enforcing *their* interpretation of the law.[75] The 420 workers who struck the three largest furniture factories in the first week of September 1935 even received the support of seventeen smaller furniture manufacturers, who allowed their workers to stay out in solidarity on the first day of the strike. In later weeks, these small employers discounted the wages of their workers to help finance the strike against their "undisciplined, greedy, and law-breaking" rivals.[76]

Yet the employers who had been struck were quick to seize the advantage offered by the state's repressive zeal following the outlawing of the ANL. Within days, the DET and the DOPS political-social police asked the local police subdelegado to investigate the strike at the employers' request. By the third week of the strike, police inspectors, soldiers, and political police had been dispatched to São Bernardo. The strikers were indignant at being labeled "extremists [simply] because we want the fulfillment of the law."[77]

To defeat such an intimidating display, all the workers at the struck factories would have had to honor the union's strike call. The response to the strike had been mixed, however, and the Corazza factory was the only enterprise that was completely shut down. The strike was weakest at the enterprise that was the cutting edge of the transformation of furniture making into a truly industrial manufacturing operation.[78] With the defeat of the three-week strike, "a conscious vanguard of one hundred or so workers" remained adamant in their refusal to give in to employer coercion. Faced with the "impossibility of the worker continuing under the growing tyranny of the bosses," these holdouts announced that they would found their own furniture factory and work for themselves. With the help of local merchants, they pooled their savings to establish a cooperative factory, the Companhia Fábrica de Móveis de São Bernardo do Campo, which, they announced, would function democratically out of the local union headquarters.[79]

Few branches of Brazilian industry offered the alternative that was chosen by the self-proclaimed vanguard of the São Bernardo furniture makers' union. Ironically enough, the option to leave the working class by becoming owners of a small shop had helped strengthen union organization and militancy among São Bernardo's furniture makers. In contrast, the 150 workers at Ítalo Setti's silk-weaving plant in São Bernardo were helpless in the face of their employer's practice of paying legally mandated vacation time in installments with a large discount.[80] The sort of militancy demonstrated by São Bernardo's furniture workers could not be sustained by the workers in ABC's large mechanized textile and metal factories. Nevertheless, these realities did not mean that ABC's industrial workers were satisfied with their lot, and in October 1935 there was another strike against the Pirelli factory in Santo André that spread to an undetermined number of workers in local textile, civil construction, chemical, and ceramics industries. All these strikes, however, were quickly defeated.[81]

A month after the defeat of the strikes in Santo André, the PCB and the remnants of the Aliança staged brief barracks revolts in Natal, Recife, and Rio de Janeiro. This insurrectional effort in late November 1935—the Communist Rebellion, as it was labeled—removed the few remaining restraints upon repressive state action against those identified with the Left. With support from all political factions of the dominant classes, a rising spiral of repression resulted in the arrest, torture, and imprisonment of tens of thousands.

Under these conditions, the fragile legality of Santo André's unions disappeared, and the public space that local unionists had sought to occupy was virtually eliminated. The return of police solutions to labor discontent resulted in a return to the unionism of activist minorities typical of the years before 1930. Santo André's metalworkers' and textile workers' unions were quickly reduced to a tiny grouping of radical worker-activists. Marcos Andreotti was forced to move to São Paulo to avoid arrest, although he retained the status of union president. As labor activists have often insisted, the Estado Novo dictatorship began for workers in 1935, not 1937.

Three • Workers, Industrialists, and the State

The popular insurgency symbolized by the Aliança Nacional Libertadora in 1935 united the government of Getúlio Vargas and the dominant faction of the Paulista oligarchy, led by Governor Armando de Salles Oliveira. Despite continuing rivalries with Vargas, the political representatives of São Paulo's planters and industrialists fully supported the suppression of the democratic rights of the mass of the population during the two years prior to the establishment of the Estado Novo in 1937.[1] Controlling the state of São Paulo and holding powerful positions in the national government, the Paulista oligarchy was convinced that its then-ally Getúlio Vargas would have to respect the planned 1938 presidential elections that it expected would return São Paulo to control of the nation.

The increased unity within the dominant classes and the lessening of internal regime dissonance between 1935 and 1938 produced a labor policy marked by the virtual demise of legal unionism, the absence of new regulatory initiatives by the state, and continued governmental non-enforcement of existing laws. The suspension of democratic and constitutional guarantees, almost two years prior to the official declaration of the Estado Novo dictatorship, further hampered the organizing efforts of labor militants like Marcos Andreotti.

As part of the conservative backlash, a cooperative chamber of deputies also established a court of exception in September 1936, the feared Tribunal de Segurança Nacional (National Security Court, or TSN), which was exempt from the restrictions governing normal legal proceedings. In addition to trying individuals who had taken up arms against the government, the infamous TSN also handled cases that had nothing to do with armed rebellion. During this witch-hunt, even the most innocuous form of labor activism could fall within the purview of the all-powerful TSN. "If in

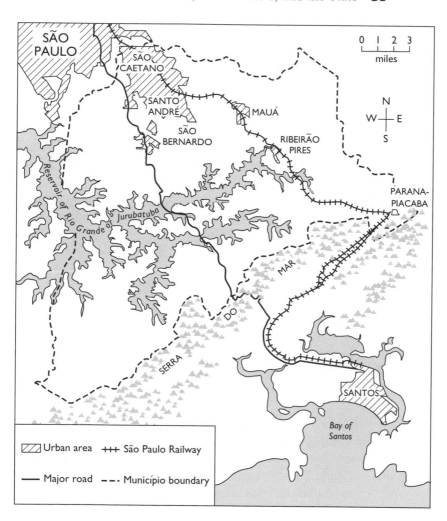

São Paulo's ABC Region, 1938 (adapted from PMSA map "Município do São Bernardo")

1920, the social question was defined as a police question," Angela de Castro Gomes has commented, "in 1935 it would be defined as a question of national security," with the Communists now targeted as the principal enemy and not the anarchists.[2]

São Paulo's regional alliance of factory and *fazenda* (plantation) fully supported repressive steps against labor. Riding high between 1934 and 1937, it had no need for the ambiguities of legal unionism or the loose prolabor rhetoric that had characterized its competitors in the early 1930s; for this alliance, class peace simply meant the employer's unchallenged domination of workers in both the factory and the community.

During this bleak period, the grievances and struggles of the workers of ABC might easily have gone unnoticed, even by historians, were it not for the police records contained in the files of the TSN, which took up the case of four workers charged with the circulation of a few leaflets in Santo André's historic Ipiranguinha textile factory (owned by the Sociedade Anônima Boyes since the 1920s). The plant's French manager called in the police on 2 February 1936 because of the circulation of "subversive bulletins" within the plant over the previous months. Having discovered an effort to approach one of his employees, René Degrave had placed the eighteen-year-old worker Maria Callejon under surveillance, and a search of her locker revealed the offending leaflets.[3]

Interrogated by the delegado, a frightened Callejon said that the leaflets had been given to her by the twenty-two-year-old woodworker Domingos Antônio da Silva at the request of her boyfriend, the twenty-year-old Spanish immigrant Eládio Ianes. A police search of the homes of these two men (who worked at a Santo André wood products factory) discovered further subversive literature. Faced with the threat of deportation, Ianes gave the police a vague lead that the leaflets had been printed by one "Marcos," a neighbor in Vila Alzira whom he had come to know while unemployed.

The involvement of Santo André's most notorious Communist, the twenty-six-year-old Marcos Andreotti, gave the February 1936 arrests added importance for the police. Andreotti had gone underground after the ANL rebellion of November 1935 and was residing in PCB-ANL safe houses in the city of São Paulo. Andreotti's clandestine activity included raising funds from sympathizers for political prisoners and in support of the Spanish Republicans. He also helped print and distribute ANL and PCB literature and worked to recruit new activists to the party's illegal network. Separated from his wife, he missed the birth of one of his children during his game of cat and mouse with the police. The former president of

Santo André's metalworkers' union was finally arrested in 1938 and spent half of the Estado Novo in prison, condemned on two separate occasions by the TSN.[4]

Yet the central focus of Andreotti's activity remained the organization of workers, even though the activities that he had engaged in openly between 1930 and 1935 were now deemed illegal. Utilizing his contacts, he traveled frequently to Santo André to oversee agitational work in local factories. Unable to appear publicly, he met clandestinely with activists like Ianes, whom he had earlier won over when the youth had lived briefly with Andreotti's family. In orienting Ianes, his friend, and his girlfriend, Andreotti directed their energies toward the main task of the workers' movement: organizing the industrial proletariat in large factories like the Ipiranguinha.

Organizing from the outside, Andreotti hoped to build the self-proclaimed "Boyes Workers' Committee" into a real organism within the factory. Although produced by a Communist cadre and sympathizers, the two factory leaflets seized by the police contained no references to the ANL, the PCB, or any other aspect of the current political situation. The two carefully prepared leaflets contained not a single word of generic anticapitalist or antigovernment rhetoric. They did, however, provide detailed descriptions of the workers' problems at the Ipiranguinha, based upon Andreotti's discussions with his informants.

Aiming at the widest level of potential agreement, the workers' committee hoped to mobilize its male and female coworkers by exposing their most immediate material needs and shop-floor grievances. "We cannot," the first leaflet said, "continue in the same situation. The salaries we are paid are not enough for anything, . . . [yet] we work like slaves." The second appeal opened: "We want an increase, we want better treatment." Judging the prevailing wages inadequate compared to the price of bread, the leaflets demanded a general pay increase as well as larger raises for teenage workers, for the spinners paid by the hour, and for those who worked in the dye shop. They also protested against management's use of fines, which resulted, at the end of the month, in the "robbery" of several hours of the workers' wages by the employer.

The leaflets gave equal prominence, however, to noneconomic issues, such as working conditions. The factory's five hundred workers, said the leaflets, had to endure filthy bathrooms, dirty drinking water, and management's refusal to open the windows despite the heat. These demands for a clean, comfortable workplace were combined with complaints about unsafe conditions and the illnesses caused by exposure to acids and chlorine in some departments. Further demands dealt with the "moral situation," the issue of management's lack of respect for the workers' dignity. Two supervisors were denounced by name as "the bandit Frankenstein" and "a Nazi pirate" for verbal threats, pushing, and even hitting employees. Workers who spent more than two minutes in the bathroom, it was reported, aroused the ire of their foreman. "We do not ask for alms," the short-lived Boyes Workers' Committee declared, "we demand our rights."

Despite charges by Degrave, the offending leaflets contained no propaganda for a strike; a strike was not feasible at this stage, given the prevailing fear and resignation among the Ipiranguinha's workers. Although mocking management's efforts to discover those responsible for the agitation, the leaflets provided their readers with no clear answer as to how management was to be made to meet their demands. The workers' committee could do little more at that moment than uphold the ideal of a "potent" organization to force concessions from management. In fact, the prospects for direct action by São Paulo's factory proletariat were no stronger in 1936 than they had been during most of the First Republic.

The workers' impotence was deepened by the prevailing governmental hostility toward labor, which eliminated even talk about forcing the government to take action to resolve workers' problems. Indeed, only one item in the 1936 leaflets dealt with state action outside the sphere of direct employer-employee relations: criticism of the company's practice of deducting Sundays and vacation days from the government-mandated annual paid vacation period.

The apparent passivity of the workers of the Ipiranguinha in 1936 gave substance to the employers' traditional public rhetoric about labor peace and the natural collaboration that existed between employers and workers. In an authoritarian and patriarchal society, the factory had long been portrayed by industrialists as a large family with a stern, but caring, father figure.[5] If this idyllic portrait were true, then discord between wage earners and employers could originate only from outside forces, the "malcontents and agitators" denounced by Ipiranguinha manager René Degrave.

Yet Degrave need not have feared the appearance of subversive leaflets by a handful of troublemakers had there been no legitimate sources of discontent. Confident of the loyalty of a truly contented work force, the factory manager would not have been concerned that the feeble efforts of a tiny minority would galvanize his employees into action. Degrave's statement to the police, however, lays bare a reality of conflict that was at variance with the claims of labor peace destined for public consumption. In sketching the relevant background to the incident, Degrave explained to the police that Boyes had recently granted the workers of the spinning section a wage increase at *their* request. "To avoid future demands" from others, management then gave a similar across-the-board increase to all workers. Yet this employer initiative, Degrave complained, had not prevented troublemakers from seeking once again "to foment *new* discontent among the workers" (my emphasis).

Being responsible for day-to-day operations, Degrave and his subordinates were familiar with the many veiled signs of discontent among the work force, including low morale, grumbling, decreased productivity, and even organized requests by small groups of workers. The appearance of anonymous but clearly well-informed leaflets alarmed Degrave because they represented a step beyond this level of conscious but unorganized resistance. Using a model of preemptive action, management may well have opened the windows after the complaint was raised in the second clandestine leaflet.

Alternate "Solutions" to the Social Question: Incorporating the Worker into the Enterprise, or into the State?

Privately, São Paulo industrialists and factory managers like Degrave had always known the falsity of their routine denials of the existence of any valid basis for labor unrest. Yet representatives of the industrial bourgeoisie in São Paulo had only publicly admitted the inherently conflictual relationship between workers and employers in response to the massive industrial strikes between 1917 and 1919.

In a famous June 1919 article, one of Brazil's leading textile industrialists had opened a more realistic debate on the origin of the social question. Worker agitation, wrote Jorge Street, owner of several large textile factories in São Paulo and Rio de Janeiro, originated in the "new and special conditions" created by the "large-scale industrialization of modern capitalism." He wrote that "inevitable, grave disagreements and antagonisms" were created because of the worker's "absolute dependence" upon his employer, which allowed management "to impose the maximum of production for the minimum of salary" while regulating wages and working conditions "at its will" and according to its "advantage and needs." The individual worker,

Street said in a comment still relevant in 1936, was impotent to defend himself against such impositions without "the help of his class *companheiros*." Speaking of the facts "known by everyone to be true," Street emphasized that employers were confident of victory in any strike because of the material deprivation of their workers' families, who were faced with the ever-present threat of hunger. "Recalcitrant" workers, Street went on, were easily replaced, and those "suspected of rebelliousness" were hard-pressed to find new jobs.[6]

Street had not been the only employer to reexamine his past practices in light of the extraordinary militancy displayed by Brazilian workers between 1917 and 1919. A number of his fellow employers also believed that a hardheaded realism was necessary if Brazil's industrialists were to overcome the crisis in which they found themselves. Like Street, the rising young São Paulo builder-industrialist Roberto Simonsen had stated his belief in 1918 that employers must "abandon the old ways" and realize that "workers' discontent [was] a new force [that] really existed."[7]

In the 1918 annual report of his Companhia Construtora de Santos, Simonsen joined Street in acknowledging the inherent conflict underlying the exchange of wages for labor power. The workers, he wrote, favored a goal of "limited output and unlimited salaries," while the employers held to a "diametrically opposed point of view." Thus the industrialist, seeking "to pay the least possible for each unit of production," confronted his workers, who sought "the highest possible pay for each unit of time." Roberto Simonsen also shared Street's belief that employers must move beyond blatant repression as the only means of handling their human capital; he too favored employer efforts to cultivate the workers' good will and "cordial cooperation." Indeed, Simonsen complained in 1918 that the "backward systems of payment and bad orientation" of many industrialists unwittingly contributed to the organization of their workers in order "to obtain improvements in pay and treatment."[8]

In 1919, however, Street had gone far beyond his fellow employers, including Simonsen, in defending what he described as the "disagreeable," "inevitable," and in the end, "just" need to accept the unionization of workers. Despite Street's several decades of leadership in the various associations of Brazilian industrialists, his acceptance of collective bargaining was not representative of the majority of Brazilian industrialists in 1919 or later. In fact, his celebrated remarks had been prompted by the division within the textile industrialists' association in Rio over the recognition of the União dos Operários em Fábricas de Tecidos (UOFT). Street's willingness to even consider such a course in 1919 was remarkable, given that most of his fellow textile employers rejected such an accommodation with their workers.[9]

The negotiated compromise that Street proposed in 1919, however, was quickly rendered irrelevant by the textile workers' defeat in 1920. Thus, the farseeing views of this humane employer had more of a prophetic than a practical significance during the remainder of the First Republic. Moreover, Street's standing with his fellows declined as his various enterprises entered into crisis and bankruptcy between 1925 and 1929.[10]

Seeking ways to mollify their workers without recognizing unions, many employers in the 1920s adopted more benevolent policies, eliminated some of the more blatant abuses, and made physical improvements in their plants in terms of hygiene and other conveniences of interest to workers.[11] But the most important employer response was the adoption of the modern techniques of personnel management that prevailed in the developed industrial countries, "welfare capitalism" as it was then called in the United States.[12]

As in the United States during the 1920s, this more enlightened brand of "open shop" antiunionism was limited to the most heavily capitalized and profitable sector of large-scale, heavily mechanized manufacturing production. Yet existing scholarship has ignored these welfare capitalist policies, which were increasingly characteristic of the most important foreign and Brazilian industrial concerns in ABC and São Paulo.

In ABC, these welfare capitalist initiatives can be exemplified by Roberto Simonsen's Cerâmica São Caetano (534 workers) and by two foreign enterprises, the French Rhodia rayon-chemical complex (1,685 workers) and the Italian Pirelli metalworking factory (638 workers).[13] Although operating in different branches of industry, these enterprises shared a range of common practices that aimed at the incorporation of the workers into the enterprise. The rational organization of material production, they believed, demanded a scientific, planned effort to understand and successfully motivate company employees.[14] The three industrial establishments adopted systematic personnel policies—such as hiring only through family ties—as well as a system of extra wages, salaries, and bonuses for veteran workers, those with young children, or especially productive or cooperative individuals. In addition to providing amenities such as filtered water and restaurants, there was also an effort to systematize the awarding of patronage—such as limited company housing—to deserving workers and supervisors.[15]

In creating a company-oriented work force, these policies provided a base for opposing independent organizational efforts. But these employers sought to go further and organize their workers outside the factory. All three companies financed athletic clubs, some with their own soccer fields for factory teams that competed in the local soccer league. These associations also organized excursions to the beaches at Santos and other recreational activities, such as dances. The Cerâmica São Caetano even held film showings for the workers in a special room at the factory. Nor were the material needs of the workers' families forgotten: several enterprises maintained their own cooperatives or warehouses to provide basic foodstuffs at reduced prices.[16]

A third major component was the provision of basic services that were not supplied by the state. Rhodia provided free medical and pharmaceutical aid, and Pirelli covered most surgical expenses in whole or in part. These companies also made special payments in the event of death or injury on the job. Finally, the manager of the Cerâmica São Caetano, Armando de Arruda Pereira, was especially proud of the school and playground the company provided on factory grounds for 120 of its workers' children. Good students received savings accounts from the company as awards.[17]

Although not yet typical of all enterprises, these progressive, even mildly reformist, management policies were seen by leading Brazilian industrialists like Roberto Simonsen as part of an effort to prevent the state intervention in industrial and labor relations that was the hallmark of Vargas's federal labor policy after 1930.[18] In a remarkable display of prescience, Roberto Simonsen in 1918 had anticipated labor's turn toward indirect action in the same company report that discussed the labor question in detail. Writing a year after the São Paulo general strike of 1917, Simonsen made the surprising claim that labor militancy and strikes were not the most important danger to industrial employers. The main threat, he wrote, was that the social question would be resolved "mistakenly, through political means," which would result in "hindrances to production." Despite labor's minimal prospects for political influence or allies during the First Republic, Simonsen warned that industrialists must, at all costs, guarantee that their workers would not form "into a hostile mass" and seek "the remedies for their malaise in political conquests that would disrupt production."[19]

The danger that Robert Simonsen anticipated in 1918 became a reality after 1930 when the national government took on the self-proclaimed role of protector of the workers. Closely allied with the dominant oligarchy in São Paulo, industrialists like Simonsen consistently opposed the Vargas regime's social and labor legislation in the early 1930s. Indeed, hostility toward such initiatives "directly contributed to the CIESP [Centro de Indústrias do Estado de São Paulo] leadership's decision to join the abortive Paulista rebellion against Vargas in 1932."[20] And the consensus of elite opinion at the state level in the mid-1930s reflected the industrialists' position: the working class did not require any special program of compensatory regulation, special governmental assistance, or state-sponsored trade unionism.[21]

The state's industrialists welcomed the de facto liquidation of legal unionism in late 1935, which was accompanied by a weakening of state interventionist tendencies. Even the de jure elimination of harmful governmental policies seemed within reach because the Paulista candidate was widely expected to win the presidential elections of 3 January 1938. A man of proven hostility toward labor, the ex-governor of São Paulo, Armando de Salles Oliveira, understood the perils of social experimentation and disdained the cheap demagoguery characteristic of the Vargas regime and its presidential contender José Américo.

Yet Getúlio Vargas, backed by the military, proved capable of an unexpected maneuver in late 1937. On 30 September 1937, the Brazilian armed forces announced to a startled nation the discovery of the "Cohen plan" for imminent Communist revolution. A crude right-wing Integralist fabrication with clear anti-Semitic overtones, the Cohen plan nevertheless convinced the Congress to once again renew the state of war on 1 October 1937. This incident also provided the pretext for the cancellation of the planned presidential elections and the establishment of a dictatorship under Getúlio Vargas.

On 10 November 1937, the Estado Novo (New State) was unveiled, with a new constitution derived from European corporatist and fascist ideas. Leaving executive powers at all levels untouched for the moment, the government dissolved the federal Congress, state assemblies, and city councils. The new constitution also specifically banned strikes as "antisocial and harmful," and those who instigated or led work stoppages were subject to automatic prison terms. Thus began eight years of dictatorial rule that has long been associated with persecution, censorship, torture, and a shameless propaganda machine singing the praises of Getúlio Vargas.[22]

Though justified as a blow against communism, the Estado Novo was in fact directed against São Paulo—and the abolition of elections weakened the agrarian oligarchies in general. Firmly in the saddle, Vargas now believed that the moment had come to resolve the problem presented by the state of São Paulo. Depriving the ruling Constitutionalists of control of the state government in 1938, Getúlio set out to win São Paulo's industrialists away from their longtime partners in the state oligarchy. For the first time, the Brazilian government put aside past rhetoric about Brazil's "essentially agricultural vocation"; the modern factory was to replace the plantation as the symbol of Brazil's future.

Having abandoned political liberalism, the Estado Novo also rejected the orthodoxies of economic laissez-faire and openly avowed the sort of state-supported push toward industrialization that had long been advocated by Roberto Simonsen. Embracing state intervention and economic planning, the new regime opened a drive to establish Brazilian basic industry—a move symbolized by the massive federally sponsored Volta Redonda steel works, which finally opened in 1943. The state's role in establishing the foundations for further Brazilian industrial development did not, however, represent an attack on private capital. Indeed, the regime's economic policy-making bodies were to be staffed by industrialists such as Simonsen and the manager of his Cerâmica São Caetano, Armando de Arruda Pereira.[23]

The fact that the Estado Novo was characterized by a nationalist industrialization policy, a new prominence of industrialists, and a vigorously repressive stance toward radical labor activism has led many scholars to classify the Estado Novo's labor policies as an expression of the interests of the industrial bourgeoisie, based upon "the complete subordination of the subaltern classes." Governmental labor policy after 1937, Luiz Werneck Vianna concludes, not only served the "primitive accumulation of capital" but provided employers with "an army of labor with a standard of discipline" far beyond their "best fantasies."[24]

Yet the industrialists' alleged identification with state policy should not obscure, as Barbara Weinstein has pointed out, the "considerable ambivalence towards the state" that continued to characterize the Paulista industrial bourgeoisie even during the most authoritarian period of the Estado Novo.[25] Although both shared a common antiradicalism and a desire to control workers, the industrialists and the Vargas regime differed in their ideal solutions to the social question: the incorporation of the workers into the enterprise, versus their incorporation into the state.

At the outset of the Estado Novo, the industrialists still hoped to preempt or neutralize positive state intervention in industrial and labor relations while limiting the state role primarily to the repression of labor agitation. In fact, the first years of the new dictatorship were marked by employers' lobbying to nullify the government's social and labor legislation. The 1939 annual report of the São Paulo industries association (Federação das Indústrias do Estado de São Paulo, or FIESP) criticized the government's social legislation, and the Paulista industrialist Morvan Dias de Figueiredo even proposed the weakening of the restrictive laws on child and women's labor. The practical counterpart to this employer agitation against existing regulations was a stubborn refusal to follow the law. In 1938, Labor Ministry officials complained about the persistent efforts by many industrialists "to escape, by all means, the enforcement of the law."[26]

State-sponsored unionization continued to be singled out by businessmen as "the gravest defect of the existing social legislation." As Boris Fausto has noted, the industrial bourgeoisie continued to view the government's unionization decrees as a "straitjacket" and resisted them even at the repressive height of the Estado Novo. Trade unions, they complained, were being sustained "artificially from above" by the government out of a mixture of "demagogic interests and lack of understanding."[27]

Nevertheless, the Vargas regime, even as it solidified its ties with Paulista industrialists like Simonsen, made clear in 1938–39 that it had no intention of abandoning its earlier social and labor legislation.[28] Indeed, São Paulo's industrial employers were frustrated by the government's stubborn refusal to draw the "proper" conclusions from its stated new focus on industrialization and economic development. Criticizing a 1939 decree requiring large factories to provide dining halls and worker training, Simonsen argued that the regime's persistence in such unsound policies was a disastrous by-product of Brazilian *bacharéis*'s (the holders of law degrees) excessive legalism, their slavish imitation of inappropriate foreign models, and their lack of a practical knowledge of economics.[29]

As the Estado Novo took shape, regime policy makers began a second and more intense phase of governmental interventionism in industrial and labor relations. Putting an end to the forced retreat that had begun in 1934–35, the government now moved aggressively to implement its ambitious corporatist scheme of incorporating workers into the state apparatus. In addition to implementing earlier promises by establishing a minimum wage and a system of labor courts, the government not only reiterated its commitment to state-sponsored labor organization but set out to expand and reorganize the system of government-recognized legal trade unions.

Yet the dictatorship was by no means immune to the argument that labor unions had proven a base for Communist subversion in the early 1930s. Thus support for legal unionism coincided with a rigorously repressive posture toward workers who could be identified, correctly or incorrectly, with a subversive approach to labor organization. Even the enlightened industrialist Jorge Street, after all, had argued, as did most employers, that legally sanctioned unionism and governmental protection of labor could be justified only if strikes and agitation were outlawed.[30]

The regime openly boasted in the late 1930s that working-class "collaboration with the state" had proved that "the unionized worker is a disciplined worker" who did not strike. The regime did not, however, depend solely on the workers' cooperative spirit to guarantee such success, and labor had by no means stopped being a police matter: São Paulo's police chief in 1939 pledged even closer coordination with the State Labor Department (DET) in monitoring trade unions. Indeed, union meetings could be held only with the authorization of the police department, which often exercised its right to send an investigator to the meetings. Candidates for union office were also required to file a "certificate of ideology" (*atestado de ideologia*) obtained from the political-social police (DOPS), and they could take office only if the election results were approved by the Labor Ministry.[31]

In the absence of guarantees of democratic rights, the police were free to persecute suspected Communists, socialists, Aliancistas, and other dissidents. Police in ABC often picked up suspected radicals from their homes or jobs and held them incommunicado, sometimes for days at a time. When Getúlio Vargas visited ABC, the police would "clean up" the area by detaining dozens of suspect workers for the duration of his visit.[32] Such police arbitrariness, although falling disproportionately on local workers, extended even to some dissident members of ABC's politically active middle class.

With time, the dictatorship even transformed the combative May Day celebrations of yesteryear, as Vargas often said, from a day of commotion and tumult into a celebration of the workers' collaboration with the constituted authorities of the nation. By the early forties, government-organized rallies were a regular feature of May Day. After watching soccer games, tens of thousands of workers would hear Getúlio Vargas announce the latest gifts from the "father of the poor." And the appearance of union leaders, as junior members of the establishment, at many ceremonial state functions had become a standard part of regime protocol.[33]

Image and Reality: Labor's Grass Roots during the Estado Novo

Scholars who stress the importance of corporatism have most often seen 1930–31 as the decisive moment of transition in Brazil, but dating the shift to the time of Estado Novo dictatorship would not seriously undermine the persuasiveness of their interpretation. For the scholarly proponents of the corporatist consensus, Brazilian labor may or may not have been effectively harnessed to the state prior to 1937. But if the corporatist schemes to control the working class failed in the early 1930s, they argue, it was due only to the absence of the powerful state apparatus that was finally established under the Estado Novo; at that point, most conclude, the unions finally passed entirely under the control of the State.[34]

As wards of the state, the trade unions after 1937 are said to have lost their independence and the workers their ability to organize collectively and autonomously.[35] For most observers, this fascist union system had reduced the "potentially dangerous trade unions" to impotence in a scheme to destroy the union as an avenue of worker protest. An independent workers' movement, it seemed, had been replaced by a statist unionism in which labor associations functioned as para-state organs providing services to the working class. Even today, most observers share the opinion of one foreign visitor who judged, in 1942, that the regime's "strict and uncompromising paternalism [left] no room for a future development of an independent labor movement."[36]

To many observers on the Left, the labor movement had exchanged its autonomy and its capacity for independent, if not revolutionary, action for a few questionable material advances and the petty advantages that the state provided to the corrupt union leadership they had foisted upon the working class. The incorporation of workers into the state, most conclude, dampened working-class action, made workers the object of Getulista politics, and cultivated widespread popular belief in illusory advances.[37] For anarchist critics like Edgard Leuenroth, the struggle to defend the principles of true trade unionism after 1937, although valiant, proved unsuccessful in the end.[38]

Not surprisingly, the typical labor leader of the Estado Novo era is said to have been a cooperative government man, a pelego "totally exempt from any larger preoccupation with workers' real needs."[39] The explanation for this outcome has varied, but most have credited the regime's repression with creating a political vacuum within the labor movement that was filled by the infiltration of men of the government into the unions. The disappearance of independent union militancy left the trade unions under the domination of a bureaucracy, supported and maintained by the government, which had eliminated oppositionist currents within the unions.[40] The dominance of these progovernment pelegos, it is argued, was facilitated by the financial stability guaranteed the unions through the state-mandated "union tax" (*impôsto sindical*), established in 1939, which financed labor organizations through an automatic annual deduction from the workers' salaries. It has also been argued that the strong state after 1937 was now capable, for the first time, of offering incentives to workers and their leaders in order to achieve its totalitarian objectives. Workers were co-opted through the establishment of a minimum wage (*salário mínimo*), an increasingly effective labor court system, and social welfare measures such as pensions.

Thus most contemporary and later observers, whether critical or sympathetic, have concluded that the architects of the Estado Novo succeeded in their stated goal of disciplining and incorporating the worker into the state. In his capacity as juridical consultant of the Labor Ministry from 1932 to 1940, the corporatist ideologue Oliveira Vianna emphasized the success of the government's campaign to eliminate the workers' "antiemployer attitudes," to resolutely suppress harmful agitation, and to create a cooperative working-class elite. Thus the Brazilian state successfully safeguarded the capitalist social order by, as a contemporary observer put it, "taking the wind out of the sails of communism."[41]

In overemphasizing the regime's grandiose aspirations and overarching ideology, both the defenders and the opponents of Brazil's corporatist labor system have continued to embrace the particularly bankrupt assumption that law equals reality, that intentions equal results, and that rhetoric equals substance. To separate image from reality, however, we must examine the impact of state action during the Estado Novo from the viewpoint of the life and struggles of labor and employers at the point of production.

As one of Brazil's top industrial areas, ABC provides an adequate test of our accepted generalizations about trade unionism during the Estado

Novo. The expanding industrial development between 1930 and the end of World War II was felt with special force in the ABC region, where some of Brazil's largest new factories had been built. Industrial employment, which was 6,000 in 1930, grew to 15,000 in 1937, to 18,000 in 1938, and to 22,000 in 1940. By 1950, 46,000 workers were employed in ABC in some of Brazil's most modern and highly concentrated industrial plants. The region's population, which was 25,000 in 1920, soared to 60,000 in 1934, 90,000 in 1940, and 216,000 in 1950.[42]

Although a superficial survey of labor in the ABC region seems to substantiate the prevailing image, a closer examination of grass-roots trade unionism suggests that appearances have too often been mistaken for realities. Following the lead of industrialists and state policy makers, we have tended to underestimate the ingenuity and persistence of those workers who sought, under even the worst of conditions, to organize their class. The centralizing state during the Estado Novo was indeed more capable of supervising and controlling union activities than in the early thirties, but it is easy to overestimate the impact of the government's greater ability to monitor and intervene within the trade unions.[43] Even the restrictive framework of legal unionism under the Estado Novo still offered working-class activists some protection from employer reprisal, while labor legislation offered a means, however restricted, to address some workers' needs.

The rebirth of the local labor movement in ABC began modestly in late 1938 and early 1939 with the reestablishment of Santo André's metalworkers' and textile workers' unions as functioning public institutions. Unlike the situation in the early 1930s, however, the leaders of the refounded unions in 1938 were consciously chosen so as to be acceptable to the authorities. In the metalworkers' union, the imprisoned president, Marcos Andreotti, was replaced by the Pirelli worker Augusto Savietto. A blacksmith by trade, Savietto had lived in Ribeirão Pires for a number of years before becoming a merchant in the Paulista city of Campinas. Returning to ABC, he had then taken a job as a maintenance mechanic at Pirelli. At his first union meeting in October 1938, he agreed to serve as union president.[44]

Savietto seemed precisely the type of cooperative working-class leader prized by the ideologues of the corporatist system. As Savietto told a local journalist in 1979, there were no strikes during his presidency between 1938 and 1942 because "we weren't discontented." Asked about the Estado Novo's "terrible repression," Savietto denied that this had affected his union. "I even think," he went on, "that the government of Getúlio Vargas did a lot for the union . . . and started many improvements for the workers."[45]

To mark their reorganization, the metalworkers' and textile workers' unions held a joint celebration at their headquarters in Santo André on 26 November 1938. Dedicating portraits of Getúlio Vargas and his new São Paulo intervenor, Adhemar de Barros, the meeting was honored with the presence of Adhemar, the head of the DET, and numerous union officials from São Paulo. This ceremony seemed symbolic of the more conformist and co-opted stance of the new leaders of Santo André's legal trade unions.[46]

Despite its unprecedented respectability, however, the refounded metalworkers' union was nearly defunct, having only thirty members. Thus, the initial focus of the diretório was the recruitment of new members, especially at Pirelli, and the regularization of the union's legal status. This working-class institution-building was characteristic of all the local unions. In 1939, the textile workers' union moved to its own headquarters, and steps were taken to establish legal unions for Santo André's woodworkers and chemical workers, and a joint organization covering workers in the civil construction and industrial ceramics industries.[47]

To renew their legal status with the government, ABC's union leaders had to learn the extralegal side of the union's incorporation into the Brazilian state. Lobbying trips to São Paulo and Rio de Janeiro, useful connections, and personal appeals to policy makers were essential, and small bribes to the appropriate functionaries were sometimes of great help in speeding up the process. From now on, union leaders would have to become adept in handling the problems of displaced files and bureaucratic runarounds.[48]

The 1938 metalworkers' constitution, incorporating the government's legal language, defined the union's purpose as "the study, coordination, protection, and legal representation" of its categoria in "collaboration with the public powers and other associations toward professional solidarity and their subordination to the national interests."[49] Indeed, most of the energies of local unionists in the late 1930s were spent in lobbying the government. In 1939, for example, ABC's unions requested the Departamento Estadual de Trabalho (DET) to open a local office to issue identification cards (carteiras de trabalho), which allowed workers to qualify for the government-mandated paid vacation time. In 1940, local unions submitted a proposal, which was later accepted, to the government's Industrial Employees' Pension Institute to build housing for workers in Santo André.[50]

Trade Unions and Indirect Action
during the Early Estado Novo

The strongly interventionist nature of the centralizing state during the Estado Novo transformed Brazilian labor relations and made indirect action, for the first time, a viable strategy for labor and not merely an aspiration, as it had been in the early 1930s. A self-aggrandizing state apparatus undertook two initiatives in 1938–39 that gave it a central role in regulating the urban labor market and employer-employee relations. First, the government introduced a legally mandated minimum wage for industrial employment, the only piece of legislation that was not foreshadowed earlier in the 1930s. The regime's second great accomplishment was the effective establishment of the system of tripartite labor courts, with labor and management representation, that had been originally proposed in the early 1930s.[51] From the regime's point of view, the former lessened the need and justification for working-class militancy, and the latter provided a legal forum where unions could defend the workers' interests in a positive and controlled fashion.

In the case of the minimum wage, unions in ABC and elsewhere participated actively in the state commissions that were formed to carry out technical studies and policy discussions designed to establish an adequate, living wage for urban workers. Composed of representatives of unions, employers, and the government, these commissions were marked, as an observer noted in 1942, by "bitter controversies" in which employers "resisted [the minimum-wage legislation] to the utmost" as "a serious drain" on their profit margins.[52]

The final minimum-wage scales announced on 4 May 1940 for the various regions of the state of São Paulo were less than the proposal supported by the state's unions. Unfortunately, we lack the empirical studies of pay systems, wage levels, and governmental enforcement efforts that would establish the exact impact of the first minimum wage,[53] but we do know that the new system did not result in lowering industrial wages, as charged by some later critics.[54]

Fragmentary evidence from ABC suggests that the minimum wage's impact varied considerably by industry, and even within a given factory. It was probably least important for the majority of those employed in the largest and most mechanized industrial enterprises, since these highly profitable firms already paid higher-than-average wages. But the lowest-paid groups in even these factories, such as women, probably did receive increases through the new minimum wage, as did workers in some of the less lucrative branches of industry.[55]

Unlike small employers or those in less profitable branches of manufacturing, São Paulo's largest industrial firms could afford the extra costs occasioned by such governmental measures. Yet they feared, quite correctly, that political calculations would in the end place the burden of these benefits disproportionately on the larger firms. The size and visibility of such enterprises, as Karl Loewenstein reported in 1942, made it virtually impossible, for example, for them to evade the minimum wage law. In addition, he noted that a 1939 law that mandated restaurants in plants with over 500 workers had been enforced "to date" primarily against large foreign concerns like General Motors in São Caetano.[56]

The second great labor relations innovation of the Estado Novo era was the organization of the system of labor courts established by Decree Law 1,237 of 2 May 1939. It would be two more years before the new labor justice system would begin to function, but it fulfilled an ambition going back to 1932: to establish a juridical framework for the resolution of the social question. Although the courts were legally endowed with the power to resolve collective disputes with employers, their practice before 1945 centered on the grievances of individual workers, especially dismissals for just cause.[57]

In focusing union attention on individual rather than collective grievances, the labor justice system has been seen by some as an instrument for "the control and repression of the working class."[58] Yet indirect action through the labor courts did, in fact, serve as a means of worker struggle against the employers. This is well illustrated by a case that Augusto Savietto still recalled with great pleasure in 1979. Fired by a large local factory, a foundry worker had filed an appeal with the labor court with no apparent success. Approached by the worker, Savietto took up the man's defense, and the court resolved the matter satisfactorily within a few months.[59] This incident shows that the union still saw itself as an adversary of management, since it took up the defense of a man who had been fired for his well-known and habitual drunkenness. In defending such a "bad worker," Savietto was not demonstrating the behavior expected by the government. From the regime's perspective, the unions were to be responsible entities striving, in a cooperative manner, to increase productivity and national well-being.

For ABC's employers, such union behavior and the unfavorable outcome in court confirmed their suspicion of the government's new labor justice system. From their point of view, the establishment of the new legal forum invited petty harassment by their employees, and especially by the unions.[60] Moreover, the outcome in a given case depended upon the decision made by a government-appointed judge, a lawyer, who lacked knowledge or understanding of the imperatives of modern industrial production. As Roberto Simonsen complained in 1939, the government's labor relations system in practice gave one party, the employers, all the duties, while the other party, the workers, had only rights.[61]

For trade unionists, the labor court system, even without the right to strike, still provided a mechanism for contesting unjust employer actions and management arbitrariness. In this regard, the workers' interests coincided with those of the growing federal bureaucracy, which sought to centralize effective control in the hands of the state. This new legal-bureaucratic empire also provided thousands of jobs for lawyers and other white-collar employees, thus guaranteeing an important base of non-working-class support for the government's labor relations system.[62]

In addition, those who administered the labor courts could not back the employers 100 percent of the time if they expected to justify their own jobs or to retain the minimum necessary cooperation of the workers.[63] Although we lack detailed studies of the institution, a labor judge from this period later recalled that he and his fellow jurists considered themselves "neutral on the side of labor." Indeed, large foreign enterprises were reported in 1942 to be critical of what they perceived as the "prolabor bias of the labor authorities" in general.[64]

Aware of the inherent conflict of interest between workers and managers, industrialists had never been convinced by the government's labor ideologues, who promised social peace and the fruitful collaboration of classes through state intervention and government-controlled unionism. However, the industrialists were realistic about their prospects for achieving a formal renunciation of misguided governmental policies, especially given their own growing dependence upon the state apparatus. Thus, by the early 1940s few industrialists publicly challenged the legitimacy of the government's social and labor laws as such. Recognizing that they lived in a less-than-ideal world, most opted for the wisdom first expressed by Jorge Street when he led employer resistance to a mandatory vacation law being proposed by the government: if the law could not be revoked, he wrote, at least it must be "rightly interpreted."[65]

Instead of a frontal assault, industrialists adopted a more circumspect and camouflaged strategy designed to frustrate the fulfillment of the new laws by using their undoubted influence within the state apparatus.[66] In some cases, they played off one government agency or level of authority against another, while cultivating individual officeholders from the highest to the lowest levels within the growing labor bureaucracy. The means used to achieve their ends also varied: at times, they engineered the insertion of crucial loopholes into the actual drafts of given laws; at other times, they waged battles, often successful, over the interpretation of the provisos of a given decree. In the day-to-day conduct of their operations, the industrialists routinely ignored laws that affected their pocketbooks, while buying de facto exemptions from enforcement by winning the support of less scrupulous factory inspectors, labor court officials, and even trade unionists. Whatever the method, the results, which were often favorable to employers, made a mockery of the law and left a bitter taste in the mouths of most trade unionists and even the many honest members of the government's labor bureaucracy.

The Impôsto Sindical, Assistencialismo, and Peleguismo

In no longer defining itself exclusively as an instrument of the employers, the state had, since 1930, opened up a Pandora's box for Brazilian employers, who remained convinced, as a disappointed Jorge Street put it in 1934, that *any* form of "collective organization of the laboring masses" inevitably resulted in a "tyrannical, disturbing proletarian autocracy."[67] Even a union oriented to the state and restricted to indirect action was, at best, a necessary evil and far from the industrialists' ideal of *no* effective organization of their workers. If labor control were the sole objective, the government would do better, from the employers' point of view, to simply maintain a repressive vigilance of labor through the police, the DOPS, and the National Security Court, while abolishing the rest of these elaborate bureaucratic structures. The employers welcomed the ban on strikes in the Estado Novo's constitution; nevertheless, they feared, quite rightly, that not all elements of the government could be counted upon to resist the siren calls of political expedience in the future. Throughout the 1930s and 1940s, as Barbara Weinstein suggests, industrialists continued to view "even the friendliest politicians as susceptible to making concessions to workers, concessions that could undermine both the economic and social objectives of the industrial bourgeoisie."[68]

It is in this context that we must analyze the controversial "union tax" established in 1939. Sometimes called the Achilles' heel of Brazilian unionism, the union tax was an involuntary annual contribution of a day's wages that the employer was to deduct from the pay of every worker. Split among the government, union federations, and the local unions, this tax is believed to have transformed Brazilian trade unions "from active, if precarious, defenders of workers' interests and rights to financially secure, bureaucratic welfare agencies."[69]

The prevailing one-sided assessment of the union tax sees it exclusively as a mechanism that undermined union independence from the state and shifted labor's focus away from the bargaining functions of union militancy toward the provision of welfare benefits.[70] Yet some of ABC's industrial employers during World War II resisted this measure because they believed, quite rightly, that the *impôsto sindical* would facilitate labor activity by strengthening the unions' economic base. Santo André's metalworkers, for example, were able to collect this assessment only starting in 1942. For Pirelli's management, this new imposition was the final straw in terms of their willingness to tolerate Augusto Savietto's union activism. Within months, the company seized upon a broken machine as a pretext to fire the metalworkers' president, despite the legal guarantee of immunity from reprisals for elected union leaders.[71]

The union tax did, in fact, provide labor organizations with a hitherto-unknown degree of financial stability. In the metalworkers' union, activists no longer had to devote their energies to fund-raising events in order to pay the rent for their headquarters each month. The new funds also allowed the metalworkers to hire a functionary to keep their office open during the day. The union was now better able to serve its members, including those who worked the night shift, which therefore meant more court cases against employers.

Further, the union tax did *not* transform ABC's unions during the Estado Novo into the organs of social assistance that have been so often described. Even before 1937, Santo André's textile workers' and metalworkers' unions had begun to contract the services of local doctors, on a part-time basis, to provide limited medical and dental services to their members—while emphasizing that this function was secondary to the defense of the interests of their members as defined by law. This stance was essential if their modest social welfare function were not to invite unfavorable comparison with the extensive, well-financed welfare capitalist programs of the biggest local employers.[72]

The scholarly description of unions as service institutions is better applied to the type of "workers' organization" that industrialists *did* favor during the years of the Estado Novo—namely, the Círculo Operário (Workers' Circle) movement sponsored by the Roman Catholic Church. Like the industrialists, Brazil's conservative church hierarchy frowned upon the legal unions and favored a Catholic organization based upon their definition of the conciliation of interests between employer and employee.[73]

Founded with 300 members in February 1940, the Círculo Operário de Santo André (COSA) grew to a claimed membership of 1,000 by the end of 1941. It received financial support from Kowarick, Rhodia, and other local employers, and the organization's ample headquarters in downtown Santo André was opened with the help of "local capitalists." Unlike the trade unions, COSA placed no emphasis on the workers' wages, conditions, or individual grievances, focusing instead on the provision of medical, pharmaceutical, and educational services to members.[74]

The Círculos Operários received governmental encouragement during the early Estado Novo, but the movement never succeeded in effectively penetrating or influencing industrial workers to the same extent as the state's legal trade unions. This is not surprising, given that the key leadership posts in COSA were held by nonworkers, including a local priest and the manager of the Pirelli factory, the former Integralist Gino Gambini.[75]

The legal trade unions, by contrast, were led by men who, whatever their orientation, were in fact workers—although most scholars routinely deny these individuals any legitimacy as working-class leaders. Those who held union positions in ABC were not bureaucrats holding well-heeled patronage appointments. Indeed, all of the leaders of Santo André's metalworkers' union remained on the job despite the legal provisions that allowed paid leave for union officials. Even during the Estado Novo, the classic phenomenon of progovernment, proemployer peleguismo flourished mainly among the paid functionaries who filled the higher, and hence more visible, state federation level of the trade union movement.

The leaders of ABC's trade unions were less a privileged union bureaucracy than a small group of volunteers struggling in the face of employer opposition and worker indifference. Unpaid union leaders like Savietto left work at the end of the day, ate a hurried dinner, and went to their office to handle workers' complaints and court cases. For these activists, the most immediate obstacle to union advances was the workers' quite sensible conviction that nothing could be accomplished against the wishes of their employers. A 1938 Santo André metalworkers' pamphlet contained a most revealing feature, "How a Member Can Contribute to Killing His Union," that provides insight into the concerns and frustrations of the minority of workers who were union members or activists. The article singled out the problem of members who failed to attend meetings, arrived late, or refused to accept leadership posts. Too many union members, it said, failed to recruit others and did little for the union beyond complaining and criticizing the mistakes of its leaders; it was "easier to criticize than to work." And too many, the article went on, refused to participate actively during union meetings but were voluble in expressing negative opinions in discussions in local bars.[76]

The qualities and motivation needed to persist in the mundane work of maintaining a local union were unlikely to be found among the more opportunistic elements, who were more likely to be attracted to the well-financed employers' athletic and social clubs or the Catholic Círculo Operário. Continued union activism demanded a concern for other people's problems, a great deal of patience with one's fellow workers, and a compensating belief in some larger purpose for unionism. This was especially true when labor leaders were still routinely subject to police harassment and retaliatory firings by their employers.

Although no particular political outlook was required, union leadership naturally attracted activist workers, including the radicals whom scholars have incorrectly assumed to have been eliminated by governmental repression. In this regard, later observers have continued to share the government's naive faith in the efficacy of the "certificate of ideology" demanded of union leaders, even though it could be used only against individuals, such as Marcos Andreotti, who had been "burned" by public exposure or denunciation. Although repression had destroyed the PCB as an organized group on the state and national levels by 1939, a handful of Communist workers did remain in ABC's factories—but their activities were clandestine in nature and were carried out without effective coordination by the party leadership.[77]

Under the repressive conditions of the first phase of the Estado Novo (up to 1942), these activists refrained from any public union leadership role out of fear of endangering the union's survival. They preferred to encourage the participation of political moderates, whose presence might lessen the prospects of repression. Augusto Savietto, for example, was invited to serve as president of the metalworkers' union at the suggestion of his seventeen-year-old son, Euclides, an enthusiast of the ANL in 1935 who eventually joined the Communist Party.[78]

The year 1942, however, was marked by a new level of aggressiveness and risk-taking on the part of the legal labor movement, even prior to the government's shift in policy. In ABC, for example, the end of the Estado Novo's most fascist phase encouraged more aggressive labor activists to assume leadership positions in several important local unions. In the metalworkers' organization, the presidency passed from Augusto Savietto to the younger and more combative Euclides Savietto, who served along with a new vice-president, the Pirelli worker Miguel Guillen, who was also a Communist. In that same year, Alberto Zamignani, a prominent postwar Communist trade union leader and politician, became even more visible as the president of the local union that covered workers in the civil construction and industrial ceramics industries.[79]

Repression had not disappeared, but ABC's unionists were able, starting in 1942, to take new initiatives to circumvent the obstacles created by the government's restrictive legislation. Barred from horizontal ties with other unions, local trade unionists formed a Consumer Cooperative of the Unionized Workers of Santo André in 1942. The government had authorized such cooperatives as a safe outlet for the energy of unionists. In Santo André and elsewhere, however, these cooperatives became the focus of a growing network of prounion workers and activists in local factories. In 1942 state-level federations of unions in different categorias were also formed. Santo André's metalworkers' and textile workers' unions affiliated with their respective federations, as did São Bernardo's furniture makers.[80]

São Paulo's unionists also became more aggressive in formulating demands directly to the government. At a statewide union gathering in Campinas in 1942, lower-level union leaders refused to endorse the efforts of conservative state labor leader Artur Albino da Rocha to limit discussion to praise of the government. That same year Miguel Guillen was part of a São Paulo union delegation that met with Getúlio Vargas in Rio de Janeiro to present their concerns. A few daring union leaders even broached the touchy issues of union autonomy and the demand for a declaration of war against the Axis.[81]

The Expanding Limits of the Possible
in the Late Estado Novo: Using
the New "Legality" in Labor
Relations to Breach the Factory Walls

Brazil's 1942 entry into World War II on the side of the United Nations
contributed to a realignment of political forces within the Estado Novo that
marginalized some of the most conservative elements who had previously
sympathized with the Axis powers. After 1942, these divisions within the
government's camp and the growing revanchism of the elites defeated in
1937, in São Paulo and elsewhere, began to cloud the prospects for the
regime's survival.

Workers now entered into the political calculations of some of Vargas's
closest supporters in a new way as they contemplated the inevitable postwar transition. Discussing the government's opening toward labor, Angela
de Castro Gomes has spoken persuasively of the "invention of trabalhismo"
during these years, in a process that led to the foundation of the Partido
Trabalhista Brasileiro (Brazilian Labor Party, or PTB) by Getúlio Vargas in
1945.[82]

This incipient populist policy gained an increasingly prominent place
under the new labor minister, Alexandre Marcondes Filho (1941–45),
who reinvigorated the regime's efforts at social reform as part of a drive to
build a working-class constituency for the government.[83] Even as economic conditions deteriorated with the complications of war, the Vargas regime
gave labor affairs and social legislation a new prominence through rallies,
radio broadcasts, union membership drives, and organized worker delegations to the president.[84] As part of this effort, the government consolidated
existing labor laws into the famous *Consolidação das Leis do Trabalho*
(*CLT*) of 1943, the bible of Brazilian labor relations to this day.

The *CLT* has traditionally been characterized in polemical terms as a
fascist labor code "copied from Mussolini's legislation for control of
unions."[85] While the Italian paternity of the labor clauses of the Estado
Novo's constitution is clear, observers have overlooked the fact that the
demise of the 1937 corporatist charter was already to be read in the text of
the new de facto labor code; rather than banning all strikes, the *CLT* now
theoretically allowed for stoppages if they had received the prior approval of
a labor court.[86]

Spurred by the sharpening of divisions among the elite, the courtship of
workers by elements of the Vargas regime after 1942 gradually loosened

repressive controls over the labor unions. Yet throughout this process, Labor Minister Marcondes Filho and his associates faced a fundamental contradiction in their efforts to instrumentalize labor. On the one hand, as Castro Gomes has acutely observed, they ardently sought ever "greater ministerial control over the labor movement . . . but on the other hand, it was necessary that the movement be significantly representative among the workers . . . [since the government] did not seek mere control but the adhesion and mobilization [of workers], which was possible only through more participatory procedures capable of generating a certain degree of real representativeness" as opposed to mere peleguismo.[87] Thus, in pursuit of its own aims, the faction of the regime entrenched in the Labor Ministry was increasingly willing to tolerate a level of aggressiveness by union leaders that would have been unthinkable during the first phase of the Estado Novo.

Castro Gomes has warned that this shift should not necessarily be seen as a sign of the weakening of the regime, much less its defeat.[88] Yet in her analysis of the regime's decomposition, she tends to overestimate the extent to which the government controlled the course of events during the last years of the Estado Novo. In fact, this liberalization of labor policy also reflected the deterioration of the regime's overall position, both internally and externally. By 1944, for example, there was considerable evidence in São Paulo of a general relaxation of control leading to a loosening of governmental restrictions on the freedoms of speech, association, and the press— all of which strengthened labor's hand.[89]

The increasing legal space for maneuver encouraged the growing ambitions of the tiny minority of trade union activists in ABC who increasingly chafed against the government's many restrictions on labor's power. After all, their own experience during the Estado Novo had taught these local labor leaders that the government by itself could not be relied upon to resolve working-class grievances and to act in their defense. Moreover, salary levels, including the minimum wage, were not keeping up with inflation despite the government's claim to guarantee a living wage. In addition, the government itself, in the interest of maximum wartime production, had suspended the bulk of the laws and regulations that were most useful to workers. And finally, the new labor courts were a far-from-satisfactory way of quickly resolving grievances; to even file a case, a worker in ABC had to take most of a day to travel to neighboring São Paulo because there was no labor court to handle the complaints of the 40,000 or more workers in this important industrial suburb.

Running parallel to this evolution among activist workers, the wartime industrial boom and its accompanying economic disruptions were altering the material conditions that shaped the consciousness of the mass of the workers. A substantial number of workers experienced an increase in their individual sense of power due to the enormous demand for labor. As the U.S. consul noted on several occasions, "the demand for skilled and semi-skilled labor in the São Paulo industrial area has far exceeded the supply," producing "competition not only between various industries but between industrial and agricultural activities."[90] During this rapid industrial expansion, workers could more easily find new employment even if they had been fired. This lessened fear of unemployment combined with "sky-rocketing prices" to produce a "growing restlessness among the working classes" in São Paulo in 1944.[91]

The increasing responsiveness of the mass of industrial workers tempted grass-roots labor activists to try to breach the factory walls, despite employer opposition and governmental prohibitions. During the first phase of the Estado Novo, by contrast, they had for the most part conducted their union activities outside the workplace. Indeed, the government's union legislation since 1931 had been consciously designed to keep the union outside the factory walls. The organization of each categoria in a single município-wide union worked in this direction, as did the absence of legal provision for union representation within the factory.[92] In this regard, the government's unionization laws reflected the employers' virulent opposition to a possible union presence within the factory. Even Jorge Street in 1919 had specifically rejected any form of union representation within his factory, despite his support for a legally sanctioned unionism. The result could only be, he wrote, "numerous conflicts" that would undermine the essential "order and discipline of the factories."[93]

Like their employers, these grass-roots labor activists were well aware that organizing workers within the factory would not only increase their power vis-à-vis the industrialists, but could also pave the way for the use of labor's ultimate weapon, the strike. In fact, the first major factory-wide strike in metropolitan São Paulo in many years occurred on 20 January 1944, among the 500 employees of the Barros-Loureiro ceramics factory in São Caetano.[94] Although it was an exceptional event, this one-day stoppage won increases for the workers and no doubt solidified the position of rank-and-file leaders like Angelo Corsato, who later ran for the local city council on the Communist Party ticket in 1947.

The massive Laminação Nacional de Metais factory in Santo André provided another, if less successful, example of the organizing efforts of activists—linked, in this case, to the local metalworkers' union. Initial meetings were held in March and April 1944 to discuss organizing the plant's 2,000 workers, but these efforts were quickly discovered, the U.S. consul reported, by the company's "private espionage services." Having identified the "Communists" involved, the factory management fired the ringleaders forthwith.[95]

The easy defeat of this initial effort at the Laminação Nacional de Metais suggests that there was still an enormous disparity of power between employers and employees. Yet a comparison with the Ipiranguinha episode of 1936 suggests that labor's prospects, though small, were still greater in 1944 than they had been immediately prior to the Estado Novo. The existence of functioning legal trade unions in 1944 provided activists with a firmer, if still precarious, perch and guaranteed that not everything would be lost as a result of the firings (indeed, the plant would be struck in February 1946). Moreover, the individuals involved in this organizing effort, although also called "Communists," were apparently not arrested by the police, as had happened to the organizers at the Ipiranguinha.

As labor pushed to further expand the limits of the possible, they also discovered that the state's strongly interventionist role had opened the way for a new labor strategy that fused the previously distinct spheres of indirect and direct action. The 1944 comments of a prominent but unnamed Paulista industrialist are revealing in this regard: he told the U.S. consul that his "secret service" had discovered that Communist meetings were being held by the workers of his plant to organize "what is termed a 'legal agitation' to force the compliance . . . [with] the so-called labor laws."[96]

This linking of the labor laws and efforts to organize workers in the shop marked the emergence of a new labor strategy made possible by the existence of a credible, if flawed, state enforcement apparatus. In both 1936 and 1944, after all, labor organizers sought access to the factory arena denied them by the union legislation. They did so in 1944, however, by trying to turn to their own advantage the "legality" defined by the government's regulatory labor laws. By concentrating their agitation around the employers' violation of the law they sought to co-opt the state as an ally, in order to shield their own efforts to organize. Thus this very unequal conflict between employers and workers could be presented as a conflict between lawless industrialists and the sovereignty and supremacy of the government, its laws, and the judiciary. The ability to anchor working-class rights in law, which gave workers a new weapon in their struggles, produced the enduring synthesis of direct and indirect action that would characterize shop-floor organizing in the future, whether such labor initiatives were connected to or independent of the legal unions.

As the Estado Novo drew to a close, labor was able to exercise increasing, if still limited, leverage over its erstwhile ally in the presidential palace. This mutual courtship was facilitated by the deterioration of relations between Vargas and São Paulo's industrial bourgeoisie. The U.S. consul in São Paulo found nothing surprising in early 1944 about the continuing hostility to Vargas on the part of many Paulista politicians and the old agrarian families from which they hailed. He noted with interest, however, that Vargas's December 1943 visit to the state had revealed a "very considerable extension of [this] hostile movement" within the state industries association, FIESP.[97] He confidentially reported that São Paulo businessmen, including industrialists like Simonsen, were showing a "very active distrust and dislike . . . for the politicians in the federal government." Although they were beneficiaries of the Estado Novo's economic policies, São Paulo's thriving industrialists were quick to complain about governmental interference, a planned federal tax on their extraordinary profits, and, according to men linked to Francisco Pignatari's Laminação Nacional de Metais, the need to expend large sums to buy political protection.[98]

This estrangement of the employers from Vargas should not be overestimated; nor should their increasing hostility toward him be principally credited to the regime's as-yet-modest opening toward labor. The deepening crisis of Vargas's regime offered Paulista industrialists an opportunity to redefine their relationship with the state on more favorable terms. At the same time, the industrialists' growing disenchantment lessened the disincentives to the courtship of labor being carried out by the more daring elements of Vargas's circle. Thus the stage was being set in 1944 for the Vargas regime's second effort since 1930 to establish a base of support among urban workers.[99]

As the end of the Estado Novo approached, Brazil's trade unions were a potential force for the political mobilization of a working class that had grown in both numbers and cohesion since the early 1930s. Moreover, the labor movement at the end of World War II was far stronger than ever before, with a nationwide network of organization, some funds and activists, and the beginnings of a real base within the industrial proletariat. By 1945, official statistics indicate the existence of 873 legally recognized unions with a claimed membership of 474,943.[100]

The alliances underlying the coming postwar confrontation, however, would be radically different from those of the early 1930s. The Estado Novo had destroyed the regionalist cohesion of São Paulo's upper classes by dispelling their collective illusions of omnipotence. During the years that followed, the state's industrialists under leaders like Simonsen were forced to become the core of a new, more truly national industrial bourgeoisie whose alliances were no longer based on strictly regionalist calculations. Thus the decisive clashes of the immediate postwar period would be characterized by the alliance between São Paulo industrialists and the elements of the Estado Novo regime, especially the military, who were not associated with Getúlio's emerging populist project.

These tensions were clear on 1 May 1944 when Getúlio Vargas appeared at a May Day rally in São Paulo for the first time. The dictator began with praise for the dedication that the workers had shown to their country during these difficult days of war. The government's initiatives, he argued, had prevented relations between labor and capital from becoming "unsolvable," as they were in so many other countries. He went on to promise more concrete action to raise the workers' standard of living and to provide more extensive health, vocational, and recreational facilities. At the same time, he called for the intensification of unionization drives in the heartland of Brazilian industry. Invoking the fight for Brazil's "economic emancipation," he argued that, with the defeat of Brazil's external enemies, the country would next face "enemies of a different and no less dangerous order . . . the discords, incomprehension, class egoism, and intransigence of private interests." Brazil must find, Vargas went on, the means of guaranteeing the cooperation and solidarity of all social groups. The "brutalizing predominance of the law of natural selection, the exploitation of man by man," he declared, must be replaced with a system of "mutual aid" in which "the absorbing preoccupation of profit" would be subordinated to the "interests of the collective." The nations of today, he declared, must find an equilibrium between those who engage in "the lucrative exploitation of the means of production and those who labor in a permanent state of need." Standing next to Roberto Simonsen, Getúlio lectured that capital need not be fearful if only it would learn the "wisdom of limiting itself."[101]

With such rhetoric, Getúlio Vargas had found a language that embodied his emerging populist project of national capitalist development with, and not at the expense of, urban working-class participation. Yet the relationship between the dictator and his working-class listeners was still flawed by the enormous inequality of power between them. For the workers' leaders, Vargas's offer had yet to prove its durability or sincerity; the ratification of this alliance could take place only after the end of the dictatorship, when democratic conditions had opened the way to free expression of the workers' will.

Part Two • Industrial Workers and

the Birth of the Populist Republic, 1945–1946

Four • The Populist Gamble of Getúlio Vargas

The United Nations' victory over the Axis powers coincided with the end of the eight-year Estado Novo (New State) dictatorship in Brazil and the reestablishment of electoral processes. In early 1945, conspiracies between the regime's top military leaders and the elite opponents of President Getúlio Vargas appeared to have set the nation on the path to an uneventful transition to a democratic republic within the traditional limitations of Brazilian oligarchical politics. Getúlio Vargas seemed to have lost control over his own succession with the military's imposition of two conservative candidates, Air Force Brigadier Eduardo Gomes (popularly known as the "Brigadeiro") and General Eurico Gaspar Dutra, the minister of war. These two candidates were alike in their adherence to the values, mechanisms, and styles of the old elite politics that dated back to the First Republic.

Vargas was an able political strategist, however, and he regained the political initiative with a bold gamble that would alter the structure and terms of Brazilian politics. Brazil's dictator saw that the nation's first presidential election in fifteen years would not be determined exclusively by the political rules of the past: industrial and urban development had created new realities and classes whose votes were not subject to the old methods of control. In slashing attacks on his enemies, Vargas issued a dramatic call in May 1945 to Brazil's industrial workers, urban laborers, and employees to enter the political arena in defense of their interests. As president, he could also alter the terms of the contest by enacting electoral legislation designed to enfranchise the working class and favor urban voter registration and participation.

Getúlio's broad populist appeal was given an independent organizational form with the founding of the Partido Trabalhista Brasileiro (Brazilian Labor Party, or PTB). Neither Getúlio nor the PTB, however, had exclusive control of this grass-roots urban political movement, whose leadership was shared by the Communist leader Luis Carlos Prestes. Released in April 1945 after ten years in Getúlio's prisons, Prestes reestablished the Partido Comunista do Brasil (PCB), which was legalized in October 1945.

Vargas and Prestes, joined by their opposition to the existing elite candidates, encouraged a popular mobilization that came to be known as *queremismo* (from *queremos*, "we want," as in "we want Getúlio" and "we want a Constituent Assembly"). The upsurge of political participation in urban and industrial areas such as ABC broke the monopoly of politics by traditional elites and forced them to come to grips with issues they would have preferred to avoid. Introducing new participants, interests, and styles into the political arena, the tumultuous events of 1945 ushered in the populist republic that lasted until the military coup of 1964.

Transition without Rupture

Maneuvers to open the issue of a successor to the fifteen-year rule of Getúlio Vargas began among a small and narrow group of opposition politicians and top military men in late 1944. As the defeat of the Nazis loomed in Europe, pressures intensified within Brazil to bring an end to a regime that had been installed in 1937 by a coup inspired by European corporatist and fascist models. After 1942, when Brazil joined the war against the Axis, the Estado Novo regime had begun to evolve away from its authoritarian origins. Such changes, however, did not still the resentment, frustration, and anger of those political and economic elites whose possibilities had been cut short by the Revolution of 1930 and Getúlio's preemption of the presidential elections of 1938.

The opening act of the drama of 1945 was shaped by the opposition's understanding of the major premise of the political game: never to cut oneself off from the ultimate source of all power—the military. Vargas's liberal opponents had always placed their hopes in the military, despite its decisive role in the cancellation of the 1938 elections, the closing of Congress, and the installation of a corporatist dictatorship.[1] Mass mobilization was never an option for these members of the "political class"; they believed that only a select minority should be allowed into the hermetic corridors of power. Their outlook was best expressed by the one-time intervenor of São Paulo, Armando de Salles Oliveira: "I do not belong," the exiled 1938 presidential candidate wrote in an illegal open letter, "to those who, disillusioned by the army, . . . appeal to the people."[2]

As the end of the war approached, the decisive pressure for change did in fact come from the top of the military establishment. Months of secret meetings came to a head in February 1945 and, with the breakdown of press censorship, reached the public's attention.[3] The powerful army general Pedro Aurélio de Góes Monteiro, a one-time sympathizer with Hitler, now called publicly for Vargas to step down, and the Estado Novo's minister of war, General Eurico Dutra, made himself available to anti-Getulista politicians and military men.[4]

The liberal civilian opposition sought to turn this military discontent to their favor by launching the presidential candidacy of Brigadeiro Gomes, a tenentista hero of the 1922 Copacabana revolt. Encouraged by Dutra's ambivalence, Gomes's backers even offered to make the minister of war the head of the transitional military junta that would replace Vargas.[5]

Faced with the deterioration of his military backing, an increasingly apprehensive Vargas moved to counter the threat. On 28 February 1945 he signed the Ninth Amendment to the 1937 Constitution, which promised that an election date would be set within ninety days. Two weeks later, the president moved to neutralize the threat of a coup by offering General Dutra his support as the "official" candidate in the upcoming elections. Research in the last decade has revealed that Dutra's candidacy was initiated without prior approval and was actually imposed on a reluctant Vargas.[6]

Brazil's future president Dutra used his unique position adroitly. To Vargas, he offered protection from a coup and from revenge by the strident anti-Getulistas. To Gomes's supporters, he held out the enticing prospect of overthrowing Getúlio prior to the elections, as would indeed happen in October 1945. To a skeptical public, he declared his support for universal, direct, and secret suffrage, freedom of expression, and amnesty for political prisoners. In his most surprising action, Dutra provided formal and public military backing for the release of the Communist Luis Carlos Prestes on 18 April 1945.[7]

The transition from a dictatorial to an electoral form of political organization thus seemed set, with the launching of two military candidates who shared conservative positions, ideas, and principles.[8] General Dutra had a clear advantage over his competitor in this contest for elite backing, however, since the Estado Novo's highly centralized state apparatus could be mobilized to create support at the federal, state, and local levels.[9] Thus, Dutra automatically received the support of the dominant local coronelistic machines, which still controlled the bulk of the nation's vote. The party structure formed to back his campaign, the Partido Social Democrático (PSD), was simply the label given to these local oligarchies in power.

The Brigadeiro's insistent demand for the resignation of Vargas and his "subdictators," by coup if necessary, flowed from these realities of oligarchical politics. Since Dutra had the political edge, Gomes demanded that power be handed to the judiciary, who were favorable to his candidacy, to prevent "interference in the electoral process" whether by pressure or by the use of governmental facilities and resources.[10] Barred access to the state apparatus until the last month of the campaign, the Brigadeiro had of necessity invested far greater energy and effort into the mobilization of middle-class public opinion in areas like the city of São Paulo. His União Democrática Nacional (UDN), founded in April 1945, took on many of the characteristics of an idealistic crusade for political morality and liberalism by the educated middle class. This emotional mass movement coexisted with outgroups of local coronelistic politicians who, in the long run, predominated within the UDN.[11]

For the architects of the Dutra and Gomes candidacies, politics was a contest for the support of the traditional local political class. In urban areas like Santo André, this conservative class was a self-conscious local elite composed of small industrialists, merchants, shopkeepers, proprietors, and factory administrators joined by the equally small number of doctors, dentists, engineers, lawyers, and teachers. In the elections of the previous twenty years, Santo André's politically connected middle class had proved its electoral decisiveness.[12]

The opening phase of the 1945 presidential campaign in the ABC region was marked by the top-down mobilization of the municipal administrations in favor of Dutra, the "official" candidate. The appointed *prefeitos* of Santo André and São Bernardo do Campo, José de Carvalho Sobrinho and Wallace Cochrane Simonsen, were present at the meeting called by São Paulo's appointed state intervenor Fernando Costa on 13 March 1945 to launch the Dutra candidacy.[13] The ABC prefeitos then energetically set out to corral support for Dutra. Santo André's politicians were soon frequenting Carvalho Sobrinho's house for political "advice." The local political class, almost to a man, joined Dutra's PSD, whose popularity was aided by the energetic support of important industrialists such as Roberto Simonsen, owner of the município's Cerâmica São Caetano.[14]

The Brigadeiro's "campaign of the white handkerchiefs," however, never got off the ground in industrialized Santo André, which had a less diversified middle class than that of São Paulo. His few supporters in ABC would have been equally at home in the PSD had it not been for patronage disputes or their state-level alliances.[15]

The natural supporters of the two candidates of the old politics in ABC shared a common political culture and outlook originating in the highly restrictive politics of the First Republic. The political class of ABC, with its feel for the electoral market of the past, was incapable of integrating workers or unionists into its closed world. Neither party included even one worker in its Santo André diretório. Lacking ties to ABC's factory workers, these experienced politicians failed to make even a pro forma appeal to the working class. Their blindness was based in part on past experience: even after the electoral reforms of the 1930s, workers had never played any significant role in elections. The political class would see no reason to challenge the wisdom of their judgment until election day 1945.

The choice of such shortsighted electoral tactics was also rooted in the deeply ingrained elitism of Brazil's traditional middle class. Their convictions were best expressed in a June 1945 editorial, "Democracy Upside Down," in the local pro-Dutra newspaper, *Borda do Campo*. Writing after new, more liberal electoral legislation had been announced, the newspaper still advanced the solution of indirect elections "with a selected electorate, that is, one conscious of its responsibilities." Such attitudes were the norm and not the exception before the advent of modern democratic, populist styles of politics.[16]

Fevered talk of elections and candidates gripped the members of the political class at the national, state, and local levels. While ABC's middle class debated the alternative candidacies in early 1945, the region's working class remained outside this narrow world of the old politics. They were not spurred to action by such talk and remained indifferent to the new party organizations being formed in ABC to back Dutra and Gomes.

Workers in ABC first entered the succession process on the evening of 18 April 1945, the day Vargas decreed an amnesty for those convicted of political crimes, including Luis Carlos Prestes. That evening a small group of local workers organized a march through the streets of Santo André to celebrate the action, carrying the banner of the wartime United Nations and singing the Brazilian national anthem.[17] This amnesty marked the beginning of the transition to democracy for Santo André's workers, ending ten years of repression in which employers and the police had never drawn too clear a line between the suppression of communism and the harassment of workers discontented with their conditions. For workers and unionists who had experienced the bitterness of arrest, imprisonment, and dismissal from their jobs, the government's move—credited to Vargas—was a further lifting of constraints and self-imposed restraints on the defense of their interests.

Facing Brazil's Future: Getúlio Vargas and His Opponents

Since the economic and political collapse of the First Republic in 1930, the whole country had undergone a profound transformation, and ABC had become the frontier of national development. There were more than 40,000 industrial workers employed in ABC's large-scale metal, chemical, electrical, and textile factories alone. In 1920, the state of São Paulo had had only 80,000 workers in all its industries, both large and small; by 1940, the state had 275,000 industrial workers—as many as the entire *country* in 1920. Brazil's million industrial workers in 1945 were concentrated in the nation's growing cities such as São Paulo, with its 1.25 million inhabitants.[18]

While the urban/industrial areas, like metropolitan São Paulo, were leading the nation's economic, social, and cultural development, the more traditional rural areas still accounted for the majority of the electorate, and Brazil's *coronéis* would deliver their votes to the PSD and the UDN.[19] Would the cities and their workers, laborers, and middle strata follow the countryside, remain politically passive, or strike out in a new direction? If the urban population *did* actively participate in the elections, would their support be decisive in bringing victory to a particular candidate? Was any leader in a position to claim this vote? If anyone was, it had to be Vargas.

Since coming to power in the Revolution of 1930, Getúlio Dornelles Vargas had presided over a dramatic fifteen-year period during which the possibilities of the 1920s had become imposing realities. A nation that had had only one line of industrial manufacturing in 1920, textiles, now had a full range of intermediate factory production. The same period had also seen the beginning of Brazilian basic industry with the construction of the Volta Redonda steel complex in 1943—the first in Latin America, and also in the Third World as a whole. Imbued with a sense of mission and a strongly held vision of future Brazilian greatness, Vargas was apprehensive as the politics of the succession unfolded in 1945. Aware that power was still based largely on the agrarian land-owning classes, he feared that the nation would move backward to all that had crippled Brazil under the First Republic.

In 1930, the economic, political, and social structure that had shaped Brazil for fifty years had entered into a profound crisis. The Great Depression that began in 1929 had shaken the foundations of a world economy that had been dominated for a century by a handful of industrialized countries with vast territorial and economic empires. It was in this context, of Brazil as a peripheral country in the world economy, that Vargas introduced a populist proposal to build an independent, industrialized economy at the end of World War II. He raised the nationalist banner of "struggle against economic colonialism" and argued that an unjust international economic order had condemned Brazil before 1930 to be a "simple semi-colonial community." Trapped in the "primitivism of monoculture and the export of raw materials," the country had been forced, during the First Republic, to import almost all of its manufactured goods from abroad. To produce in this "colonial manner," Vargas believed, meant low profits and wages and the impoverishment of the nation. Brazil's economic emancipation, he said, could only be based upon a policy of industrialization aided by the state and protected from international competition and interference.[20]

The rejection of the liberal dogma of comparative advantage in international trade was part of Vargas's vigorous attack on the theories of laissez-faire liberalism that had characterized Brazilian political discourse for a century. Liberalism's "disordered individualism," with its "myth" that labor was "a simple commodity," bred social injustice and communism, he said. "Exclusively political equality" was inadequate to guarantee "social equilibrium." The liberal ideal of state nonintervention in social affairs was a mask for a selfish policy that would have the government sustain "the rich against the poor, the powerful against the humble."[21]

Vargas's populist project of an autonomous capitalist industrialization no longer implied a zero-sum game among the different social classes.[22] An expanding economy grounded in industry, Vargas believed, could and should provide a share, even if unequal, to all who produced. In 1945, such populist policies and views were also part of a tide of social reform sweeping the United States and Western Europe, where liberal certainties had been shaken by depression and war. The landslide defeat of Winston Churchill, Britain's conservative wartime leader, in July 1945 astonished the world, as the socialist Labour Party took over the reins of power. In the words of Franklin Delano Roosevelt and the New Deal, this did indeed seem to be the age of the "four freedoms," the beginning of the "century of the common man."[23]

Stereotypes ill prepare us for the curious figure of Getúlio Vargas in 1945, the populist dictator who displayed neither the charismatic magnetism, the spellbinding oratory, nor the eclectic thinking that one tends to associate with populist politicians. Rather, he was a profoundly intelligent and private man, an enormously skilled politician with an integrated and coherent worldview, which he confidently believed to represent the collective interest and future of his country. Aspiring to be a leader who embodied the interests of the nation and not merely of one class, Vargas was willing to take risks, sure of his own judgment and ability to control the events he set in motion.

Faced with strident enemies and dubious friends, the dictator decided on an unexpected course that was to profoundly affect both the 1945 electoral campaign and Brazilian history: to rely on the nation's working people. If a return to elections were not to mean a return to the vices of the First Republic, the political arena would have to be broadened to include the people of the new urban-industrial Brazil, who were absent from the PSD and the UDN. During his May Day 1945 speech in Rio de Janeiro's Vasco da Gama Stadium to an audience of workers and unionists, Vargas forthrightly projected the nation's urban workers into the center of the succession process.[24] With the defection of his more conservative civilian and military supporters in early 1945, he was free to formulate his populist appeals in a more uncompromising manner.

Referring to the disloyalty and disillusionments he had suffered, he said that he had never been disappointed by the workers, and he attacked his elite opponents—both hidden and open—with ferocious sarcasm and scorn. Today's self-proclaimed "champions of democracy," he said, had not enforced the eight-hour day or even their own feeble labor legislation before 1930. These "opportunists and reactionaries," he went on, had for decades supported the "policy of the police state, called upon to intervene only when necessary to constrain and forcefully stifle the demands of the people, of the laborers—the true producers of the wealth of the nation."

Having cited the bitter past, the president then hailed the achievements of his own administration in passing social and labor legislation. The Vargas regime could, in fact, claim credit for many laws that had begun to meet some of the workers' needs: laws establishing legal unions, labor courts, vacations, pensions, and workmen's compensation; laws setting maximum hours and minimum wages; and protective laws to govern child and women's labor. These gains, he went on, constituted a veritable "code of rights" that guaranteed the workers' "economic emancipation."

What he did not mention, of course, was that his fifteen-year rule had had more than its share of police-state measures against the workers. The very constitution of the Estado Novo, still in effect in 1945, outlawed strikes. Getúlio's prolabor rhetoric on May Day 1945 was also exaggerated, since his regime's social legislation was often insufficient, full of loopholes, loosely enforced, or contradicted by other governmental actions. Cries of hypocrisy were not unfounded—but his frustrated opponents' charges of inconsistency, opportunism, and demagoguery carried little weight with Getúlio's audience. He said he was confident that the people knew that "they had never received anything nor could they expect any benefits" from his enemies.

The stakes involved in the coming elections were high, Vargas told the workers. A victory for the Brigadeiro and the UDN, representing the "retarded mentality" of the First Republic's "provincial party spirit," would be a disaster for the workers and the nation, a return to the days when "oligarchical groups made the country a colony of international finance," which sucked the nation dry and pushed it toward disintegration.

On the "official" candidate of the government, Vargas was restrained. General Dutra, he said, deserved the confidence of the nation as a representative of a political current that incorporated the "conquests of our social policy." This mild endorsement would be Vargas's only public reference to the imposed candidacy of his minister of war until the last weeks of the campaign. At the same time, he referred to the prevailing military discontent by defying the "*golpistas* [coup-makers] and reactionaries of all species" to test his will.

Getúlio's rhetoric in May 1945 was not, of course, totally new or untested in Brazilian politics. Vargas had himself pledged the passage of social and labor measures in his 1930 presidential platform. Populist rhetoric was not, however, the same as actually delivering concrete benefits, and much of Getúlio's vaunted social and labor legislation of the early 1930s had remained so many paper promises during the first decade of his rule. Nevertheless, whatever their practical impact, Getúlio's innovative social policies and rhetoric had brought hope to the masses and aroused the suspicion of many members of the conservative classes, especially after 1942. "I have never proposed," Vargas had hastened to assure such an audience in 1944, "to foment class struggle, but rather peace, harmony, and collaboration among them."[25]

All Brazilian politicians, naturally enough, shared this common rhetoric of "class cooperation" and "social peace." For most, however, "class peace" was a convenient shorthand for denying the legitimacy of any conflict between workers and their employers. Vargas, for his part, gave these clichés a different emphasis because he did not equate the interests of the state, the employers, and the workers. He recognized the divergence of sectoral interests between workers and industrialists but deemed both inferior to the collective interests of the nation as represented by the state. Social injustice, class rivalry, and subversion stemmed, he believed, from a failure to meet the workers' legitimate needs. With labor's rights guaranteed by the state, class struggle would be eliminated and the "bonds of solidarity" would be strengthened as each group contributed to the supreme goal of national development.[26] In this approach, the key concept was that of the social integration of workers, while maintaining the flexibility necessary to justify action against a strike or other workers' protest.

In his policy of working-class inclusion, Vargas had the inevitable political objective of winning workers' support. He was conscious of the natural repulsion that existed between this potential working-class constituency and the PSD, which he had helped found, with its conservative politics and elitist style. To guarantee the desired popular participation, it was essential to establish a separate political vehicle.

On 15 May 1945, a new party was formed that would play an enduring role in the history of the following two decades. Although it could have simply been called the People's or Popular Party, Labor Minister Marcondes Filho chose a more daring and class-tinged name: the Brazilian Labor Party (Partido Trabalhista Brasileiro, or PTB). The PTB was to be a classic populist party that spoke to class differences without proclaiming itself a class party. Its name, while excluding employers and the rich, was designed to appeal to a wide audience of urban laborers and members of the lower middle class. Getúlio Vargas, that "loyal and dedicated friend of the laborers," was named the party's "president of honor." In implicit references to the PSD and the PCB, the PTB's founding platform argued that laborers' interests clashed with those of the "moderate right" and the "extreme left." Praising the existing social and labor legislation, the PTB called for greater union autonomy and the political representation of working people by the workers themselves.[27]

Getúlio's ambitious plans for the PTB could easily have come to naught, given the political marginality and electoral inexperience of its proposed constituency. If an opening to urban laborers was to bear fruit, it would be necessary to foster their participation in the coming elections. To achieve his objectives, Vargas had unilaterally to alter the terms of the upcoming election. The electoral legislation that emerged from his cabinet, Decree Law 7,586 of 25 May 1945, differed radically from earlier Brazilian laws: in every regard, it was systematically designed to enfranchise the working class and favor urban over rural voter registration and electoral participation.[28]

Vargas sought to prevent the return to political power of the conservative landed classes with their millions of dependent voters.[29] As part of his effort to create an urban-industrial counterweight to the coronéis who still ruled the countryside, he maintained the literacy requirement for suffrage, which discriminated against the rural population,[30] while making voting obligatory for virtually all literate Brazilians (only women who did not work outside the home were free from a fine if they did not vote).[31] Even more importantly, the law established an ex officio group voter-registration procedure specifically designed to favor urban areas.[32] While others had to request registration directly, all full- or part-time employees of public offices, professional associations, and private, mixed, or state businesses were registered automatically through submission of their names to an electoral judge by their enterprise. When Vargas had promised a "simplified registration procedure, accessible to all classes," he had meant accessible to urban classes.[33]

This astute maneuvering by Vargas posed new and difficult challenges for the anti-Getulista opposition headed by Brigadeiro Gomes. Until June 1945, Gomes's campaign had focused almost exclusively on the demand for the deposition of Vargas prior to elections.[34] Moreover, progress in the powerful world of military politics had been checked by Dutra's ability to consolidate military backing for his ambitions to succeed the president.[35] These setbacks, combined with the establishment of direct presidential elections with judicial oversight, led the UDNistas to try to shift their emphasis toward a broader audience beyond the barracks. Vargas forced Gomes, who was most secure on the terrain of purely political and juridical matters, to confront broad issues of national development and social and economic policy.[36]

The ensuing debate between Vargas and Gomes over Brazil's past and future was marked by an ironic reversal of roles. The impassioned enemy of the old Brazil, the large ranch-owner Getúlio Vargas, had been one of the First Republic's beneficiaries as a loyal member of the corrupt political machine of Rio Grande do Sul. And the persecuted tenente revolutionary who had helped bring down the First Republic, Eduardo Gomes, was arguing in 1945 in defense of the agrarian Brazil of his youth and attacking Vargas for blaming Brazil's "errors" on the "representative regime in force until 1930."[37]

The UDN's candidate, Gomes, campaigned openly in defense of the plantation owners and the export agriculture that had sustained Brazilian society for centuries.[38] Casting himself as the defender of the "rural producer," the Brigadeiro presented himself as the voice of an aggrieved majority that had been neglected and exploited since 1930. In his second major address, he emphasized that, contrary to currently fashionable ideas, the "basic wealth that sustained Brazil as a civilized nation" still flowed from extractive and agricultural activities. Citing census data, he argued that the million Brazilians involved with urban industry lived and prospered only at the expense of the majority in the countryside.[39] Victimized by the government's bureaucracy, deficit spending, and the unjust "confiscatory foreign exchange rates" instituted in 1931, the agricultural producer had seen his "considerable influence" in public affairs decline since the onset of the "industrial boom" of recent decades. The plantation owners, Gomes went on, had been relegated to an even more secondary role after 1937 when the weight of the votes they controlled no longer concerned a dictatorship that had abolished elections.[40]

In his commitment to agricultural interests, Gomes went far beyond the customary sensitivity shown by all Brazilian politicians toward large landowners and their interests.[41] Vargas's government, he said, based its policies on the false theory that "we must break our armature as an agricultural country, because only industrialized nations are strong and rich." Echoing the free-trade arguments used by past opponents of industrialization, Gomes argued that tariff barriers and the disruption of normal trade during the war had fostered an unnatural industrialization based on "excessive profits." The rural producer was thus forced to pay artificially high prices for inferior Brazilian manufactured goods.[42]

Brigadeiro Gomes also eloquently denounced the havoc wreaked on agriculture by the unprecedented growth of industry and the cities. Adopting an antiurban stance, he decried the depopulation of the rural areas. The workers who were desperately needed by the planters, he went on, were being drawn to the cities by the government's public works and the "higher and higher wages" and fewer hours of labor offered by industry. This unfair competition was intensified by the "policy of fascinating the city's multitudes with costly and luxurious projects," resulting in a "veritable exodus" from rural areas and the "overcrowding" of the urban centers.[43]

The UDN's presidential contender also took a clear stand against Vargas's assertive nationalism. Quietly favored by U.S. Ambassador Adolph A. Berle, Jr., Gomes stressed that an alliance with the United States was the foundation stone of Brazil's foreign relations. While Getúlio sounded an aggressive note of aggrievement toward foreign powers and economic interests, the Brigadeiro thanked them for their economic, political, and cultural contributions to Brazil.[44]

Gomes was vigorous in denouncing the regime's economic nationalism as well. Beyond favoring industrial imports through low tariffs, he argued that "the collaboration of foreign capital" was essential for the development of industry and even of Brazil's oil reserves. These issues were catapulted to prominence in late 1945 when Vargas issued a famous antitrust law (the *Lei Malaia*, Decree Law 7,666), which was seen to portend a move against foreign economic interests. Gomes called this "nazi-like" attack on free enterprise the fruit of a "thoughtless opinion of a current hostile to foreign capital," which believed that such investments "make us poorer."[45]

It proved difficult for Gomes to accept the incorporation of workers and their interests into politics under Vargas.[46] Lacking the empathy and understanding that Getúlio projected, the UDN's candidate was received with an instinctive antipathy by the workers.[47] His opening campaign rally of 16 June 1945 provided dramatic proof of their indifference, if not hostility: São Paulo's Pacaembu Stadium was only half-full, with an exclusively middle- and upper-class audience.[48]

Eager to counter the popular appeals of Vargas and Prestes, the Brigadeiro sought to incorporate workers into his speeches but not his program. Praising the "resistance" to the dictatorship offered by workers, intellectuals, writers, journalists, teachers, and students, he claimed that the workers had never been won over by the Estado Novo. Brazil's workers, he went on, had understood the need to "divorce themselves" from the fascist state—language that betrayed his resentment against the apparently happy marriage of the workers and Vargas. Citing Catholic social theory, the Brigadeiro said that Brazil must move toward a society where "the sad spectacle of the excessive opulence of some does not confront the extreme misery of others, . . . in which the rich would be less powerful and the poor less suffering." Beyond this note of paternalistic concern, the UDN candidate pledged to perfect the existing social legislation with the elimination of its "fascist" features.

Later observers, however, have incorrectly credited Brigadeiro Gomes with the defense of trade union autonomy and the right to strike in 1945. In an often-cited and little-understood passage, Gomes did say that the worker needed "trade union freedoms and the right to strike," the "two weapons essential to the defense of his interests." Far too many later commentators have taken this statement at face value because of *their* concerns about the link between the Brazilian trade unions and the state. In fact, the Brigadeiro consistently advocated a conservative approach to the labor question. And the very next sentence in his speech countered his apparent appeal for worker support with language appealing to Brazilian entrepreneurs: "However, state intervention should have in mind the stimulation of personal initiatives and activities and not their destruction."

Brazilian workers were not taken in by Gomes's opportunistic maneuver to consolidate support among the middle-class socialists who had joined his crusade.[49] Six months later, Gomes would reveal his true outlook toward labor in a 22 November 1945 speech in the São Paulo textile city of Sorocaba. His remarks there were so damaging that he was forced to disown them in a later speech after they were extensively exploited in his opponent's radio broadcasts.

Brazilian workers, he announced, were not "so lacking in the elements of resistance" as to require "vigorous state intervention" in their defense. With this hearty advice to stand on their own two feet, Gomes blithely ignored the bitter realities that the nation's working people had so long experienced. Unlike Vargas, he did not criticize or even refer to the repressive realities that had stymied workers' past efforts. Employers and wage earners, he explained, could "loyally" work out an understanding without state intervention beyond the most "cautious and prudent" of limits. Gomes also emphasized the need to protect capital from "confiscatory assault by the state" and made an ambiguous comment that he would preserve everything "beneficial" in the existing social legislation. While talking of "conciliating" and "harmonizing" capital and labor, Brigadeiro Gomes seemed to bluntly threaten the gains, however small, that workers had made in the past fifteen years.[50]

Gomes's idealized world of labor relations was based on the "natural" economic order of classic capitalist theory, where the formal equality of the two contracting parties, employers and workers, was unsullied by the gross differences in power that existed in reality.[51] He emphatically denied the existence of any objective basis for conflict between employees and employers. The source of the labor problem, he argued, lay in the subjective and unfounded "belief" by both groups that their interests clashed.[52] His "free trade unions" with full "autonomy," he made clear, would be led by men "conscious of their duties and not just their rights." Disagreements with their employers would be resolved without "disturbing the social order or the always-pernicious recourse to general or partial strikes"—a clear contradiction of his earlier pledges.[53]

Unlike Vargas, who recognized the inevitability of conflict, the Brigadeiro wanted labor relations without disturbances. It would take little for someone who heard him to imagine Gomes, as president, calling in the police to restore things to their "natural" and nonconflictual state, and blaming the disturbances on the interference of agitators and their wrong "beliefs."

This opponent of the "fascist" Estado Novo offered the Brazilian working class a form of free-enterprise trade unionism whose "independence" and "autonomy" from the state could have only meant, at that time, the virtual destruction of unionism in the face of intransigent employers. The workers' opinion of these hollow promises would soon be made very clear.

The Brigadeiro's opponent, General Eurico Dutra of the PSD, showed a similar lack of sympathy toward labor.[54] While Gomes opposed state-supported unionism, the Estado Novo's minister of war saw himself as the potential beneficiary of Getulista influence among the workers. A man of notoriously conservative leanings, Dutra contented himself with vague talk of the "economic unification," "adjustment," and even "complete assimilation of classes," while pledging that labor problems could be resolved through the "impartial organs" established by "our social law."[55] As president, Dutra would have ample opportunity to show his opposition to strikes and leftist activism among Brazilian workers.

Although based on the dominant agrarian oligarchies, Dutra's coalition included Brazil's rising class of industrialists who feared the backward-looking policies of Brigadeiro Gomes almost as much as Getúlio's unreliable and potentially threatening trabalhismo. Thus General Dutra did differ markedly with his UDN opponent over the role that industry should play in national development. Asked about agriculture and "incipient industry," he responded that Brazil "was on the road to industrialization. The 'essentially agricultural' epoch is passing. Such countries . . . are countries of pauperism."[56] This development-minded military leader also called for the "industrial utilization" of the nation's natural resources and the mechanization of agriculture. Brazil should develop its export of manufactured goods, he indicated in a nationalist thrust, despite possible opposition by the already industrialized countries.[57]

Luis Carlos Prestes, Queremismo, and the Fall of Vargas

In mid-1945, neither declared presidential candidate appealed to the nation's urban workers, whose potential impact had been increased by Getúlio's electoral legislation. May 1945 would show, however, that Vargas was not to go unchallenged as the leader of the new popular politics. Emerging from ten years in the regime's prisons, the hero of the tenentista Long March of 1924–27, Luis Carlos Prestes, was to prove that at forty-seven he had not lost his formidable popularity.

The 18 April release of one of South America's most famous political prisoners came at a very special moment in world history. The Second World War had seen the weakening, if only momentarily, of the rigid divisions of Left and Right. If Great Britain, the United States, and the Soviet Union could put aside past hostility and work together as loyal allies, then surely a similar tolerance was demanded on the domestic front. Prestes and those who followed him felt vindicated in 1945 and operated in a more open public atmosphere than at any other period of Brazilian history.

Prestes's position on the succession was eagerly awaited by all the contending camps. Courted for his support, Prestes would make his final decision clear in the spectacular rally that the Communists organized on 23 May 1945 at the Vasco da Gama Stadium in Rio de Janeiro. To the surprise of the anti-Getulistas, Prestes began his first public speech by rejecting the UDN's demand for the immediate resignation of Getúlio Vargas as a condition for the maintenance of internal peace. Decrying the "spirit of unrestrained and threatening party feeling with which the campaign had begun," the PCB leader declared that the solution to Brazil's severe problems would not be found in "civil wars nor in redeeming coups."[58] Prestes then spoke of the thousands who had been jailed, tortured, and killed by the dictatorship. Yet "hatreds" and "personal resentments," he went on, had no place in his politics if the government was truly willing to liquidate the "decrepit remains of reaction." The personal drama of the ex-prisoner made a large impact. Not only had Prestes been a prisoner of Vargas's regime, but Vargas had also been personally responsible for sending Prestes's pregnant German-born wife to her death in a Nazi concentration camp.[59]

At the same time, the PCB's secretary general was careful to position himself to the left of Getúlio Vargas and independent of him. Like the Brigadeiro, he categorically rejected the president's exaggerated claims and pretensions. Nor did South America's leading Communist renounce the 1935 effort to resolve the problems of Brazil's "archaic economic structure" in a revolutionary way through the Aliança Nacional Libertadora (ANL).

Prestes was unrestrained in his attack on the "painful" situation and "miserable" standard of living of the "poorest strata of our people." But unlike Gomes, he combined his criticism of the misery of the working class with concrete proposals for radical change. Among other measures, his immediate program called for land redistribution and credit to foster the production of foodstuffs; the elimination of taxes on necessities; a 100 percent increase in the minimum wage; and a progressive income tax with emergency levies on capital and the extraordinary profits of the few. With such a program, he said, the working class could unify the popular masses and point national politics in a truly democratic direction.

Prestes and Brazil's thousand Communists in 1945 had not, of course, delivered benefits to millions of people. Nor did they have a network of paid state employees, like Dutra, or the financial support of elements of the dominant classes, like the Brigadeiro. To an even greater extent than Vargas, Prestes was making an audacious gamble that the people would provide all that he lacked.

The two elite candidates ignored the workers, and Vargas denounced past but not present problems. While Vargas promised state action to resolve workers' problems, Prestes argued that the people could help solve their own problems. Grass-roots organization, he emphasized, was the key to reshaping Brazil to meet their needs. "Broad committees or commissions," Prestes proposed, should be established "in the workplaces, streets, and neighborhoods." Uniting "bit by bit, from the bottom up," these democratic popular organizations would help elect "genuine representatives of the people."[60] Such popular organization was conceived within the framework of the Communist policy of "national unity" around the governments that were fighting Hitlerite fascism. These moderate organizations, of even greater breadth than the "popular fronts" of the thirties, were to be open to all except "reactionaries" and the "fascist fifth column."

Within the next six months, thousands of such committees were established, and the Communist Party, operating freely for the first time since 1927, gained tens of thousands of new members. With enormous energy, the followers of Prestes, whether Communist or not, tried to break down the barriers that separated them from sectors of the working class, the middle class, and even the capitalists. Their moderation also served to neutralize the fear of extremism that had inhibited the participation of many in the past, proving that the November 1935 adventure of barracks revolts was not about to be repeated.

On the pressing political issue of the day, Prestes had clearly sided with Getúlio Vargas. And in seeking working-class support, Prestes had to allow for Vargas's popularity among those his party saw as their own potential constituency. As Prestes informally told his supporters, "You can't throw stones at the people's idol."[61] While many "patriots," especially intellectuals, were disenchanted by what they saw as Communist collaboration with a loathsome regime, Prestes faced a different problem among the workers: many working people and unionists tended to see Prestes as merely an ally of Vargas, a leader they respected and believed in.[62]

Although he was preparing to move into closer alliance with Getúlio and his followers in late July and early August, Prestes was driven to clarify his position, and PCB policy shifted toward a harder line against the legacy of the Estado Novo. The upcoming presidential elections, Prestes now said, would not guarantee the real "democratization of the country," since the February 1945 constitutional amendment implied recognition of the 1937 Estado Novo charter. The road forward, Prestes concluded, lay in the nullification of the 1937 Constitution and the establishment of a freely elected Constituent Assembly.[63]

Armed with this new political line, Prestes's followers were now equipped to work within the broader current that was taking shape in response to Getúlio's new course. The Communists' slogan, "We want a Constituent Assembly!," distinguished them from the Getulistas with whom they worked, whose cry was "We want Getúlio!" or "We want a Constituent Assembly with Getúlio!"[64]

The 1945 alliance between Prestes and his ex-jailer Vargas has always aroused heated debate. Was it the result of a prearranged deal by which Prestes received his freedom in exchange for his support? Was this a case of two totalitarians brought together by their xenophobic nationalism and hatred of liberal democracy? Was this surprising coalition merely the Brazilian translation of a general policy directive of world communism? Or was it a sell-out of the Communists' revolutionary calling?

With so much passion invested in the debate, it may seem less than satisfying to say that the answer lies in the practical needs and congruent goals, however short-range, of these two politicians and the urban masses they sought to lead. The two men had a common interest in overturning the political scenario dictated by the elite conspiracies of early 1945. Noting the people's "manifest disinterest," Prestes rejected the Gomes and Dutra candidacies, both built "from the top down" around a candidate rather than a party or a program.[65] Prestes also shared with Vargas certain nationalist prescriptions for Brazil's future, and both leaders sought to awaken the sleeping giant of Brazilian politics, the "people."

Getúlio moved with confidence in dealing with the Communists. As he told the U.S. ambassador, he was sure that the masses followed him and not Prestes or the PCB.[66] The support of the popular Prestes could nonetheless help Vargas by facilitating his access to certain urban constituencies, including labor. Friendly treatment by his regime's most persecuted opponent could also neutralize the "fascist" label that was putting the president on the defensive in 1945. Vargas was even willing to pay a price for this support, although the hazards seemed less in 1945 than at any earlier time, since legalization of the Communist Party was part of the democratic package of the wartime alliance. After all, the U.S. ambassador himself had received Prestes in April 1945, and the photograph of the two men on the embassy's balcony was taken by Brazilian public opinion as symbolic of Communism's newfound respectability.[67]

The tacit cooperation that emerged between the two leaders, who had not met personally, was a radical departure in Brazilian politics, although it fell far short of a true alliance of forces. Conducted at arm's length through intermediaries, the relationship involved parallel action rather than formal, negotiated agreements.[68] Getúlio, it is clear, set the terms under which Communist participation took place.[69] Furthermore, no Communist spoke at a Getulista rally, just as PTB leaders did not appear at the PCB's mass functions and events.

Vargas openly reentered the political equation in the summer of 1945 through the "we want Getúlio!" ("queremos Getúlio!") movement, or queremismo. The idea that the president might be the third presidential candidate had first surfaced in late May 1945 in Getúlio's home state of Rio Grande do Sul. As an organized movement, however, queremismo took shape only in late July when a committee was organized in Rio de Janeiro by previously unknown individuals. Within days, the public organization of this movement for "a civilian candidate of the people" reached São Paulo, with employees of the Ministry of Labor in the lead.[70] August 1945 saw queremismo burst onto the scene with large demonstrations of workers, Getulistas and Prestistas alike, in the nation's urban areas. Requests for permission to hold queremista marches and rallies had been denied by Rio's police chief at first, but intercession from above soon caused the prohibition to be lifted there and in other urban areas.

For the first time, groups from the lower reaches of Brazilian society were invited, by the president no less, to have a say in the affairs of state. Addressing a 30 August queremista rally in Rio de Janeiro, Vargas hailed the "protest of the people" as a response to the "invective" of his opponents. Deepening his identification with the outcasts of national politics, he said that his enemies were those who, "living in abundance, do not wish to pay the men who work a just remuneration for their services."[71] The "laboring man," Vargas said, was "no longer dependent on his boss or the state," in the cities at least.[72]

Spontaneous popular action was combined with careful organization by the Getulista faction, which believed that the time was ripe for mass urban politics on a national scale.[73] The well-financed movement fully exploited the possibilities of mobilization offered by radio, the first modern form of mass communication in Brazil; for example, rallies were broadcast throughout the nation by simultaneous national radio hookups. In addition, paid advertisements were placed in the universally hostile print media that served a select literate audience.[74]

The unruly demonstrations by tens of thousands of urban working people caught the conservative classes by surprise.[75] A dictatorship that had been installed as the definitive answer to class struggle and social disorder was now disintegrating in the largest popular mobilization in a decade. As one scholar has noted, Vargas was in effect divorcing himself from the Estado Novo, leaving its legacy to General Dutra and the PSD. At the same time, queremismo was driving General Dutra and the Estado Novo's most vocal opponent, Brigadeiro Gomes, "into a common camp, and probably with them the Army," as U.S. Ambassador Berle noted.[76]

The dominant social classes represented by the UDN and the PSD shared a deeply rooted revulsion against this explosion of unruly plebeian participation. The elites' response reeked of inbred superiority and disdain for those below. Speaking in Bahia, the Brigadeiro cited Rui Barbosa, a famous statesman of the First Republic, who had spoken of the "unconscious masses" that "oscillate between bondage and disorder."[77]

After an August incident in which queremistas stoned UDN supporters at the Rio law school, the traditional center of elite culture, the UDN called it "one of the saddest, most degrading and grotesque spectacles" in all of Brazil's history as a "civilized nation." Although the UDN denounced Communist participation in such disturbances, they found the subversive activities of their leftist enemy less disturbing than Getúlio's instigation of the disorders. The most regrettable aspect of the affair, they concluded, was that "such rabble" had been received in the palace of the Brazilian president. Vargas, after all, was a member of that elite, and they saw his actions as a betrayal of group norms and loyalty. His irresponsible and "subversive" behavior would be condemned as "Communism" or "communo-queremismo"—labels with which his enemies sought, then and later, to discredit Getulista populism among the upper classes.[78] Anticommunism, long before the cold war made it de rigueur, was the shared language of an elite eager to defend its power and privileges. Vargas would be the only politician who refused to engage in anticommunist polemics in 1945.

The raucous outbursts of sympathy for Vargas and Prestes were a rude shock for the conservative middle-class politicians of ABC. When the queremista agitation reached their community, the local political class had already begun to gather support for Dutra in the traditional ways in which politics had always been conducted. They had planned no rallies, marches, or other forms of mass participation as they campaigned for Dutra, the sound candidate of transition without rupture.[79]

From the beginning, *Borda do Campo*, the PSD's mouthpiece in Santo André, had been especially concerned by the legalization, de facto or otherwise, of the Communist Party. Although initially encouraged by the poor turnout at the PCB's first public rally in Santo André in July, the paper's editors became more and more alarmed by the progress of "communism" during the months when queremismo took to the streets.[80] By September, not an issue appeared without denunciations of Prestes, the PCB, and their proposed "democratic progressive committees." Rabid anticommunist propaganda, drawn from Catholic and Integralist sources, became characteristic of this backward-looking newspaper. Reckless charges of sexual perversion, murder, and atheism made it clear that the propaganda of the Estado Novo was not yet dead in Santo André.[81]

The UDN's candidate also began energetically raising the communist specter in September 1945. Gomes now classed the Soviet Union, a wartime ally that Brazil had just recognized, with the defeated regimes of Hitler and Mussolini.[82] Having been freed from the constraints of political expediency by Prestes's rebuff, Gomes now exploited the "communist" issue to mobilize his conservative military colleagues in order to achieve his original goal of deposing Vargas prior to elections.[83]

Despite the UDN's allegations that queremismo was merely a mask for Getúlio's desire to stay in office, it is clear that Vargas had no illusions in late 1945 that he would be able to cancel the elections as he had done in 1937.[84] With his loss of military backing, he could not fail to see that he continued in office only at the sufferance of the armed forces led by General Dutra.[85]

Dutra resigned as minister of war on 9 August 1945, but he had chosen his own successor over Vargas's opposition. General Góes Monteiro, one of the military strongmen of the 1937 coup, accepted the post only on condition that the elections be held and that Getúlio avoid "ties of any sort" with the Communists.[86]

Dutra's candidacy was secure as long as he maintained his firm grip on the military. In September and October 1945, he concentrated on warding off Vargas's probings in military and political circles. The Estado Novo's top military man did not favor a coup unless absolutely necessary, especially if it meant a weakening of PSD control over the government. Nor did he share the Brigadeiro's degree of concern about queremismo, which he called "a sentimental movement." On 28 September and 3 October 1945, the ranking representatives of the armed forces publicly affirmed that the elections would be held as scheduled. Dutra's military colleagues also rejected the call for a Constituent Assembly, and once again endorsed the PSD candidate as the representative of the "conservative currents of national politics."[87]

Yet queremismo had clearly unsettled Getúlio's opponents and restored the political initiative to him. Unleashing new forces in the political arena, the movement had altered the terms of debate by encouraging the emergence of a third popular camp in national politics, following Vargas and not his elite opponents. It also increased the president's leverage over his "official" candidate Dutra, who was reminded of his need for the votes of Getúlio's urban supporters. Yet, while placing Vargas squarely back in the center of the succession process, queremismo had deepened his rift with traditional conservative elites, both civilian and military. On 29 September 1945 U.S. Ambassador Adolph Berle gave a speech that directly commented on the succession process. His intervention, which was interpreted as hostile to Vargas, was welcomed by the UDN as the atom bomb that ended queremismo.[88]

Vargas in 1945 had never relied solely on popular mobilization, yet his attempts to reopen the succession process with talk of a third elite candidate had been rebuffed. By late 1945, he realized that it would be impossible to span the chasm between the old elite politics and the new popular politics he was creating, and he settled instead for the more modest goal of building a popular electoral following to preserve the advanced nationalist economic and social policies that he had come to see as central to Brazil's future.

After the deadline for Vargas's resignation in order to become a candidate for president had passed on 2 September 1945, queremismo continued with the demand for a Constituent Assembly. The fifteenth anniversary of the Vargas-led Revolution of 1930 would become the next great queremista mobilization. On 3 October 1945, 100,000 people gathered at the Palacio Guanabara in Rio de Janeiro. The impassioned crowd urged Vargas to stay on in what has come to be known as "the demonstration of *Fico*" (I Stay).[89] Getúlio Vargas, however, was too realistic to be swept off his feet by applause. Once again, he reiterated his noncandidacy while endorsing the people's right to demand the convocation of a Constituent Assembly. Yet, conscious of the climate of elite opinion, he also warned that "powerful reactionary forces, some hidden, others ostentatiously visible," were opposed to this "genuinely democratic process." Without naming the U.S. ambassador, Vargas said pointedly that Brazilians did not need foreign examples or lessons from abroad on how to conduct their own affairs.[90]

Seven days later, Vargas would sanction Decree 8,063, which added gubernatorial contests to the scheduled December elections. This measure revoked a concession made to the UDN opposition in February 1945 and has often been incorrectly cited as a cause of the coming coup against Vargas. Serving the interests of the PSD, the dominant military faction backing Dutra was able to prevent any immediate response to Decree 8,063.[91] Yet the Brigadeiro's military backers gained strength in the following weeks, while Dutra became increasingly uncertain about the attitude and ambitions of Minister of War Góes Monteiro. Both factors played a role in the military crisis of 27–29 October 1945.[92]

Unrestricted popular mobilization was the proximate cause of Getúlio's downfall. On 26 October 1945, police authorities in Rio and São Paulo canceled planned demonstrations for a Constituent Assembly by supporters of Vargas and Prestes. The president responded the following day by ordering his brother, Benjamin Vargas, to take over as Rio police chief from João Alberto Lins de Barros, a measure rejected by an emergency meeting of generals. Confronted with an ultimatum to rescind the appointment, Vargas refused and was deposed by the military with singular lack of ceremony. General Dutra himself helped lead the coup against Vargas, although, fearing a threat to his candidacy if power were passed to Góes Monteiro, he accepted the Brigadeiro's long-standing proposal to turn power over to the nation's judiciary led by Supreme Court Justice José Augusto Linhares.

In the first days of this "coup that restored democracy," the power structure instinctively struck back against the popular forces whose entrance on the scene had seemed so threatening. National leaders of the Labor Party were arrested, and military and police raids took place against the Communist Party throughout the country. In Santo André, the *Borda do Campo* was exultant, reporting that the local Communist "bosses" had been picked up by the police.[93]

The day of the coup, 29 October 1945, was a moment of triumph for Eduardo Gomes who, against all odds, had achieved his year-long goal of ousting Vargas. While repealing Decree 8,063 and the controversial Vargas antitrust law, the new government agreed to transform the Congress, to be elected in December, into a Constituent Assembly. Linhares chose UDN members and supporters to serve as cabinet ministers, military officials, state intervenors, and local prefeitos. The Brigadeiro's denunciations of the political misuse of government office, it was clear, were questions of opportunity, not of principle.

For Dutra the coup was unfortunate but survivable. Although he would soon object that the Linhares government was "totally hostile," his contribution to the coup had been recognized with the appointment of the PSD's José Carlos de Macedo Soares as intervenor in São Paulo, the nation's most populous state.[94]

"Getúlio Says": The Newfound Power of the People

Getúlio Vargas would appear to have been the greatest loser of 29 October 1945. Despite popular support and some military backing, he had not chosen to resist the coup. Talk of strikes, demonstrations, and fighting was in the air, but his many followers and allies, including Prestes and the PCB, did not receive the call to action that they expected.[95]

Vargas had never believed in futile actions in politics. He knew that popular mobilization in 1945 could provide only a moral counterbalance to those who, as he told Santos dockworkers in July, "threaten the nation with movements of force and coups d'état, whether in secret meetings, in speeches in public squares, or in the articles of mercenary journalists."[96] Leaving office in "an agreed-upon deposition," he was aware that there were measures of power and influence in 1945 that did not derive solely from the military or the dominant classes. In fact, his being forced out of office for the "subversive character" of his appeals would help him win the support of a massive new constituency.[97]

Having avoided the sanctions urged by many of the generals who overthrew him, Getúlio now retired silently to his ranch in Rio Grande do Sul. The ex-president refused to endorse his betrayer, Dutra, for president, despite the advice of many of his associates. Instead, he advised the people to reinforce the PTB, inheritor of the principles of the Revolution of 1930, so that it could "fight and survive." Talk circulated that the PTB, which had not endorsed a candidate for president at its founding convention, might run a third civilian candidate.[98]

Debate raged within the party. Many noted that the PTB's "enormous numerical force" was matched by its equally "enormous weakness as an electoral organization." Alliance with the PSD would defeat the worst enemy, many argued, while providing time, money, and patronage to allow the PTB's consolidation as a real political power. Vargas, however, still held back.[99]

After the initial days of repression, the Communist Party soon reemerged, having gained legal recognition two days before the coup. In a statement of 3 November, the PCB declared that the 29 October coup had been only "apparently" against Getúlio, being directed, in reality, "against the people and democracy, against the proletariat and its organization," the PCB. The result, despite the illusions of some democrats, they said, was merely the substitution of one de facto government for another. While pledging support of the "democratic" elements of the government, the party of Prestes criticized Getúlio for his "vacillations" and attacked him for "betraying the people" by refusing to resist the "fascists." The PCB's position, unfair as it was, reflected the party's growing confidence and a continuing rancor against its rival, Getúlio.[100]

These feelings at the leadership level did not, however, truly reflect the sentiments of the rank-and-file working people whose hopes and desires had sustained the popular movement of 1945 in both its trabalhista and Communist variants. They were united in their condemnation of the coup that had overthrown Getúlio.

The Communist leadership sought a way to exploit these mass realities. Since it was now a legal party, the PCB could field a slate of candidates, and it decided to run a non-Communist candidate for president. After negotiations with the famous urban planner and ex-prefeito of São Paulo, Prestes Maia, broke down, they announced on 18 November the nomination of Yedo Fiuza, an engineer and one-time Petrópolis prefeito who had been close to Vargas. In a whirlwind two-week campaign, the Communists would place hundreds of thousands in the streets in support of their civilian candidate of the people. Getúlio's continuing silence would help them attract the support of a large body of popular opinion that strongly repudiated the two conservative military candidates. In what Prestes now calls an error, the PCB did not, however, directly approach Getúlio to support Fiuza.[101]

Although the PSD's campaign had been dealt a blow, its local machines were too deeply rooted to be successfully dislodged by a few appointed officials in the month remaining before the election. Yet Dutra's backers had lost certain advantages and faced the hostility of Getúlio's supporters because of their candidate's participation in the coup. João Neves, one of the PSD's more farsighted leaders, was convinced that Getúlio had called onto the scene powerful "unknown forces" whose strength, which was "not yet revealed," could mean the difference between victory and defeat for the PSD. To Vargas, he wrote that support for Dutra was essential to "impede a return to the old and ingrained conservatism" and the "oligarchical system of the politics of governors" against which they had fought in 1930.[102]

Convinced of the need for a deal, Dutra made a formal public agreement with the PTB on 21 November. Pledging support for existing social and labor legislation, Dutra promised to select a minister of labor agreeable to the PTB and to fill appointed positions in accordance with their share of the vote. Within days, arrangements were worked out for financial subsidies and votes for PTB candidates. To exploit the Brigadeiro's antilabor speech in Sorocaba on 22 November, Dutra even pledged action against those employers who defrauded their workers of their rights.[103]

On 27 November, Vargas provided the message that the PSD needed so badly. In a short text distributed by the millions under the slogan "Getúlio Says," he called for an end to recriminations and blamed the coup on "errors and confusions." Declaring abstention from voting to be an error, he reminded the poor and the humble, the workers, and the people in general that "one does not win without struggle" and urged them to vote for General Dutra.[104]

If 29 October had proved the strength of the traditional holders of power, the elections of 2 December 1945 showed that Vargas had gambled correctly on the existence of something radically new in the politics of 1945. Defying the elitist "common sense" of most politicians, Vargas had opened the way for the participation of millions of Brazilians from the urban popular classes in the affairs of politics and government. In 120 years of elections, Brazil's economic and political elites had grown accustomed to a highly restricted politics of the few. The electoral marketplace in 1945, however, was totally transformed as participation increased from 10 percent of all adults in the 1930s to 33 percent in 1945, out of a population that was about 50 percent literate.[105]

As intended, electoral participation increased most dramatically, by 400 to 500 percent, in the country's urban and industrial heartland. For the first time in Brazilian history, the state of São Paulo displaced Minas Gerais as the nation's largest state contingent of voters. As the centers of Brazilian industry, São Paulo and Rio de Janeiro (the national capital) also had the highest percentage of ex officio voters: fully 33 percent of the Paulista and Carioca electorate had been registered ex officio, compared to only 15 percent for the less developed state of Minas Gerais.[106]

Mass enfranchisement clearly meant that electoral politics was no longer the exclusive realm of the traditional rural oligarchies. Ex officio registration also combined to dramatically increase the clout of urban areas within a given state. While holding only 23 percent of the state's population, greater São Paulo provided 44 percent of the total electoral turnout. Half of the voters in the state's urban and industrial centers were registered ex officio, compared to only a fifth of the electorate in rural areas.[107]

The final presidential results for the nation were: Dutra 56 percent, Gomes 35 percent, and Fiuza 10 percent.[108] Brigadeiro Eduardo Gomes, the hope of the UDN's liberal opposition, was the great loser of 1945 despite his supporters' genuine conviction, until the last, that Vargas's dictatorial regime was indeed without support among Brazil's people. The results were a shock to all partisans of the noble democratic campaign of liberation, still discussed and debated years later.[109]

Dutra, backed by the PSD's local machines, had put together the winning combination in 1945 by being willing to ally with the new urban forces represented by Getúlio's PTB. Dutra's calculating behavior throughout the turbulence of 1945 gave him the victory he desired over Gomes. However, the election of the conservative former minister of war was also a clear demonstration of Vargas's political leverage. After refusing to endorse the man responsible for his ouster, Vargas's successful last-minute appeal for Dutra showed that he could deliver support among the urban masses even to a candidate repudiated by many of his own followers.[110]

Getúlio Vargas was aptly called the "great elector" of 1945. He was elected senator by São Paulo and Rio Grande do Sul, and nine states also elected him federal deputy. As a result, the PTB made a surprisingly strong showing in its first elections and emerged as the nation's third-largest party. When Vargas turned down the São Paulo senatorship, the post fell to the PTB's primary architect, ex-minister of labor Marcondes Filho.[111]

For Luis Carlos Prestes, the elections also represented a moment of triumph. His symbolic presidential candidate, Fiuza, received 10 percent of the vote nationally and the PCB emerged as the fourth-largest party in the nation—a solid accomplishment for a party without money, with fewer than a thousand members, and with no past history of electoral success. Prestes's personal popularity was attested by his receiving the second-highest number of votes in the country; he was elected senator by the Federal District (Rio de Janeiro), federal deputy by three states, and alternate deputy (*suplente*) by another three.[112]

The results in ABC indicated that local electoral politics had been transformed by this precipitous expansion in participation. After dominating electoral politics for decades, ABC's politically active middle class found its small and narrow patronage networks overwhelmed by a mass of new working-class voters. From 6,000 voters in 1936, electoral participation in ABC jumped fivefold to 28,000 in December 1945.

In the município of Santo André, the unanimity of support by the political class for the PSD, combined with Getúlio's support, gave Dutra 63 percent of the vote—while Gomes virtually disappeared as a candidate, receiving only 9 percent of the vote, compared to his state-wide average of 28 percent or his urban/industrial average of 24 percent.[113] Santo André favored the PCB's candidate Fiuza with 28 percent, twice as much as in the state as a whole, so that he came in second. The same pattern was shown in other major Paulista industrial cities like Sorocaba, where Fiuza came in second, or São Paulo itself, where he tied Gomes. In the most dramatic result, the famous port city of Santos gave the PCB's candidate a first place, with 42 percent of the vote, over Dutra (32 percent) and Gomes (26 percent).[114]

The Santos workers would also elect one of their own, dockworker Osvaldo Pacheco, to be federal deputy for the Communist Party. Pursuing a similar tactic in Santo André, the PCB had nominated the president of the local metalworkers' union, Euclides Savietto, who received 5,647 votes to become second alternate federal deputy for the PCB.[115]

The 1945 election results in the nation's major urban center were startling in their uniformity, with the PTB and the PCB receiving an absolute majority of the votes cast for federal deputy. In the município of Santo André, the two class-identified popular parties received fully 71 percent of the total vote (compared to only 32 percent on the state level).[116] Participating in electoral politics for the first time, working-class voters had shown a unity of purpose that heralded the coming of a new day for politics in Brazil.[117]

Vargas had indeed won his gamble of mid-1945. His populist appeals had been met with an impressive popular response. New forces were unleashed that could no longer be controlled in the manner of the past. Having examined the politics of 1945 at the top, I shall next turn to the factory districts of ABC, to investigate the grass-roots dynamics of this surprising upsurge of working-class activism and unity.

Five • Popular Getulismo

and Working-Class Organization

The birth of the Populist Republic has long been seen as merely a change of the juridical forms of elite rule in Brazil. Most have failed to appreciate the radical break of 1945–46 that was marked by the dramatic entry of the urban working class into Brazilian political life.[1] Consciously focusing on the state, trade unions, and political parties, even the best existing scholarship has failed to explain the outlook and behavior of the masses of Brazilian industrial workers.

The absence of serious, month-to-month studies of industrial working-class communities in 1945–46 has left us with little understanding of the dynamics of this remarkable upsurge of popular activism. To approach such an understanding, one must examine the workers' material conditions and explore the contours of working-class consciousness: its characteristics, psychology, and direction of development. We can then explain why workers responded with such startling unanimity to the mobilizational appeals of Getúlio Vargas and Luis Carlos Prestes in 1945.

To understand the development of postwar trabalhismo/Getulismo and communism/Prestismo in ABC, we must also address the crucial question of organization, the means through which change was wrought, which provides the key to working-class political practice and the politics of the labor movement itself in 1945.

The Workers' Material Conditions

The ABC working class had not lacked economic complaints during the war, even while they responded enthusiastically to Getúlio's appeals. Although work was plentiful in expanding local factories, the region's wage earners were hurt by the severe disruptions that accompanied the war effort.

Wartime industrial expansion had intensified the in-migration to greater São Paulo. Hundreds of thousands from the state's interior coffee regions poured into the metropolitan area, and makeshift settlements sprang up overnight as the factories' new recruits settled as near as possible to their places of work.[2] These new workers and their families had to be fed and clothed at a time when the state's agricultural, commercial, and industrial life was in disarray. Shortages and spiraling prices for foodstuffs and other necessities accelerated each year of the war. The federal government, in a futile effort to control the high cost of living (*carestia*), had established an elaborate price-control mechanism in 1942: prices were fixed for alcohol, kerosene, coffee, sugar, and salt, and all major foodstuffs were soon included as well.[3] Various rationing schemes were worked out by local and state price-control authorities but had only moderate success, if any.

An understated measurement of the food-price spiral in São Paulo can be found in the official, state-approved price increases for basic foodstuffs, such as macaroni, beans, rice, bread, milk, and potatoes. During one year, from 1943 to 1944, the increases ranged from a low of 24 percent to a high of 115 percent, with most foodstuffs going up 30 to 60 percent. The rate of food-price increases intensified between mid-1944 and early 1945: the rise in prices for macaroni, beans, and bread in one month, from July to August 1944, for example, was half the total increase during the 1943–44 period.[4]

Minimum wages, first set in May 1940, had failed to keep pace with this inflationary price spiral. While they increased by approximately 30 percent in January and May 1943, they then remained stationary through the end of the war—which suggests that the drop in the real wages of some workers may have been substantial.[5]

Bread-and-butter issues like wages would seem a natural object of collective bargaining by trade unions, but Vargas's legislation gave the government the primary responsibility for setting the basic wage framework and wages were always set below the level of inflation. When Santo André's textile workers received a wage increase in July 1945, for example, their wage was still only 26 percent above the official governmental minimum wage for the São Paulo region, which had been set in mid-1943—an increase that barely recouped the 30–60 percent increase in the cost of living in 1943 and 1944.[6] Families with multiple wage earners and overtime work (paid at time-and-a-fifth) probably lessened the impact of these economic trends, but the workers' situation was clearly precarious. The situation was so bad that even the industrialists saw the need to improve it. In November 1943, the Federation of Industries of the State of São Paulo (FIESP) formally recommended immediate increases in industrial wages.[7]

The effort of working-class families to stretch already inadequate budgets was made even more unbearable because of manipulated shortages and rampant black marketeering. Acquiring foodstuffs, even at black-market prices, required personal connections, luck, and hours of standing in lines—a burden that fell on the housewives of ABC. By mid-1945, nationwide shortages led Santo André's prefeito to complain that he was able to acquire only 50 percent of the flour needed by local bakers and merchants.[8]

The pressing problems of urban supply prompted ABC's employers and unionists to search for solutions. In 1942 the government authorized the Consumers' Cooperative of Unionized Workers of Santo André, but it could assist only 3,272 family members in 1946; it was clearly insufficient to meet the needs of some forty thousand local workers.[9] During the first years of the war, ABC factory managers had fought individually for access to limited stocks of rationed foodstuffs in an effort to maintain their hard-working employees. To overcome the anarchy that resulted, the government authorized "provision posts" in large factories in 1944, allowing 10 percent over wholesale prices for overhead. The new posts were established in most large ABC factories, including Firestone, Rhodia Química, Pirelli, Aliberti, and Cerâmica São Caetano.[10] Although the posts were an improvement over the prior system, this direct distribution scheme rarely provided foodstuffs at less than retail prices.

The chaos spawned by an unplanned, unregulated urbanization process added to the problems of scarce foodstuffs and other supplies. Most working-class neighborhoods, even established ones, lacked electricity, running water, sewage systems, and dependable mass transportation. While Santo André's *prefeitura* was proud to point out that ABC generated more taxes than the capital cities of twelve states, very little of the money was used to resolve the pressing needs of such working-class neighborhoods.[11]

The deterioration of economic and living conditions was accompanied by intensified on-the-job pressures. The disruption of the export of developed countries' manufactured goods had created new export markets for Brazilian manufacturers. The United Nations' "total war" against the Axis powers required the expansion and deepening of Brazilian industrial manufacturing—yet there was no possibility of increasing production by importing new machinery from the metropolitan centers. Even in the textile industry, the nation's largest employer of industrial labor and the trend-setter for Brazilian manufacturing as a whole, output could be increased only by lengthening working hours and freezing workers in their jobs.[12] Most of the measures hailed by Vargas in 1945 as the "workers' code of economic emancipation" had in fact been suspended as part of the wartime industrial production drive. After the declaration of war in 1942, for example, the Ministry of Labor, Industry, and Commerce had moved immediately to revoke the legal eight-hour day in enterprises vital to "national defense." The decree authorized up to ten hours of labor, even for unhealthful occupations. A subsequent proviso allowed a workday of more than ten hours in cases of urgent necessity.[13]

Industrial expansion increased the competition for labor, but the government intervened in the labor market to lessen the workers' bargaining power. The difficulties of textile manufacturers had been intensified by the workers' preference for better-paying industries like metalworking. To counter this trend, the government declared the textile industry of military interest in July 1944 and eliminated freedom of contract. Henceforth, governmental permission was required in order for textile workers to leave their jobs, or for manufacturers to hire workers without proper papers. Under the new provisions, textile workers could be shifted from one place to another without appeal, and restrictions on night work for women were lifted.[14]

To meet wartime production goals, industrial machinery was pushed to its limit; and as working conditions deteriorated and the hours of labor were lengthened, the workers were pushed to *their* limit. The importance of industrial production to national security under conditions of total war also encouraged the expansion of the Brazilian army's role in industrial and labor relations. Military oversight of industrial production existed in ABC industries only indirectly linked to war production, as well as in munitions factories like the Companhia Brasileira de Cartuchos.[15]

In 1945 the Estado Novo's minister of war, General Eurico Dutra, proudly emphasized the military's central responsibilities in industrial matters. The military's vision of national security, hierarchy, and Brazilian development was shaped by its wartime ties with industrial management at every level.[16] Seeing the world of the factory from the employers' point of view, the top military leadership favored repressive antilabor solutions to disputes between the factory owners and their employees.

The Nature of Popular Getulismo

Content with references to the popularity of the "charismatic caudillos" Getúlio Vargas and Luis Carlos Prestes, few scholars have provided detailed explanations for the degree of support these two men received in 1945. While the power of propaganda is still cited by some scholars, most have simply taken mass support for Vargas and Prestes at face value. They have thus been unable to explain the motivation of urban voters as a whole, or the relationship between support for the PTB versus that for the PCB.[17] Even the authors of two excellent local studies of workers in postwar Minas Gerais merely note but do not explain the origin of this political and trade union militancy.[18]

In many discussions, commentators seem to have accepted the Getulista explanation that support flowed from the material benefits provided to workers under the Vargas regime's "advanced labor legislation." Yet, as we have seen, the government's social programs, as experienced by ABC's workers, were largely promises, and few workers had received actual benefits at war's end. Some retired workers, for example, received modest stipends from the Industrial Employees' Retirement and Pension Institute (IAPI), and four hundred working-class families in Santo André had new homes as the result of an IAPI housing project inaugurated in 1943—but this small number of direct beneficiaries clearly cannot explain Vargas's popularity among ABC's workers.

Others have visualized a patronage chain extending from the national Ministry of Labor, which organized the PTB, down through the bureaucratic trade union hierarchy to the local unions, and thence to the workers. Pension payments from the IAPI and trade union assistencialismo (medical/dental/social welfare programs) were the patronage benefits for which votes for Vargas were exchanged. But the simplicity of this explanation fails on many fronts. There were few Labor Ministry or IAPI functionaries in ABC in 1945; and as for the trade union structure, none of the paid union functionaries at the state federation level had any direct ties to the unpaid local union leaders in ABC. Nor did ABC's trade unions, plagued by employer refusals to pay the required union tax, have the funds to support any extensive program of medical/dental assistance to their members. And finally, the diminutive membership of local unions in 1945 could not account for the results of the balloting.

The Getulismo of ABC's workers cannot, therefore, be explained as the result of direct material benefits, or of the patronage exercised by the bureaucracy that was said to staff the corporatist state-linked trade unions. Perhaps one might then accept the oldest and most common explanation for popular Getulismo: that ABC's workers had been won over by Vargas's propaganda and loose prolabor rhetoric. Indeed, susceptibility to populist "demagoguery" has long figured in explanations from both the Left and the Right. Unaware of their own interests, it is said, inexperienced workers were manipulated by a dictator who had done nothing real for them and had repeatedly crushed their efforts at independent organization.

The use of populist techniques of manipulation and political control, it has often been said, resulted in the loss of class autonomy and left urban workers as a mass base for maneuvers by bourgeois groups. The PCB's decision to cooperate with Vargas in 1945, it is further argued, contributed to the workers' dependence upon the state and their mystification by nationalist developmentalist ideologies. The failure of these postwar workers to develop independent class politics, as conceived by later writers, is then explained as a result of misleadership or betrayal.[19]

Lacking a firm foundation in empirical research, these explanations fail to illuminate the political or trade union behavior of São Paulo's urban workers precisely because they overlook the specific political dimension of the special circumstances of World War II. The world conflagration was not an abstraction for the people of ABC and other urban areas: their everyday lives were affected in fundamental and visible ways. No worker could fail to see the direct tie between the war and the expansion of industry, with its corollary of near-full employment. Although distant, the war involved local residents in activities such as collecting scrap iron and rubber, soliciting contributions for the Brazilian Expeditionary Force (FEB), and practicing blackouts. The news of the war was followed anxiously by ABC's populace, who felt—as did much of humanity—that their fate was being decided on distant battlefields.[20]

The unanimity of support for the war crossed class lines in ABC, while the war's political tenor discredited the right-wing and Integralist politics that had, in the past, been associated with the management personnel of many local factories. Popular involvement in the war was dramatically expressed by the explosive public celebration, on 8 May 1945, of the news that Hitler's "thousand-year Reich" had come to an end.[21]

Moreover, within the wartime context the workers' ongoing problems— economic difficulties, the high cost of living, high-handed employers, and repressive governmental authority—were invested with a broader and potentially political meaning. World War II was sold to the world's peoples as a "democratic" war in which the defeat of a common menace required the sacrifice of all—even if the burden was clearly unevenly distributed, as in Brazil. The workers' reward would come—so they expected—at the conclusion of the war, an understanding fostered and encouraged by the regime's wartime promises. If the measures taken by Getúlio were still small, the workers accepted them as a good-faith down payment on what was due them after victory had been achieved. In his classic study of the strike of 400,000 U.S. steelworkers in 1919, David Brody showed that the combination of wartime grievances and hope for postwar change, whether realistic or not, was an explosive combination that led easily to labor militancy.[22]

In heightening popular expectations, the war increased popular hostility toward speculators and the rich. The breadth and simplicity of this grassroots sentiment was eloquently captured by a rural metaphor chosen by Gonçalo Baptista dos Santos, a Santo André worker, during an October 1945 rally: "The rain that fertilizes the soil is not sent to favor only the rich and powerful"; all human beings have equal rights to the gifts of nature. Speaking for the Democratic Progressive Committee (CDP) of the IAPI housing project in Vila Guiomar, Santos stressed that "disunity and calamity" were being bred by "the retention of needed bread by selfish people."[23]

Indeed, a heightened, almost millenarian, sense of the possibilities of change gripped ABC's workers in mid-1945. Although the exact road to a better life was unknown, there were few workers who did not feel that they were heading toward a promising future. Their feelings of political efficacy were enhanced by the division of Brazil's ruling groups that led Vargas to opt for building a popular urban electoral base.

To achieve his goals, Vargas consciously encouraged and stimulated these popular expectations. While he sought to blur the lines between social classes by using the term "laborers" (*trabalhadores*) and not "workers" (*operários*), the *effect* of Getúlio's rhetoric was to foster a common group identity among ABC's discontented but expectant factory workers. For them, the distinction between "laborers" and "workers" was academic, since either term translated into "us and them" in their own lives.[24]

Rather than hindering the development of class consciousness among workers, these populist appeals actually served as a rallying point that helped to unify the working class and increase its confidence. Vargas's rhetoric would have had less of a mobilizational impact if he had been able to maintain unchallenged control of the urban popular arena. Yet despite his publicly avowed intention of preempting leftist extremism among the workers, the peculiar context of elite division and conflict in 1945 brought him into a de facto alliance with the Communist Prestes. This alliance of convenience precluded the anticommunist attacks and rhetoric that might have turned Getúlio's followers against the PCB.

Working parallel to Vargas, the PCB avoided open collision with popular Getulismo while establishing a fruitful dialogue with this powerful current of working-class self-assertion. Placing itself on the same side of the barricades, the weakly organized PCB grew as an expression of a class appeal to the left of trabalhismo, yet within the more general unity expressed in the broader queremista movement. The evidence bears out the critics of Francisco Weffort in their characterization of the PCB's policy in 1945–46 as one of "competition in alliance with Varguismo."[25]

The emergence of a rival to the left of the PTB spurred a competition for the workers' support that forced Vargas to go even further in emphasizing his commitment to working-class interests. The avoidance of fratricidal divisions among the workers had a powerful impact on mass consciousness during these crucial months. The lines of division were not drawn between workers of different outlooks, but between workers and industrial employers with their conservative middle-class allies. This reinforced the workers' sense of a common identity and united and invigorated their movement in ABC.

This dynamic of mass opinion among the workers provides the key to understanding the political crystallization that took place in ABC in 1945–46. Support for Getúlio, whether grudging or enthusiastic, served as the single most important defining point of popular sentiment—as shown by the PTB's 43 percent share of the total vote in the heavily industrialized município of Santo André. Yet even Getúlio, it must be emphasized, did not *control* these working-class voters. Even though 63 percent of the voters voted for Dutra, fully 28 percent ignored Getúlio's well-publicized appeals by voting for a Communist presidential candidate in 1945 who had no chance of being elected. Clearly, many workers, despite the general enthusiasm for Getúlio, were fully capable of making their own decisions.

It would be easy, perhaps, to see these 7,000 votes for the PCB's candidate Yedo Fiuza as a protest by class-conscious workers against the demagoguery of the former dictator Vargas. But although for some it was an expression of dislike for Vargas, for most the Communist presidential vote was the strongest possible protest against Vargas's ouster by Dutra and the military. Thus even the PCB's share of ABC's vote was shaped by Getúlio's popular appeal, as even the Communists grudgingly admitted at the time.[26] Ironically enough, the Communist voter may well have been the strongest Getulista in 1945.

To achieve their goals, both Getúlio Vargas and Luis Carlos Prestes would have to come to terms with these currents of mass consciousness—which they had not created and did not control, despite the charges of their conservative opponents. Indeed, the striking labor rhetoric of these two leaders would have been meaningless without a working class ready to respond to their message of struggle. While decisively influenced by Vargas and Prestes, these new working-class voters were already demonstrating that they were far from being automatic followers simply manipulated from above.

The Dynamics of Working-Class Politics: Trabalhismo versus Communism

Enjoying massive working-class support, Getúlio's PTB should easily have established its dominance in ABC's political and trade union affairs. Yet the PTB was weak in postwar ABC, and support for organized trabalhismo would consistently decline over the next two years vis-à-vis the PCB. Why did this occur, and what did it imply about working-class sentiment?

First, we must put aside the idea that the PTB/PCB split coincided with a distinction between migrants and "class-conscious," second-generation industrial workers.[27] The collective biography of ABC's Communist militants of this period reflects the same demographic reality to be found in marriage samples and factory payrolls: the majority of ABC's industrial working class was from the Paulista countryside.

Rather, the crucial weakness of the populist PTB was conceptual and organizational. Energized by the queremista agitation of late 1945, the PTB in São Paulo combined daring populist appeals with a style of mobilization and organization still shaped by traditional Brazilian politics. Innovative in its choice of themes, its targeted audience, and its creative use of the new medium, radio, the PTB still relied on older techniques of bureaucratic patronage to build its new "popular" party.

Like Dutra's PSD, the PTB was built through the Getulistas' control over a part (although not the most powerful part) of the state apparatus. To guarantee success in the nation's most important industrial state, Labor Minister Marcondes Filho called upon the employees of the Labor Ministry, the labor courts, and pension agencies.[28] Direct dependence upon their bureaucratic superiors guaranteed substantial support from this group, much as the PSD's control of jobs, favors, contracts, and deals won the overwhelming adherence of ABC's political class. To this base of support, the incipient PTB added trade union functionaries, especially the small group of individuals who held bureaucratic positions in the state union federations.[29]

The prominence of labor and trade union functionaries in the state PTB would seem to complete the patronage chain that led from the federal government to support for the trabalhistas in industrial areas like ABC. And indeed, like many later observers, the architects of the PTB assumed in 1945 that patronage would flow smoothly downwards within the official Labor Ministry and trade union hierarchies to the workers themselves. Yet such traditional patronage chains broke down at the local level where the PTB had to connect with the workers. Despite ostentatious official encouragement, only Santo André's textile workers had a vigorously PTB leadership under Henrique Poleto—while the most influential local trade union, the metalworkers', was a stronghold of the Communist Party.

In fact, the PTB's organization in ABC was so precarious that it proved impossible to mount a serious campaign for the December 1945 elections. The PTB's problems in Santo André were exacerbated by the local party's control by ambitious middle-class individuals with few ties to labor. These political unknowns were eager to ride the wave of Getúlio's popularity for their personal advancement and had no interest in connecting the PTB with even its union supporters. Consequently, labor participation in Santo André's PTB was minimal in late 1945 and early 1946; Henrique Poleto, the trabalhista president of the textile workers' union, did not even serve on the diretório of the local PTB.[30]

Moreover, the Getulista faction's skill in maneuvering at the national level was not matched by an equal understanding of the very different rules that governed urban working-class life and politics. Urban workers had collective needs that could not be met simply by the individual favors that satisfied traditional political constituencies. These urgent working-class needs for better wages, hours, and working and living conditions could only be met at a cost to other, far more powerful interests.

The fear of upper-class retaliation, to which even Vargas was not immune, explains in part the unwillingness of the local political class to take up the workers' grievances, as well as the cautious approach of state-level union functionaries. A different sort of party organization with far greater latitude for movement from the bottom up was required in order to force concessions in these touchy areas.

Vargas had spent much of 1945 urging Brazil's laboring classes to involve themselves in politics. His appeal was mobilizational, yet the Getulistas lacked an efficient vehicle to give shape to this popular participation. As Ricardo Maranhão has pointed out, the result was a curious paradox: the PTB was weak at the grass roots, in ABC and elsewhere, although it represented the broadest current of working-class opinion.[31] Even though Getúlio's popularity guaranteed the PTB the largest bloc of working-class votes, that mass Getulista sentiment failed to become an effective, sustained force in ABC's political and trade union life.

Instead, the effective mobilization of the workers' inchoate desire for change fell to the Communists, who helped to give organizational expression, at the grass-roots level, to the popular participation encouraged by Vargas. While lacking bureaucratic and monetary resources, the Communists emerged as the heart of a whirlwind of activity conceived from the base upwards. In contrast, the PTB's greatest weakness in 1945 was precisely its inability to conceive of politics on such a participatory basis. The builders of the Labor Party came from a tradition of top-down politics in which parties were fictions without lives of their own at the local level. The PTB also lacked any conception of a possible link between electoral/political activity and trade unionism—once again in contrast to the PCB.

In ABC as elsewhere, the Democratic Progressive Committees (CDPs) proposed by Prestes in his May 1945 speech in Rio de Janeiro proved vital to popular mobilization over the next four months. By October 1945 these nonpartisan, although PCB-led, committees were functioning in nine neighborhoods in the district of Santo André, and others in Utinga, São Caetano, and Mauá. With two rented headquarters, the committees and their elected leadership bodies provided a first experience in democratic politics for hundreds of local residents.

These CDPs were an important avenue for Communist recruitment, but their success depended, above all else, on their dedication to the resolution of working people's urgent problems in their neighborhoods. When ABC's workers returned home after a hard day of labor, they faced grossly inadequate living conditions spawned by haphazard urbanization and the indifference of the PSD-controlled municipal administration. The CDPs provided a flexible form through which community members could be organized to resolve their pressing complaints.[32]

The problems were commonplace, but the grass-roots CDP was an innovation in Brazilian associative life. Through their CDPs, the residents of Vila Guiomar won better garbage pick-up and lower water and sewer fees, while São Caetano's residents, presenting the São Paulo Railway with 5,000 signatures, succeeded in winning more frequent train service to and from São Paulo. The São Caetano committee carried out mass campaigns for a district hospital and a night school for those over fourteen years of age. The CDPs also held literacy classes and organized Christmas parties for poor children. In Santo André, they took up the case of a black street sweeper who was arbitrarily fired by the municipal administration after thirty years of devoted service.[33]

Local committees also carried out more consciously political tasks, such as registering voters and organizing rallies to oppose the "fascist" constitution of 1937. Special efforts were made to organize women, and the first meetings to that end were held in late October 1945 in Santo André. Plans were announced for the município's First Convention of Popular Organizations to be held in early November 1945.[34]

The PCB itself grew rapidly in the turbulent months of heightened politicization and activism that marked the emergence of queremismo on the national scene. By early October 1945, PCB district committees were functioning in the two factory districts of Santo André and São Caetano. Under their guidance, Communist organization was quickly established in the smaller districts such as the railroad center, Paranapiacaba, and Mauá. By February 1946, there were seven functioning PCB cells in the district of Santo André alone.[35]

Unlike the local PTB, the PCB also benefited from its overwhelmingly working-class composition and its support by a group of highly motivated activists with proven records of service to workers. The political secretary of the PCB's municipal committee in Santo André, for example, was the son of the Santo André metalworker Epímaco Frati, who had distinguished himself in the region's labor struggles since the time of the União Operária after World War I; in 1945, Rolando Frati was head of the Consumers' Cooperative of Unionized Workers of Santo André.[36]

The Dynamics of the Postwar Labor Movement: Left, Right, and Center

The Brazilian trade union movement that emerged in 1945 would play a crucial role in determining the direction of working-class politics over the next two years.[37] If political parties and factions were the favored vehicles for action by ABC's middle class, it was the trade union even more than the CDP that provided the major locus of organization for ABC's workers. Yet the nature of postwar trade unionism has been obscured by an excessive preoccupation with the legalisms of Getúlio's *Consolidação das Leis do Trabalho* (*CLT*) which survived, as countless scholars have pointed out, the end of the dictatorial regime that gave it birth.[38]

If we are to grasp the evolution of postwar trade unionism, it is vital that we understand the consciousness of the core of working-class activists who had been attracted to the local unions during the Estado Novo. This group of activist workers did not reject Vargas; they perceived the positive elements of his new direction. Responding enthusiastically to his populist appeals, they welcomed the loosening of repressive control over unions in mid-1945 (such as ending the requirement of police attendance at union meetings). Their Getulismo strengthened their confidence and encouraged them to push harder as conditions improved with the end of the Estado Novo. Nothing, after all, is achieved without struggle, they thought, and even Getúlio needed help in order to defeat labor's many enemies.

Having won the allegiance of an activist minority, and with the encouragement of the president, the unions set out in mid-1945 to broaden their ranks by recruiting and involving a larger circle of workers. While ABC's handful of veteran Communists might find them naive, the unions' emerging activists were expressing the very illusions that characterized the mass mood of their fellow workers. They may have been open to "manipulation" by Vargas, but only because they were sincerely concerned about resolving the grievances of their fellow workers, even if uncertain as to how to go about it in mid-1945. Employer resistance to the legal trade unionism promoted by Vargas reinforced their willingness to accept what their ally Getúlio said at face value.

This amorphous group of activists, lacking self-proclaimed labels, encompassed a range of implicit views and outlooks in political terms. Easily ignored by contemporary polemicists and later scholars, they have been subsumed under a two-camp characterization of trade union leaders as either class-conscious radicals, like the Communists, or pelegos (a derogatory term for union "sell-outs"). To understand postwar unionism, we must go beyond this simple dichotomy that lumps all nonradicals into one negative reference group.[39] This largely unorganized grouping is best understood if it is characterized as the labor Center, as distinct from the labor Left or the labor Right (the classic pelegos). The existence of these Center forces, if not the label, has been noted in several studies. Describing Juiz de Fora's postwar unions, Maria Andréa Loyola has insisted that these non-Communist leaders, although Getulistas, were not pelegos and are best called union independents.[40]

The labor Center was neither static nor monolithic but encompassed a variety of perspectives. The postwar political and trade union experiences of these activists resulted in a political crystallization in late 1945 and early 1946 that determined the direction of the postwar trade union movement.

The handful of Communists in ABC were ideally situated to benefit from the process of political definition undergone by these activist workers. Long active in the unions, Communist workers had established their credibility with this Center group through close cooperation in union affairs and during the queremista movement of 1945. Although only a minority of ABC trade unionists became Communists, many union activists and workers who did not join the party nonetheless voted for the PCB presidential candidate Fiuza as a protest against Dutra. Others welcomed the candidacy of the metalworkers' union president, Euclides Savietto, who received 5,647 votes in Santo André in December 1945 as a PCB candidate for federal deputy.[41]

The coalition nature of this postwar union upsurge has often been overlooked by past observers. Many have talked of the new opportunities for Communist "infiltration" created by the connivance of Vargas and the legalization of the PCB.[42] Others have assumed a general PCB predominance—which was, in fact, far from a reality in most union leaderships.[43] The first view overlooks the Communist presence in union diretórios before 1945; the second ignores the clear evidence that the effectiveness of PCB leadership stemmed from the Communists' ability to win over some non-Communist unionists while working with other centrist forces within the unions.

While the Communist Party benefited from its union ties, Getúlio's PTB again suffered the negative impact of having tied its fate in the trade union movement to a narrow stratum of union functionaries that comprised the main base for the labor Right. Peleguismo did not, however, characterize ABC's trade union leadership as a whole in 1945, which was rank-and-file oriented and alive with new ideas.

In ABC, the isolated PTB-led Santo André textile workers' union best exemplifies the policies we have come to associate with peleguismo. While the textile workers sought an increase in union dues in 1946, other ABC unions declared dues amnesties, abolished entrance fees, and sought to encourage involvement even by those who had not yet joined.[44] While the textile workers held few general meetings, ABC's other unions organized dozens of general assemblies and factory meetings open to both members and nonmembers in late 1945 in order to discuss the demands to be presented as part of the new procedure for collective bargaining, the *dissídio coletivo* conducted through the labor courts.

Henrique Poleto's textile workers' union never approached the mass support or influence of the Left/Center metalworkers' union of Santo André, which was not only the largest and most active local union but also the only one to possess its own building. The union's new facilities at Rua Dona Gertrudes 202 were shared by the chemical workers' union, the civil construction/industrial ceramics union, and two associations covering the food products and pottery industries. Similar professional associations were later established for leather products and tanning workers.[45]

Trade Unionism and the State in 1945

The radical changes in Brazilian politics in early 1945 had been quickly felt in the trade union movement. Within two weeks of the April 1945 amnesty of Prestes, the establishment of the Unifying Movement of Workers (Movimento Unificador dos Trabalhadores, or MUT) marked the first public stirrings of those who were eager to escape the restrictions of the dictatorial regime. The national MUT manifesto was signed by three hundred trade unionists, including both holders of official union posts and the left-wing activist elements whose persecution had been a major focus of the Ministry of Labor and the political-social police (DOPS). The MUT's legitimacy was further enhanced in late 1945 when Vargas publicly shook hands with the national MUT president, Communist João Amazonas.[46]

The importance of the events of 1945–46 and the MUT itself were first discussed in Francisco Weffort's widely translated essay on "the origins of populist unionism in Brazil." In his forceful polemic, Weffort attacked the Left for having forged the fetters of governmental control of the trade unions by breathing life into the fascist official trade union structure. The Communist Party in 1945, Weffort argued, repressed working-class demands and subordinated labor to Vargas. Indeed, he claimed to see little difference between the trade union practice of the PCB in 1945 and the "politics of class collaboration" and peleguismo that characterized the Estado Novo. The only qualification in his indictment was that the PCB's erroneous policy did finally shift at some point in early 1946 under the new presidency of General Eurico Dutra.[47]

Thus it is of exceptional interest to find that in late 1945 state tutelage of labor was rejected by all levels of the Left/Center trade union movement in São Paulo. The criticism of the existing labor relations system by these trade unionists sheds much light on the meaning of state intervention in industrial relations for the working class. While Vargas and the PTB paternalistically emphasized what the state had done and could and would do for the workers, São Paulo's Communist and centrist unionists emphasized what workers could do for themselves through their class associations. The trade union philosophy shared by the dominant Left/Center coalition was well captured by state MUT leader Hugo Albertini during an official interunion conference in Santo André in October 1945. The workers, he said in summing up the meeting, must join their unions en masse, participate in the life of their class associations, study their problems, unite themselves, and, so united, peacefully demand their rights.[48]

The Santo André meeting was a high point in the revitalization of local trade unionism in 1945. Sponsored by the MUT and all but the local textile union, the gathering of five hundred workers in the Carlos Gomes Cinema debated the theses to be presented as ABC's contribution to the planned state union congress. Unions from both São Paulo and Santos sent high-level representatives to attend. The meeting addressed a wide range of issues of concern to local workers. The president of Santo André's downtown CDP, the socialist medical doctor Ari Doria, presented a paper on the problems posed by the unhealthy conditions under which so many workers labored, with special attention to children's and women's labor. The fifteen days of paid vacation mandated by governmental decree in 1925 and 1932 also received attention. The gathering pointed out that when vacation time was not paid at double the normal rate, few workers actually used the time for needed rest and recreation: the workers' economic need impelled them, in many cases, to accept the offers of unscrupulous employers who paid cash if they would work during their vacation days. The attorney for local unions, Communist Lázaro Maria da Silva, spoke on the urgent need for a local labor court to handle the grievances of ABC's workers and thus avoid the inconvenience, lost time, and delays caused by the need to travel to São Paulo.

Trade union freedoms and rights received special attention as the unionists sought to define their relation to government. The union pluralism preached by the UDN was rejected as an effort to create many small and weak unions and thus destroy the workers' unity. Yet the Estado Novo's union structure did not, despite Getúlio's belief, represent the trade union ideal of these local labor activists. They rejected those aspects of the law that restricted their freedom of action, although they did not waste time objecting to the CLT's legal definition of unions as "collaborating organs" with the state. Nor did they reject the state-collected union tax that financed their institutions. Rather, the assembled unionists asked that the state fully respect the autonomy of union assemblies and their right to debate any and all relevant economic questions. On the powers of oversight granted the state, they proposed that governmental intervention should occur only when expressly requested by the union entity itself. Rejecting ministerial control over budgetary projections, they called for a simplified accounting system, study of the establishment of a national trade union body, and revision of the Labor Ministry's arbitrary power to define each union's constituency (*enquadramento sindical*).

The October 1945 ABC union congress, spurred by the MUT, was a move toward establishing a broader and more representative organization of the state's unions. The First Union Congress of São Paulo's Workers, which opened in the capital on 9 January 1946, represented a further step in unifying the trade union movement on the basis of a common platform of struggle. The congress was sponsored by a diverse group of labor organizations from some of the state's major industrial cities: at least thirty-nine entities from Santos, twenty-eight from São Paulo, ten each from Campinas and ABC, four from Piracicaba, two from Sorocaba, and three from other places in the interior. A variety of union-related institutions were also represented, including the state textile workers' federation, union consumer cooperatives, professional associations, MUT groups in unions that had not endorsed the meeting, and even the São Paulo Catholic Workers' Circle. The metalworkers and construction, chemical, and rubber workers of ABC were represented, along with the stonecutters of Mauá and Ribeirão Pires, associations of workers in pottery, leather products, and food products, the local union consumers' coop, and São Bernardo's furniture makers.[49]

Opening the congress, the secretary of the preparatory committee, printer Humberto de Fazzio, rejected paternalistic dependence on the state, noting that the labor courts, retirement institutes, and social assistance services did little in practice. The challenge, he stressed, was to make the unions representative of the working class. Abelcio Bittencourt, youthful Communist leader of the bank workers and the MUT, summed up the five-day state gathering as part of an effort "to unify the great mass of workers [to] defend their legitimate interests and prepare them to fight for better conditions of life."[50]

The congress debated dozens of proposals, large and small—from theses on tips and piecework schemes to ABC proposals on vacations, Christmas bonuses, and improvements in the labor justice system. While endorsing consumer cooperatives, the meeting rejected a proposal to encourage the establishment of production cooperatives as well as proposals favoring profit sharing by workers. Women's labor prompted a heated discussion, and a proposal for day-care in the factories was endorsed by the meeting. On the government-collected union tax, the state meeting argued that the unions should receive all of the proceeds. The participants also recommended direct election of workers' representatives in the labor courts.[51]

As in Santo André, the assembled unionists sought to preserve what had been gained under existing legislation, while demanding the end of all restrictions on their freedom. "Freedom for us," as a national MUT leader would later say, means "union self-determination, . . . that the workers should be left to organize themselves without interventions of any sort, by the government or other social classes."[52] If the link to the government could be redefined on the unionists' terms, there would be no grounds for further objection to the existing labor relations system.

Not everyone, of course, was pleased by the consolidation of trade union strength represented by the January 1946 congress. The state Secretariat of Public Security, under the PSD intervenor José Carlos de Macedo Soares, refused to authorize a planned outdoor rally that was to close the meeting. In addition, five rightist-led state union federations issued a public manifesto against the gathering, while trying, at the last minute, to organize a competing First National Congress of Workers' Union Entities that would reflect the Brazilian workers' "pacific" and "disciplined" habits.[53]

Despite the grandiloquent title, the labor Right's rival meeting was a strange affair that opened and closed in São Paulo on the day before the Left/Center state gathering and illustrated the relative weakness of the labor Right in São Paulo. While most federation-level entities endorsed the meeting, the majority of the local union endorsers were small and insignificant organizations from the interior or from nonindustrial occupations in the capital. No sponsorship was received from the union stronghold of Santos, but the São Paulo metalworkers' union, which had recently suffered an intervention by the government, gave their endorsement, along with three unions representing workers in ABC: the textile workers, the São Paulo/Santo André rubber workers' union, and the São Bernardo furniture workers—both of the latter groups also being represented at the rival Left/Center congress.[54]

The labor Right's weak influence in the lower levels of the trade union movement was clear: representativeness could not be guaranteed solely by bureaucratic fiat. These indirectly elected federation leaders operated in a world once-removed from that of their lower-level union compatriots, who dealt directly with rank-and-file workers and their concerns. The bureaucratic labor Right was characterized by an unscrupulous careerism, sycophancy to those above, and arrogance to those below. These paid functionaries depended upon their superiors in the Ministry of Labor for their continuation in office. They tended to be inveterate followers of whoever was in power: Getulistas while Vargas was in office, and Dutristas in 1946.

The PTB's cadre of leading unionists could have worked to consolidate Getulista union supporters by operating within the broader currents of postwar labor. Instead, the labor Right sought to pit the PTB and Getúlio's prestige against the majority of the union movement, including the centrist Getulistas. Nurtured under the noncompetitive conditions of the Estado Novo, this stratum of functionaries feared that the new ferment in labor would cost them their salaried positions. Indeed, rightist PTB unionists like Deocleciano Hollanda de Cavalcanti perceived such local Getulista unionists as an even greater threat to their positions than actual Communists.

In incorporating such rightist labor figures into the party's structure at the national and state levels, the PTB weakened its own influence within the labor movement. Union Getulismo in ABC was not, after all, limited to the isolated rightist PTB leadership of Henrique Poleto in the textile workers' union; even the leftist metalworkers' leadership contained many enthusiastic Getulistas. In forcing a choice upon them, the labor Right isolated itself from many centrist Getulista sympathizers who sought to straddle both Left and Right—like ABC's rubber and furniture workers—as well as from those who embraced unity with the Left—like the chemical workers' and metalworkers' unions.[55]

The labor Right's selfish and divisive policies polarized a labor movement that sought, above all else, to gather and unite its forces in order better to serve the workers' interests. If the repressive Estado Novo era had dictated caution, the new, more favorable conditions prevalent after mid-

1945 were explicitly cited as the spur to a bolder and more ambitious trade unionism.[56] Thus the aggressive trade union movement that emerged from the Estado Novo was the product of a broad coalition of the Left and Center, of Communists and Getulistas, which isolated the peleguista current of upper-level trade union functionaries. Ironically, a system designed to domesticate and control labor had created a working-class leadership that was far from tame.

Membership card in São Bernardo's furniture makers' union, 1933. Armando Mazzo, future Communist state deputy from ABC, was a leader of São Bernardo's Union of Furniture Makers, Carpenters, and Related Classes in the early 1930s. (Courtesy Serviço de Documentação da História Local, Prefeitura do Município de São Bernardo do Campo)

"Workers' Mass" in Santo André, 1938. This mass was held on May Day 1938 at the Church of Carmen in Santo André. Note the simultaneous display of the flag of Brazil and that of Santo André's recently refounded metalworkers' union. (Courtesy Sindicato dos Metalúrgicos de Santo André, Mauá, Ribeirão Pires, e Rio Grande da Serra; reproduced by Nogueira and Araújo Imagem, Santo André, São Paulo)

Santo André metalworkers and their union, 1940. This painting honors the metalworkers of Santo André and was donated to their union by the artist, Jorge Vernik, on
31 May 1940. It is still on display in the union's headquarters. (Courtesy Sindicato
dos Metalúrgicos de Santo André, Mauá, Ribeirão Pires, e Rio Grande da Serra; reproduced by Nogueira and Araújo Imagem, Santo André, São Paulo)

Santo André metalworkers in the shop, 1942. Workers at an unidentified local metal-working factory. (Courtesy Projeto Viva Cidade, Prefeitura Municipal de Santo André)

May Day 1944 rally in São Paulo. Government-sponsored May Day rallies such as this one in São Paulo's Pacaembu Stadium were common during the Estado Novo regime. In a speech to the rally, Brazil's dictator Getúlio Vargas laid the groundwork for his emerging populist project. (Courtesy Iconographia-Pesquisa de Texto, Imagem, e Som S/C Ltda.)

São Paulo rally celebrating Germany's surrender in World War II. News of the surrender of Nazi Germany was met by an outpouring of popular sentiment such as this celebration of 8 May 1945 in the Praça da Sé in the center of the city of São Paulo. (Courtesy Iconographia-Pesquisa de Texto, Imagem, e Som S/C Ltda.)

Luis Carlos Prestes in São Paulo. Former tenentista "cavalier of hope," Communist leader Luis Carlos Prestes (shown in center, shaking hands with supporters) was at the height of his popularity between 1945 and 1947. The exact date and locale of this photograph of a Communist rally in postwar São Paulo are unknown. (Courtesy Iconographia-Pesquisa de Texto, Imagem, e Som S/C Ltda.)

Populist pioneer Antônio Braga. Despite being a small manufacturer, veteran politician Antônio Braga actively courted the labor movement after World War II as a supporter of Adhemar de Barros. (Courtesy Museu de Santo André)

São Paulo rally celebrating Adhemar de Barros's election in 1947. A traditional site of mass rallies, the Anhangabaú Valley in downtown São Paulo was packed for this 11 March 1947 celebration of the election of Adhemar de Barros as state governor. (Courtesy Iconographia-Pesquisa de Texto, Imagem, e Som S/C Ltda.)

Luis Carlos Prestes and Adhemar de Barros in March 1947. An ecstatic Luis Carlos Prestes (fourth from left) and other Communist leaders compliment the new PSP/PCB governor Adhemar de Barros (far right). (Courtesy Iconographia-Pesquisa de Texto, Imagem, e Som S/C Ltda.)

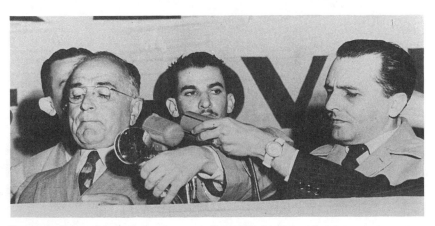

Getúlio Vargas and Luis Carlos Prestes in late 1947. In their only joint appearance, Senators Getúlio Vargas (left) and Luis Carlos Prestes (right) address a 4 November 1947 rally in the city of São Paulo during the campaign for vice-governor. (Courtesy Iconographia-Pesquisa de Texto, Imagem, e Som S/C Ltda.)

Nº **9119** ★ **Cr$ 10,00**

vide verso

GRANDE TOMBOLA POPULAR ELEITORAL

Correrá pela Loteria Federal do dia 29 de Novembro de 1947

PREMIOS: 1.º — 1 Dormitório completo;
2.º — 1 Máquina de costura «SINGER»;
3.º — 1 Rádio cabeceira;
4.º — 1 Bateria de alumínio;
5.º — 1 Relógio de pulso «TISSOT», anti-magnético.

N. B. — Os números que não forem pagos, até a vespera da extração, perderão o direito ao premio.

Grande Tombola Eleitoral Popular

A realização desta Tombola tem como objetivo uma Campanha de Finanças para custear as despesas de propaganda da "Chapa Popular de Vereadores" à Camara Municipal, para o próximo Pleito Eleitoral de 9 de Novembro.

VOTEM nos Candidatos Operários que sempre lutaram intransigentemente na defesa dos direitos do Povo e da Classe Operária!

Santo André, Setembro de 1947

September 1947 Communist lottery ticket from Santo André. Funds for PCB/PST municipal candidates in Santo André were raised through grass-roots initiatives such as this lottery. "Vote," the message on the ticket appealed, "for the Worker Candidates who have always fought intransigently in defense of the rights of the People and of the Working Class!"

Inauguration Day 1948 souvenir for Communist candidates. Foreseeing no obstacles, Santo André's elected Communist prefeito Armando Mazzo and the thirteen PCB/PST vereadores printed souvenirs to mark their expected inauguration on 1 January 1948. When they were denied the right to take office at the last minute, the planned celebration turned into a day of clashes between police and protestors. (Courtesy Serviço de Documentação da História Local, Prefeitura do Município de São Bernardo do Campo)

Populist pioneer Anacleto Campanella in 1948. At the start of a career that would take him far, Anacleto Campanella of São Caetano rejected the cassação of the Communists in January 1948 and pioneered a new style of urban populist politics. (Courtesy Museu de São Caetano do Sul)

Communist labor leader Marcos Andreotti in 1982. Founder of the Workers' Union of 1928, industrial electrician Marcos Andreotti was the most important leader of ABC's metalworkers prior to Luis Inácio ("Lula") da Silva in the 1970s. (Photograph by the author)

Six • Reading a Strike

• Direct Action in Early 1946

The general mood of protest and expectation among São Paulo's industrial workers led to a strike wave in 1946 that involved, at its height in February and March, perhaps 100,000 workers in the metropolitan São Paulo region. In ABC at least 10,000 workers, a fifth of the total work force, joined this upsurge of industrial militancy between 23 January and 15 March 1946.

This generalized strike movement was the first large-scale use of direct action within the new legal and institutional labor relations framework established during the Estado Novo. As such, these industrial conflicts offered workers, employers, and the state an opportunity to redefine their relationships in the first open test of their respective power since the strikes of 1934–35. When given the opportunity, it became clear, neither Getulista workers nor their union leaders proved willing to forgo the use of strikes—thus revealing the limits of the workers' absorption into a corporatist state that had sought, above all, to limit labor exclusively to indirect action.

This "explosion" of strikes in early 1946, which demonstrated the workers' capacity for "independent" action, has been commonly interpreted as an implicit rejection of the corporatist industrial relations system. A careful reading of the strikes, however, suggests that use of the strike weapon was closely linked, for both workers and their emerging leaders, to the new state-sponsored mechanism for collective bargaining, the dissídio coletivo, which was implemented for the first time in 1945–46.

At the same time, the strike movement represented a challenge to organized labor since it was, in its origin, more a product of mass initiative from below than a result of conscious decisions by union leaders. Thus this episode of collective action allows us to explore the moment when important currents of mass consciousness came to coalesce with the region's Left/Center labor leadership to produce a new and far more deeply rooted trade union movement based on a synthesis of direct and indirect action.

Avoiding "Spontaneous but Disorganized Movements"

Discontent among the workers had been building for a long time in the face of a continuing inflationary price spiral, shortages, and black marketeering, especially when the end of the war eliminated the major justification for working-class sacrifice. Moreover, the workers' political victories of December 1945 had generated a sense of unity and newfound power, and Getúlio Vargas's overthrow had generated anger at the powerful distant forces of the rich.[1]

The volatility of this mass sentiment was not formally encompassed by the existing trade union structures, despite their growth in 1945. A highly laudatory October 1945 article in the Communist newspaper *Hoje*, for example, proudly claimed that 10,000 workers related, in one way or another, to the unions and associations that shared offices with ABC's metalworkers' union.[2] Yet this exaggerated figure, even if accepted as an estimate for the membership of the entire union movement in 1945, would still mean that no more than a fifth of all industrial workers in ABC belonged to a union.[3] A more conservative estimate would give a maximum of 2,000–3,000 union members in 1945, although most of these workers were not well integrated into the structures of the trade union movement.[4]

While working aggressively to increase the representativeness of their institutions, labor's Left/Center leadership remained acutely conscious of the precariousness of their mass support. By late 1945, the gap between union leaders, labor activists, and workers had narrowed somewhat, at least in some factories, but ties between the organized minority and the rank and file as a whole remained problematic.

Having just emerged from a dictatorial regime, São Paulo's unionists were also acutely conscious of the fragility of their newfound freedoms during this transition to democratic rule.[5] They feared precipitate action that might bypass the protection, however frail, that established legal procedures offered the workers. They sought above all else to avoid, in their words, the "outbreak of spontaneous but disorganized movements" by ABC's workers.[6]

Attuned to such realities, Left/Center union leaders and the PCB emphasized the avoidance of strikes, or even talk of strikes, in late 1945. In this instance, the Left/Center's policies coincided, at least momentarily, with those of the labor Right. When a few individual strikes began to occur in the first ten days of January 1946, a group of unions of all persuasions, including the MUT, the Santo André chemical workers, and the Santos central labor body, signed a common statement urging the use of pacific means to resolve the workers' complaints. This antistrike manifesto urged that delegations be sent to negotiate with employers before striking, and that workers press the government for action on food prices.[7]

For Francisco Weffort, this policy of "order and tranquility," which led Communist leaders to urge workers to "tighten their belts," reflected the PCB's class collaborationist bent and its deference to Soviet foreign policy needs. Yet his excessively politicized explanation overlooks the positive trade union rationale that lay behind the cautious stance adopted by the youthful trade unionists.[8] Firm partisans of organized struggle based on careful preparation, Left/Center labor leaders believed in late 1945 that a cautious policy of methodical organization and growth would best strengthen the union, influence the employers, and facilitate success through the established bargaining procedures of the existing labor legislation.

In addition, ABC's labor leaders hoped that the democratic spirit of the time and a respect for the unions' newfound strength would induce the employers to negotiate in good faith and peacefully accede to their demands. The apparent willingness of Pirelli's management to grant a union request for wage increases, for example, was publicly praised by the newly elected metalworkers' president Victor Gentil Savietto at a 29 January 1946 mass meeting of perhaps two thousand Pirelli employees. The management, he reported, was even willing to discuss establishing a union factory council.[9] These optimistic hopes were enhanced by small victories for which the unions hoped to claim credit, such as the decisions of Firestone, Rhodia, and Pirelli to grant a requested Christmas bonus. A similar demand at the financially troubled São Caetano Electro-Aço factory was also brought to a successful conclusion after a one-day strike by the firm's 335 employees on 23 January 1946.[10]

Such employer cooperation provided the sort of easy victories that ABC's unionists hoped would solidify their position as the workers' representatives. The unions could only gain in popularity among the rank and file as a result of winning such benefits without recourse to strikes, thus encouraging more workers to join and become active in union affairs. Furthermore, peaceful bargaining would promote the unions' acceptance as a legitimate and respectable force within the broader social and political arena.

The unionists had, however, overlooked the employers' interest in preventing an invasion of their long-established managerial prerogatives. From the employers' point of view, the atmosphere that had developed since Vargas's incitement of queremismo and the legalization of the Communist Party did not bode well. For them, the new labor activism of 1945 represented a potential threat. Acceding to union demands, many powerful managers felt, could only encourage the unions to press harder in the future for input in setting the workers' terms of employment and remuneration.

Striking in a "Peaceful and Orderly" Manner

The workers' new assertiveness and desire to influence the world around them was thus on a collision course with the authoritarianism of the managers of ABC's powerful industries. For many factory administrators, these new pressures were intolerable affronts that would have to be dismissed out of hand. On 24 January 1946, Firestone's North American administrator, William Richard Clark II, eager to "teach the workers a lesson," locked out the plant's 1,200 rubber workers, a day after the Electro-Aço strike. Cutting off the supply of foodstuffs, Firestone posted armed guards at the gate. Mr. Clark, refusing to meet with the thirty-man delegation selected by the workers, said he would keep the plant shut for thirty or even sixty days rather than give in.[11]

The strike against Firestone grew out of the management's refusal in December 1945 to accede to a request from the workers that Firestone pay a Christmas bonus like other firms. After denying initial requests for a meeting, company representatives finally agreed to talk with a delegation of workers on 31 December. They promised that the matter would be considered once instructions were received from the United States. Faced with stalling tactics over the next three weeks, the increasingly discontented Firestone workers finally struck when confronted with Mr. Clark's arrogant threat. Meeting at the local metalworkers' union hall, the strikers, backed by the rubber workers' union of Greater São Paulo, demanded payment of a Christmas bonus and wage increases of from 20 to 30 percent.[12]

On the following day, the 223 workers of the historic Ipiranguinha textile plant, now owned by Moinho Santista, became the third group of workers to strike their employers in ABC. As with Firestone, the workers had made repeated but unsuccessful efforts to convince the company to negotiate prior to undertaking an in-plant work stoppage at 10:00 A.M. on 25 January. With the workers standing by their idled machines, management reiterated its refusal to talk and then ordered the factory evacuated after a fifteen-minute deadline had passed.[13]

The residents of Santo André were stirred by these strikes, the largest since 1935, and eagerly awaited the news from the two evening assemblies scheduled for early the following week. Meeting on 28 January, four days after the strike began, the Firestone workers first heard from José Gurgel, leader of the local strike commission, who attacked the company's refusal to negotiate and mocked management's claim that it lacked the autonomy necessary to resolve the workers' problems. Speaking at a time when the dictatorial Estado Novo constitution was still in force, Gurgel sought to minimize any unease felt by Firestone workers in contemplating their role as strike pioneers. His praise of the "peaceful and orderly" manner in which the workers had struck appropriated the rhetoric of social peace so often evoked by nonworkers, while simultaneously emptying it of meaning. Responding indirectly to the charge that the strike was illegal, he branded Firestone itself a lawless enterprise for defying Brazilian law when it threatened to lock out its workers—employer lockouts being barred by the same clause of the 1937 corporatist constitution that outlawed strikes by workers.[14]

The next to speak was Lázaro Maria da Silva, the Communist lawyer of the rubber workers' union, who gave a long and reportedly inflammatory speech in which he attacked the swindling bosses for having provoked the strike. Like Gurgel, he insisted that the stoppage was, in fact, "a typical lockout, a strike of the employer and not the worker." And after all, he emphasized, the workers' demands were extremely modest: they asked only that their wages be made "a little higher, [and] a little more respectable" so that they could live decently. While granting that the Christmas bonus was not yet a written law, Silva argued that it was nonetheless a natural right of the workers.[15]

Silva explained to his audience that it was up to the courts to take the necessary steps to resolve a work stoppage, and that the dissídio coletivo provided the appropriate legal mechanism to win workers' demands. Proposing a commission of thirty members to oversee the negotiations, Silva made clear that he was not advocating passive reliance on the good faith of judges. If there were court delays, which always benefited employers, Silva said, then "we will all go en masse to knock on the doors of the labor court." Speaking in terms of an implied bargain, the union attorney emphasized, however, that the workers must conduct themselves within the legal boundaries set by the labor justice system. Indeed, while the first of five substantive resolutions adopted at the meeting reiterated the strikers' determination not to return to work under orders from the employers, the second countenanced the possibility of returning to work if so ordered by the court. If this occurred, the meeting resolved, the workers would comply—but only if no police were present on the day of the return to work.

Yet the third, fourth, and fifth resolutions made clear that the union did not expect such an unfavorable development. If management stubbornly ignored a labor court decision favorable to the workers, they resolved, then the union would press for full payment of the hours lost during the strike. If employers refused to settle the dissídio at the lower level of a conciliation (*conciliação*), they also resolved to demand higher wage increases in the resulting labor court judgment (*julgamento*); and if pleased with the latter, the union reserved to itself the right to ask the courts to extend the julgamento to cover the entire categoria in greater São Paulo.

In his speech, Silva emphasized the union's unconditional solidarity with the striking Firestone workers since, as he put it, "a union only exists to serve its class or else it's not a union." The striking rubber workers also heard pledges of support from the MUT and from Leonardo Vitor Molinaro, a leader of the rubber workers' union from São Paulo. Aware that most strikers were not yet union members, the rubber workers' official used his speech to urge workers to join and thus strengthen the union, which, he explained, had now dropped the initiation fee previously required of new members.

On the evening after the Firestone gathering, the textile workers' union of Santo André and the local branch of the greater São Paulo union of textile foremen and supervisors (*mestres* and *contramestres*) organized a meeting of the Ipiranguinha strikers at the headquarters of a local sports club. Rejecting management's demand that they return to work prior to negotiations, the gathering resolved to open a "dissídio coletivo, Ex Officio," based on the memorandum submitted to the factory three days earlier. Beyond a central demand for a 30 percent wage increase, the strikers requested greater ventilation, more bathrooms, paid leave for proven sickness, and an end to the use of children to do the jobs of adults. They also asked that the cloth the factory sold to its workers be provided directly and not through intermediaries.[16]

A closer examination of union practice during the Firestone and Ipiranguinha strikes suggests both similarities and differences in approach between the Left/Center rubber workers and the Right-led textile workers' union. Faced with the de jure illegality of the strikes, both groups sought to balance the scales by stigmatizing their employers for *their* "lawless" behavior.[17] Both groups also embraced the dissídio procedure and accepted the legitimacy of the government-established industrial and labor relations system; they differed radically, however, in terms of *how* to use the system, and to what ends.[18]

Left/Center labor leaders welcomed the workers' spontaneous mobilization, which they saw as a precious opportunity to gain leverage and thus enhance their bargaining power with employers and the state. The textile workers under Henrique Poleto, by contrast, were discomfited by this insurgency from below and adopted a far more timid and strictly legalistic stance. Like the rubber workers, the textile strikers' assembly had agreed to return to work if so ordered by the labor courts, but it did so without *any* stated preconditions. Moreover, the rightist textile workers' union was unwilling to encourage or build upon grass-roots initiative and organization. The rubber workers' union, by contrast, entrusted the leadership of the Firestone strike to José Gurgel and his local factory committee, two of whose leaders were arrested at the end of the first week. Indeed, the textile workers' union adopted a hands-off stance throughout the dramatic events of February and March 1946, while the Left-led metalworkers' and civil construction workers' unions took the lead, along with the chemical and rubber workers, in aiding strikers no matter what their categoria by providing facilities, lawyers, and doctors, and raising funds through street and factory collections.[19]

With the Firestone and Ipiranguinha strikes holding firm, strike activity in ABC took a decided upswing on 6 February 1946, when 1,000 workers at the Santo André Rhodia Química factory struck after the director fired thirty members of their negotiating committee and rejected a demand for wage increases of from 30 to 50 percent. Although this French chemical concern had paid a Christmas bonus, the management insisted, like Firestone, that it could not negotiate without outside guidance—in this case, from the new government of President Eurico Dutra.[20]

With the strike at Rhodia, an episode that had begun as individual stoppages at particular plants had clearly given way to a more generalized strike movement, a rolling wave of uncoordinated strikes that spread with no immediately apparent logic from one factory to another. The first four strikes touched both large and medium-sized enterprises, and in very different industrial sectors (metalworking, textiles, rubber, and chemicals). Nor were the stoppages themselves explainable by the political complexion or mobilizational strategies of the unions involved—which included two firmly Left/Center unions (metalworkers and rubber workers), a divided but predominantly Left/Center union (the chemical workers), and a rightist union.[21]

This has led analysts, starting with Francisco Weffort, to speak of the "explosive" nature of this "eruption" of strikes in São Paulo in 1946.[22] Weffort argued that they were largely prompted by a sharp deterioration in the workers' real wages.[23] Ricardo Maranhão, in his analysis of the strikes, has quite correctly emphasized their "spontaneous" nature; they did not occur as part of any preconceived plan by leaders of the trade unions or working-class political parties.[24] Finally, it has also been suggested that the workers' "extremely radical" mood made these stoppages a prime example of autonomous working-class action, "independent of the state," organized primarily by rank-and-file "factory commissions."[25]

Yet these generalizations represent at best a partial and superficial analysis of the 1946 strike wave.[26] In fact, the most remarkable aspect of mass behavior during these labor conflicts lies in the boldness with which significant numbers of factory workers acted prior to the strikes. In case after case, the actual work stoppage was preceded by organized worker requests to management, originating from within the shop. In December 1945 and early 1946, delegations of workers—in some cases as many as thirty— formally presented demands to management and refused to be put off by employer stalling.[27] Such widespread public delegations, speaking openly and forcefully as representatives of their fellow workers, were without precedent in São Paulo (nor did they occur again on such a scale after this period). This behavior contrasted sharply with the informal, often indirect, communication of discontent to management that had always been part of industrial life. Thus, these actions provide dramatic proof that a profound revolution in mass consciousness had occurred among significant numbers of workers since 1945.[28]

Such mobilizations presupposed a breakdown of the atmosphere of fear and intimidation that had for so long permeated the industrial workplace. The minority of workers who participated in these delegations, after all, were willingly running the risk of employer retaliation; it is doubtful whether these grass-roots leaders, some in contact with the unions and some not, would have done so if they had not believed they had the support of the overwhelming majority of their fellow employees. Thus, the thirty workers fired by Rhodia Química had to have had confidence that their colleagues would back them up in the event of company reprisals—which they did.

Yet it is also doubtful whether most of these rank-and-file leaders expected such repression; their behavior suggests that most thought management would accede to their requests, at least in part. They acted not so much out of sharp anger or desperation as from feelings of hopefulness, empowerment, and legitimate rights that grew out of the events of 1945.[29] At the mass level, workers and their potential leaders within the workplace were responding to the same positive stimuli that had influenced union activists and leaders to push for a stronger and more independent labor movement. Like their leaders, large numbers of industrial workers in early 1946 really believed that things had changed, and they made history because they were prepared to act upon what would prove, in hindsight, to have been illusions.

Thus, our reading of the strikes will be distorted if we divorce the economic component of the workers' motivation from its political dimension: their newfound democratic conviction that they had the right to a say in the conditions of their lives and labor, whether at the ballot box, in the community, or in the workplace. This sentiment was not derived from antistatist, much less anti-Getulista, sentiment; instead, it drew sustenance from the legitimacy and legal sanction that the government of Getúlio Vargas had given to workers' efforts to advance their collective interests.

The *CLT* of 1 May 1943, after all, had not only made provisions for *dissídios individuais* (individual disputes) but had also established the *dissídio coletivo* (collective dispute) procedure through which unions representing workers and employers would resolve disagreements over wages and working conditions—with the final decision rendered by the labor courts.[30]

Within four months of promulgating the *CLT*, however, the Vargas regime on 16 September 1943 effectively suspended the dissídio coletivo—in an effort, they said, to avoid disturbances in areas of production vital to national security. (The dissídio individual, by contrast, was left untouched, since it did not "affect the structure of the economy" to the same extent.)[31] Thus the new dissídio coletivo mechanism set forth in the *CLT* languished throughout the war (there were 30 nationwide in 1943, only 1 in 1944), and it was only in 1945 (134), and especially 1946 (420), that it became relatively common before declining sharply again as part of the Dutra government's antilabor drive of the late 1940s.[32]

The Labor Ministry's toleration of this new collective bargaining procedure represented a radical innovation in Brazilian labor relations that was received unfavorably by employers in ABC.[33] To judge solely from newspaper reports, several dozen dissídios covering individual enterprises occurred between December 1945 and March 1946, as well as one dissídio covering the entire textile industry.[34] Most interestingly, in ABC the dissídio coletivo was not used solely as a mechanism for resolving strikes: at least thirteen, covering 3,000 workers, occurred at enterprises that did not experience work stoppages.

Although workers did not form delegations to management or strike *because* of the new procedure, dissídios coletivos unquestionably heightened workers' expectations and affirmed the legitimacy of their actions. Starting in October 1945, Left/Center unions had held some individual factory meetings to encourage worker participation in the formulation of demands. In other plants, the process of forming internal delegations to negotiate with management flowed very easily—under union direction once strikes occurred—into enterprise-level dissídios coletivos. Indeed, there is no evidence of any objections being voiced in strike meetings against the use of this government-linked procedure as a means of winning workers' demands.

"The Strike Is Not Disorder"

The labor conflicts in ABC in late January and early February 1946 were part of a growing wave of strikes in the município of São Paulo, and in urban Brazil as a whole—including a nationwide bank workers' strike beginning on 27 January—that posed challenges to labor's would-be leaders. São Paulo's right-wing federation leaders responded on 30 January by forming the Union Coalition for Salary Increases and a Decrease in the Cost of Living to lobby the industrialists and the government. The Right's succession of meetings with the state industrialists' association (FIESP) starting on 2 February were not negotiating sessions, however, and they served only to emphasize the Right's hands-off policy toward the spreading strikes.[35]

By contrast, the rival Left/Center "Permanent Committee" of the state union congress offered the strikers its unrestricted solidarity. And the PCB's National Committee, on the very day that strikes began to break out in ABC, issued a statement, "The Strike Is Not Disorder," that defended the strike as the workers' ultimate recourse. Referring to Santo André, Senator Luis Carlos Prestes would explain that the PCB's call for "order and tranquility" should not be confused with "passivity or submission."[36]

Yet for São Paulo's highly centralized police apparatus, controlled by the appointed PSD intervenor José Carlos de Macedo Soares, strikes were by definition disorderly. As the superintendent of the political-social police (DOPS) explained from the outset, all measures necessary to guarantee the right to work of nonstrikers would be taken.[37] Since the pressure of disrupting production by striking was the workers' only weapon when negotiations failed, conflict was inevitable.

At the end of the first week in February, police inspectors, soldiers of the state militia, and DOPS agents were rushed to Santo André in response to unfounded rumors of plans to attack the Ipiranguinha factory. Beginning on 7 February, they were aggressively deployed throughout downtown Santo André, where they began to harass and sometimes beat strikers or suspected strikers. Indeed, at least five workers, interviewed at the local union cooperative, willingly gave their names to a newspaper reporter to protest police actions that included detaining, verbally abusing, and beating them—in one case, with rubber truncheons.[38]

The antilabor mission of the police was very much on the minds of the workers who gathered in Santo André later that day to greet state Communist leader Mario Scott, a railroad worker, and PCB secretary general Luis Carlos Prestes. The large crowd, perhaps as many as 20,000, chanted "Prestes, Prestes" as the Communist leader approached the podium during this second visit to the city. Reiterating his party's "decided support," Senator Prestes denounced the continued use of the "savage" and "barbarous" methods of the Estado Novo by a police apparatus still infested with corrupt "fascist" elements. While steps toward democracy had been taken, Prestes said, the people had not yet been assured "the right not to go hungry."[39]

The Santo André rally also heard an impassioned speech by Lusia de Lurdes Gonçalves, a young leader of the Firestone strikers. Denouncing the police as "students of Felinto Muller" (the infamous Nazi sympathizer who served as Rio police chief in the late thirties), she denied that strikes were a crime and blamed their occurrence on the reactionary "fifth columnists" who directed local factories. Citing police statements that they had written proof that the PCB had taught the workers to strike, the young rubber worker defiantly declared that if this were true, she would join the Communist Party forthwith.[40]

The strikes in ABC were an integral part of a broader upheaval within the São Paulo metropolitan region that involved 50,000 workers by the second week of February and 100,000 by the third week, a powerful and spontaneous movement that showed no signs of abating.[41] The intense climate of mobilization in ABC also contributed to the further unification of the region's labor movement. Meeting the evening before Prestes's visit, directors of all ten unions and professional associations—including Poleto's textile workers' union—agreed to form a local central labor body, the União Sindical of Santo André and São Bernardo do Campo.[42]

The further broadening of the strike movement in ABC was aided by what was judged to be the success enjoyed by the Firestone strikers in their dissídio coletivo. After both Firestone and the Ipiranguinha had refused to enter conciliatory proposals, the two *processos* were sent to the Regional Labor Council where, on 7 February, the final julgamento awarded the rubber workers wage increases of 10 to 30 percent. Although they had failed to win the requested Christmas bonus, the striking rubber workers judged the outcome satisfactory and voted to return to work the following day after having held out for two weeks.[43]

The 1,000 Rhodia Química strikers, under increasing pressure again in mid-February, were soon joined by workers from other factories whose efforts at direct negotiation had failed. After twenty days of futile meetings with management, the hundred workers of Santo André's Sociedade Industrial Tetracap went on strike on 11 February 1946, having grown frustrated with stalemated negotiations and "disbelieving" the construction union's efforts to negotiate an agreement.[44]

On 14 February the 1,200 employees of Companhia Brasileira de Mineração e Metalúrgica also struck, after four months of fruitless negotiations. The workers of the São Caetano metalworking firm were not only demanding wage increases, but they also complained of dirty bathrooms, polluted drinking water, and the lack of a lunchroom. Forced to eat in an uncomfortable locker-room area, they charged that the women who brought their lunch pails were often embarrassed by men changing their clothes.[45]

The 2,000 to 3,000 employees at the Pirelli metalworking factory in Santo André struck on the same day, clearly illustrating the limits of welfare capitalism as a strategy for avoiding labor conflicts. The Pirelli management reacted with surprise and pointed to their enlightened policies, which had provided new buildings; a subsidized restaurant and facilities to heat lunch pails; medical, hospital, and dental aid; some company housing, and loans to build homes; a foodstuff post; Christmas bonuses; prizes; and, they claimed, the highest wages in the region.[46] The workers' spokesmen, denying that the strike was a surprise move, pointed out that five efforts had been made to reach an agreement. The workers' views of the conditions of work at Pirelli, they pointed out, were clearly shown by the fact that all but one worker had joined the strike.[47]

While recognizing the movement's broad support, Pirelli managers disputed the strikers' claim that most office employees had also joined the strike on its first day although at least half the white-collar employees had joined the factory workers' dissídio coletivo prior to the strike. Meetings of Pirelli office workers were called the day after the strike began to neutralize this possibility, with employee representatives informing an expectant strike assembly of their decision not to strike. This remarkable development testifies to the severe economic strains that brought wage earners and salaried employees together, at least temporarily, despite the enormous social distance between the factory floor and the office.[48]

Throughout the industrial regions of ABC, employer recalcitrance helped spread the strike movement, while working-class militancy spurred the industrialists of São Paulo and ABC to call for more decisive repressive action. Despite Communist protests in the Constituent Assembly, ABC's 5,000 strikers in mid-February faced an escalation of threatening actions by the police, including the menacing display and even discharge of firearms. The DOPS inspectors were especially brutal as they engaged in their longtime specialty of Communist and labor affairs.[49]

A policy of no negotiations had been adopted by the textile industrialists' association on 9 February, and by the FIESP on 18 February. Employer intransigence found a convenient cover in charges that it was the Communist Party and its "professional agitators" that were responsible for the strikes, and not the workers' admittedly difficult economic conditions. Speaking informally for the Pirelli management, an office employee denounced the infiltration of alien "undermining elements, true anarcho-syndicalists," who were disturbing the "orderly, pacific, hardworking, and patriotic" workers.[50]

As proof of the predominance of the "political factor," the FIESP's acting president, Morvan Dias de Figueiredo, cited the case of his brother's textile firm, Indústrias Nadir Figueiredo: when asked why they were on strike, the firm's workers, he claimed, said that they had no demands to make but were acting "in solidarity with their fellow workers on strike." While solidarity strikes are not proof in themselves of Communist agitation, Morvan Dias's comment points out the powerful, spontaneous fellow-feeling that surged among São Paulo's workers. Indeed, the Mineração e Metalúrgica workers also claimed to have struck in support of the workers in the company's other factories in Jundiaí and São Paulo.[51]

The strike experience itself spawned an almost instinctive solidarity as the workers learned that success depended, in the end, on their ability to halt production. Rhodia's strikers, having observed work being carried out on the factory's railroad loading docks, publicly criticized the nonstriking São Paulo Railway workers for scabbing. Concerned railroad workers quickly hurried into print to explain that they were scrupulous in refusing to carry out such work and that the loading in question was being undertaken by independent labor gangs hired by Rhodia.[52]

These expansive impulses and the sense of collective identity were encouraged by the unprecedented freedom of the press that had resulted from the end of the Estado Novo. While strikes did not fit into the UDNista *Estado de São Paulo*'s notion of news, at least two metropolitan newspapers covered the strikes in detail. The most extensive coverage appeared in the Communist daily newspaper, *Hoje*. The pro-Dutra *Diário de São Paulo*, owned by the eccentric newspaper magnate Assis Chateaubriand, also opened its pages to such news, as did the weekly newspaper *O Imparcial* in Santo André. Information, in many cases, came from worker delegations who made the rounds of the capital's newspapers in order to explain their demands and complaints; at times, as many as one hundred workers were involved, often insisting on the inclusion of their names or photos in the published stories.[53]

The workers' challenge to the industrialists was not blunted by the additional economic distress caused by the strike. Nor did the employers' refusal to negotiate or the police's routine harassment discourage the strikers. The industrialists, for their part, made further efforts in mid-February to coordinate their stance toward their workers. "No employer," the FIESP formally reiterated on 23 February, should "enter into agreements with workers on strike or under threat of strike." But the employers could not long maintain a united front. In the third week in February,

ABC's unionists welcomed the decision of one local metalworking firm to break ranks. The Companhia Brasileira de Construção Fichet Schwartz-Hautmont, they said, had shown its humanitarianism by granting its 304 workers a 30–50 percent wage increase without a strike. The workers were also pleased with the management's agreement to permit initiation of a union factory committee.[54]

Conciliation was not, however, the course embraced by most of ABC's industrialists. Industrial magnate Francisco Pignatari was personally involved in the conflicts at his Laminação Nacional de Metais factory in Santo André's Utinga district. His only response to two months of attempted negotiations had been an effort to bribe two of the representatives chosen by his 1,931 workers. Meeting with another workers' commission on the morning of 20 February, Pignatari threatened to hold those thirteen workers personally responsible for instigating a strike. Detaining them in the office area, he informed the workers on the shop floor of his planned action and the impending arrival of the police. At noon, the factory's workers refused to go back to work; the strike was on, despite Pignatari's belated release of their leaders. Within days, workers at five other Pignatari factories, in Santo André and elsewhere in the state, had joined the strike.[55]

Despite the encouraging news of the 25–35 percent wage increases won by Rhodia Química workers on 19 February, the Santo André workers who struck Pignatari's Laminação Nacional de Metais and the Companhia Brasileira de Cartuchos would find that the employers' and the government's resistance had stiffened. Incidents with the police, including a bayonet charge against strikers, became more common, and two arrested workers "disappeared" for a day when neither the São Paulo DOPS nor the local police would admit holding them. While arrests in Utinga continued, Pignatari announced the firing of twenty-six "agitators," including six workers with job tenure (*estabilidade*), on the third day of the strike. Others, he said ominously, were being closely watched.[56]

Pirelli, Laminação Nacional, Mineração e Metalúrgica, and Ferro Esmaltado Silex followed the aggressive stance of noncooperation with the dissídio coletivo process adopted earlier by Firestone and the Ipiranguinha. In São Paulo, the metalworkers' union's lawyers were told that all four firms refused to negotiate as long as the workers remained on strike. The representatives of the Ministry of Labor's regional office took a similar tack, recommending a return to work in order to initiate negotiations.[57]

The employers' hard line in the third week of February was also embraced by the labor Right's Union Coalition for Salary Increases. Eager to curry favor with the employers and the government, leaders like Deocleciano Hollanda de Cavalcanti, Artur Albino da Rocha, and Santo André's Henrique Poleto publicly opposed and sabotaged the strikes.[58] In doing so, the Right was betraying obvious workers' interests that mattered a great deal to the average union activist.

The labor Right's position clashed head-on with the views of both rank-and-file workers and the predominant Left/Center leadership of the lower levels of the union movement. As one Pirelli striker pointed out, the workers' only means of confronting rising prices was by demanding increases in wages, their "only source of income." And the São Paulo MUT, in a 26 February 1946 manifesto, disagreed with those who said that controlling prices was the first step in halting carestia; provide immediate relief with wage increases now, they said, and then the government can move to control prices. The Union Coalition's advocacy of factory foodstuff posts as the solution to carestia, they said, was unrealistic and could easily lead to a company-store situation that would also hurt small shopkeepers.[59]

The Communist Party and the Left/Center labor leaders were clearly more responsive to the needs and desires of their working-class constituents than the labor Right. Yet, despite charges to the contrary, they had not created and could not necessarily control this mass movement. The Communists, for their part, were uncomfortable with the impromptu speeches by anonymous worker orators who blamed the bad situation on the ousting of Getúlio Vargas, the "father of the poor," from the presidential palace.[60]

The impetuous actions by many factory workers, especially in São Paulo, tended to disconcert even Communist trade union leaders whose clear notions of *organized* struggle were sometimes swept aside in the reigning strike fever. On 19 February, the MUT's state president Roque Trevisan told the press that some of the present strikes were untimely and had been declared without the knowledge of the unions. Public criticism and the employers' efforts to involve the Dutra government also worried Trevisan, the PCB, and other union leaders. They suspected that conflicts were being instigated by the industrialists or unnamed provocateurs to create pretexts for a crackdown on the union's newly won freedoms.[61] Acutely conscious of the power of the conservative military establishment, for example, the Laminação Nacional strike committee announced on the second day of the strike that in order to show their patriotism, workers should report to Pignatari's automatic arms factory for a planned visit by an army general.[62]

In the end, however, union fears and discomfort with the workers' head-strong actions did not prevent them from embracing a massive movement whose legitimacy came from the streets. The workers, the MUT said on 26 February, should return to work only after victory had been achieved. To this end, they systematized their strike experiences into the following recommendations to the unions: mass unionization, the development of general demands for the categoria, the establishment of strike funds, and the formation of union factory committees. Such factory committees, they said, should be linked to the union leaderships and, in the event of a strike, should take joint responsibility for the holding of strike assemblies.[63]

Union preparations for further strikes were matched by an employer offensive to prevent labor agitation through highly visible repressive measures. In ABC's São Caetano district, the local police subdelegado, Eduardo Gabriel Saad, a DOPS labor specialist, went on the offensive in the last ten days of February. Soldiers of the state militia began to carry out searches of workers in the street and raided the local headquarters of both the PCB and the MUT in a search for arms and weapons. Saad's police tactics were designed to intimidate the workers of Roberto Simonsen's Cerâmica São Caetano and of Louças Adelinas, whose dissídios were scheduled for the end of the month.[64]

The managers of the Cerâmica São Caetano, which employed 1,225 workers, also sought to guarantee labor peace by attempting to thwart any sort of union activism. Some workers were encouraged to circulate a petition to withdraw the dissídio, while others were threatened with retaliation for supporting the union's dissídio. Reporting for a union meeting, Cerâmica São Caetano workers were forced to submit to searches by the police; a company spy was expelled from the meeting itself. Armando de Arruda Pereira, longtime head of the firm, angered ABC unionists by taking an especially strong position against the strikes during February FIESP meetings.[65]

On 25 February, the workers went on strike at Swift, the North American meatpacking plant in the Utinga subdistrict of Santo André where the Laminação Nacional strike was still in progress. Swift's management, the workers alleged, refused to follow existing labor legislation, which demonstrated, they said, the need for more efficient enforcement of the labor laws.

The police responded with the use of more aggressive tactics. On 26 February, two Laminação strikers were seized and held in the factory building before being sent to DOPS holding cells in São Paulo. Police began to visit the homes of strikers, while the company reiterated its refusal to negotiate as long as workers disregarded Article 724 of the *CLT*, which banned strikes. Workers, observing the arrival of what they called "phantom trains," also suspected that Pignatari was going to try to operate the factory with strikebreakers.[66]

The Mixed Legacy of the Estado Novo Era: Labor Courts and "Fascist Decrees"

The February 1946 strike wave in metropolitan São Paulo took place in an unsettled political atmosphere. The new presidential regime of General Eurico Dutra, who had been inaugurated on 31 January 1946, was marked by a fundamental constitutional and institutional ambiguity: while Dutra had been elected on the basis of an amendment to the dictatorial 1937 Constitution, the freely elected Constituent Assembly had not yet drafted a new, democratic charter for the nation.

With Dutra as president, the PSD's absolute parliamentary majority could be expected to favor the maintenance of the dictatorial powers accorded the executive under the Estado Novo's charter. The debate over the 1937 Constitution spread throughout the country. In ABC, Santo André's prefeito José de Carvalho Sobrinho, a member of the state PSD executive committee, favored his party's solution of maintaining the 1937 Constitution until the passage of a new one.[67]

The strike agitation in ABC thus coincided with a fundamental political and institutional debate that was far from a meaningless abstraction for ABC's trade unionists or their employers. During a February labor court hearing, one management lawyer taunted ABC union representatives by reminding them that the 1937 Constitution made by their "friend," Getúlio Vargas, banned strikes.[68] For the labor movement, however, queremismo and Getulismo did not mean support for the Getúlio Vargas who had instituted the 1937 charter with its absolute ban on strikes—their support in 1945 was for the new Getúlio who had opened political participation to the people. In responding to the attorney's taunt, the union representatives cited the 1945 Chapultepec accords, signed by Brazil, which pledged recognition of the right to strike. This international legal document symbolized the coming of a new day in which, to use Getúlio's words, there would no longer be a "police state" approach to the social question in Brazil.

Speaking to a rally of thousands of São Caetano residents against the 1937 Constitution, the representative of ABC's unions emphasized that "the day is gone when workers were treated under horses' hoofs. Today," he continued, "we have a Constituent Assembly where we can unmask the fascists and the enemies of the people and the workers." Indeed, police repression against ABC's strikers could not fail to become an issue of public debate as Communist deputies repeatedly brought the strikes to the attention of the Assembly. "The strike," PCB deputy João Amazonas said, "is a just right of the workers as their ultimate recourse to make their rights respected."[69]

The workers' power to denounce antilabor measures and activities by the police did not, of course, constitute real political influence or effectiveness. While the PCB could win Constituent Assembly approval of a request that the government clarify its position on the right to strike, the industrialists of São Paulo exercised far more effective influence with their direct access to the seat of power.[70]

From the onset of the strike crisis, São Paulo's industrialists had looked to the federal government for help in setting strict limits upon the workers' newly won freedoms. Rhodia Química, as we have seen, rejected negotiations out of hand in early February, arguing that nothing could be resolved "without knowing the orientation of the new government of the country and the attitude of the present Ministry of Labor." At its mid-February meeting, the FIESP voted to send a delegation to meet with the federal government.[71] As powerful constituents of the governing PSD, they were confident of a warm reception by President Eurico Dutra. The employers' anticommunist appeals, although sincere, were no doubt tailored to the conceptions of the Estado Novo's preeminent military strongman. The leaders of the FIESP were reported in mid-February to believe that Dutra favored measures to strip the Communist Party of its legal status as soon as the evolution of the international situation made such a move feasible. The elites were also reported to be pleased by the appointment of General Canrobert Pereira da Costa, a strong anticommunist, as Dutra's minister of war.[72]

The FIESP delegation arrived in Rio de Janeiro on 19 February 1946, to request "governmental measures" against the current strikes. Led by Morvan Dias de Figueiredo, these self-styled representatives of the conservative classes harped on the value of order and discipline. As for the right to strike, "without doubt a conquest of our times," they argued that it could not "be invoked to the detriment of the nation's legitimate interests." The response of President Dutra and Minister of Labor Octacílio Negrão de Lima, a banker, was warm, and the delegation returned to São Paulo confident that action would be taken to meet their demands.[73]

In ABC, the conflict between Pignatari and the local metalworkers' union was quickly emerging as the crucial test of strength between industrialists and workers. At the first hearing of the Laminação dissídio, Pignatari's lawyers reiterated their argument about the illegality of the strike under the *CLT*'s antistrike proviso. They charged that the union had fomented the trouble, and they spoke of a case they had filed against the union's leaders with the DOPS. For Pignatari, the social and labor legislation of the Estado Novo era had value only as a means of repression and control of the working class—a conviction he would cling to even after the end of the strike on 2 March 1946.[74]

The trade unionists of ABC gave an equally partisan interpretation to the labor laws passed during Vargas's rule. They had never accepted the government's bargaining apparatus in the sense in which it had been formulated by the regime's corporatist ideologues. Labor courts and governmental conciliation procedures were not *the* solution to the workers' problems, but a means to be used along with other weapons such as the strike. The unionists had never counterposed direct action to the use of the labor court procedures set forth in the *CLT*. The strike, in their eyes, could be legitimately used as a last resort to pressure both employers and the government for more favorable treatment of their demands.

The labor movement did not expect the federal Conselho Regional do Trabalho in São Paulo in 1946 to resolve their problems for them; yet neither did they treat it as a tool of the employers against labor. As the Santo André unionist Armando Mazzo, a Communist, explained in 1945, the *CLT* contained some fascist articles, which must be rejected, along with other items of great benefit to the workers. He credited these governmental concessions to labor's struggle in the early thirties, victories that had not been destroyed despite the vicious persecution of labor leaders later in the decade.[75]

The labor court system in 1946 was, unionists stressed, "one of the few organisms in which agents of reaction" were not powerfully entrenched. The conciliatory procedure set forth in the law, if executed at all honestly, meant that it was possible for mobilized workers to win something more than the employers were willing to grant. If some labor judges and government attorneys were dishonest and subject to employer suasions, others were sympathetic and helpful. If proceedings were slow and subject to bureaucratic mishap and stalling, the end results in February and March 1946 were good enough, from the workers' point of view, to be rejected by virtually all of ABC's companies, which had to be forced to comply.[76]

The employers' provocative behavior in the first month of Dutra's rule stemmed, to a great extent, from the political realities of the government's labor establishment. Not even Pignatari could deny the legitimate need for wage increases to deal with the decline of real wages during the war—at a time when the industrialists' profits were soaring. As it was, the settlements that the workers had won—from 10 to 40 percent, in most cases— barely made up for what had already been lost and could not have diminished manufacturers' profits significantly. The general crisis caused by carestia in urban areas also attracted broad public sympathy and support from even non-working-class citizens, as reflected by the office workers' behavior during the Pirelli strike and the attitudes of some government labor officials.[77]

To prevent the consolidation of the labor apparatus on terms unfavorable to the employers, the industrialists needed a certain atmosphere of crisis and upheaval; while they did not instigate the strikes in any conspiratorial fashion, they would at least use them to gain as much as they could from the new, more conservative federal government of General Dutra. This interpretation is strengthened by the employers' behavior two weeks after they had invoked the issues of communism and national security in their meetings with Dutra.

Despite pledges to resist to the end, São Paulo's industrialists, one after another, came to terms with their employees. On 28 February, an agreement was reached between textile industrialists and their workers, while the dissídio of the Pignatari group was decided on 1 March as hundreds of workers gathered outside the Conselho Regional do Trabalho: the Laminação Nacional lawyers agreed to the compromise proposed by the labor court, and the workers returned to work the following day on the basis of this "victory." In early March, the Pirelli strike was resolved on a similar basis, thus ending the two largest strikes in ABC. Despite complaints and stalling, the industrialists accepted these judgments, which fell far short of resolving the "Communist" question or of purging the unions.[78]

In ABC, the resolution of the Pirelli and Laminação Nacional strikes left only the Swift meatcutters and a few other small factories on strike in early March 1946. Swift used tactics similar to those of the neighboring Laminação plant, sending dismissal notices and having gun-carrying police visit strikers at their homes.[79] The two-week stoppage at Swift differed from the other strikes in the region, however, because it did not receive universal support among the plant's 870 employees. The slaughterhouse continued to operate, albeit on a reduced scale, by using nonstrikers and newly hired personnel, especially young girls.[80] The embittered strikers, who frequented the plant gate with the cudgels and clubs they used to control the cattle, seemed most bitter at the betrayals they suffered at the hands of nine male strikebreakers. While arresting strikers, police allowed some of the more aggressive strikebreakers to go around armed with knives.

Although the Swift strikers were aided by Santo André's Left/Center unions, they apparently received no guidance, whether positive or negative, from the official trade union that had jurisdiction over the industry. The weakness of the strike's leadership was also revealed by the high degree of internal dissension among the group's initial leaders. In addition to attacking two obnoxious guards, the strikers vigorously denounced three belligerent "traitors" who had been vocal advocates of the stoppage at the outset. In a comment reflecting a degree of cultural, religious, and perhaps racial disdain, they repeatedly identified one turncoat, "Macumbeiro Tito," by referring to his practice of Macumba—an Afro-Brazilian religion that would not have been common among ABC's overwhelmingly white workers of southern European descent.

Finally, the strike against the Fábrica de Porcelana Piratininga, which began on 27 February, illuminates the conditions in the region's less modern industries. The thirty strikers, many of them minors, complained of leaking roofs, a lack of drinking water and medical assistance, and the absence of a time clock. When payday arrived at the end of the month, workers were often uncertain of what they were due, especially since they were often dismissed without pay on days when there was no raw material to use in the furnaces.[81]

But São Paulo's industrialists in early March were increasingly willing to resolve the outstanding economic questions and end the strikes because they were confident that they could achieve their primary goals through the Dutra administration. On 2 March, the Constituent Assembly voted 140 to 94 to accept the 1937 Constitution as the law of the land pending the promulgation of the new charter. Equipped with the dictatorial powers of the Estado Novo, President Dutra's authority would meet no challenge by the Assembly.[82]

On 15 March, Dutra issued Decree Law 9,070 regulating the right to strike. This measure adopted the industrialists' position and created the legal basis for governmental action against virtually any strike. Strikes were categorically banned in all fundamental economic activities, including any "industries basic or essential to national defense." Even in "accessory" economic activities, the strike was restricted to the enforcement of a labor court decision. As for dissídios coletivos, the decree held that their resolution should be subordinated to the "collective interest, since no right can be exercised contrary to or offending this interest."[83]

The antistrike measure would remain the law of the land for the next twenty years, despite the formal guarantee of the right to strike in the democratic constitution eventually promulgated in 1946 by the Constituent Assembly. The PCB and the union leaders violently criticized this "fascist decree." Although it was not immediately used, the decree was a clear indication of Dutra's loyalty to his industrialist backers: it was the symbol of a far more wide-ranging governmental commitment to clipping the wings of labor.[84]

The Strikes and the Crystallization of Labor Politics

Like a spotlight, São Paulo's generalized strike wave had illuminated the realities of power for many workers and trade unionists. As the movement subsided in ABC, one final strike served to underline a fundamental division that had developed within the labor movement over the previous two months. On the same day as Dutra's antistrike decree, 973 workers struck the Louças Adelinas factory in São Caetano in an effort to force the labor courts to handle their dissídio coletivo with greater dispatch.[85]

Like the Firestone workers, the employees at Louças Adelinas were legally represented by a São Paulo–based trade union that covered workers throughout the metropolitan region who made ceramic dishes and other cookware. Unlike the Left/Center São Paulo rubber workers' union, however, their official class organ was controlled by one of the most prominent and long-lasting rightist PTB labor leaders, Artur Albino da Rocha.[86] Frustrated by the union's refusal to support their demands, local activists in ABC formed a Professional Association of Ceramics Employees in early 1946. As the first legal step to the creation of a separate union, their association represented a significant threat to Albino da Rocha, whose union received the annual impôsto sindical payments collected from the São Caetano workers for whom it provided neither services nor support.

On the first day of the Louças Adelinas strike, Albino da Rocha appeared at the factory in the company of the notoriously repressive police sub-delegado Eduardo Saad. Denouncing their professional association as "an appendix of the Communist Party," he was booed when he urged the strikers to return to work. The failure of his mission was followed by police harassment of workers at the association's local headquarters.

Albino da Rocha's impolitic actions were all the more remarkable be-cause they were unnecessary. In making such a public avowal of his loy-alties to the government and the police, Rocha made clear that he lacked the scruples of even Santo André's Henrique Poleto. Although Poleto signed denunciations of strikes in general, the president of the local textile workers' union had at least given his support to the Ipiranguinha strikers in January. In doing so, Poleto had shown some sense of loyalty to the workers he represented, however well or badly.

Yet even Poleto himself, as the most prominent trabalhista labor leader in ABC, had been compromised by his willingness, less than a week before the São Caetano incident, to use the police to maintain his control over a tumultuous union meeting. Starting in mid-February, twenty-six oppo-nents of Poleto had pressed for a union meeting to consider their demands for a dues amnesty, a general membership drive, and support of the initia-tives of the state's Left/Center labor movement. When a meeting was finally held on 8 March 1946, Poleto had police in attendance and refused to recognize the opposition motions presented by the Communist electri-cian Marcos Andreotti, first president of the Santo André metalworkers' union in the 1930s. In an atmosphere of general chaos and physical con-frontations, the demand of Andreotti and his supporters for a vote was refused by the president, whom they labeled "a police agent of the Labor Ministry" who refused to recognize "the sovereignty of union assem-blies."[87]

The opprobrium that accrued to prominent PTB trade union leaders for such self-serving actions had a very negative impact on the development of the incipient Labor Party. For rightist PTB labor leaders like Albino da Rocha, who had flourished during the Estado Novo, nothing seemed more natural than to continue collaborating with the government and the em-ployers in 1946. Yet their stance weakened the ties between the PTB and the Getulista Center forces within the labor movement. At the same time, it strengthened the Center's alliance with the Communist-led Left that claimed for itself the banner of loyalty to the workers' interests and support for internal union democracy and fair play.

Moreover, the agenda of the PTB's rightist trade union leaders did not necessarily coincide with the needs of the PTB as a labor-identified political party. If electoral calculation alone had dictated party policy, the PTB would have been wiser to avoid such trade union ties in 1946. With each incident, the possibility of a lasting political alliance between the parties of Getúlio Vargas and Luis Carlos Prestes also declined, despite the promising precedent afforded by the queremista agitation in 1945.[88]

The PTB's internal contradictions thus provided the Communist Party with an excuse to move away from the uncomfortable queremista alliance and invited Communist efforts, both fair and unfair, to claim the mantle of the "workers' party" for themselves alone. The Communists claimed, for example, that a PTB deputy, Romeu José Fiori, had refused to accompany strikers past the police posted at the Santo André railroad station. While Fiori denied the incident, *Hoje* called it symbolic of the "racketeers who use the name of our class to defend their shameful hidden interests."[89]

The PCB justified the hardening of their attitude as an effort to "clarify" for the workers the identity of their true friends. This increasing sectarianism reflected a growing Communist conviction that they alone had a rightful claim to labor's leadership. The PTB seemed, to the Communists, at best an uneasy mixture, a "bag of cats," that combined reformists and various interests who had benefited from the Estado Novo, like Albino da Rocha or the banker and cotton speculator Hugo Borghi. The deepening Communist intolerance is suggested by the mid-March 1946 visit to Santo André by national Communist leader Carlos Marighela. Denouncing the "traitorous" PTB, the Bahian federal deputy was especially irked by the trabalhistas' "demagogic attitude" of claiming "to represent the workers in order to attract them."[90]

The Aftermath: Strikes, Activists, and "Reactionary Bosses"

By mid-March, 10,000 of ABC's industrial workers at fourteen enterprises had gone on strike, most for at least two weeks. Although strikes occurred in almost all branches of local industry, half of the participants were metalworkers, with the remaining 50 percent divided almost equally between six other industries.

The strikers represented a fifth of the entire industrial labor force in the município of Santo André. The percentage of participants varied somewhat between the município's three major industrial districts:17 percent in São Caetano, 24 percent in Santo André, and 38 percent in the Utinga district, where some of the newest and largest enterprises had recently been built. Moreover, an additional 2,693 workers were employed at thirteen nonstriking enterprises that experienced some degree of mobilization regarding the dissídios coletivos covering their plants. Thus, almost a quarter of the total industrial labor force in the município of Santo André had been touched by the labor mobilizations that spanned late 1945 through the first quarter of 1946.

Yet the strike movement, despite the expectations of some sympathetic local observers, had not reached all, or even most, large factories.[91] For example, the rayon and ceramics factories operated by the Indústrias Reunidas Francisco Matarazzo in São Caetano, which together employed 3,365 workers, were untouched by the labor mobilizations of early 1946.

Although four-fifths of the industrial workforce did not directly participate, those who did represented a critical mass large enough to constitute an industrial, social, and political fact of first rank. By their numbers and the visibility and novelty of their actions, the strikers touched the lives of many thousands, both workers and nonworkers, throughout the region.

Moreover, the strike as a form of collective action was a major step in the constitution of a self-conscious class identity among local industrial workers. After all, the last significant strikes in the region—which were small and largely concentrated in São Bernardo and not Santo André—had taken place more than a decade earlier when the local labor force was less than 15,000. Over the intervening years, the region had experienced a net gain of 30,000 jobs as factories expanded and proliferated in the region. Since the new workers were drawn almost exclusively from the rural regions of the interior of São Paulo, only a very small minority of local factory workers could have ever participated in such an action in the past.[92]

Although the actual economic result of the stoppages is impossible to establish, especially in comparison with nonstriking enterprises, it is more important that the movement was widely perceived to be successful. The strike movement also brought workers into motion who were not part of the existing trade union movement. Only rightist labor leaders failed to see that the strikes represented a golden opportunity for unions to recruit many thousands of new members.[93] Furthermore, the new activists who emerged from the delegations and strike committees would provide the main recruiting ground for both the trade unions and the Communist Party over the next year.[94]

Finally, the strikes also confirmed most trade unionists in their views about the complementary relationship between direct and indirect action. Expressing the question in the minds of many nonworkers, a Santo André journalist asked, in March 1946, why workers struck if a solution to their problems could be reached through the dissídio coletivo procedure. Exposed to the views of labor's leadership, he explained to his readers that workers had learned that a dissídio without a strike could take months and even years to resolve. The experience of February 1946, he went on, demonstrated that a strike combined with a dissídio produced a rapid solution by the otherwise slow-moving labor courts.[95]

But there was a downside to the work stoppages of early 1946. While the strikes had imparted a new dynamism and élan to union life and introduced many workers to struggle, they had also revealed the network of union activists and militants, new and old, who had led the strikes at the plant level. All of ABC's big industrial firms had long maintained security departments charged with monitoring such rebellious and disruptive activities—often headed, as in the case of Laminação Nacional, by ex-delegados of the police. As the factories returned to normal in early March, the major ABC industries that had been struck, including Pirelli, Mineração e Metalúrgica, Laminação Nacional, Rhodia Química, Firestone, and Swift, began dismissing the newly exposed rank-and-file leaders. At Pignatari's Laminação Nacional plant in Santo André, hundreds were dismissed with notices stating that they had been fired for violating the antistrike provisions of the *CLT*—although only the labor courts could legally exact such a penalty. At Pirelli 100 workers were fired, including the worker who had led the strike assemblies, Miguel Guillen, the union vice-president. Angry workers discussed striking to defend their compatriots, but union leaders advocated caution, seeking to avoid compounding the problems through an unsuccessful strike.[96]

Feelings ran high as thousands of workers gathered on 19 March 1946 at a mass meeting called by the central labor council of ABC. Shouting "Down with the fascist Pignatari," the workers heard their leaders blame the strikes on the employer intransigence that had even led local firms to initially refuse to honor the judgments of the labor courts. In a protest eventually read from the floor of the Constituent Assembly, ABC's unions denounced these employer actions as an attack on Brazil's new democratic era and labor laws. In all, they said, 1,400 had been fired and blacklisted so that even industries hiring new workers refused to give them jobs. In the case of Laminação Nacional, they further alleged, Pignatari was using the strike as a pretext for firing even nonstrikers, including many older employees with job tenure.

Euclides Savietto, the metalworkers' past president, vigorously denounced the "reactionary bosses" who charged that it was the Communists who were responsible for strikes. "Pure farce," he declared. "Strikes are the result of the high cost of living, of the miserable life that the proletariat has in Brazil. No one goes on strike because they like to, but only out of the need for more bread, so as not to die of hunger." Attacking Dutra's antistrike decree, the rally decided to send a commission to Rio de Janeiro to bring the workers' problems to the attention of President Dutra, despite his refusal to meet other such worker delegations.

The industrialists, the assembled unionists said, were provoking disorder and civil war by their unpatriotic actions; they were creating a spirit of revolt within the working class. Casting themselves as representatives of the national interest, the unionists stressed that workers knew that the road forward lay through the "evolution and equipping of national industry" and "greater agricultural production." In this way, Brazil could become "completely emancipated," eliminate inflation, and "escape from this state of hunger and misery."[97]

Seven • We Have

Reached the Age of Consent

• Labor and the State

n 1945, Brazil's military, economic, and political establishment had seemed impotent to hold back the popular tide. The democratic explosion had swept away much of the repressive past, while promising a radically new order. As the new republic began to take form, the urban popular classes enjoyed a freedom of expression and organization the breadth and vigor of which were unknown in the nation's history. The resulting widespread popular insurgency, symbolized by popular Getulismo and the strike, prompted efforts, once the turbulent succession crisis was over, to clamp down upon these new forces.

The Brazilian government, the federal intervenor in São Paulo, and the state's industrialists pursued a consistently repressive policy throughout 1946 in an effort to demobilize the newly militant postwar trade unionism. This resort to repression, however, intensified the workers' determination to guarantee their newfound rights and to bar a return to the past so many had thoroughly rejected. President Dutra's break with the Vargas regime's paternalistic courtship of labor also paved the way for the consolidation of a stronger and more independent trade union movement that rejected state tutelage.

The Logic of Repression

"What kind of democracy is this in which the workers cannot even demand their rights from the government?" Alberto Salvadori, the head of Santo

André's central labor council, asked in April 1946. Despite ten days of lobbying in the nation's capital, a delegation of four trade union leaders from ABC had failed to get an appointment to see President Eurico Dutra. Although they were successful in arranging a meeting with Dutra's labor minister, Octacílio Negrão de Lima, it had hardly been satisfying. The banker from Minas Gerais had been openly skeptical of their charges that local employers were boycotting the labor justice system and carrying out widespread reprisals against participants in the strikes of early 1946. In an interview after their return, the four labor militants declared that such inaction demonstrated that the president's campaign pledges to respect the workers' "sacred rights" were words without consequences. A government that gives in to "the enemies of the proletariat," metalworkers' treasurer Alberto Salvadori went on, "does not deserve the workers' confidence."[1]

The unionists of ABC had not been naive about President Dutra's inclinations toward labor, but they also knew that working-class voters had contributed, at Vargas's direction, to his election in 1945 over the UDN's Brigadeiro Eduardo Gomes. Once freed of the electoral constraints of 1945, however, Dutra lacked Vargas's motivation to build an urban popular base for his rule.

With the solid backing of the military, Dutra's PSD enjoyed an absolute majority in both the Senate (62 percent) and the federal Chamber of Deputies (53 percent). The commanding majority produced by the Estado Novo's coronelistic political machine was occasionally supplemented by support from the formally allied PTB and the more pliant members of the opposition elite party, the UDN.[2] Moreover, the president still had the power, pending state elections, to appoint the state intervenors who, in turn, appointed all of the nation's municipal and law enforcement authorities.

Given such a firm and unchallenged control over the levers of power, the nation's democratically elected chief executive had no compelling need to tolerate the "agitation" or "disorder" that followed the easing of dictatorial control. His general crackdown on labor and the Left was justified through heightened anticommunist rhetoric based on an exaggerated notion of the "Communist threat." The shifts in the international arena symbolized by Winston Churchill's March 1946 "iron curtain" speech merely reinforced Dutra's determination. The anticommunist theme had the added advantage of placing Getúlio Vargas and his trabalhistas on the defensive. And the PCB's centrality to the new trade union movement guaranteed that anticommunist repression would hit the primary target, the newly militant Left/Center labor movement.

The political forces most opposed to the changes of the previous year began to move into action as the strikes of early 1946 came to an end. On 23 March, a challenge to the registry of the Communist Party as a legal political party was filed with the Supreme Electoral Court (Tribunal Superior Eleitoral, or TSE). The PCB, it was charged, was "a foreign party at the service of Russia" that was "instigating class struggle, fomenting strikes [and] seeking to create an atmosphere of confusion and disorder."[3]

While the Communists and their labor allies pressed their campaign for "national unity," the partisans of the Estado Novo rejected any concept of unity that included the Left and its subversive ways. In May 1946, Santo André's PSD newspaper attacked a local celebration of the allied victory over Germany as a "Communist gathering," despite the presence of local PSD Prefeito José de Carvalho Sobrinho. Russia was the true "motherland" of these Communists, the *Borda do Campo* article went on, and Brazil's patience with the Communist program of "disorder, revolution, dynamite, and destruction" was wearing thin. When the day came for the army to hunt them down, it warned, not many Communists would survive to tell the story.[4]

The powerful ABC employers did not passively wait for an apocalyptic day of reckoning. Emboldened by the backing of the new government, they were determined to reassert their authority and put an end to the "agitation" they associated with communism and the new trade unionism. With the end of the strike wave in ABC, they embarked on their own hunt for "Communists" among their workers. Dozens of activist workers, whether Communists or not, were fired or otherwise penalized for their participation in the PCB, the Democratic Progressive Committees (CDPs), or trade unions.

Repressive measures such as demotions, fines, or dismissals were most successful if the majority of the other workers in the shop responded with neutrality or even acquiescence. This was achieved by stigmatizing the activist elements as "Communists" so that the dispute would appear to be a conflict between managers and Communists, and the nonaligned workers would not feel they had a stake in it. Yet the efforts by ABC's industrialists to conduct a carefully targeted repression were inevitably compromised in 1946 by the realities of managerial behavior. Not only did the employer have to contend with the fact that the PCB was legal in 1946, but he also needed to know who was and who was not a Communist in order to conduct such a strategy with total success. Although there were self-proclaimed PCBers in local factories in 1946, there were also others who were not open in their affiliation. While employer infiltration of the Communist Party could identify many in both these categories, there were further complications.

Employers faced difficulties in isolating openly Communist workers from their fellow employees. The majority of those who called themselves Communists in ABC had joined the PCB after its legitimation as a political party in 1945. Thus, their shopmates could easily identify with these new PCBers, most of whom had less than a year of party affiliation; this might not have been the case had the only Communists been the veteran revolutionaries who had been underground or in prison during the Estado Novo.[5] The election of avowedly Communist union leaders in ABC's factory districts in 1945–46 also indicated that many workers felt that these radicals made sense. Moreover, the Communists had received 7,000 votes in ABC in December 1945, and hundreds of non-Communist workers were active in organs linked to the PCB, such as CDP neighborhood associations. How were these sympathizing but non-Communist workers to be handled? If a decision was made to extend the circle of repression this far, there remained further cases of non-PCBers who were active in the trade unions led by the Communists.

Since certainty was not possible, the industrial managers running ABC's factories had only one real test: what an individual had actually done. Had the worker challenged the foreman's authority? Had the worker led or actively supported a strike or a dissídio? Had the worker tried to recruit new members for the union? The indiscriminate repression based on such activities gave credibility to the victimized workers' charge that the bosses were trying to eliminate those who led their fellow workers in struggle.[6]

An alternative repressive strategy for ABC's industrial employers would have been the wholesale replacement of all suspect workers with newer and hopefully more pliable employees. This policy was pursued by at least one Santo André employer in 1946—namely, Francisco Pignatari, owner of Laminaçao Nacional de Metais.[7] More commonly, however, the imperatives of production and profit-making in 1946 made across-the-board firings difficult, if not impossible. This strategy made sense only in a time of economic crisis, retrenchment, and unemployment—but the period was still one of high employment and economic boom.

The wartime economic expansion had also intensified the long-standing shortage of skilled workers in Paulista industry, and a significant number of skilled workers were Communists or union activists. The companies would have lost more than they would have gained if they had fired Communist skilled workers at a moment of great demand for their skills.[8] As a result, some Communist and leftist workers were spared while other non-Communist activists within the same factory were penalized. These inconsistencies based on monetary considerations served to further undermine the anticommunist justifications the employers gave for their actions.[9]

Industrialists in 1946 also used their political clout to win governmental action to curb aggressive trade unionism. The PSD's monopoly over the machinery of government and law enforcement, the industrialists believed, could guarantee the success of their assault upon Brazil's labor movement and its leftist leaders. Dutra's March 1946 antistrike decree was the first clear payoff to this key PSD constituency. In the following month, the federal government intervened to prevent the registry of the Unifying Movement of Workers (MUT) as a legally recognized association. The ends of the MUT, it was charged, were illicit, dangerous, and contrary to the *CLT*.[10]

The federal government's turn to confrontation with labor activists was paralleled by the decidedly hostile actions of São Paulo's PSD intervenor José Carlos de Macedo Soares. The state's Communists were not completely wrong when they charged in mid-1946 that Macedo Soares still believed that "the social question is a police matter, and the strike, Communist agitation."[11]

Officials of the political-social police in São Paulo (DOPS) were encouraged by their return to official favor in 1946 after having suffered a momentary eclipse the year before. The highest state police officials began to consciously reward those who had shown personal initiative in the new campaign against the Left. During the summer of 1946, Eduardo Gabriel Saad, São Caetano's repressive police subdelegado, was promoted to interim police delegado for the whole município of Santo André.[12]

The conflict between labor and the state in São Paulo was the most intense in the port city of Santos, the only Paulista município where the Communist Party candidate came in first in December 1945. In May 1946, local dockworkers refused to unload two Spanish vessels in protest against the Franco regime. The conflict escalated into a full-scale clash when soldiers occupying the port opened fire on the strikers, killing at least one. The stevedores' union was intervened in by the Labor Ministry, and twenty-five local union leaders were jailed to await trial before a military court.[13]

These violations of the guarantees of freedom of assembly and expression reflected the firmly and publicly expressed convictions of many powerful military and government officials in mid-1946. Army General Oswaldo Cordeiro de Farias, for example, head of the Third Military Region, openly regretted that excessive toleration allowed Communists to hold seats in parliament. That these were not empty words became clear on 23 May 1946, when Rio de Janeiro's police authorities banned a planned Communist mass meeting. When a crowd gathered despite the contested order, the police opened fire, leaving at least one dead and dozens wounded. The Massacre of Largo da Carioca, as the incident came to be known, spurred nationwide protest even from many who were unsympathetic to the PCB.[14]

The bloodshed in Rio was symbolic of a vigorous antileftist offensive from which President Dutra was not inclined to call a retreat.[15] In the following month, São Paulo's intervenor began a further crackdown on labor and the Left when the workers of the Sorocabana railroad line went on strike. Police raided the Communists' state headquarters in the capital, and soldiers were deployed in ABC's main railroad stations for three weeks. This intimidating display of force by the state militia and the DOPS was paid for with municipal funds authorized by Santo André's PSD Prefeito Carvalho Sobrinho—much as Prefeito Saladino Cardoso Franco had done during periods of labor agitation before 1930.[16]

On 6 July 1946, police arrested three local union activists for their part in an alleged conspiracy to organize a work stoppage in solidarity with the railroad strikers. Among those arrested were João Fuchs, a São Caetano labor activist; Pedro Calzolari of Santo André; and the metalworkers' new president, Victor Gentil Savietto. Savietto, who was detained during his Saturday office hours at the union's headquarters, had earned the ire of local employers as leader of the region's largest and most aggressive union.[17]

Many times earlier that year, ABC's labor movement had raised funds, passed resolutions, and organized meetings to protest other violations of. union and democratic rights. The response to the arrest of their own leaders was immediate: a defense committee was quickly formed, protest meetings were held, and numerous delegations were dispatched to São Paulo newspapers and state authorities. In an effort to involve the labor rank and file, petitions were circulated in dozens of major factories in Santo André and São Caetano, demanding freedom for the jailed unionists.[18]

In defending their leaders, Santo André's Left/Center trade unionists could legitimately frame their appeals as a defense of the government's own system of legal trade unions. As thirteen São Paulo union leaders wrote, the "illegal" arrests in Santo André were the work of "powerful employers and obdurate adversaries of normal legal union activities." The protests and petitions circulated in dozens of ABC factories were phrased in eminently practical terms: an honest, democratically elected leader was being penalized for defending the workers' interests within the government's own labor relations structure.[19]

There was further police harassment of Left/Center unions in ABC during July. Warrants were issued for the arrest of João Leocadio da Silva and Alberto Zamignani, presidents of the greater São Paulo rubber workers' union and the Santo André civil construction workers' union, respectively. The Labor Ministry used the arrests to bar Zamignani from office while punishing Leocadio da Silva for his denunciation of a fraudulent union antistrike manifesto that the Delegacia Regional do Trabalho (Regional Labor Delegacy, or DRT) had sponsored the previous month.[20] Four days after the arrests in Santo André, interim delegado Saad and four subordinates invaded the PCB's Santo André headquarters during a public meeting. The assembled Communists rejected Saad's ultimatum that they seek police permission for future indoor meetings, citing legal provisions that required prior authorization only for street gatherings. Similar orders were nonetheless issued to the metalworkers' union, and Saad posted policemen at the entrance of the union hall. Even workers attending the local labor court to monitor their dissídios had to pass by armed police at the entrance, a clear attempt to intimidate activist union members.[21]

The ostentatious use of the police to harass labor and the Left emphasized the close link between developments in the economic and political spheres, between attacks on unionism and attacks on the PCB. The parallels were all too obvious between the repressive actions of employers within the workplace and the police actions against trade unions and a party, the PCB, that had much working-class support. For this reason, the repression in mid-1946 did not have the desired demobilizing effect; rather, it more firmly united the labor Left and Center and spurred a general movement of unionized workers to rally around their trade unions and Left/Center leaders.[22]

At one stroke, the government had done away with the mythology of the state's allegedly neutral role in labor relations that had developed during Vargas's last years in power. Charged with overseeing the legally recognized labor movement, Dutra's administration acted as if the trade unions were merely a facade designed to facilitate the control of labor for the purposes of public order, the government, and the employers. The government, in other words, had reverted to an older pattern in which the state was openly identified with the industrial employers against the working class.

On 1 August 1946, this process was carried to its logical extreme in Brazil's most industrialized state when, for the second time since 1930, São Paulo was made the only state not subject to the oversight of the federal Labor Ministry. The responsibilities, personnel, and facilities of the federal Regional Labor Delegacy were transferred to the State Labor Department of São Paulo (DET).

São Paulo's trade unions had no illusions that this move heralded a more vigorous enforcement of existing labor laws. They immediately denied official claims that they had requested this change and complained about the lack of consultation in a matter that directly affected their constituents. Although they had criticized the federal DRT in São Paulo in the past, most unionists rightly suspected that the DET under intervenor Macedo Soares would be even more inimical to their interests.[23]

The government's open defense of the employers' interests repelled the many workers who had emerged from the December 1945 elections and the ensuing strike wave with an enhanced sense of class identity and solidarity. Most felt closer to a Communist fellow employee with whom they might vigorously disagree politically than to those who persecuted him. In addition, it was not forgotten that Dutra had helped overthrow Getúlio in October 1945—and the rift between the two men became an open break in August 1946 when Labor Minister Negrão de Lima was expelled from the PTB by both its Minas Gerais and national leaderships.[24]

The Dutra government, the PSD, and their intervenors were not deterred by the negative reaction to their policies in the nation's industrial areas. Responsive only to traditional elite constituencies, the government saw the dramatic changes of 1945 as mistakes to be rectified at the earliest possible opportunity. The PSD's electoral victories in the countryside led many party strategists to discount the importance of the new urban vote. If the maintenance of order required a sacrifice of popularity in the cities, so be it. Indeed, the Dutra government raised the stakes of its confrontation with the Left in August 1946 when formal action was approved at the cabinet level for further measures against the PCB.[25]

The police, the attorney for the arrested Santo André trade unionists charged, still acted as if democratic freedoms were a gift from the police and not a right of all citizens. The most politicized workers were quick to see such behavior as a continuation of the Estado Novo and the dictatorial 1937 Constitution. The promulgation of the new democratic constitution on 18 September 1946, they believed, would help guarantee real freedom of speech, association, press, and assembly.[26]

On Sunday, 22 September 1946, the PCB and other local organizations called for a mass celebration of the new Constitution at the central railroad station in Santo André. In doing so, the local PCB was defying a DOPS order banning the meeting, an action that it viewed as a restriction on democratic rights.[27] Twenty militants preparing the meeting were arrested and the PCB sound truck was seized. Within the hour, dozens of soldiers and police from São Paulo joined in a raid on the local Communist headquarters and arrested PCB political secretary Armando Mazzo.[28]

Less than a year after the end of the Estado Novo, repression under the new democratic regime already far surpassed the level that had existed during the last years of the dictatorship. For ABC's Communists, at least, it appeared as if nothing had been essentially changed by the institutional transition from tyranny to democracy. Yet, such a pessimistic view overlooks a number of important realities in 1946. The large-scale repression of the early Dutra regime was required precisely because the workers were mobilized to a degree unknown during the Estado Novo.

Repression might have succeeded if ABC's workers had not been convinced that a new day had, in fact, arrived. If this belief was in good part an illusion, it served them well, nonetheless, by generating anger and the determination to make the promise of 1945 a reality. Throughout 1946, the rhetoric of democracy and antifascism would provide them with simple and powerful responses to the ironies of transition; the people would not be turned back by the remnants of the past dictatorship.[29]

At the same time, the government's freedom of movement was limited by the democratic transition that had spurred the popular militancy they sought to quell. There were new legal barriers that, although they were only partially effective, had a real significance in the lives of ABC's workers. The restoration of the rule of law, for example, restricted some police actions that would have gone unchallenged under the dictatorship.[30]

Moreover, the new Brazilian democracy met the labor movement's historic demand for the freedom to print and distribute its own newspapers and magazines. Flourishing and partisan prolabor newspapers like São Paulo's daily, *Hoje*, were a powerful weapon against the employers and their government allies. While the fate of a victimized worker during the Estado Novo had been known only to a few individuals in his family, factory, or neighborhood, the relatively free press in 1946 meant that individual stories could be publicly exposed, protested, and debated—easing the individual worker's sense of isolation and futility.

To achieve unanimity of governmental action was also far more difficult under democratic than under dictatorial forms of rule—even in the case of the Dutra government's anticommunist campaign. To achieve its objectives, the government coalition had to contend with a range of counterpressures of electoral, institutional, and even personal expediency. The revocation of the PCB's registry as a legal party, for example, had to proceed through the uncertain channels of the electoral court system.[31]

Unexpected obstacles to the government's plans even surfaced within the hierarchical structures of the military. In August 1946, the military tribunal of São Paulo's Second Military Region found no evidence for the charges against ABC trade unionists Savietto, Calzolari, Zamignani, and Leocadio da Silva. Whatever the explanation, this act of simple justice was warmly welcomed by the workers of ABC who saw it as proof of the democratic inclinations of the military. In the acquittal's aftermath, Communists Savietto and Zamignani resumed the presidencies of their respective unions.[32]

"Union Politics": Founding the General Confederation of Brazilian Workers

The government's inability to demobilize the workers was compounded by the lack of a positive role for the Labor Ministry, the major weapon for sophisticated intervention in the trade union movement. Dutra's top labor policy maker, Negrão de Lima, had little understanding of the contemporary politics of labor, and his uninformed actions actually jeopardized the regime's declared objective of containing labor militancy. The federal minister of labor, industry, and commerce apparently believed the conservative rhetoric that blamed labor turbulence on the actions of a handful of unrepresentative malcontents and subversives who had infiltrated into union leaderships. A logical conclusion drawn from this line of thinking was that left-wing trade union leaders, because they had gotten their power illegitimately, could be replaced through union elections. Therefore, four months after the suspension of union elections, federal Decree 9,502 ordered the holding of new elections in all unions and federations on 6 September 1946.[33]

Decree 9,502 was an unexpected blunder that alienated the government's natural allies, the labor Right. At a gathering of thirty-eight Paulista union bodies, the panicky rightist leaders of the state union federations joined their Left/Center rivals in opposing this "fascist" violation of union autonomy. Decidedly on the defensive, Deocleciano Hollanda de Cavalcanti, president of the São Paulo Federation of Workers in the Food Industry, summarized the Right's mood when he declared that President Dutra could not allow such an "unjust measure" to stand.[34] This fragile unity of all factions of organized labor paved the way for the greatest victory of labor's Left/Center leadership in 1946: the convocation of a National Union Congress of the Workers of Brazil, which founded the General Confederation of Brazilian Workers (Confederação Geral dos Trabalhadores do Brasil, or CGTB). Although often mentioned, the origin and politics of the meeting have been little understood.

The national gathering was originally proposed for 20 August 1946, in Rio de Janeiro. The congress was to be conducted in accordance with the militant spirit and grass-roots orientation of the activist Left/Center coalition that led the majority of Brazilian unions. Such a national meeting, they had long argued, must be representative of more than just union leadership bodies acting without the involvement of their members. Participation in the congress and the selection of delegates should be decided through carefully prepared democratic elections by union assemblies.[35]

Minister Negrão de Lima and the labor Right naturally opposed these efforts to create formal national linkages between union organizations. To counter the planned Left/Center labor conference, the government banned its discussion from the agenda of union meetings and announced a competing official conference to be held in Recife in September. To succeed, the counterconference would require a semblance of labor support that could only come from the labor Right now antagonized by Decree 9,502. The Right, however, withdrew its support from the minister's project, and instead joined the organizing commission for the Left/Center Rio conference.[36]

Thwarted by this defection, Minister Negrão de Lima was forced to cancel the Recife meeting and he finally agreed, in last-minute negotiations, to sanction a single unified congress. The first session of the National Union Congress of the Workers of Brazil was opened on 19 September

1946, by Negrão de Lima. Rio de Janeiro's municipal theater was packed with almost 2,000 delegates along with government ministers, military men, leaders of the National Labor Council, and a delegation of parliamentarians, including Senator Luis Carlos Prestes. The Rio meeting was the largest and broadest trade union gathering in Brazilian history to date, representative of the geographic, political, occupational, and organizational diversity of the postwar labor movement.[37]

The gathering brought together full-time functionaries, local union leaders, and elected rank-and-file activists. Politically, the delegates represented trabalhismo in both its bureaucratic rightist form and its Center/Left Getulista form. As an organized force, the Communist Party was undoubtedly the most influential political party represented among the delegates assembled in Rio. From ABC, trade unions of all political colorations were present: the São Bernardo furniture workers, Santo André's metal, chemical, rubber, textile, and civil construction workers, as well as the professional associations of bakers and leather and ceramics workers.[38]

The congress's deliberations reflected a consensus among labor activists that rejected state tutelage of the labor movement.[39] The meeting was unequivocal in rejecting the corporatist thesis, embraced by the labor Right, that trade unions should be "integrated with the state as an arm and organ of the state." In the words of the U.S. labor attaché, Edward J. Rowell, the CGTB founding meeting was a defeat for those forces who "accepted ministerial interpretation of the Labor Code and ministerial direction" of labor's activities—thus marking a triumph for those forces who sought "to create an independent and autonomous labor movement" modeled after labor's "status and activities" in the "Western democracies."[40]

The resolution on trade union freedoms and autonomy adopted by the meeting reflected the conviction that workers, in one delegate's words, had reached "the age of consent." The Paulista leaders were not alone in their strong proprietary feelings toward their trade unions, whose authority, they believed, derived from the sovereign decision of the members and not the provisions of the legal labor code.[41]

The delegates were acutely aware of trade unionism's limited penetration inside the nation's factories and the need to strengthen the union's direct bargaining power through more comprehensive workplace organization. The system of union factory commissions pioneered by Paulista trade unionists in 1946 had demonstrated the advantages and feasibility of such a grass-roots base.[42] The aftermath of the strikes had shown, however, the discouragingly high price that many such factory activists had to pay in the face of employer hostility. To remedy these problems, the congress proposed a system of "union delegates" with power to handle grievances through direct negotiations with the employers. Their proposal, if legally enacted, would have institutionalized a strong shop-steward system with legal protection from the employer reprisals that unionists knew so well.

On the "sacred and inalienable right to strike," the delegates emphatically rejected both the spirit and the letter of Dutra's antistrike Decree 9,070 of March 1946. Strikes, they argued, were a legitimate last resort in defense of the workers' vital interests. When necessary, work stoppages should be decided by the democratic decision of the workers concerned and should be carried out through the unions.

The resolutions on existing social and labor legislation and its enforcement suggest that labor saw considerable grounds for improvement in the "world's most advanced labor legislation." Vacations, it was proposed, should be doubled in length and paid at twice the normal wage. All organs of the labor justice system should be constituted on the basis of trade union parity rather than the existing tripartite system of union/management/government representation. Labor inspectors, they proposed, should be elected by the vote of union assemblies. They also suggested that legal job tenure (*estabilidade*) in employment should be attained by the worker after five and not ten years.

While union dependence on the state might have been feasible if Vargas had remained in power, the trade unionists fully realized that a reliance on government was foolhardy, if not suicidal, in light of Dutra's antilabor policies of 1946. Yet if alliance with Dutra was out of the question, the assembled unionists were equally chary of aligning themselves publicly with the Communists or even the PTB, which had recently broken with Dutra. Therefore the congress not only did not endorse any political party but even proposed a legal ban on "propaganda" of any political party or religion within the trade unions. If this was not done, the resolution warned, agitation by discontented minorities would threaten the labor movement with organizational disintegration.

At the same time, the delegates recognized that politics—in the "higher sense"—was a necessary dimension of labor's struggle. Their own experience in 1945 and 1946 had provided dramatic proof that labor's progress was inseparable from the overall political climate of the country. To advance, or even to prevent setbacks, it was essential that workers attempt to influence the country's direction through alliances with non-working-class groups. The resolution, therefore, did not reject political struggle, but accorded a valid place for a specifically "union politics" if conducted "in the interests of the class itself"—that is, a politics designed to unify and strengthen the workers' struggle for their demands. This special realm of "union politics," it was clear, would be arrived at by negotiation among the diverse forces of labor. This non-political-party formula avoided conflict between the PTB and the PCB, the two strongest political groupings within labor, and eased the way for further cooperation between grass-roots Getulista and Communist labor leaders. The more cohesively organized PCB was required to renounce overt efforts to capitalize on its leading role, while trabalhistas were inhibited from using their grass-roots support against the PCB.

The final order of business before the assembly in Rio was the creation of a national trade union federation, the General Confederation of Brazilian Workers (CGTB) so vigorously rejected by Labor Minister Negrão de Lima. Failing in his efforts to sway the delegates, the minister decided to close the meeting with the help of the bureaucratic labor Right, which had lost its motivation to continue its alliance with the Left/Center forces on 30 August when Negrão de Lima suspended the disputed union elections scheduled for 6 September 1946—a measure that brought vigorous protest from Left/Center labor.[43]

On 20 September 1946 a São Paulo PTB leader, Orval Cunha, created a tumult when he read a denunciation of Communist "coercion" signed by two hundred delegates from a group of rightist labor factions. The representative of São Paulo's Union of Traveling Salesmen led a walkout of a "not small" number of delegates from several state delegations. In a telegram to Dutra, the dissidents requested that the labor minister close the congress, which, they said, was dominated by an "anarchic current." Meeting with Negrão de Lima, these dissident delegates became the nucleus for the foundation of the National Confederation of Industrial Workers (Confederação Nacional dos Trabalhadores na Indústria, or CNTI).[44]

The thousands of Left/Center delegates who remained, however, defied orders to disperse and went on to found the CGTB, which was to be tied to subordinate state and local central labor bodies. The president of the newly formed CGTB was Roberto Morena, a legendary labor activist and former furniture maker from Rio de Janeiro. He had moved from anarchist activism in the First Republic to Communism and the PCB. The president of São Paulo's state union body, Communist weaver Roque Trevisan, was to be the state's representative on the CGTB's fifteen-member executive committee.[45]

In the aftermath of the Rio congress, the balance sheet showed a decisive defeat for the government's efforts to control the majority of the existing legal labor movement. In his message to the congress, Dutra had explicitly warned of the risk that the unions, like a young tree, would be "deformed" by "foreign" and "anti-Brazilian" influences. Unions, the president said, should not be "links of discord, agents of agitation [and] instruments of struggle." Rather, Brazil needed an "apolitical" unionism that would be "exclusively apparatuses of assistance to those who work . . . and organs of cooperation."[46]

In rejecting such a subordinate status, the Rio congress confirmed the lack of mass influence of the labor Right, the *ministerialistas*, who were, in the words of the U.S. labor attaché, "amenable to direction, control and domination" by the Ministry of Labor. The Left/Center coalition that triumphed, he went on, should be "classified as 'independent' in terms of its objectives [for labor] and 'Communist' in terms of its sponsorship and orientation."[47]

Yet attaché Rowell, a close observer of the Brazilian labor scene, was quick to remind his superiors that not all of the members of this "independent current" within the labor movement were Communists, although "its most articulate, most aggressive, and, in general, most popular leaders undoubtedly are." As Robert Alexander, who attended the meeting, observed, the CGTB founding convention was divided, in political terms, into "the Communists and their friends, [and] the Vargas people and their friends"—with both groups united against "those who were unconditionally at the beck and call of the Ministry of Labor no matter who was president of the Republic."[48]

As 1946 drew to a close, Dutra's minister of war continued to denounce communism as an "exotic ideology," while the minister of justice publicly advocated a ban on PCB participation in elections. This anticommunist rhetoric coincided with new examples of official hostility to trade unionism at all levels. On 25 October, Dutra replaced Labor Minister Negrão de Lima with Morvan Dias de Figueiredo, a Paulista industrialist who had long advocated a crackdown on labor. And in São Paulo, the State Labor Department (DET) was placed in the hands of Santo André's former police delegado, the repressive DOPS official Eduardo Gabriel Saad.[49]

The intent of Brazil's governing elite was transparent, and unionists became increasingly convinced that labor's fate was bound up with that of the Communist Party. United by the manifestly hostile actions of Dutra's PSD, the Paulista labor movement turned its attention toward the elections scheduled for 19 January 1947. Whether Getulista or Communist, São Paulo's organized workers had a clear and immediate interest in seeing the PSD ousted from the executive branch in São Paulo, while electing as many labor state deputies as possible.

Part Three • The Promise

and Pitfalls of Democracy, 1947–1953

Eight • Workers and

the Rise of Adhemarista

Populism in São Paulo

Labor's potential for political influence in São Paulo had greatly increased since the oligarchic First Republic (1889–1930). At that time, labor's prospects for any state-level alliance had been nil, given the integration of political and economic power under conditions of unchallenged one-party rule. Overturning the Paulista domination of national politics, the Revolution of 1930 led to the first courting of urban workers by chief executives appointed by Getúlio Vargas. This relationship, however, was more a function of the regime's conflict with São Paulo's ruling groups than of labor pressure. Despite the rhetoric of intervenors in the early 1930s, these ties were not defined by working-class leaders, since labor had no real leverage—a situation that continued during the Estado Novo.

The representative democratic system of the postwar period offered, for the first time, the possibility for labor to advance its interests by electoral means, working through the PTB and the PCB. In both trabalhista and Communist variants, the labor-oriented parties of postwar São Paulo had decided advantages over the fragile organizations of the previous decade. Not only was Paulista trade unionism immeasurably more massive, firmly rooted, and powerful, but this successful economic organization went hand in hand with an unprecedented degree of political unity among urban workers.

When they surveyed the political scene in late 1946, furthermore, labor leaders had grounds for optimism, because almost half of the Paulista electorate was now located in the six industrial cities that were the center of trade union strength. As election fever grew, the state labor movement hoped to punish its enemies and guarantee the election of a candidate sympathetic to its interests. Although defensive in origin, the unions' political initiatives were also an offensive effort to alter the political environment in which future collective bargaining would take place.

For the Communist Party, the approaching elections were crucial because of the looming threat of being outlawed by the government. A favorable outcome in São Paulo might determine whether their formidable organization there could survive such an adverse development. Too small to aspire to the governorship for one of its own, the PCB watched as Paulista politicians went through a dizzying routine of negotiations, rumored deals, and betrayals between and within each party.[1]

Having won the votes of 180,000 Paulistas in 1945, the Communist movement represented a new and potentially decisive element in the electoral calculations of the aspirants to state office. To increase its leverage, the PCB did not include a gubernatorial candidate on the slates that it filed on 19 October 1946, and it did not make an endorsement until two weeks before the elections scheduled for 19 January 1947.[2] The final line-up in the gubernatorial race included two traditional candidates, Mario Tavares of the PSD and the UDN's Antônio de Almeida Prado, and two figures oriented toward the newly enfranchised popular sectors: the trabalhista Hugo Borghi, and Adhemar de Barros.

Statesmen and Demagogues: The Candidates

The conservative PSD of State Intervenor Macedo Soares was the only party that showed no interest in negotiating with the Communists. Its repressive course toward labor indicated the intervenor's belief in the traditional power of incumbency. To knowingly alienate a large block of urban voters, PSD strategists must have been confident of electoral support from the state's rural coronéis. Generations of boss rule on the state level had proved to their satisfaction that the incumbents who controlled the state and local governments never lost elections.

The state's political and economic establishment thus demonstrated little insight into the political changes of the past year that had emboldened urban workers. The direct gubernatorial elections of 1947 would not be based on the restricted suffrage and fraud that had sustained boss rule in the First Republic. And unlike its predecessors during the 1930s and early

1940s, the Paulista PSD faced the prospect of popular electoral retribution for the antilabor policies it had openly pursued over the previous year.

In urban-industrial areas such as Santo André, appointed PSD prefeitos like José de Carvalho Sobrinho also had to contend with the continuing climate of ill will generated by the high cost of living (*carestia*), the black market (*câmbio negro*), and the monopolization (*açambarcamento*) of essential goods. Popular anger focused on the incumbent municipal administrations of the PSD that were entrusted with the thankless task of rationing essential foodstuffs and other goods.[3]

A popular explosion was widely expected, and the PCB and its allied organizations sought to give this discontent an organized form with marches and protest demonstrations. Yet the Communists were not alone in their efforts to use the issue of carestia for political gain.[4] Industrialists from São Caetano opened two provisioning posts in the district in an ambitious effort to win votes by alleviating the problem. For the manager of the Cerâmica São Caetano, Armando de Arruda Pereira, the motivation was straightforward, since he and Roberto Simonsen, the owner of the enterprise, were PSD candidates for state deputy and federal senator, respectively.[5]

Simonsen's heavily financed campaign made highly visible, if awkward, efforts to win popular support throughout ABC. An advertisement in the *Jornal de São Caetano*, for example, declared: "Worker, your vote belongs to Roberto Simonsen and Armando de Arruda Pereira."[6] The propaganda for the PSD gubernatorial candidate Mario Tavares was equally inept and lacked the popular touch. Some proudly hailed his service in the government of the last Partido Republicano Paulista (PRP) president of the First Republic, Washington Luis, who had been deposed by Vargas in 1930. Another advertisement called the PSD candidate "the symbol of São Paulo against Communism."[7]

The PSD's difficulties might have provided the opposition UDN, the state's second-largest party, with a golden opportunity to overcome its minority status. The supporters of Brigadeiro Eduardo Gomes had long denounced the "regime of chronic hunger" caused by Getulismo and the Estado Novo. Moreover, socialist and Communist intellectuals had helped to found the UDN. Yet, like the PSD, the state UDN nominated a highly respectable politician of impeccable credentials and little popular appeal, Antônio de Almeida Prado, a liberal professor of medicine at the University of São Paulo.

In opening his campaign, Almeida Prado showed an acute intellectual awareness of the crisis of his style of Brazilian liberalism. In a hurried judgment in December 1945, he said, the people had unjustly perceived the UDN's presidential candidate Brigadeiro Gomes as "a plutocrat . . . [and] an exponent of the refined classes remote from the working and humble masses."[8] Yet the state UDN and its candidate were to prove incapable of moving beyond the restricted social boundaries of their 1945 electorate. For all his sympathy, this intellectual advocate of a reformist and mildly socialistic liberalism still spoke of the workers as the "others." Does not the fault for the 1945 defeat, he asked, lie with those of us who failed to provide them with education, exploited their ingenuousness, and failed to fulfill our promises? We must, he declared, "give up, without reserve and with our heart in our hands, a little of that which our privileges have granted us."[9]

However irritating Almeida Prado's sense of noblesse oblige may have been, the Communists had by no means ruled out the possibility of supporting the candidate of the state's second-largest party. Negotiations continued until the first days of January, when the state UDN leadership finally decided not to match the latest competing offer made to the PCB. This failure to effect a PCB-UDN alliance involved far more, however, than the mere breakdown of the negotiating process; it also involved questions of tactics and purpose.[10]

Almeida Prado was trying to confront a sense of loss and confusion shared by his stratum of São Paulo's high intelligentsia. The exodus from the interior to the capital, he said, had brought with it far more than just the "abandonment of agriculture" and urban overcrowding: it had unleashed a whole series of "social and economic maladjustments," such as "the housing crisis, strikes, popular agitations, [and] all sorts of unrest and disturbances."[11] While recognizing that it was impossible to stop these processes, Almeida Prado understood the threat they posed to the role that his group of native-born Paulista intellectuals had played in the past.[12] Faced with an agonizing choice, this group sought to stand aside from the dramatic confrontations around them. "In an epoch agitated by the most violent and controversial social demands," Almeida Prado said in his last speech of the campaign, "when all the classes have risen, attacking each other, fighting for their rights, it is extremely difficult for a statesman who does not wish to exploit any sentiment of hate on his behalf."[13]

The lesson of postwar politics demonstrated, however, that not everyone was willing to forsake the political advantages to be gained from existing social cleavages. In Almeida Prado's eyes, a new type of politician, "disreputable and irresponsible," had erupted onto the scene—populists such as Getúlio Vargas, Hugo Borghi, and Adhemar de Barros. These "unscrupulous adventurers" and "demagogues," he complained, have turned the people into "a faithful flock of sheep." Speaking in "the simplicity of their language and needs," they promised the people "everything to which they aspire."[14]

The competing gubernatorial candidacies of trabalhista Hugo Borghi and Adhemar de Barros for the new Partido Social Progressista (PSP) were an affront to the elitist sense of political propriety shared by supporters of the PSD and the UDN. The shocking characteristic of these controversial politicians had nothing to do with their social origin or upbringing, however. Hugo Borghi was an industrialist, banker, and cotton speculator, while Adhemar de Barros was the son of a politically well connected family of coffee planters active in the PRP. Educated as a medical doctor, Adhemar was involved in numerous entrepreneurial ventures, including several factories.[15]

Having established himself as São Paulo's most visible PTB leader, the flamboyant federal deputy Hugo Borghi represented a formidable threat to the PSD's Mario Tavares and the UDN's Almeida Prado. As financier of the queremista movement in 1945, the controversial Borghi had been a key speaker at the climactic 3 October 1945 rally in Rio de Janeiro where 100,000 demonstrators had called on Getúlio Vargas to become a presidential candidate.[16]

Like the PSD industrialist Roberto Simonsen, Borghi used his personal financial resources and connections to the maximum. Since the PTB lacked a São Paulo newspaper, Borghi's radio station became the party's most important means of communicating with its urban constituency. As president of São Paulo's Radio Clube, Borghi arranged for the nomination of the station's director, Gabriel Migliore, on the PTB slate for state assembly in 1947. Like Simonsen and Arruda Pereira, Borghi also sought votes in ABC by establishing a food distribution post of his Popular Provisioning Tents of the Workers of Brazil in November 1946.[17]

As the Paulista personification of trabalhismo, Borghi had no opponents for the gubernatorial nomination of the PTB. Yet his ambitions went beyond what Vargas and the national PTB were willing to countenance, so they canceled the state PTB diretório that had registered Borghi's candidacy. On the eve of the January 1947 election, the Supreme Electoral Court upheld the national PTB's position against Borghi.[18] By then, however, his candidacy had momentum, and he received PTB votes despite his formal registration as the nominee of the newly formed National Labor Party (Partido Trabalhista Nacional, or PTN).

While this PTB factional conflict was of little significance at the mass level, Borghi's trabalhista candidacy was unlikely to win the support of the Communists despite their cooperation with the queremista movement in 1945. Deteriorating relations between the PTB and the PCB reflected the bitter trade union conflicts that pitted the PTB's rightist union leaders against the Left/Center forces allied with the PCB. While the exact course of the negotiations is unclear, the PCB apparently ruled out the trabalhista option at an early point. Thus, twenty days before the election, the PCB was engaged in negotiations only with the UDN and with a small party, the PSP, that belonged to a competing candidate: Adhemar de Barros, another onetime protégé of Vargas.

A reluctant backer of Brigadeiro Gomes in 1945, Adhemar was isolated from the major currents of postwar Paulista politics because of his role as Vargas's intervenor in São Paulo during the Estado Novo. Ousted by Vargas in 1941, Adhemar was unwelcome in the PTB, while the Paulista PSD was led by former members of the traditional PRP irritated by his independence and antiparty behavior as intervenor. For the anti-Getulista UDN, which in São Paulo inherited the tradition of the anti-PRP Democratic Party, Adhemar's past association with Vargas (and earlier with the PRP as well) was sufficient to keep him marginalized within their party.[19]

In September 1945, Adhemar formed the Republican Progressive Party, based on the ties in the interior that he had cultivated as intervenor. In June 1946 he merged his skeletal organization with two other tiny parties, the National Union Party and the National Agrarian Party, to found the PSP as the vehicle for his candidacy for the governorship of São Paulo.[20] An improbable candidate, Adhemar nonetheless saw the electoral advantages to be gained by exploiting the clash of the elite parties, the UDN and the PSD, in the interior, and the bitter rivalry of the PTB and the PCB in the cities.

Adhemar's Search for Urban Allies: Populists and Communists in the Elections of January 1947

Adhemar drew important lessons from the failure of the UDN's "campaign of the white handkerchiefs" in 1945. Single-mindedly devoted to returning to the post of Paulista chief executive, he was realistic enough to recognize that a triumphant return could not be based solely on support from the interior of the state. The experience of 1945 convinced him of the need to penetrate urban areas, and he quickly realized that a radically new and pragmatic approach was needed in order to compete successfully in the urban electoral marketplace.

A man of enormous ambition, Adhemar was willing to take great risks in pursuit of the main prize. Although he was a product of the conservative PRP and the Estado Novo dictatorship, he had positioned himself to the left of center in the immediate postwar period. When Communists in ABC and elsewhere were jailed following the 29 October 1945 coup against Getúlio Vargas, Adhemar announced his support for the continued legality of the PCB. Over the next year, Adhemar's PSP would also cosponsor and participate in many activities with the PCB.[21]

Adhemar quite correctly perceived that the control of the established urban "political class," as exercised by the PSD and the UDN, would yield far less in electoral terms than it had in the past—a conclusion strengthened by the results of the 1945 voting. In early 1946, Adhemar began to seek out other leaders in urban areas, however unconventional, who could demonstrate any degree of popular support. Unlike the UDN's Almeida Prado, he was fully willing to exploit the hostilities generated by various sorts of social cleavage, as he did in the ABC municípios of São Bernardo do Campo and Santo André.

Although São Bernardo was less urbanized than the rest of ABC, its 18,000 residents had also suffered from black marketeering and shortages of essentials such as sugar, lard, cooking oil, and soap. The ongoing provisioning crisis in 1946 gave rise to a charismatic leader, the dynamic and pugnacious twenty-seven-year-old Tereza Delta, who to this day remains a controversial figure in local history. Known to her partisans as the Joan of Arc of São Bernardo, she was attacked as an irresponsible and demagogic carpetbagger by the local establishment.

A native of the state capital, Delta had been born to a single mother and had married and separated at an early age before opening the Delta Beauty Institute. She eventually went to live with the owner of the neighboring Castro House of Sewing Machines, and in 1943 she moved to São Bernardo where her companion had business connections. She quickly established a reputation as a pretty and unpredictably brash young woman prepared to take on anything and anybody.[22]

On Monday, 5 August 1946, Delta led a protest march to the São Bernardo *prefeitura municipal* (city hall). Anticipating trouble, police had already been posted at the prefeitura and the bigger local shops. The crowd of angry housewives, their children, and some local workers were confronted by the local police delegado who displayed orders banning the parade. With tempers rising, PSD Prefeito Wallace Cochrane Simonsen finally agreed to meet a small delegation if the crowd would disperse. In the meeting, Prefeito Simonsen argued that the problem was beyond his control, while denying the committee's right to speak for the people. The wealthy São Paulo banker, landowner, and industrialist was unprepared for what followed. Hundreds of workers from local factories took their lunch breaks on the streets and resolved not to return to work until the committee's demands had been met. With these additional demonstrators, the crowds began to canvass the local shopkeepers, demanding that they display all of their stocks and sell them at the official price. Intimidated, the merchants hastened to produce some scarce products, while those without invited the crowd to search their premises.[23]

For the small, peaceful village of São Bernardo, the events of August 1946 were unprecedented—guarded in the local memory as a veritable upheaval that marked an epoch. Indeed, São Bernardo's traditional way of life was already undergoing rapid change in 1946 with the construction of Brazil's largest and most ambitious highway project, the Via Anchieta from São Paulo to Santos. Initiated when Adhemar de Barros was intervenor, the Anchieta had destabilized the social hierarchy of São Bernardo by bringing several thousand construction laborers to the region. Scattered in camps along the highway's route, they were largely recruited from Minas Gerais and the northeast region of Brazil.[24] They were also active participants in the August turbulence, and they were central to Delta's emerging constituency. Without established ties in São Paulo, the laborers on the Anchieta lived in makeshift camps and were subject to arbitrary treatment by the State Department of Roads.[25] Unskilled, poor, and often darker-skinned, they were the object of disdain by longtime residents, including the skilled local furniture makers. Their local reception reflected the gap between São Bernardo's cohesive and rather conservative community of the past and these recent migrant laborers, carriers of new problems and difficulties.

The Communists had been quick to realize the political potential of the São Bernardo movement, which they hailed as the state's first "general strike against hunger."[26] Although the PCB was the first to court Delta, however, it did not long remain alone in seeking her support. In the latter part of 1946, Adhemar de Barros approached Delta with an eminently practical proposal: a future appointment as prefeita of São Bernardo in exchange for persuading her popular following to vote for him. In doing this, Adhemar co-opted an insurgent local leadership, without concern for the normal proprieties of elite politics or the established norms of respectability among the "conservative classes."

For São Bernardo's middle class and many of its tightly knit residents, including some workers, Tereza Delta was an outsider who violated all of their most cherished norms of female behavior and decorum. From their point of view, she was a disreputable character who was legally separated in a society still imbued with a very conservative Catholic morality. Moreover, she identified with and defended social outcasts such as those involved with the numbers game (*jogo de bicho*), whose abolition was the objective of a major "moralizing" campaign by the postwar Paulista UDN.[27]

Delta represents the epitome of many established ideas about populism and populist politicians. Demonstrating great personal courage, she used a militant but nonclass rhetoric that cast the people against the villains. While avoiding any systemic critique, she focused her attacks against merchants far more than employers. This strategy avoided any emphasis on class struggle in favor of a mobilization based on the general populace as consumers. A "courageous fighter for the cause of the humble ones," Delta also maintained the sort of patron-client relationship with her supporters that has often been described in the literature on populism. Of recent rural origin, her supporters were highly vulnerable to abuse and found in her the sort of patron they were looking for. While the Communists sought to politicize popular anger and direct it against the PSD intervenor, Macedo Soares, the tone of the protest was best captured by a worker who complained that "no one takes the side of the people; no governmental authority, that is."[28]

Yet the aptness of an illustration such as Tereza Delta has too often led scholars to ignore the variability of the populist phenomenon at the grass roots. If the São Bernardo case stands at one end of a continuum, very different populist dynamics can be found at the other end in the more heavily industrialized districts of Santo André and São Caetano do Sul. With a population of well over 100,000, these districts represented a far greater challenge for Adhemar de Barros, given the preexisting political and trade union mobilization of their 46,000 factory workers.

In Santo André, Adhemar could count on a small but experienced group of supporters, affiliated with his own political party, who, although electorally insignificant, were more open to the new political realities than any other group within the local political class. "A new world is being born" in the agitations of the postwar period, their second vice-president, Edmundo Soares de Souza, wrote in February 1946. "The old ideas, prejudices, and injustices are tumbling down." While "disillusioned statesmen find themselves at an impasse," he concluded, "only the aristocracy of money remains unshakable and without understanding, immune to the red injunctions of the present."[29]

The consciously innovative stance of this small middle-class faction, willing to court the Communists and labor, is exemplified by its Santo André party president, the forty-three-year-old Antônio Braga. Active in the local PRP in Ribeirão Pires before 1930, Braga had served as a city councilman in Santo André from 1936 to 1937 and remained politically active in opposition to the appointed prefeito Carvalho Sobrinho throughout the Estado Novo. In 1943, the local newspaper of Braga's faction, *O Imparcial*, was confiscated by censors, and several of its journalists were briefly imprisoned by the police.

Since 1940, Antônio Braga had owned a small pharmaceutical laboratory, which in 1945 employed ten workers. A visit by an Uruguayan trade union leader, the Communist Enrique Rodriguez, provided this small industrialist with his first opportunity to set himself off from his fellow employers and their political allies. On 9 January 1946 he published an article in the Communist newspaper, *Hoje*, in which he discussed his favorable impressions of the meeting. Braga reported that some workers viewed him with a certain distrust and others with curiosity, intrigued at the paradox of an industrialist attending a meeting to discuss "genuinely working-class interests, notably unionism," the "bugbear" of his fellow employers. Decrying the "unbridled ambition and greedy spirit" of the typical employer, he denounced the "false thinking and inhospitable pride" that led them to oppose the just demands and "perfectly rational and profoundly human aspirations" of their workers. Braga combined this carefully crafted rhetoric with an open admission of truths about employer-employee relations that must have easily won the approval of *Hoje*'s readers. Describing a "sad and revolting truth" about the labor justice system, Braga said that many "bosses prefer to spend 'one hundred' on able lawyers so as not to pay 'ten' to the worker who demands it with reason."[30]

Braga eschewed the condescending tone that infected the discourse of UDNistas like Almeida Prado, and flatly rejected the use of terms such as "philanthropy, altruism, or charity" that only increased "the vanity of the rich." He emphasized the need to make the ideals of equity, justice, and, above all, fraternity a reality, and concluded that it was simple justice to give the workers a little of what they were owed.[31]

Braga's discourse offered an alternative to the Left's rhetoric of class struggle, the PSD's overtly anticommunist, antiworker polemics, and the elitist condescension of Almeida Prado. In both tone and stance, Braga's rhetoric also presented a striking contrast to his fellow Adhemarista in São Bernardo, Tereza Delta. The astute Braga avoided depicting himself as the workers' patron, while his more substantive discourse went beyond Delta's simple opposition of good versus evil men. Accepting the equality of the parties involved, at least at the level of rhetoric, Braga and his group proposed a partnership between themselves and the workers who now possessed something that these professional politicians needed: their votes.

From the point of view of Santo André's Communist Party (which, as we have seen, had 28 percent of the local vote), Antônio Braga's remarks, while flattering, served at most to illustrate the feasibility of the party policy of "national union." They no doubt facilitated the PCB's eventual alliance with the PSP in January 1947, but there was no evidence of any mass response to or enlistment in the PSP in Santo André in the aftermath of such appeals. The Braga episode was thus of less significance for the workers than for the local political class of Santo André. These PSP initiatives represented the first, isolated dissent from the hegemony of conservative, elitist, and anti-labor ideas among local politicians.

To credibly seek the governorship, Adhemar realized that he needed far more substantial support in urban areas like ABC than could be offered by Tereza Delta and Antônio Braga. Delta's ability to turn out voters at the polls had never been tested, and Adhemar's Santo André supporters had mustered a mere 4 percent of the total votes in 1945. The PTB and the PCB, by contrast, had gained 71 percent of the vote, while Santo André's most voted-for candidate for federal deputy had been the Communist president of the local metalworkers' union, Euclides Savietto.

A formidable political operator, Adhemar was shrewd enough to turn his own lack of support in urban areas to his advantage, since the Communists did not see him as competition for their electoral base (as they did Hugo Borghi and the trabalhistas). In addition, Adhemar's imperative need for Communist support increased the PCB's confidence that it could, in fact, dictate terms in the event of victory. As a consequence, on 4 January 1947 the sensational news was released that an agreement had been reached between the PSP and the PCB. Prestes's followers nominated Adhemar as their candidate for governor, while the PSP agreed to a joint slate for federal deputies and the nomination of a Communist as one of the PSP candidates for senator. The alliance of the two parties was formalized in a published exchange of letters in which Adhemar pledged to defend the constitution, respect the legal existence of all parties, and take action against carestia and inflation.[32] This public agreement was supplemented by various secret assurances of positions for the PCB in his administration.

There was a great public furor over Adhemar's alliance with the Communists. São Paulo's Archbishop Carlos Carmelo de Vasconcelos Mota and the Catholic Electoral League immediately released a letter saying that no Catholic should vote for any PSP candidate. President Dutra openly criticized politicians who let electoral considerations tempt them into negotiations with those whose loyalties lay elsewhere. The PSD's call for a fight against communism was shared by many UDN leaders and voters, horrified at the alliance of leftist subversion and Getulista corruption.[33]

In breaking ranks with the state's political and economic establishment Adhemar was taking a serious risk, and his audacious gamble would test the loyalty of his supporters throughout the state. By the date of the election, 19 January 1947, political opinion in São Paulo had divided into two camps: all those oriented toward the urban working class, whether backing Adhemar de Barros or Hugo Borghi, were united in their rejection of the backward-looking formulas of the PSD; the overwhelming majority of the Paulista middle and upper classes, by contrast, were equally convinced that victory for the PSD was not only inevitable but essential.[34] Despite official harassment, the PCB retained its bold optimism.

The Election Results

Election day was calm and the voting took place without disruption. Voter turnout was less than in 1945, but the urban electorate had gained in importance: while urban industrial areas accounted for 44 percent of the state electorate in 1945, they had grown to 48 percent in January 1947. When the count ended, Adhemar had scored a major upset with 35 percent of the vote for governor, followed by the trabalhista Hugo Borghi with 31 percent, the PSD's Mario Tavares with 26 percent, and the UDN's Almeida Prado with a mere 8 percent of the statewide vote.[35]

Adhemar owed his triumph to a massive urban vote that gave him twice the support in urban industrial areas that he received in the rural interior. Contemporary observers were quick to credit these results to the generalized atmosphere of conflict between workers and employers. Writing in the business magazine *Digesto Econômico*, one analyst argued that the election demonstrated "the accentuated progress of class consciousness and the growing antagonism of the proletariat."[36]

In giving their votes overwhelmingly to the PSP/PCB or PTB candidates, urban voters punished the PSD of Intervenor Macedo Soares for its antipopular sins of omission and commission. Indeed, the major weakness of the conservative parties was their lack of support in urban areas like greater São Paulo, where the PSD vote declined by two-thirds and the UDN vote by one-fourth compared to the elections of 1945. The candidates of the PSD and the UDN received insignificant support in São Bernardo and Santo André, where the votes for Adhemar de Barros and Hugo Borghi were 79 and 91 percent of the total.[37]

In the most dramatic local development, a Communist trade unionist from Santo André became the only state deputy elected from the ABC region. A furniture worker, Armando Mazzo had led a major 1934 strike in his trade in São Bernardo; in later years he worked with the Santo André metalworkers' union. Arrested and manhandled by the police in September 1946, Mazzo could be said, in a sense, to have gone from jail to parliament.[38]

The state assembly results in ABC demonstrated a modest increase of PSP support to 11 percent, while the PTB lost ground to the Communists compared to 1945. With 22 percent of ABC's total vote, Mazzo came in first among PCB state assembly candidates with 5,175 votes, followed by the Communist lawyer for local unions, Lázaro Maria da Silva, with 1,330 and the leading female Communist, Carmen Savietto, with 650.[39]

With 15 percent, the most voted-for trabalhista candidate for state deputy was lawyer Gabriel Migliore, who won election with 3,468 ABC votes out of a statewide total of 6,628. As a director of Borghi's São Paulo radio station, Migliore was associated with a message of militancy and protest; being a nonresident, however, he would come to defer to Mazzo as the authentic representative of local workers.

The voters provided further evidence of class-based electoral behavior in decisively rejecting the extravagantly financed campaigns of Roberto Simonsen and Armando de Arruda Pereira, the owner and the manager of the Cerâmica São Caetano. Despite employing 1,378 workers in their factory in São Caetano, both men lost by wide margins, with Simonsen receiving only

326 votes for senator and manager Arruda Pereira a mere 112 for state deputy. Their top Communist competitors, by contrast, won 1,576 and 806 votes respectively in the district of São Caetano.[40]

The election of Adhemar, two PCB federal deputies, and strong PTB and PCB delegations to the state assembly promised a new beginning for labor in São Paulo. The workers, it seemed, would finally be accorded the recognition due them after decades of struggle. Emerging as the state's third-largest party—ahead of Adhemar's PSP—the PCB included in its eleven-member state assembly delegation Santo André's Mazzo; rubber worker Lourival Vilar, a state and national labor leader as well as a member of the PCB's National Committee; textile worker Roque Trevisan, head of the state trade union federation; and the noted Marxist historian Caio Prado Júnior.[41]

For Adhemar de Barros, the elections were a personal triumph. Although his party elected only nine deputies to the state legislature, his wide knowledge of the politics of the interior and his control of the state apparatus afforded him the means of consolidating his political base. His populist rival Hugo Borghi also had reason to be happy, although his hold over the second-ranked PTB delegation was shaky. The results were most discouraging for the UDN, which dropped from second to fourth place, while the PSD's control of the largest number of deputies did not make up for their catastrophic loss of the executive branch.

For Brazilian President Dutra, the victory of Adhemar de Barros and his PCB allies was the government's biggest political setback of the January 1947 elections. In Brazil's other nineteen states, the ruling PSD had done very well, winning the governorships of five states on its own and an additional six in coalition.[42] Only Brazil's most populated and industrialized state had elected a governor who was not only backed by the Communists but who had won without the support of either of the two elite parties, or of Getúlio's PTB.

The Paulista rebuff of Dutra's anticommunist campaign sent a resounding message to the conservative classes who had remained confident to the end that the PSD's Mario Tavares would win. Indeed, the decline in the UDN's vote compared to 1945 reflected a shift in political support that was meant to guarantee the victory of the lesser evil, the PSD, over the greater one, Adhemar and the Communists.[43] Moreover, the gubernatorial defeat of the government party itself, the PSD, was without precedent in Paulista history. The conservative classes and landowning oligarchy could no longer dictate the outcomes of state elections through rural coronelismo, as in Brazil's less-developed states, nor did they have the urban and working-class support that was now the key to winning political control of Brazil's richest and most populous state.[44]

Adhemar's victory fragmented the state's political and economic establishment and ended the tight top-down control that had been the essence of traditional boss rule in São Paulo.[45] At the same time, his triumph marked the emergence of a new type of political boss willing to court, even if opportunistically, the state's urban and working-class population. By changing the rules of the political game, Adhemar's election helped create the state's unique political system during the Populist Republic that ended in 1964.

To be sure, the upper-class establishment was far from resigned to its loss of control. In the storm that followed January 1947, it remained an open question whether Adhemar de Barros would even be allowed to assume the governorship in March 1947.[46] Less than twenty years earlier, the Brazilian political system had regularly "beheaded" less controversial candidates whom the establishment did not want in office. If Adhemar did finally take office, how would he conduct himself in relationship to his new working-class constituency? What meaning if any did his rhetoric of collaboration with labor hold for Paulista workers, their trade unions, and their political leaders?

Labor and the Populist Statecraft of Adhemar de Barros

The inauguration of São Paulo's first popularly elected governor on 14 March 1947 was a time of great jubilation with victory parades and celebrations throughout the capital. Having mollified his elite enemies enough to be inaugurated, Adhemar savored his triumphant return to the post of state executive that he had exercised, through dictatorial appointment, between 1938 and 1941.[47] Yet he faced difficult challenges as a democratically elected governor at a moment of great working-class mobilization and employer-government resistance. Improvising in unknown terrain, Adhemar elaborated a populist statecraft toward labor between mid-March and early May 1947 that illustrates both the innovations and the tensions of the populist enterprise.

For Adhemar's Communist and labor allies, the new governor and state assembly were the start of "a government of collaboration" in which the working class would have a major role. Three days after the inauguration, the state affiliate of the young Left/Center General Confederation of Brazilian Workers (CGTB) launched its nationwide unionization drive with a rally of tens of thousands of workers in São Paulo. Aiming at 200,000 new union members nationwide and 50,000 in the state, the CGTB sought to exploit the newly favorable conditions under a governor who it hoped would remove the obstacles to labor action. In particular, Paulista unionists were hopeful that the new democratic state government meant the end of the treatment of labor disputes as police questions. The governor, rumor had it, was even seriously considering the abolition of the São Paulo arm of the hated DOPS.[48]

The shift in the political arena left Paulista industrialists rightly apprehensive, since the federal government's labor relations responsibilities had been transferred to the State Labor Department in 1946. This powerful lever was now in the hands of the Communist/Progressive governor. It appeared that the strategy of resolving labor conflicts through governmental intervention and police repression was about to backfire on the industrialists. In a telegram hailing the prospect of Adhemar's "governing with the people," the president of Santo André's metalworkers' union, Victor Gentil Savietto, urged the governor to dismiss the head of the Labor Department, Eduardo Gabriel Saad, whose past involvement in antilabor violence and union interventions in São Caetano had earned him the hatred of trade unionists.[49]

Animated by their deepest hopes, São Paulo's Communists and the state's Left/Center labor movement were justly proud of their extraordinary victory. Indeed, Communist Senator Luis Carlos Prestes warned the Paulistas against allowing their triumph to go to their heads.[50] Yet the heady self-confidence of labor's leadership was directly in tune with the mood of the state's rank-and-file industrial workers, including many who had not dared to join in the strike movements of early 1946. In the general euphoria, even workers who had voted for Borghi could not fail to see the defeat of the PSD and UDN as heralding a new day for "the people."

Encouraged by Adhemar's inauguration, a small strike wave spread among the state's workers that combined the ongoing organizing efforts of labor activists and initiatives by rank-and-file workers. Four days after the inauguration, 1,500 Santo André textile workers began a week-long strike against the Rhodiaseta spinning and weaving division of the French-owned Rhodia company. Unlike the Rhodia chemical workers in Santo André, the predominantly female textile workers had not struck in 1946 and were not well integrated into the local textile workers' union headed by the rightist PTB leader Henrique Poleto. Fearful that their union leaders would mishandle the 1947 negotiations, several hundred textile workers, led by the union's Left/Center opposition, gathered on Sunday, 16 March 1947, to formulate their own demands, which were presented to management the next day.[51] When a meager wage increase was offered, the workers struck and received the immediate support of the factory's unionized foremen and supervisors (*mestres* and *contramestres*) as well. Parading from the factory to the union headquarters, the strikers convinced Poleto to call an official assembly that evening, at which the Rhodiaseta strikers were joined by activist textile workers from other plants.[52]

The strikers demanded 20–50 percent increases to be calculated on a wage base that included all bonuses paid to the workers. They also sought the paid weekly rest mentioned in the Constitution's Article 157—a demand raised at the 16 March meeting by the metalworkers' president Victor Savietto—and complained of dirty and insufficient bathroom facilities and dressing rooms, the lack of showers for blue-collar workers, and the twenty-minute lunch period. They also criticized the management's speed-up of production accompanied by repeated threats of suspension if workers failed to make their required quotas.

Women, who made up two-thirds of the Rhodia workforce, played a prominent role in Santo André's most important strike of the year.[53] Two women weavers chaired the gathering, which heard rank-and-file leaders like Tomas Delamo and Isoldina Pinto as well as union presidents Henrique Poleto and Otaviano Rocha Leme, the head of the metropolitan union of foremen and supervisors.

The unity and organization at the rank-and-file level was strong enough to force even a hostile PTB labor leader like Poleto to back the strike. Poleto's decision to cooperate reflected his recognition, once the strike began, of the legitimacy of the action despite the fact that it was being led by his militant union opponents.[54] Poleto's stance was also politically motivated, given his new responsibilities as president of the PTB diretório in Santo André.[55]

The political dimension of the strike was underlined by the appearance of ABC's newly sworn-in Communist state deputy Armando Mazzo. The former furniture worker spoke of the looming industrial crisis that made it imperative for the proletariat to defend "our national industries." The workers, he insisted, would be the first victims of the failure of any branch of industry as a result of renewed North American competition.[56]

In their advocacy of a nationalist drive to industrialize Brazil, postwar Communists and unionists like Mazzo shared common ground with politicians like Getúlio Vargas, and with Brazilian industrialists, who were also convinced that the nation's future lay in manufacturing.[57] Yet broad cross-class agreement over the path for national development did little to assure tranquil relations between employers and workers. For both groups, the immediate issues at stake were far more prosaic, with each seeking to use the shared patriotic goal to advance its own distinct interests.

In his comments to the Rhodiaseta strikers, ABC's first successful worker-politician favored increasing workers' productivity but argued that this must go hand in hand with fighting for better living and working conditions. One of the strikers made the implicit bargain even clearer. Acknowledging the need "to defend our industry and cooperate with the government for the progress of our country," José Rodrigues emphasized that "those who give also want to receive." To guarantee "the best, most rapid and active workers," he concluded, employers should provide "a just increase in our salary [as well as] working conditions fit for human beings and not cargo animals or slaves."[58]

The conflict in the postwar period revolved precisely around the employers' rejection of such a proposed bargain with labor. During the week-long Rhodiaseta strike, national Labor Minister Morvan Dias de Figueiredo explicitly attacked the "exaggerated" requests for wage increases in current labor court negotiations. Calling for increases that did not diverge from "economic reality," the Paulista manufacturer spoke of "a plan of agitation" designed to create "economic disequilibrium" and "confusion" in order to facilitate an unnamed group's sinister aims. Brazil must be careful, he warned, that the labor justice system not be converted into a disorganizing force in the national economy.[59]

As the new governor of Brazil's most industrialized state, Adhemar de Barros too had to deal with the frontal clash of material interests between workers and employers—and the style that he adopted for handling trade unionists and their political representatives was very different from that of his conservative predecessors. The PSD's identification of the state with the employers' side in labor/management disputes gave way to a new, more neutral stance and rhetoric.[60] On 24 March 1947, for example, Adhemar received delegations from the central labor councils of the state and city of São Paulo, accompanied by the national CGTB president, Communist Roberto Morena. Advancing demands for change in the State Labor Department, the trade unionists received a warm reception in which the governor expressed his full confidence in unionized workers and their leading organs. Adhemar promised action against the high cost of living and the people's "misery" and said he would devote his attention to the Labor Department within the week. He asked, in exchange, their cooperation in explaining to workers the need to avoid strikes. Police violence against workers or interference with union meetings, he further told his listeners, should be reported directly to him for action.[61]

Adhemar's meetings with such trade union and worker delegations were conducted on a far less paternalistic basis than in the past. Moreover, the labor delegations that trooped to the governor's mansion were far more assertive in their presentations, a reflection of trade union strength and labor's newfound political influence. In a symbolic departure, Adhemar even promised aid for strikers engaged in a bitter conflict with the São Paulo–Goiás Railroad.[62]

Yet Adhemar's unwillingness to identify automatically with employers, in the manner of the previous PSD state executive Macedo Soares, did not mean that he unequivocally identified with the workers and their unions and political parties. In fact, he had no interest in being the spokesman for the workers and little desire to accept the controversial PCB as a true partner in the state administration. Once elected to office, the governor sought to placate every interest without decisively alienating any single group—a populist hallmark. He publicly wooed workers with such gestures as a pledge of official support for a planned union May Day rally, and secretly made deals with the industrialists. Whatever the appearances, he had no intention of following a consistently prolabor course that would further harm his relations with the state's conservative classes, a decisive political constituency that could influence his ability to stay in office. Responsive to the industrialists who had opposed his election, a cautious Adhemar left the highly sensitive positions of secretary of public security and secretary of labor unfilled on inauguration day, when he announced his appointees to all other top posts.

As the weeks went by Paulista employers were displeased by the new governor's rhetoric but were reassured that he had not adopted, in practice, the wholeheartedly prolabor stance expected by the trade union movement. Despite earlier pledges to the unions, Adhemar did not immediately replace the antilabor Saad as head of the State Labor Department. A week after the inauguration, the hated Saad struck a blow against Santo André's labor movement when he ruled that local chemical industries must transfer their "union tax" payments from the more representative Left/Center chemical workers' organization to his favored group of former leaders of the chemical union.[63] Nor could he be expected to show much sympathy for the Rhodiaseta strikers.

A strike like the stoppage at Rhodiaseta placed Adhemar in a difficult situation by demonstrating that not all conflicts could be avoided or finessed. Consenting to an interview with the strikers, Adhemar sought to curry favor with a delegation led by state deputies Armando Mazzo of the PCB and José Alves da Cunha of the PTB. But he avoided assuming any direct responsibility for the outcome of the strike, despite his control over the Labor Department, which in turn exercised decisive influence in labor court proceedings.

Opening the Rhodiaseta hearing on 24 March 1947, Eduardo Saad endeavored to use Adhemar's popular support to convince the striking workers to return to work without a settlement. Encouraged, the lawyers for the employers refused to budge from their initial offer of a 10 percent wage increase and no provision for paid weekly rest. Unable to find a conciliatory formula, another Labor Department official asked the strikers, "Do you want Adhemar to defend you?" They answered that they did, and he counseled them again to return to work. While some workers accepted this as a pledge of the governor's personal intervention to resolve their complaints, most expressed surprise that a representative of Adhemar would want the workers to return to work "with their eyes on the floor." Other unionists pointed out that two of the officials present had participated in a raid, earlier that month, on the chemical workers' union headquarters in Santo André.[64]

In the aftermath, the Communists were quick to criticize the State Labor Department for contradicting what they believed should be the policies of the "democratic" governor who met with and verbally supported strikers. The discontent was focused on Saad: had he or had he not been truly authorized to act in Adhemar's name? Thus, from Adhemar's point of view, criticism was conveniently diverted from himself; at the same time, labor discontent with Saad provided him with an excuse to replace the latter with his own appointee in early April.

The Rhodiaseta episode revealed the inherent tensions between organized workers and populist politicians. When faced with hard choices it was clear that Adhemar's administration preferred to avoid a clear-cut decision as long as possible. As an initial response to grass-roots pressure, it preferred a vague message of "trust me," suggesting that the populist politician alone could resolve the workers' problems. When faced with sufficient pressure, however, Adhemar did in fact move toward meeting the demands of the workers' representatives. In the case of Rhodiaseta, higher-level negotiations resolved the strike on terms more or less favorable to the textile workers—a net gain for labor.[65]

On the whole, the previously stigmatized PCB and its labor allies found the events of March and April 1947 to be the auspicious beginning of a new era in Paulista politics and labor relations. Speaking on behalf of the PCB state assembly delegation on 30 April, Armando Mazzo proudly hailed the proletariat's decisive contribution to the "democratic conquests of the last years." While warning that the "forces of retrocession" had not given up "their reactionary aspirations," Mazzo optimistically celebrated the heightened organization and consciousness of the workers, "the class of the future."[66]

Yet these inexperienced newcomers to politics were far from controlling the unfolding political scenario. Indeed, the election of Adhemar de Barros and labor's new political influence posed a difficult challenge for the workers' movement in São Paulo: how to maintain and exert influence within a populist alliance. In this regard, the Achilles' heel of the entire postwar upsurge of labor militancy in Brazil lay in the absence of significant organized support in the countryside.[67] The dramatic entry of workers and the urban populace into politics in 1945, after all, should not obscure the continued centrality of the rural voters who still made up 52 percent of São Paulo's electorate.

The key to immediate postwar electoral success therefore lay with politicians like Adhemar who could combine elements from the two worlds of Paulista politics. As an experienced politician, Adhemar understood these realities and immediately set about broadening and consolidating his base of support in both rural and urban São Paulo. In the interior, he strengthened his following by winning over many traditional local political families and machines, thereby virtually liquidating the PSD. Simultaneously, he wooed trabalhistas by incorporating Hugo Borghi into his governing coalition. Adhemar's unexpected victory in 1947 thus prompted a reorganization of party allegiances in which the PSP won over elected officials and supporters of the PSD, the PTB, and even a group of UDN dissidents led by Paulo Nogueira.[68]

This display of political virtuosity and "unprincipled" flexibility could not be matched by the Communists, who were increasingly dependent on an ally whose need for their support was decreasing. During March and April 1947 the PCB's leverage in its dealings with Adhemar was, therefore, weaker than it might have been. The ousting of Eduardo Saad from the DET, for example, was not followed by the expected prolabor policies. The Communist newspaper *Hoje* was critical of Adhemar's new secretary of labor for his stance on such key issues as the department's autonomy from the federal government, union interventions, and freedom of association. Although he was eventually overruled by Adhemar after union protests, he even retreated, at first, from the governor's pledge of official support for the May Day rallies being organized by a Left/Center interunion commission.[69]

São Paulo's May Day celebrations of 1947 were nevertheless a hopeful moment for the state trade union movement and the PCB. Whereas planned rallies the year before had been banned by Intervenor Macedo Soares, the 1947 gathering of tens of thousands in the capital's Anhangabaú Valley was addressed by the governor and his new secretary of labor. In São Caetano, PSP Prefeito Alfredo Maluf also appeared at the unions' May Day celebration in a further display of governmental support for the workers' movement.[70] Before long, there would be somewhat less to celebrate.

The End of a Populist Interlude: Adhemar's "Betrayal" of the Communists

During the first months of his administration, Adhemar de Barros pioneered a new approach to the problems of organized labor. Whatever its limitations, his ambiguous stance reflected the strength of working-class mobilization and represented a net gain for labor. Yet his exercises in symbolic politics were viewed with a jaundiced eye by his conservative opponents at the national and state levels. Former Minister of War General Pedro Aurélio de Góes Monteiro, newly elected senator from Alagoas, would even claim to find "an imminent danger for democracy" in São Paulo's May Day celebrations.[71]

The conservative parties that had lost to Adhemar, the Paulista UDN and PSD, were quick to challenge the legitimacy of his electoral mandate. Formal appeals for presidential intervention were matched by a frenzy of informal conspiracies to the same end; thus survival was a principal preoccupation as Adhemar began his term in office. These escalating pressures from the Right were not easily neutralized by the popular support cultivated by Adhemar in the months after the January 1947 election.

The Communist/Progressive victory in São Paulo had reinforced the conviction of President Dutra and his powerful backers that decisive action was needed to restore discipline and hierarchy. The central thrust of this conservative counteroffensive, which coincided with the onset of the cold war, was the year-long drive to outlaw the Communist Party. By early May 1947, the Dutra administration was exerting intense and open pressure on the one undecided judge of the Supreme Electoral Court in an effort to break a two-to-two deadlock in the court.[72] On 7 May 1947, Judge Francisco de Paula da Rocha Lagoa finally announced his vote for cancellation (*cassação*) of the PCB's registry as a legal political party—an action followed by governmental interventions against militant labor unions.

Granted the power to oust state governors in the 1946 Constitution, President Dutra used the threat of intervention to pressure Adhemar to ally himself with the Paulista PSD and to support the cassação. Thus Adhemar de Barros faced the possibility of being removed from power if he stood by his campaign pledge to support the legal existence of the PCB. Faced with a threat to his political survival, he quickly capitulated and reached an agreement with Dutra to maintain himself in office by breaking with his leftist allies and backing a PSD candidate for vice-governor in November 1947. Starting two days after the decision to outlaw the Communist Party, Adhemar's state police raided hundreds of offices of the PCB and allied organizations throughout the state—a measure duplicated nationwide. The government's seizure of PCB records was followed by interventions, carried out by Adhemar's State Department of Labor, that ousted Left/Center leaderships in thirty-six Paulista trade unions, including several in ABC.

Adhemar's betrayal in May 1947 came as a surprise to the Communists and their Left/Center trade union allies and has gone down in Brazilian political history as the most dramatic demonstration of Adhemar's unprincipled opportunism. In perfunctory comments on the episode, commentators have generally chided the Communists for their own "opportunism" and "naiveté" in believing that anything but betrayal could ensue from an alliance with Adhemar de Barros. Most have assumed that Adhemar's break with the PCB was inevitable and had been planned by him from the outset.[73]

Yet there is no evidence that the Paulista governor would have turned on his leftist labor allies so decisively in May 1947 had it not been for the threat of federal intervention. Indeed, Adhemar's behavior in the six months after the cassação suggests that he would have preferred to continue his ambiguous policy of muddling through, conciliating all groups and alienating none. Although cooperating with the crackdown on labor and the Left, he had no intention of converting himself into a new version of the state's previous PSD intervenor, Macedo Soares. Adhemar was too realistic to adopt the PSD's brand of ideologically consistent conservatism untempered by electoral calculation. Indeed, the January 1947 elections clearly indicated that a vigorous antilabor stance was the road to political disaster—as it would be in São Paulo throughout the Populist Republic of 1945–64.

Past observers have also assumed that the raids of 9 May 1947 marked a definitive position taken by the Paulista governor vis-à-vis the PCB and labor. This impression is based largely on Adhemar's vigorous and murderous repression of suspected leftists in 1948 and 1949.[74] Yet such a repressive policy, as advocated by Dutra's PSD and the state's industrialists in late 1947, made no electoral sense in terms of Adhemar's key short-term political objective: winning the state's November 1947 municipal elections.

Eager to consolidate his rule in the face of entrenched and by no means resigned elite opponents, Adhemar was aware of the widespread working-class disapproval of the cassação of the PCB and the union interventions. A calculating politician, he was not about to assume any larger onus of blame than was absolutely necessary to satisfy his new "partners," Dutra and the Paulista PSD. Adhemar simply could not afford to squander whatever political capital he and his supporters might still retain in the state's urban industrial regions—especially since the final outcome of the PCB's supreme court appeal of the cassação was still uncertain.

From the governor's point of view, it was best to avoid the additional controversy that an extensive and intrusive anticommunist repression would have created in the state's urban areas. Indeed, police intervention against the PCB and its members was less between May and November 1947, a period in which the party was outlawed, than it had been during 1946 when it was legal. And the de facto legality enjoyed by the Paulista PCB greatly facilitated the victories of Communist slates, running under other party names, in the November 1947 municipal elections in industrial centers such as Santo André.[75]

The electoral calculations that motivated Adhemar at the state level were felt even more strongly in the micropolitical arena in urban areas. Eager to win over the Communists and their working-class voters, all of Santo André's middle-class political factions (except Dutra's PSD) actively courted the PCB. Even Santo André's PSP prefeito, Alfredo Maluf, joined in the protests against plans to oust elected Communist officials and invited Communist participation in Independence Day celebrations. Moreover, the prefeitura agreed to distribute special lower-priced textile goods through the Union of Democratic Women of Santo André, led by Communist Carmen Savietto.[76]

As intended, the Adhemaristas' opportunistic behavior created a difficult tactical problem for the Communists as they sought to marshall public support against the betrayal they had suffered at the hands of a man they now labeled a "reactionary capitalist politician." Adhemar's deliberately ambiguous stance was brilliantly designed to weaken the effect of these attacks at the level of mass popular opinion. By September 1947, Pedro Ventura Felippe de Araújo Pomar, a prominent PCB leader, felt compelled to criticize the widespread belief that "Adhemar did not betray the people" but had been forced to do what he did "by the fascists." He declared this an "illusion" of those who still believed in Adhemar's "demagoguery."[77]

This deliberately two-faced and opportunistic conduct represents an important dimension of the populist phenomenon as we have come to know it in postwar Brazil. Yet it is important to realize that São Paulo's conservative establishment was equally horrified by the behavior of Adhemar and his ilk in late 1947. While loudly claiming to fight communism, he was forsaking the demands of class solidarity and violating the spirit if not the letter of his deal with Dutra. As leaders of the previous PSD administration had warned Dutra in late January 1947, Adhemar's "known untrustworthiness and wild ambition" made any talk of a deal with Adhemar "to abandon the Communists" a dangerous proposition.[78]

These morally censurable tactics did indeed work for new-style politicians like Adhemar de Barros and were an endless source of frustration to both Left and Right, workers and industrialists, in postwar São Paulo. Unlike politicians definitively identified with one or another group, Adhemar founded his success on eschewing firm loyalties in order to maximize his flexibility in the free play of electoral politics. His calculatingly inconsistent behavior in 1947 captured the essence of his new approach to politics: "Don't expect me to be consistently on your side, but if I'm against you today, don't assume that I will not be with you tomorrow." If offered a deal more advantageous to his interests, Adhemar was fully prepared to change positions. But when carrying through his side of an agreement, he avoided precluding any of his options for the future. Always gauging the prevailing political winds, he sought, whenever possible, to anticipate their future direction.[79]

Nine • A Free Workers'

Movement in a Constitutional

Democracy

The PSP-PCB victory of Adhemar de Barros in January 1947 was greeted with euphoria among the state's urban working people, and the election of eleven Communist state deputies, including six workers, took on great symbolic and practical significance for São Paulo's trade unionists. The workers' movement, it seemed, was no longer a pariah but had finally attained a new status in Brazilian politics and industrial relations. Operating under new and more favorable conditions, the Left/Center trade unions set out to strengthen labor's grass roots while defending the movement's newfound autonomy from state control.

Election to the state assembly on the PCB ticket posed new challenges for experienced trade unionists like Santo André's Armando Mazzo or Roque Trevisan, head of the state labor federation. Yet scholars have paid no attention to the political practice of these working-class leaders and none have grappled with their hopes, ideals, and illusions in early to mid-1947. The briefness of this episode, which lasted less than a year, may explain in part the scholarly neglect of this early effort to unify the workers' economic and political struggles. Yet the recent prominence of labor-based political action in Brazil suggests that there is much to be learned from the efforts of these trade unionists to link the workers' immediate grievances to a broader program for the social and economic transformation of Brazilian society.

The outlawing of the Communist Party in May 1947 and the governmental intervention in the trade union movement that followed was a decisive blow to the postwar political opening and sheds light on the limitations of democracy during the Populist Republic. At the same time, popular resistance to the suppression of labor and Left produced the Communists' greatest political victories when they swept the November 1947 municipal elections in most of the state's industrial centers, including Santo André.

A Constitution that "Guarantees Us Our Rights": Communism, Nationalism, and the Defense of Working-Class Interests

Tens of thousands of Paulista workers attended the 17 March 1947 rally in downtown São Paulo that kicked off the union membership drive sponsored by the General Confederation of Brazilian Workers (CGTB). The CGTB's Secretary General Roberto Morena, who was from Rio de Janeiro, hailed the working-class vote that had given victory to Adhemar de Barros. At the same time, Morena emphasized that effective support for the new administration demanded a working class that was "united and organized in trade unions within a free workers' movement."[1]

Labor activists such as Morena were far from satisfied, however, with the state of the trade union movement in 1947. The small size of the unions during the Estado Novo, Morena said, might be explained by the police infiltration and repression of the period, but there were no such excuses in 1947. São Paulo's Osvaldo Pacheco, a dockworker and a Communist federal deputy, also talked of the need to neutralize the "opium injected" into the unions "during so many years of dictatorship." In a similar vein, PCB state deputy Roque Trevisan, president of the state union federation, had earlier criticized the bureaucracy that still predominated in the unions, which had failed "to [effectively] organize the working class in the workplace."[2]

These self-criticisms reflected the optimism of leftist labor leaders in early 1947 who sought to fill the political space created by the January 1947 electoral victory with a carefully planned and executed drive to win 50,000 new members for São Paulo's unions. At the same time, these union leaders sought to perfect the mechanisms for penetrating the workplace and actively involving the rank and file in the trade unions.[3]

The goals and techniques of this concerted unionization drive can be seen in the ABC industrial district of São Caetano. The central labor council president for ABC, Agobar Corrêa da Silva, reported on efforts to establish union commissions in *every* local factory in order to orient and direct the workers' struggle in the workplace. In this regard, Corrêa da Silva cited the Cerâmica São Caetano where, after a year, the union commission had won recognition and was meeting with management every week to resolve disputes.[4]

Yet recruiting union members was not enough in itself, Corrêa da Silva went on. All new members, especially the youth, must be given concrete tasks to encourage them to stop by the union headquarters every day. As leader of the civil construction and ceramics union, Corrêa da Silva emphasized that closer links could best be guaranteed if branch leaders were elected in every district where ABC's unions had members. Designed to build rank-and-file involvement, such tactics proved themselves in late February 1947 when hundreds of São Caetano General Motors workers, organized by the metalworkers' union, attended the local labor court's hearing on their dissídio. These mobilizational efforts met with considerable employer resistance, however. In March 1947, for example, forty-eight workers at Pignatari's Laminação Nacional de Metais factory were fired after they defied orders not to attend their dissídio.[5]

Increasingly confident, this generation of trade unionists emphatically rejected the government's continued interference in labor's affairs. On the eve of Adhemar's inauguration, the antilabor DET Director Eduardo Gabriel Saad seized the headquarters of the Santo André chemical workers' union on the day of scheduled union elections. The 1 March 1947 police occupation was the final step in a conflict involving a union diretório that, with one exception, had been ousted in mid-1946 by a membership dissatisfied with their behavior during the strikes earlier that year.[6]

The DET "invasion" in Santo André quickly became the object of the sort of protest that had met the arrests of local trade unionists the previous year. Within a week, worker delegations were visiting newspapers and government officials in São Paulo. Petitions were once again circulated in dozens of factories of all branches of industry to protest this arbitrary and unconstitutional measure. On 19 March 1947, 958 chemical workers signed protests in a display of support that the DET-backed leaders were unable to rival.[7]

"As workers conscious of our rights and determined to fight for respect of the Constitution," said local mason Antônio Cabrera in commenting on the intervention, "we will not permit our union organizations to continue under the threat of brutal interventions. The Constitution," he went on, "guarantees us the right to direct that which belongs to us and, within our unions, the decisions are made by assemblies of members."[8]

The invocation of the 1946 Constitution in this way was a new element in working-class discourse in Brazil. Before 1930, anarchist labor militants had often referred to the 1891 Constitution, especially its guarantees of free speech, press, and association, but only in a bitterly sarcastic sense. And the short-lived 1934 charter was quickly followed by the repression of 1935, while the phantom 1937 Constitution of the Estado Novo never became a major theme in workers' rhetoric. By contrast, the Constitution of 18 September 1946 was the first to have been formulated with substantial working-class participation and input.[9] Labor's leaders, the contemporary debate demonstrates, truly believed the Constitution's pledge of freedom of trade union organization, which, they thought, revoked those aspects of the *CLT* that violated trade union autonomy and freedom. They were equally certain that Dutra's unilateral antistrike decree of March 1946 had been rendered illegal by the Constitution's explicit guarantee of the right to strike.

Working-class activists also valued the document's formal democratic norms and its explicit endorsement of historic working-class demands. The 1946 Constitution of the Populist Republic was officially pledged to such labor goals as the eight-hour day, equal pay for equal work, minimum wages, night-work differentials, and restrictions on women's and children's labor. The Constitution also established the right to a safe workplace, pregnancy leave, restrictions on the employers' right to fire employees, and nationalist job guarantees for Brazilians. It even went beyond existing laws by promising, in its more visionary clauses, legal recognition of collective bargaining agreements, aid for the unemployed, general rights to sanitary, hospital, and medical assistance, and social security coverage against sickness, old age, disability, and death.[10]

In formulating these promises, the Constituent Assembly of 1946 proved, once again, that politicians who had never met industrial payrolls were willing to promise anything to the electorate in order to curry favor. Incorporating workers' demands into the Constitution did not, however, result in immediate change, and most of labor's gains were destined to remain paper victories. Nevertheless the constitutional guarantees gave legitimacy to the workers' claims and created new conditions for their struggles. For the first time, the fruits of a strategy of indirect action were rooted in the fundamental law of the land. From that point on, organized labor faced the challenge of generating the economic and political pressure to turn these abstract promises into reality.[11]

Operating as labor's de facto political arm, the PCB of São Paulo was well placed to defend workers' interests in mid-1947. Having won 173,647 votes, the Communists emerged from the January 1947 elections with the state assembly's third-largest delegation. Moreover, the Communist Party had experienced spectacular growth, from 1,000 members nationwide in early 1945 to 180,000 by May 1947, perhaps 60,000 of these in the state of São Paulo.[12]

The growth of the PCB was equally breathtaking in ABC: from under twenty members to close to 1,000. Present throughout the region, the PCB was especially strong in the heavily industrialized districts of Santo André and São Caetano, with eight and eleven active party organisms, respectively. Activity in the newly legal PCB was conducted on a completely public basis. The names of members were used in *Hoje*, and many of the more enthusiastic members even wore PCB buttons and decorations to work in local factories.[13]

It was not a knowledge of socialism or a special interest in Marxism-Leninism that drew workers to the Communist Party, however. In part, the PCB grew as a result of the enormous personal popularity of its leader, Luis Carlos Prestes. For twenty years, stories of the heroism and self-sacrifice of the "cavalier of hope" had circulated among both urban and rural populations. The popular image of Prestes was of a perpetual underdog persecuted for his actions on behalf of the people. Even many non-Communists spoke of his purity of purpose (though most thought it ill-directed), a quality unsullied by the compromise or ambiguity of normal politicians.[14]

Yet the role of personal charisma in party success can be easily overestimated. Ultimately, the PCB owed its postwar electoral success to its responsiveness to the prevalent mood of working-class self-assertion and its pragmatic emphasis on resolving workers' immediate problems.[15] Based upon the experience of the CDPs, the PCB Municipal Committee of Santo André drew up a detailed "Minimum Program" in March 1947, a good eight months prior to the municipal elections. Addressed to the "workers and people," the manifesto was a down-to-earth document that summarized the immediate grievances of the local citizens: the black market; high food prices and bus fares; the lack of a public swimming pool; inadequate schools, day-care centers, clinics, and hospitals; poor sanitary conditions, street lights, and upkeep of the roads; inadequate housing; and insufficient salaries for municipal workers. Specific neighborhoods were cited, and special attention was demanded for the district of São Caetano, which had suffered, the manifesto said, years of administrative neglect.[16]

This eminently practical program of municipal administration, however, did not exhaust the politics and strategy of the Communist Party, which claimed to stand for a larger program of radical social and economic reform. Indeed, top PCB leaders criticized excessive faith in the resolution of the problems of the people through the "simple realization of administrative plans"—evidence of "reformist tendencies" within the party's ranks in São Paulo. The people's problems, they emphasized, could never be resolved as long as the economic basis of reaction was left untouched.[17]

During the ten months that he exercised his electoral mandate, Santo André's Armando Mazzo was charged with making the connection between the workers' immediate interests and the problems of "imperialist exploitation" and "the monopoly of land." As the only deputy from ABC, Mazzo used the state assembly above all as a forum from which to call attention to the workers' grievances. While performing individual services for constituents,[18] he focused on the central concern of ABC's workers: an economic crisis in which the cost of living continued to rise, while some industries closed and others laid off workers and reduced the hours of work.

On two occasions, the Communist deputy presented long, well-researched reports and petitions that documented the "destruction" of Brazilian industry by the foreign competition. On 30 July 1947, Mazzo declared that 1,500 to 2,000 families in Santo André were without work "because of the entry of foreign products that we could make here like dishes, textiles, shoes, combs, etc." By 5 September, he presented an updated list of factories in ABC that had cut normal overtime, reduced working hours, laid off workers, or gone bankrupt. The workers, he declared, were suffering from an economic crisis that his colleagues preferred to ignore—a criticism seconded by PTB deputy Gabriel Migliore elected with votes from ABC. Layoffs alone, Mazzo reported, had hit 3,549 workers in ABC, a small but significant portion of the region's total industrial workforce of 46,000. The federal government, he charged, had artificially restricted credit because of Dutra's ties to the "imperialist trusts." Rather than capitulate to these interests, he suggested, the government should adopt the Communist program to save national industry through cheap credit, tariff barriers, and the widening of the internal market through agrarian reform.[19]

Such nationalistic themes were not new in Communist and labor discourse in 1947.[20] "Colonizing foreign capital" had been defined by the state PCB as the main enemy of the nation and the working class as early as June 1946. The reemergence of foreign industrial production, especially in the United States, the PCB argued, deprived Brazilian firms of foreign markets and even threatened to "invade" the national market as in the case of leather and shoe production. The rising unemployment that accompanied the industrial recession of 1947 seemed to give credibility to this antiimperialist rhetoric.[21]

The Communists sought to make their nationalist case to ABC's workers by highlighting working-class suffering that could be linked to the crisis of "national industry." Nationalist themes were tied to mass sentiment by politicizing the economic difficulties that followed the end of the wartime industrial expansion and prosperity. In ABC, Communists seized on the case of São Caetano's Electro-Aço factory, founded during the war, whose 335 workers were the first to strike in ABC in January 1946. By May, the company had gone bankrupt, leaving its newly unemployed workers with salaries due.[22] Workers were led by the PCB and the unions to suspect, as Electro-Aço worker Manoel Carreiro Gonçalves declared, that the plant had been targeted by "the imperialists who want to enslave our country" because Electro-Aço "produced steel as good as any foreign steel." Framed in this way, the working-class complaint about unemployment became a matter of national security. In reporting this "fight against imperialism," the PCB's newspaper *Hoje* cited the dictum of the nationalist military colonel, later general, Anapio Gomes, who declared that a country that did not "produce its own machines" was "practically a semicolonial one."[23]

Yet the Communist Party's nationalist stance was itself contradictory in the context of working-class life in ABC since it did not, in practice, result in any hostility to the foreign-owned enterprises that employed thousands of workers in the region. For local workers and trade unionists, the defense of Brazilian industry often seemed to refer less to actual foreign factory ownership than to the defense of "our" jobs.[24]

Agrarian reform was the second major theme of Communist propaganda in 1947. The PCB argued that semifeudal agrarian relations, based upon the concentration of land ownership, resulted in low income for the majority of the Brazilian population. Urban workers, they argued, then suffered from the increased labor competition fostered by rural migration to the cities. At the same time, these conditions held back the further expansion of industrial employment opportunities because they restricted the internal market for goods manufactured by ABC's workers.[25]

Haunted by a Specter: The Government's
Repression of Labor and the Left

For the three judges of the Tribunal Superior Eleitoral (TSE) who supported the cancellation (*cassação*) of the Communist Party's electoral registry, the PCB was a foreign-oriented "Communist fifth column" that threatened Brazil's survival. Judge José Antônio Nogueira, citing the *Communist Manifesto*, argued that the "specter" that had haunted Europe alone in 1848 had finally reached the shores of these Americas.[26]

The international dimension of intensifying cold war also cast its shadow over the decision of 7 May 1947. Two days earlier, the Communist ministers had been ousted from the French government. The TSE decision, as one judge pointed out, had "enormous national and international repercussions." The voluble rightist Senator Pedro Aurélio de Góes Monteiro was quick to point out that Brazil was the first postwar Latin American government to outlaw the Communist Party, an action that would be noted throughout the continent.[27]

In mid-1947, however, it was not at all clear that Dutra's bold initiatives would succeed in driving Brazilian politics to the right. The precarious three-to-two margin on the TSE was, in itself, a sign that the outlawing of the PCB was far from winning general political acceptance. To outlaw a political party that had signed and helped draft the 1946 Constitution, it seemed to many observers, was a dangerous step toward dictatorship—a charge repeatedly made by Senator Luis Carlos Prestes and other Communist deputies.[28]

The PCB national executive committee's immediate response was to call for calm while advising compliance with an unjust decision, which they denounced as an "assault on democracy." In fact, the practical consequences of the TSE action were not immediately clear to contemporaries. The PCB would be barred from running candidates for elective office on its own slate, but the TSE said nothing about Communists' running under other party labels. As the Communists emphasized, the cassação did not legally affect the PCB's other activities as a duly registered nonelectoral organization (*sociedade civil*). Even the party's official organ, *A Classe Operária*, they at first believed, would be allowed to reopen as a nonparty newspaper.[29]

The Communist Party was quickly disabused of its belief that the Dutra government would allow them to function as usual as long as they did not run candidates under their own name. Under a questionable interpretation of the TSE ruling, Dutra's minister of justice decreed that the loss of legal registry meant that all Communist activity should be halted and the PCB's property and records confiscated. On 9 May 1947, the police began a series of raids on the offices of the PCB and its related organisms throughout Brazil.

In São Paulo, governor Adhemar de Barros quickly pledged his support for the cassação and ordered the police to raid and seal all offices belonging to the PCB and related organizations. At 8:00 P.M. on Friday, 9 May 1947, Santo André's police delegado oversaw the lowering of the big sign at 41 Industrial Avenue that marked the headquarters of the Communist Party of Brazil, Santo André Municipal Committee. Following orders from the São Paulo DOPS, the police ended the one brief period of legal Communist activity in ABC. As elsewhere, the PCB made no attempt to offer physical resistance to the raids, and party officials were posted to oversee the legal inventory of their seized records and property.[30]

The police inventory told the story of an energetic movement that had made its presence felt: a large amount of printed matter, along with posters, buttons, photo badges of Prestes, a megaphone, and large placards and banners sporting the hammer and sickle. One stack of pamphlets contained the "theses" of the fourth PCB congress, which had been scheduled to begin three weeks after the TSE decision. On the walls were the framed portraits of Joseph Stalin, Constantino Castellani, Santo André's labor martyr of 1919, and Saint Sebastian—a selection that suggests the curious mix of elements that was postwar communism in ABC.

In the neighboring município of São Bernardo do Campo, Communist activities had been conducted on a far more modest scale by Antônio de Oliveira Marques, a local hardware merchant who served as the PCB's political secretary. The police delegado sealed the small party office that he had operated out of his home. In Santo André, by contrast, the closing of the central PCB headquarters was followed by raids on the offices of district committees in the neighborhoods of Utinga, Vila Camilópolis, and São Caetano. In heavily industrialized São Caetano, police officials followed in the belligerent footsteps of former subdelegado Eduardo Gabriel Saad. They officially warned the Communists present at the party headquarters at 102 Rua Pará that, from this date on, "no political meeting sponsored by any organ of the PCB" could be held in São Caetano.[31]

The raids in Santo André showed, once again, the close ties that bound the PCB with major local trade unions. The president of the metalworkers' union, Victor Gentil Savietto, was present during the raid on the Santo André PCB headquarters as an official party representative; and the branch office of his union in São Caetano was located in the same building as the district PCB headquarters, separated by only an interior door. In outlawing the PCB, the government clearly did not intend to spare the trade unions from which the Communist Party derived its strength. Indeed, the TSE majority justified the outlawing of the Communists by referring to the unparalleled postwar agitation that had seen, in the words of Judge Cândido Mesquita da Cunha Lobo, the growth of "strikes, restlessness, the virus of disobedience and unmeetable demands, crimes and revolts."[32]

On 8 May 1947, the government issued Decree 23,046, declaring that the unions must be kept "apart from all political and social movements." The decree stated that elected trade union diretórios were to be replaced by appointed juntas if the organization had given support to the CGTB or to its subordinate state and municipal central labor councils.[33] "I know that once again I will be labeled a reactionary," Labor Minister Morvan Dias de Figueiredo said in presenting Decree 23,046, but order could only be established by ousting those "whose only preoccupation is to agitate."[34] Yet Morvan Dias, a prominent Paulista industrialist, was quick to deny that the government planned to revoke Getúlio's *Consolidation of Labor Laws* (*CLT*) outright—a disclaimer that was proof of the legacy of Vargas's populism.[35] It was now impossible to entirely ignore the workers who wished to retain the advantages symbolized by the *CLT*.

At the same time, the surprising strength and independence of the postwar labor movement had reminded employers like Morvan Dias de Figueiredo that the maintenance of the *CLT* served important interests of theirs as well. With the government's labor relations system directly in the hands of the industrialists, Morvan Dias saw no reason to act upon his earlier public pledges to liberalize Brazil's labor legislation by removing "the corporative aspects" of the *CLT*. By late 1947, the U.S. labor attaché reported that his labor ministry sources were now convinced that any weakening of governmental controls over labor would inevitably produce a "Communist-dominated" labor movement.[36]

One day after Decree 23,046, the diretórios of thirty-six São Paulo trade unions had already been ousted. The labor movement of the left-wing stronghold of Santos was especially hard hit, with governmental intervention in sixteen unions in all, followed by fourteen in the city of São Paulo, four more in the metropolitan region including ABC, and two in the interior of the state. In all, the government had intervened in up to a quarter of São Paulo's legally recognized trade unions, especially those in major urban and industrial areas.[37]

The governmental interventions of 1947, as the U.S. scholar Robert Alexander has written, affected "virtually all unions led by members of the Communist Party, as well as many which were non-Communist, but militantly led." In the end of August, unofficial Labor Ministry estimates indicated that the government had already intervened in 170 trade unions with 300,000 members—more than a third of the nation's total union membership. And on 10 July 1947, the possibility of legal recourse against the government's action was ended by a Brazilian Supreme Court ruling that the trade union autonomy guaranteed by the 1946 constitution was "not a clear and unrestricted right."[38]

In ABC, the Santo André metalworkers' and civil construction/industrial ceramics workers' unions were turned over to appointed juntas under the terms of Decree 23,046, while the Santo André chemical workers' union was still under an intervention declared in March 1947. In late May, the diretório of the rubber workers' union of São Paulo and Santo André, headed by a non-Communist, was also ousted, as was the São Bernardo furniture workers' union, which initially had been left untouched despite its endorsement of the CGTB.[39]

In one stroke, the majority of ABC's industrial work force had been stripped of its right to representation by elected union officials. The nature of the juntas appointed to run the intervened unions increased the unease of local workers. Most juntas contained no former union officials because non-Communist Center forces refused to participate and thus give legitimacy to the government's actions. Lacking personal stature in the categoria, the new intervenors came to depend upon support from the security departments of various local factories. The least credible junta was appointed to take over the civil construction/ceramics union formerly headed by the Communist Alberto Zamignani: none of the three appointees had ever been workers in the categoria, and the junta's key figure was a youthful former student named Milton Miguéis who was linked to the political police and would in later years be charged several times as a confidence man. Vocal protests were soon being heard from ceramics workers, who felt that their dissídios were being mishandled due to the inexperience of the union intervenors.[40]

Turning Setbacks into Victory

Stripped of their institutional structures, the Communist and labor movements and their broader constituency had been defeated, but not routed. While awaiting the results of their appeals to the Supreme Court, the Communists sought to demonstrate, in the summer of 1947, that a political movement was far more than the sum of its property and offices. Forced to rely more on human than on material resources, the PCB made efforts to reestablish legal and only slightly camouflaged forms of organizational activity.

An alternative political party framework to replace the PCB had been established at the national level prior to the TSE decision. By early June, the Popular Progressive Party (PPP), headed by Army Major Henrique Oest, a World War II hero, was well on its way to meeting the legal requirements for registry. Collecting local signatures for recognition, Santo André's Communists continued their activities as representatives of the new PPP. On 28 June 1947, the Association of Paulista Workers (Agremiação Paulista de Trabalhadores) was also registered as the organized expression of Left/Center trade union activism.[41] These transparent maneuvers were easily thwarted by the government. The TSE simply refused to register the new PPP, while the founding meeting of the short-lived workers' association in September 1947 was broken up and the home of its secretary, Moacir Ramos, raided by the police.

Organization at the grass-roots level in areas like ABC, however, was not as easily controlled. Local unionists and workers continued to accept the legitimacy of their ousted leaders, while rejecting the government's intervention against the PCB and the unions. Despite the government's claims, Brazilian union members saw the intervened unions not as "Communist" organizations, but as institutions that served their needs and met their interests.[42] For thousands of ABC industrial workers, bewilderment soon gave way to a powerful sense of anger at the sudden seizure of "their" trade unions.

In spite of having been outlawed as a party, the Communists were far from isolated and found themselves the object of intense courting by other political forces. Although anticommunism had not disappeared, many local politicians could see little to be gained from openly supporting the unpopular TSE decision banning the PCB. The Communists were out, which was just as well, but there was no compelling reason to applaud the act if it might cost their party the support of the PCB's 6,000 voters.

This opportunistic tendency was strengthened as the issue shifted from the cassação of the PCB's electoral registry to the *cassação de mandatos* (cancellation of mandates), which was sought by Dutra and the PSD. Eager to oust those elected in 1945 and 1947, the government argued that the electoral mandates of Communists had been automatically canceled when the party lost its legal registry; this novel legal interpretation was rejected by even the TSE in early August.[43]

Actively competing for PCB support, local middle-class politicians in Santo André quickly adopted a stance of outright opposition to the cassação de mandatos. By 8 July 1947, the new consensus was formally expressed in a joint protest by six Santo André political parties that represented 90 percent of local voters. They vigorously objected to the efforts to oust Communist elected officials and attacked Dutra's proposed National Security Law (Lei de Segurança Nacional, or LSN) as a "blow to our young democracy." With only 6 percent of the vote, Dutra's PSD was the only party in Santo André to maintain a continuing loyalty to conservative orthodoxy.[44]

Like their competitors, São Paulo Communists focused their attention on the upcoming municipal elections. In late September 1947, PCB federal deputy Milton Caires de Brito laid out his party's plans for the state. Barring a statewide alliance with a single party, the PCB would negotiate agreements in each município with parties willing to accept its Minimum Program in whole or in part. In the areas with the greatest Communist strength, like Santo André, Caires de Brito said, the Communist Party claimed the right to name the candidate for prefeito and a common slate of *vereadores* (councilmen).[45]

The disappointment of local politicians over the PCB's refusal to support non-Communist candidates for prefeito was tempered by the widely shared conviction that Santo André's largest party would never be allowed to register its own candidates, as indicated by the TSE's refusal to register the PPP. Searching for a legally recognized party, the state PCB came to an agreement with the state diretório of the minuscule Partido Social Trabalhista (PST) in early October.[46] On 12 October 1947, fifteen local Communists met in Santo André to found a local diretório of the PST to nominate a complete slate of Communist candidates for the municipal elections. At least one ABC newspaper, *O Município*, foresaw voter confusion in the appearance of the candidates of Prestes running under the label of a national party that backed President Eurico Dutra.[47] The Santo André PCB, at least, avoided possible confusion by proudly listing "Communist" among the attributes in the candidate biographies that appeared in its campaign literature. The region's Communist state deputy Armando Mazzo headed the PST slate as candidate for prefeito municipal in Santo André.[48]

The developments of the second half of 1947 placed the Communists in the center of the electoral campaign in Santo André and São Caetano. An energized PCB quickly reestablished a commanding presence in ABC's industrial districts. Since there were no longer any PCB headquarters, PST shacks were set up in early November, with municipal permission, as centers for the storm of campaign activity that engulfed the region. Graffiti for the "candidates of Prestes" appeared on the walls of factories, bars, and even private homes, while a crescendo of rallies, door-to-door visits, and factory-gate appearances led up to election day. A truck equipped with loudspeakers and posters incessantly toured local neighborhoods. The Communists printed five times more sample ballots than there were voters and distributed over two thousand fund-raising lists to gather campaign contributions.[49]

Of the PCB's local competitors, only the Santo André PTB had a chance at winning the elections on its own. Yet the Santo André PTB, despite having received 34 percent of the January 1947 vote, was poorly positioned for the municipal race under its new leader, Henrique Poleto, the rightist president of the textile union. Unable to compete successfully at the grass-roots trade union level, Santo André's labor Right had used its bureaucratic ties to win appointments for several of its members in the newly intervened trade unions. Gervasto Maschio and Rafael Martins da Silva, intervenors in the chemical workers' and metalworkers' unions, respectively, were both members of the local PTB leadership in 1947.[50]

Although the PTB protested the cassação de mandatos, the party's complicity with the governmental interventions embittered independent Getulistas and undermined its credibility with thousands of local workers. Moreover, Santo André's PTB was also wracked by internal disputes over candidacies that were linked to factional conflicts within the state party.[51]

The efforts to establish a united front against the Communists among other non-Communist political parties were undermined by intensified competition within the local political class. Such individualistic proclivities and personal rivalries had always characterized middle-class politics, but in the past they had operated within a framework that discouraged the total dispersal of efforts. The defeat of the local PSD in postwar elections, however, resulted in a loss of the political discipline that had flowed from a middle-class unity around the political/economic establishment.[52] After an eleven-year wait for elections, no politician was willing to forgo his right to run for the highly coveted municipal offices in Santo André.

As the date grew near, the statewide elections of 19 November 1947 in São Paulo were the object of national attention, being widely viewed as a test of the relative strength of each political current. In the major statewide contest for vice-governor, Dutra, Adhemar, and Hugo Borghi backed the candidacy of PSD leader Luiz G. Novelli, Jr. Important factions of the Paulista PSD, discontented with this "imposed candidacy," backed PSD federal deputy Carlos Cyrillo, Jr., in a candidacy also endorsed by Getúlio Vargas's PTB.

In this context, the Communists had difficulty in developing an electoral policy for statewide contests, but in the end they campaigned for Cyrillo along with Vargas. As Prestes himself admitted, it was difficult for Communist voters to support a man so recently "at the service of reaction," but he argued it was essential in order to defeat Adhemar and Dutra. Eager to avoid abstentions among PCB supporters, party leader Pedro Pomar declared that "to vote is to resist."[53]

Campaigning in São Paulo, Getúlio Vargas concentrated his fire on the federal government, which had "given nothing to the workers" and now sought "to take away their jobs." "Reaction," he went on, hoped "to break down the unity of the proletariat" that was "an imperative of the national conscience today." In their only joint appearance, Getúlio addressed an Anhangabaú rally in the company of Communist Senator Luis Carlos Prestes on 4 November 1947. Getúlio declared that Dutra did "not wish to govern with the people," as president Juan Perón was doing in Argentina. While that neighboring nation prospered with the help of the workers, Brazilian industry, agriculture, and stock breeding were being annihilated by a government that left the workers with only one legacy, hunger.[54]

However great their prestige, the politicians recognized that the outcome of the elections would be determined, in the end, by the strength of their local supporters. Both Vargas and Prestes spoke at rallies in Santo André, the state's second-largest industrial center. The Communists also dispatched many other top leaders to campaign in ABC. In October, the Communist vereadora Arcelina Mochel from Rio de Janeiro appeared in São Caetano to appeal for female support for the candidates of the Left. The PCB's federal deputy from Pernambuco, Gregorio Bezerra, also campaigned in Santo André. Bezerra, a legendary leader of the 1935 Aliancista uprising, was accompanied by important São Paulo Communists such as federal deputy Diógenes de Arruda Câmara.[55]

As the campaign reached its climax, Santo André's Communists continued to benefit from the general conviction that the Communist/PST slate would be banned, in the end, from participation in the elections. This belief was strengthened by developments in October 1947: Brazil broke off relations with the Soviet Union, and the office of the Rio Communist newspaper, *Tribuna Popular*, was attacked by a mob. Rumors circulated that Santo André would be declared "a military base" and hence stripped of its right to elect its own prefeitos. These uncertainties guaranteed that the divided opponents of the PCB would continue to mute their fire in an effort to curry the favor of Communist voters.[56]

Sixteen days after the registry of the PST (PCB) municipal slates, the TSE informed its regional affiliate that the national PST had canceled its Paulista state diretório. In so doing, the conservative PST Senator Victorino de Brito Freire and the federal government believed that they had resolved the problem of Communist candidates in São Paulo. They had not, however, counted on the unexpected resistance of the regional electoral court (Tribunal Regional Eleitoral, or TRE) in São Paulo, which failed to carry out its responsibility to the anticommunist cause.[57]

The TRE did cancel the PST state diretório but, in accordance with a strict reading of the law, upheld the validity of the candidacies filed by that diretório when it had been legally recognized. The TRE decision of 7 November 1947 was hailed by the PCB's *Hoje* as a defeat of the last maneuver of the "small group close to the dictator." This unexpected development, two days before the scheduled elections, testified to the dispersal of power under the new democratic system that, as in January 1947, frustrated the plans of the central government.[58]

Electing "Fitting Representatives of the Working Class": The Municipal Elections of 9 November 1947

When election day arrived on 9 November 1947, the voters of Santo André and São Caetano were asked to choose from the full spectrum of political alternatives and candidates. In the end, a total of eight parties or coalitions presented slates for municipal office. An analysis of the occupations and origin of the candidates sheds light on the nature of the contending parties in Santo André's first fully democratic and representative municipal elections.

To legally register their slates, parties were required to file basic biographical data on their candidates with the electoral justice system. Surviving records enable us to establish the occupations of 129 nominees of five political parties, 58 percent of the total of 221 candidates presented by eight local parties. The available data include the two popular parties— PTB and PST (PCB)—and three major elite parties—PSP, UDN, and PSD. Together these parties won 75 percent of the total November 1947 vote.[59]

For this study, the declared occupations are divided into two broad categories: workers and nonworkers (including salaried employees, industrialists, liberal professionals, and merchants). Although acuity is lost in the latter category, this two-class scheme best reflects the polarized nature of the contemporary status system. Whether skilled or unskilled, the working class was still rigidly separated from the nonmanual higher social strata. The candidates' occupational composition will then be compared with the declared occupations of the local electorate in the município of Santo André as of 31 December 1948.[60]

The selection of people to run for office reflects a party's operational philosophy. Although not surprising, the underrepresentation of workers among the candidates of the elite parties is striking: while 60 percent of the adjusted electorate (excluding housewives) were workers, workers made up only 14 percent of the candidates of the elite parties. The fact that 86 percent of their candidates were nonworkers reveals the continued predominance within these parties of the traditional political constituency of the past—the politically active middle class.[61] Whether they were unable or unwilling to recruit worker candidates, the elite parties' strategy was potentially self-defeating during an election year in which workers were politically highly mobilized.

Santo André's Labor and Communist Parties, by contrast, were much more representative of the occupational distribution of the local electorate. Workers made up 36 percent of the PTB slate, which included three trade unionists who supported SESI (Serviço Social da Indústria), the industrialists' social service organ directed by Armando de Arruda Pereira. The PTB's eight working-class candidates included two unspecified workers, two furniture makers, a textile worker, a stevedore, a driver, and a baker.[62]

The Santo André PST (PCB) slate stands alone in overrepresenting workers among its candidates: fully 81 percent of its candidates were workers, versus 60 percent of the adjusted local electorate. The Communist (PST) slate also was far more representative of industrial workers than the PTB: the candidates included eight metalworkers, four unspecified workers, three ceramics workers, two chemical workers, two weavers, and one furniture worker. The remaining working-class candidates included two stonecutters, one bus driver, one tinsmith, one electrician, and one baker. Three small merchants and two "employees" completed the slate.[63]

The nomination by the PST (PCB) of eight metalworkers, the single most common occupation, demonstrates the central importance given by the party to Santo André's largest trade union. Both the former treasurer of the metalworkers' union, Alberto Salvadori, and a former vice president, Miguel Guillen, were chosen to run for vereador. Miguel Guillen had been a key rank-and-file leader at Pirelli and had lost his job in mid-1946 as a result of his leadership in the strike against the company. Another nominee, Carmen Savietto, had long served as unpaid accountant for the metalworkers' union headed by her cousins, Euclides and Victor, before May 1947.[64]

The composition of the PST (PCB) slate in Santo André might be explained by a hypothesis that the PCB's national self-image as the "party of the working class" led to candidate lists with disproportionate working-class representation. The evidence demonstrates, however, that Paulista Communists outside of ABC were not at all adverse to nominating nonworkers for office. Indeed, the Communist slates elsewhere in São Paulo were marked by an overrepresentation of nonworkers: half of the candidates on the PCB slate in the statewide contests of December 1945 and January 1947 were nonworkers, and so were six of the eleven PCB state deputies elected in January 1947.[65]

A comparison of the PST (PCB) municipal candidates nominated in Santo André and in the município of São Paulo in November 1947 suggests that the Communist Party in ABC was a more purely working-class organization than it was in the state capital. Half of the PST (PCB) slate in São Paulo, the state's largest concentration of industrial workers, were nonworkers, compared to only 20 percent of Santo André's slate.[66]

The skewed occupational breakdown of the PCB in the município of Santo André compared to that in São Paulo reflected the PCB's lack of appeal among the 40 percent of the local adjusted electorate that was non-working-class. Unlike the situation in the city of São Paulo, the smaller middle class in Santo André was part of the highly polarized and rigid social structure of ABC's industrial districts. Nonworkers in Santo André, moreover, were more tightly linked to the world of commerce, industry, and government than in São Paulo, and thus tended to identify more closely with the dominant elites. In São Paulo, by contrast, a minority of a larger and more diverse middle class was able to escape the bonds of patronage in the 1940s and to build ties with the labor movement and even the Communist Party.[67]

These conditions also encouraged Santo André's Communists to adopt an aggressive class identification that alienated the party's few local middle-class allies, such as the medical doctor Ari Doria, the former president of the Communist-led Comitê Democrático Progressista de Santo André in 1946. Four days prior to the election, Doria, running as Socialist candidate for prefeito, engaged in a noisy confrontation with aggressive Communist campaigners whom he found painting-over PSB slogans. In commenting on the incident, PST (PCB) candidate Iguatemy Lopes de Oliveira charged that the doctor was angry because the PCB refused to support the candidacy of a nonworker like Doria. The PCB and other "respected worker leaders," Lopes went on, had rejected Doria's invitation to run on the PSB slate because workers refused to serve as a "trampoline" to facilitate the election of an "outsider."[68]

The occupational division between workers and nonworkers among the nominees of Santo André's political parties also coincided with differences between those of rural origin and those born in urban areas. Data on the place of birth, an indicator of migratory flows, is available for the candidates of the PST (PCB) and two elite parties, the PSD and the PSP. All three parties were of overwhelmingly native-born Paulista origin (90–96 percent); however, half of the candidates of the elite parties were born in metropolitan São Paulo, including the 21–35 percent born in ABC itself, while three out of four of the Communist candidates in Santo André, by contrast, were born in the rural interior of São Paulo.[69]

In Santo André, the PCB sought to use the rural origin of its candidates to appeal for the votes of the majority of local industrial workers who were born in the interior. The PST (PCB) campaign propaganda listed seventeen of their thirty-two candidates as "of peasant origin" on their biographies—a further effort to identify their party with those who had migrated from rural areas.[70] Thus the automatic association of rural origin with less "class conscious" political behavior is clearly inadequate to explain working-class political dynamics in Santo André, where many workers of rural origin supported the Communist Party.

The working-class character of the postwar PCB in Santo André is abundantly clear, but the party's composition did not guarantee that workers would vote for the illegal PCB in November 1947. Although the PCB had 1,000 members in ABC in mid-1947, many were only loosely integrated into party life.[71] Of a possible electoral turnout of over 22,000, only 6,000–7,000 Santo André residents had voted for the PCB in the past. Would the PCB be able to mobilize their past voters and win new supporters? Would the non-Communist parties sufficiently fragment the remainder of the votes to facilitate a Communist victory?

A total of 21,000 residents of Santo André turned out to vote in the third postwar election on 9 November 1947.[72] Although the candidate for vice-governor backed by the PTB and PCB, Cyrillo, was defeated at the state level, he still commanded 56 percent of the total vote in Santo André.[73] In the more important municipal contests of November 1947, there was no similar trabalhista/Communist unity. Running against the slate of the PST (PCB), the PTB's candidate for prefeito, Ícaro Sydow, an outsider from São Paulo, received only 13 percent of the vote, tied for third place with the UDN's Luiz Meira. Even the PTB's slate of vereadores received only 15 percent of the total vote, demonstrating that the party's problems involved more than the nomination of Sydow, a man without local roots.[74]

The PTB's disastrous decline is especially significant given the composition of the party's candidates and the continued popularity of Getúlio Vargas. The November 1947 PTB vote in the município represented a drastic decline in support from the high point of 1945, when the trabalhistas had received 43 percent of Santo André's vote. Over the next thirteen months, the PTB's local electorate had declined by a moderate amount to 34 percent of the vote. During the ten months after the January 1947 election, however, the party vote shrank to less than half of its earlier share of the local electorate. This outcome reflected working-class unease with the PTB's cooperation with the government's unpopular union interventions and assault on the PCB.

If the PTB was the most dramatic loser in the November 1947 elections, the illegal PCB emerged as the biggest winner. Statewide, PCB slates, running under other party labels, came in first in the *câmara municipal* (municipal council) elections in the industrial centers of Santos, Sorocaba, São Paulo, and Santo André, as well as electing 145 vereadores in the rural interior.[75]

In Santo André, the Communist Party remained the largest vote-getter, despite its travails. Communist state deputy Armando Mazzo easily won election as prefeito municipal with 33 percent of the total vote. The PCB's slate of vereadores also came in first with 26 percent. With thirteen of thirty vereadores, the PCB would need only three allies on the câmara to completely dominate municipal administration. Illegality, union interventions, and anticommunist propaganda had not succeeded in defeating the PCB. Although the number of Communist votes for câmara (5,162, or 26 percent of the total) in November 1947 was a third lower than the PCB's vote for state assembly ten months earlier, the total of 6,483 votes received by the Communist candidate for prefeito, Mazzo, was virtually the same as he had received in January 1947 when elected on the PCB ticket; these results gain in significance due to the 8 percent decline in overall electoral participation between the two elections.[76]

The PSD and the PSP, "parties of government" past and present, did poorly on the whole. Internal divisions within Adhemar's PSP undermined support for the PSP candidate for prefeito—a mere 6 percent for Antônio Braga—although the power of incumbency was shown by the PSP's 19 percent of the vote for câmara municipal. Having thrown its support to the PDC candidate Antônio Flaquer, the PSD ran candidates only for câmara, maintaining the 5–6 percent vote share that it had registered in January 1947—a two-thirds decline from its vote in December 1945.

Rumors of the Communist victory in Santo André, despite the secrecy of the ballot count, were already circulating by the middle of the week after the Sunday, 9 November 1947, election. A sense of exaltation, tension, and apprehension built, until the official and final results were released on Saturday, 15 November. In a "Manifesto to the Laborers and People of Santo André," Armando Mazzo, Marcos Andreotti, and Carmen Savietto hailed, on behalf of the PST (PCB) slate, the "great victory" over Brazil's "reactionaries and fascists. For the first time in the history of Santo André, the workers have the opportunity of electing a worker as the chief of the local executive power . . . [and] fitting representatives of the working class and the people, men and women from within basic industry" to the câmara municipal.[77]

The consolidation of this victory, the writers of the manifesto went on, "depends upon the workers and people. The presence of men of confidence in the posts of government undoubtedly means a great deal. But it is the support of the organized people, above all, that allows popular governments to overcome the hindrances and obstacles of reaction." Citing Senator Prestes's appeal for "resistance, unity, and organization," they called for popular organization in unions, neighborhood groups, clubs, and guilds to guarantee this victory and the success of the Minimum Program of the new prefeito and câmara. "The proletariat and people of São Paulo and Brazil," they concluded, "have their eyes turned toward this great industrial center." With the people's support, they pledged "an administration equal to the level of industrial development in the município, the first among those that represent the progress and greatness of São Paulo, in the fight for the independence and happiness of Brazil. Viva Brasil! Viva São Paulo! Viva Santo André! Viva Democracia!"[78]

Ten • The Election

of 1950 and the Consolidation

of the Populist Republic

n 19 November 1947, five days after the release of the official election results, Santo André's Communist municipal officials and supporters traveled to São Paulo's Palace of Justice to receive the legal certificates verifying their election victory. The new Communist prefeito and thirteen vereadores spent the following six weeks in constant activity as they awaited their formal inauguration on 1 January 1948. With confidence in Brazil's new democracy, they paid only perfunctory attention to the electoral court appeals that were filed by the Partido Democrata Cristão (PDC) and Adhemar's Partido Social Progressista (PSP) in Santo André on 17, 19, and 22 November 1947. The general euphoria in Santo André was not disturbed even when the police intervened on 23 November to prevent a planned celebration rally.[1] For the first time in Brazilian history, workers were going to demonstrate their capacity as elected municipal officials in one of Brazil's most important industrial centers.

Brazil's political, military, and economic elites, however, were far from willing to accept the PCB's electoral victories of 9 November as the inevitable price of democratic rule. If the elected Communists were permitted to take office, the PCB's control over the prefeitura and the câmara municipal would allow them to consolidate their mass electoral base, thus nullifying the government's repressive drive. It was inconceivable, the Santo André PDC argued in its appeal to the São Paulo Tribunal Regional Eleitoral (TRE), "that the government . . . of the heart of the Paulista industrial park . . . [would] be turned over to the Communists."[2]

In certifying the PST (PCB) electoral victories, the São Paulo TRE reaffirmed its principled legal position of early November 1947—but the final decision would be made by the federal Tribunal Superior Eleitoral (TSE), which had outlawed the PCB in May 1947. Meeting a day before the scheduled inauguration in Santo André, a divided TSE overturned the São Paulo TRE ruling and sustained the PDC/PSP appeal, ordering that the votes cast for the PST (PCB) candidates in Santo André be invalidated. In so doing, the TSE gave the prefeitura to the PDC's losing candidate, Antônio Flaquer, and, calculating new electoral quotients, gave half of the PST's câmara seats to the PSP, with the rest to be distributed among the losing candidates of other parties.[3]

The TSE thus embraced an unusual and controversial interpretation of the law by creating a new class of voters whose ballots were essentially annulled. Many parties and jurists interpreted the relevant law to require the holding of new elections for prefeito and câmara without the participation of the PCB or its candidates.[4] But this procedure, although democratic, had serious limitations from the point of view of the Dutra administration: holding new elections would unleash a competition for the support of the PCB and its sizable bloc of voters among the other parties. The TSE's decision to divide the PCB's seats among the losing candidates, on the other hand, gave the non-Communist parties a stake in the cassação of the PCB and would make alliances more difficult in the future.

Thus the final, municipal, stage of the democratization process that began in December 1945 witnessed the discarding of tens of thousands of votes in the state of São Paulo that had been cast for legally registered candidates whose election victories had been sanctioned by São Paulo's electoral justice system. The inauguration of Santo André's first postwar prefeito and câmara municipal on 1 January 1948, less than twenty-four hours after the TSE's decision in Rio de Janeiro, took place in an atmosphere of shock, disbelief, and, for some, relief.

Informed of the TSE's decision by telegram on 31 December 1947, São Paulo's TRE played less of a role in the events of the following day than the state government of Adhemar de Barros. The residents of Santo André awoke on 1 January 1948 to find the downtown area occupied by the soldiers and cavalry of the state militia, while policemen with dogs patrolled the streets. Water trucks with hoses were positioned at strategic points, and the crowds that gathered for a protest march to the site of the inauguration were dispersed. With tempers rising, the downtown area was soon transformed into a battleground in which protestors were beaten and arrested, rocks were thrown, and blows were exchanged with the police over a three-hour period.[5]

Communist state deputy and prefeito *cassado* (canceled) Armando Mazzo was physically barred from entering by the police, while a reporter from the PCB's daily newspaper, *Hoje*, was ejected from the inauguration. With the dispersal of the crowds, the police continued to patrol the streets and visited the homes of known Communists. In at least one instance, the police fired into the empty house of the unemployed metalworker and vereador cassado Miguel Guillen, who had already gone into hiding.[6]

Two days after the ouster of the PCB's elected municipal candidates, the police raided and closed the offices of *Hoje* in São Paulo. On 12 January, Senator Luis Carlos Prestes and the PCB's fourteen federal deputies appeared for the last time in the federal parliament. In São Paulo, the PCB's eleven state deputies were likewise ousted from the state assembly.[7] Not all of the practices of the First Republic, it was clear, had been ended; means could still be found to "behead" elected officials who were out of favor with those in power.

On 22 January 1948, three conservative parties signed a national interparty accord that formally allied the liberal opposition União Democrática Nacional (UDN) and the small Partido Republicano (PR) with the PSD of President Eurico Dutra. In Santo André, the inauguration of Antônio Flaquer as prefeito marked the return of the Flaquer family to control of the local prefeitura, which it had last held in 1914. The inauguration of Fioravante Zampol as president of Santo André's câmara returned control to yet another conservative political veteran.[8]

The views of Santo André's new leadership on the social question also suggested a return to an idealized past. In campaigning for office, Antônio Flaquer, praising his grandfather, had invited the support of all who valued "their Christian faith" and refused "to make common cause with disorder." Fifty years of industrial progress, he argued, showed that capital and labor could cooperate harmoniously without "social convulsions." Later in 1948, Zampol was unsuccessful in convincing the câmara to pass a resolution against the enforcement of existing social and labor legislation. The Flaquer/Zampol team chose the conservative *Borda do Campo* newspaper to publish the official notices of the municipal government. In 1949, the former PSD organ still publicly lamented the enfranchisement of ABC's workers. "Today," the newspaper remarked bitterly, "everything that says it is democratic attracts like a magnet. Even if it is a totalitarian fable."[9]

Santo André's câmara and prefeitura had thus been returned to the hands of the politically active, conservative-minded middle class, which had failed, for the first time in local history, to win control at the ballot box in 1947. The ouster of half of the elected câmara also dramatically altered the social composition of the município's legislative power. Ten of the thirteen PST (PCB) vereadores cassados were workers, while only one of the eleven new vereadores for whom occupations are known was a worker; six of the replacement vereadores were self-described industrialists, capitalists, or proprietors.[10]

The government's labor relations system in the late 1940s was also transformed and bent to the will of industrial employers. Even the rightist PTB trade unionist Henrique Poleto, who had supported the government's union interventions the previous year, was angered in 1948 by the blatant perversion of the labor justice system.[11] The significance of the government's minimum wage legislation was lessened by Dutra's refusal to support any increases; minimum wages remained unchanged between 1943 and 1951 despite the ongoing inflation that ate into workers' real wages.[12] And with control of the trade unions placed firmly in the hands of procompany elements, ABC's labor organizations now discouraged membership involvement and favored the harmless pursuit of welfare programs and sewing and typing classes.

The late forties were thus marked by the triumph of the police approach to labor matters. Under the conditions of escalating cold war, dozens of activist workers, including Marcos Andreotti, were fired, and an array of legal and extralegal harassment was used against many of the PCB's most widely known figures—including a ninety-day imprisonment for Santo André's Armando Mazzo in 1948. Both the regular and the political-social police were once again given free reign to pursue all those whom they considered subversives and agitators. In November 1948, police invaded the Vila Assunção cemetery to disperse a crowd that had gathered to commemorate the death of Constantino Castellani, Santo André's labor martyr of 1919.[13]

The collapse of the workers' earlier, exaggerated hopes, combined with these repressive new conditions, resulted in the disappearance of Santo André's previously vibrant Left/Center trade unionism and mass Communist movement. The PCB's elaborate organization in ABC's factory districts did not survive this massive defeat. Within a year, the PCB was reduced from one thousand members to several dozen activists, often unemployed, who functioned as a militant minority acting outside the official structures of legal trade unionism. As in the First Republic, ABC's radicals maintained an independent União Geral dos Trabalhadores (UGT) in Santo André whose grandiloquent title was no substitute for its limited influence and lack of a significant following.[14] The dissolution of the unprecedented labor militancy of 1945–47 left a legacy of widespread cynicism, apathy, and fear, and many workers felt they had been misled by their radical leaders.

A Return to the Past? Placing Postwar Defeats in Historical Perspective

The great mass movements of 1945–47 had been, it seemed, a mirage that was rudely dissipated by the victories of Dutra and the conservative classes in 1948. The postwar illusions of labor radicals now gave way to an equally strong belief that Brazilian democracy was merely a false name for the continuation of the dictatorship of the Estado Novo. Had democracy truly proved itself a mere illusion that beguiled the masses with fictitious freedoms? Did the return of the police approach to the social question after 1947 reveal the unchanging and unchangeable essence of capitalism? Was it indeed possible to return to a time when workers had been ignored or handled solely in a repressive manner?

These depressing questions haunted ABC's handful of activist workers after January 1948. Yet the government-employer drive against working-class political militancy and aggressive trade unionism could not nullify the vast changes that had occurred since the opening of ABC's first large-scale factories at the turn of the century. From 1,000 workers in 1900, ABC's industrial employment had grown to 4,300 in 1920, and 22,000 in 1940, and would grow to 46,000 by the end of the decade.[15] And Brazil's industrial revolution was not limited to a numerical increase in the number of industrial workers or to the growing importance of industrial production within the national economy: industrial production itself had been profoundly transformed during these fifty years. In 1920, ABC's industry had still been marked by the predominance of the partially mechanized small shops characteristic of the era of competitive capitalism; by the 1940s, however, factories employing 300 or more workers accounted for the bulk of the industrial labor force.

During the early decades of Paulista industrialization, the ties of craft and ethnic loyalty had obscured the divisions between social classes.

Large-scale factory production undermined this world and put an end to the democratic character of the skilled worker/small shop nexus. The sort of paternalistic authority and influence wielded by small employers in the past was no longer possible. Indeed, it was the rise of factory production and the consequent threat to the semiartisanal conditions prevalent in São Bernardo's furniture industry that fueled the militancy of local furniture makers in the thirties.

The factories of Santo André and São Caetano, by contrast, had long been characterized by a widening gap between the employers and their workers with the growth of the bureaucratic and impersonal forms of management demanded by modern corporate enterprise. Large-scale mechanized industry also reinforced the factory's internal hierarchy by institutionalizing very different roles for workers and management.

As the factory destroyed opportunities for skilled workers, São Paulo's anarchists had led an emerging labor movement toward a radical break with the classless ideologies of immigrant progress. In emphasizing a strictly economic form of struggle, the labor radicals of the first decade of the twentieth century had found a common ground with the militancy of São Paulo's skilled workers who, like the stonecutters, were best situated to strike successfully. Yet this sort of strike militancy—"direct action," in anarchist parlance—was far more difficult for the factory proletariat at that time. Even those factory workers who possessed the leverage of skill, like the weavers, proved unable to prevail over their employers in this manner. To strike successfully required factory workers to organize in much larger numbers under workplace conditions in which leadership was very difficult to sustain. Moreover, their powerful and wealthy employers were able to mobilize the oligarchical state on their behalf—a police approach to labor affairs that further lessened the prospects for an exclusive reliance on direct working-class action.

At the same time, the factory environment generated a growing feeling that workers had little in common with their managers or the distant corporate owners. The end of the illusion that a worker might become an employer allowed the new factory proletariat to develop a more global sense of "us" versus "them." This development was further encouraged by the numerical predominance of unskilled labor and the inability of skilled workers to exercise independent power in the new factory environment.

The adoption of welfare capitalist measures by many larger industrial employers was an attempt to neutralize the negative impact of the increasing depersonalization of the relationship between employers and the work force. While removing some of the workers' most elementary grievances, this new approach to labor relations could not fully neutralize labor discontent. Indeed, the greater intensity and pace of work of these mechanized factories itself created powerful shared complaints.

These transformations in the nature of industrial production had a profound impact upon the prospects for working-class struggle as well as upon the ideologies orienting the labor movement. The potential cohesiveness of the new industrial working class was amply demonstrated by the labor militancy that swept metropolitan São Paulo between 1917 and 1919. The anarchist-led workers' movement of that period reflected this shift in the mass base of labor militancy. For the first time, labor's leadership looked favorably upon means of resolving workers' grievances other than strikes, boycotts, demonstrations, and other forms of direct action. The formulation of demands for state regulation of the conditions of employment and consumption represented an important step toward the acceptance of new forms of indirect action.

Industrial workers thus sought to outflank the employers' overwhelming power within the workplace by calling on forces outside the private sphere of employer/employee relations. This course of action was thwarted in São Paulo, however, by the long-standing alliance between the factory owners and the ruling Partido Republicano Paulista that prevented any intervention by the state government or politicians on the workers' behalf. When repression destroyed the state labor movement after 1919, surviving labor radicals quickly embraced the tenentes' political revolution with the objective of overthrowing the oligarchical state.

Working-class activism on a significant scale did not reappear in the state until the eve of the Revolution of 1930 that ousted São Paulo's rulers from national dominance. The regime of Getúlio Vargas, although it was by no means hostile to industry, advanced the sort of state intervention in labor affairs that was not favored by the industrialists. Imbued with a less elitist conception of the role of the state, the new regime sought to reconcile conflicting interests rather than simply translating private economic interests into public policy. While not abandoning coercion as an option for handling workers' discontent, the new government added co-optive mechanisms to forestall labor unrest and gain popular allies.

Governmental initiatives in social legislation and the creation of an arena of legitimate trade union activity radically altered the form and nature of working-class action. Further opportunities were created by the turbulent political disputes of the early thirties that pitted São Paulo's dominant elites against the federal government of Vargas. A new generation of labor militants was quick to exploit these openings as a means of facilitating the organization of the industrial working class. At the same time, the radically new conditions of struggle demanded a modification of the ideas of labor's activist minority.

By 1933–34, São Paulo's new legal labor movement reflected the numerical predominance of the industrial working class and the defeat of the forms of revolutionary unionism that had long predominated in the Paulista workers' movement. The new state-sanctioned trade unions, no longer restricted to a radical minority of activists, were to become mass working-class institutions without stated revolutionary goals. The lessening of the disincentives to involvement also increased the degree of political pluralism within the union movement.

During the First Republic, the labor movement had been wracked by impassioned debates over the utility of direct action (such as strikes) versus indirect action (through political means). The innovative approach of the Vargas regime after 1930, as both an ally and an opponent of labor, rendered this dispute irrelevant: both direct and indirect action were necessary in this new setting. In fact, the political conflicts of the thirties made strikes easier to undertake, even if success was still problematic.

For the first time, the Paulista labor movement confronted the need for a political strategy. How was labor to gain the political influence needed to win the enforcement or improvement of the government's social and labor legislation? Since industrial workers were a minority of the population even in São Paulo, alliances with other social groups and political forces would be necessary in order to influence the state.

The new legal labor movement developed an approach that distinguished between economic action, which was the sphere of the trade union, and political action, for which parties and electoral alliances were necessary. Labor-based political action in São Paulo, however, remained largely a theoretical matter in the thirties because of the absence of any significant working-class electoral participation. Therefore, the most important example of labor's new politicized approach could be found in union support for the Aliança Nacional Libertadora (ANL, or Aliança) in 1935. Advocating a nonelectoral, revolutionary route, the Aliança, during its brief existence, pioneered a nationalist rhetoric with social overtones combined with new techniques of popular agitation.

This ill-conceived alliance with the radicalized middle-class ANL ended in defeat and repression by the state. Unlike what had happened in 1919, however, labor's rout in the mid-1930s was not followed by a period of complete disorganization. Rejecting the industrialists' appeals, the federal government retained the legal union structures and allowed the reemergence of a chastened labor movement in late 1938 under stricter governmental control.

Far from homogeneous in outlook, the government apparatus of the Estado Novo era pursued diverse approaches to labor affairs. While independent labor militancy was repressed and union affairs were monitored, important elements allied with Getúlio Vargas were also conscious of the political possibilities of the growing industrial proletariat. They were eager to expand the state's role in labor relations and were prepared to intervene far more actively in the previously private sphere of employer/employee relations.

Brazil's workers shared a partial coincidence of interest with Vargas, their powerful new ally, who brought the working class important advances between 1938 and 1940. A more effective enforcement of existing social legislation, the establishment of an extensive system of labor courts, and the setting of minimum wages brought some real benefits to ABC's industrial workers despite the repressive conditions of the early Estado Novo.

Although these material gains were later nullified during the economic mobilization of World War II, the freer wartime political conditions made possible a more expansive self-organization of the workers. The ABC unions exploited these new possibilities by constructing a small but important network of union activists within local factories, an undertaking facilitated by the demand for labor generated by the wartime industrial expansion.

Brazil's industrial employers did not accept the naive theories of the regime's labor ideologues who preached class peace based upon the incorporation of the worker into the state. They remained convinced that the creation of any form of trade union organization benefited those who preached class struggle in Brazil. Even elements within the government foresaw dangerous side effects of the state's sponsorship of working-class organization. "The process of unionization," some members of the government told a foreign observer in 1942, "might render the laboring masses more class conscious," and the legal trade unions might provide an organizational framework for radicalism.[16]

Getúlio Vargas and Labor Minister Alexandre Marcondes Filho hoped to minimize this threat by controlling the political potential of Brazil's million industrial workers through a top-down form of mobilization. Their plans were frustrated, however, by the divisions within the Estado Novo regime brought on by the succession process in 1944 and 1945. In response to the conservative alliance of top military men and the elite opposition organizing against him, Getúlio sponsored the entry of urban workers into national politics. In mid-1945, Vargas made an unprecedented appeal for popular political mobilization through queremismo and an alliance that included even Luis Carlos Prestes and the PCB. At the same time, he ended the elitist electoral system of the past by enfranchising urban workers through ex officio voter registration and the compulsory vote. In an unprecedented demonstration of popular energies, urban workers emerged from the elections of 2 December 1945 as a dynamic political force of considerable influence.

The transformation of the electoral marketplace in industrial areas like ABC ended the political monopoly long enjoyed by the conservative and elitist middle class. Galvanized into motion during the queremista upsurge, ABC's industrial workers had displayed a strong loyalty to Getúlio Vargas, which was not, however, wholly transferred to his newly created Labor Party (PTB). Encouraged to make labor's voice heard in 1945, Santo André's workers and union members also gave their votes to PCB candidate Euclides Savietto, the president of the local metalworkers' union, who received more votes for federal deputy than any other candidate in ABC. Popular Getulismo, it was clear, did not mean automatic working-class support for the candidates of Getúlio's PTB.

Contrary to the scholarly consensus, Getúlio's populist policies and appeals had not demobilized the working class. As one contemporary observer wrote in 1947, São Paulo's workers, "animated by unionism and a labor legislation that gave them a sense of class," had attained a high degree of political consciousness by 1945.[17] The dictator's labor-oriented rhetoric encouraged the workers' sense of collective identity and helped give it a unified political direction.

In December 1945 the PTB and the PCB together received 71 percent of the vote in Santo André, a level of combined support that the two popular parties sustained in the elections of January 1947. The industrial workers of Santo André and São Caetano thus made their economic status as wage earners the basis for a common political identity at the voting booth. This unusual degree of working-class unity was indicative of a profound working-class discontent but fell far short, at the mass level, of expressing an antisystemic or revolutionary ideology—a "reformist" reality that influenced the policies of the Communist Party.

The spirit of working-class self-assertion that mobilized thousands of workers laid the basis for the expansion of ABC's unions into mass institutions. Freed of the repressive restrictions of the Estado Novo, the corporatist unionism of class peace and collaboration with the state was transformed, almost overnight, into a grass-roots trade unionism of struggle. Labor sought to use the new freedoms of the democratic era and the resultant mass backing to establish collective bargaining relationships, on a plant-to-plant basis, through the dissídio coletivo procedure allowed by law.

The perceived success of working-class mobilization in 1945 led, in February and March 1946, to a mass strike wave by 100,000 industrial workers in metropolitan São Paulo. A fifth of ABC's workers joined the strikes against the region's largest industrial employers. Unlike the industrial militancy of 1934–35, however, that of 1946 was most characteristic of the industrial proletariat and not the furniture workers of São Bernardo; for the first time, the industrial working class was unquestionably the dominant force within the organized workers' movement. The unsuccessful Pirelli strikes of 1934 and 1935 had shown the difficulty of sustaining worker morale during work stoppages in a single factory. A strike movement common to the workers of many factories, however, helped to lessen the sense of isolation and hopelessness that had undermined the earlier movements. As in 1917 and 1919, generalized strike movements increased workers' confidence that victories could be won despite employer and police coercion.

The postwar upsurge was marked, above all, by the direct leadership of Paulista workers and was, in this regard, quite different from the ANL ten years earlier, in which a radicalized middle class had provided the key leadership cadre. Moreover, in contrast to the events of 1935, the existence of a mobilized and relatively united working class in 1946 enabled labor leaders to make electoral struggle a focus of this new phase.

The workers' postwar economic and political struggles in ABC were led by an ambitious group of Left/Center trade unionists who sought to establish a comprehensive class politics. The concept of labor-based political action had remained a theoretical matter in the early thirties, despite the acceptance of the distinction between the union and the political party. After 1945, theory became reality in the form of a mass-membership Communist Party in São Paulo led by activists who had emerged from the struggles of 1930–35. Continuities could also be found in Getúlio's new Labor Party (PTB) in São Paulo, which combined some of the surviving leaders of the state's Socialist Party of the early 1930s with some rightist trade union leaders who had emerged during that period.

Faced with newly militant unions and an assertive labor politics, São Paulo's industrialists turned to their political allies in the state and federal governments. President Dutra and his São Paulo PSD intervenor, José Carlos de Macedo Soares, moved in mid-1946 to resolve the industrialists' problems through a repressive antistrike law. They also outlawed the PCB, intensified police harassment of the Left, and endorsed governmental intervention in the unions. The employers used their disciplinary powers to punish activist workers in ABC, at the same time that they established the employer-administered social service agency Serviço Social da Indústria (SESI), designed as an extension, outside the workplace, of their welfare capitalist measures inside the factories.

In adopting a repressive approach to labor militancy, the São Paulo PSD satisfied an important elite constituency but did not perceive the political price of this approach under Brazil's new democratic conditions. The PSD's open identification with the interests of a handful of employers alienated the 275,000 or more Paulista industrial workers who made up the largest single group within the 50 percent of the state electorate to be found in urban areas. Because they still held to the political wisdom of the past, the state's political and economic establishment failed to anticipate the damage that a cohesive anti-PSD vote by urban workers could do to the party's chances in the gubernatorial elections of January 1947. Retaining its confidence in the rural vote, the PSD did not foresee the possibility that this large urban voting bloc would erode the rural foundations of conservative political power. But in fact, the existence of a prospective ally in the cities cleared the way for a splintering of the vote in the interior of São Paulo, which had been, for so many years, under the exclusive control of those with power over the machinery of government.

Under the new political conditions of postwar São Paulo, the key to statewide victory would be found in some combination of urban and rural backing. The conservative vote of São Paulo's traditional political forces was divided between the PSD's and the UDN's gubernatorial candidates in the face of a formidable challenge by the PTB's Hugo Borghi. Yet the prospects of the Paulista PTB were weakened by internal divisions and by its bitter split with the PCB, which barred the sort of urban labor unity that had guaranteed the relative success of the queremismo movement of 1945.

These circumstances opened the way for an ambitious and experienced former intervenor, Adhemar de Barros. In 1947, he made a bold gamble modeled after that of his onetime mentor Getúlio Vargas. The son of a coffee planter and himself a factory owner, Adhemar was fully prepared to place his personal objectives as a political entrepreneur ahead of those of the state's conservative classes. With cool realpolitik, he signed a formal pact with the Paulista PCB, and the PSP-PCB alliance then fielded a joint slate of candidates.

The united effort of the state's political and economic establishment was not sufficient to defeat the combination of Adhemar de Barros and the Communist Party. In January 1947, São Paulo was the only state in Brazil where the gubernatorial candidates of the conservative parties were defeated in the elections. Not only was the PCB to be a formal participant in the government of Brazil's largest state, but the Communists were also the third-largest party in the state assembly. The processes of urban and industrial development, which had gone their furthest in São Paulo, had clearly unleashed new electoral dynamics that were very different from those in Brazil's less developed states.

Analyzing the elections for an audience of São Paulo businessmen, a Paulista academic, Clovis Leite Ribeiro, argued that under conditions of universal secret suffrage, the proletarian majority tended to use its numbers "to seize economic power from the minority." While the events of 1945 to 1947 were far from portending revolution, working-class voters could directly infringe upon the power, wealth, and authority of São Paulo's industrial employers. If state intervention in labor relations had stirred employer opposition even when undertaken by a dictatorial regime, the prospect of these powers being wielded by a government dependent in whole or in part upon working-class votes was intolerable. Ribeiro continued his analysis by observing that, when faced with this threat, those who hold economic power tend to defend their wealth by usurping political power "by fraud or violence."[18] And Paulista industrialists did indeed appeal for support of their interests from the federal government of President Dutra, whose electoral base was in the conservative agrarian elites of the less developed regions of Brazil. With the transformation of politics in São Paulo, Paulista industrialists found their interests best protected by a national alliance with the military and the conservative politicians of those poorer regions.

With the May 1947 cassação of the PCB, Dutra forced a choice upon

Adhemar de Barros under the threat of federal intervention in São Paulo. Adhemar had allied with the PCB earlier that year for strictly pragmatic reasons in pursuit of his goal of returning to control of the state government. There was little question, therefore, as to where São Paulo's most enduring populist politician would stand when the PCB tie endangered his political survival: he was fully prepared to turn on his onetime allies in exchange for a pledge of nonintervention by the Dutra administration.

Yet Adhemar was too sly and ambitious a politician to become subservient to employers or the federal government. During his early months in office, for example, he sought to have it both ways by pleasing Left/Center labor while at the same time doing as little as possible to antagonize the state's employers. In a similar fashion, in late 1947, acutely aware of the upcoming municipal elections, he had no interest in carrying out the sort of ideologically consistent repression that the PSD's Macedo Soares had directed in 1946. Keeping his options open, Adhemar proved an only partly faithful ally of the PSD, whose candidate for vice-governor he backed in November 1947.[19]

Dutra's anticommunist policies in the late forties were increasingly in tune with an elite backlash against the disruptive consequences of Getúlio's populist gamble of 1945—a reality perceived by the PTB, which was the only party in January 1948 to vote solidly against the cassação of the PCB's deputies in the federal parliament.[20] The attack on the PCB, which had received only 10 percent of the national vote, served a larger purpose of rolling back the changes associated with the new urban popular politics of the postwar period.

The threat from below, especially the Communist Party's postwar electoral victories, led to the national interparty accord of January 1948 through which the liberal opposition backers of Brigadeiro Eduardo Gomes, the UDN and the PR, formally allied themselves with Dutra's majoritarian PSD, the party of the Estado Novo dictatorship. In discussion since mid-1946, the agreement symbolized the elites' yearning for a return to power through a conservative consensus. Whatever their differences with each other, the signatories were united by their distaste for trabalhismo and a refusal to tolerate a working-class movement like the PCB that aspired to power—whether for reformist or revolutionary ends—in the name of democracy. This violation of generally accepted democratic theory did not, however, necessarily mean a return to dictatorship, as was charged by Brazil's Communists.

There was a historical precedent to the PCB's warning that the outlaw-

ing and persecution of their party might be the first step in the destruction
of Brazil's new electoral democracy: in 1937, at a time of far less working-
class mobilization, Brazil's postwar president Dutra had used an anticommunist fabrication as a pretext for dictatorship. In the end, however, the
memory of 1937 would itself set limits to the president's antidemocratic
actions. The coup that had established the Estado Novo, after all, had been
designed to prevent, not a Communist revolution, but an electoral triumph
of competing elite factions.

To win parliamentary backing for the outlawing of the PCB, Dutra would
have to overcome the suspicions of his elite opponents who feared that this
extraordinary measure might establish a precedent that could be used
against their own elected officials.[21] Democratic rule, moreover, guaranteed a greater role for even the minority factions of the elite and gave the
government's supporters in parliament a greater degree of personal power
and prominence than would have been possible under a discretionary
regime.

The road to dictatorship in the late forties was further blocked by the
existence of millions of Brazilians of all classes who believed in democracy.
In 1937, public opinion had been an amorphous force, and most of the
people had not had the experience of direct political participation. The
Estado Novo dictatorship had been followed, however, by an extraordinary
outburst of political mobilization in which millions had become convinced
that each citizen had a right to a say in who would govern the country. In
deference to this sentiment, even among supporters of the government,
the Dutra administration had to defend the cassação of the PCB as a
defense of democracy—a pledge that implied important restrictions on the
government's freedom of action.

Thus there would be no moves in the late 1940s to end secret suffrage.
Brazil's experienced men of government, formed under less than fully
democratic conditions before 1945, would have felt more comfortable with a
return to the restricted political participation of the past, and to this end,
Brazil's elite parties did abolish the ex officio voter registration procedure
that allowed the automatic enrollment of workers through their place of
employment.[22] However, moves to discourage popular participation
through more extreme alterations of electoral rules, such as restricting
eligibility or abolishing the compulsory vote, carried the risk of serious
electoral damage to their proponents. Moreover, there was no guarantee
that the enactment of such measures would actually reduce the electoral
participation by those new sectors of the population who had recently

acquired the right to vote. And indeed, abolition of ex officio registration, the elite's miraculous panacea, did not have the expected result after 1950.

Under these conditions, the conservative counteroffensive of 1948–50 did not, in the end, severely restrict popular participation in Brazil's new electoral democracy. The preservation of democratic forms of rule did not prevent the Dutra government from halting the advance of the Left, but it did guarantee that there would be no wholesale return to the closed and elitist political system of the past. Basic rights were cynically distorted and rendered almost meaningless, but they could not be publicly disavowed. A similar logic applied to Brazil's labor relations system: there could be no return to the days when labor was handled strictly through repression. The government could intervene in the unions, and the labor justice system could be tilted against the workers, but it was impossible to abolish Brazil's array of social and labor legislation even at a moment when its progressive potential was being suppressed.

We Are All Populists Now: A Profile

Thus the conservative triumph after 1948 was never as complete as it seemed. Beneath the surface, new forces were at work whose full impact had not yet been felt. In São Paulo the existence of a massive urban popular constituency led to a widening divergence between the politicians based in the rural interior and the growing number of politicians responsive to an urban constituency. In São Paulo, trabalhismo had become a profession.[23]

These realities were demonstrated during the state assembly debates over the cassação of the PCB's elected officials in late 1947. One PTB state deputy, Gabriel Migliore, an attorney and a radio station operator elected largely with votes from Santo André, freely used an expansive democratic rhetoric to denounce the threatened cassação of elected Communist officials: "I never understood democracy," he declared, "to be the will of the powerful." He condemned the robbing of election mandates as a return to the past when elections "were fabricated in cabinet offices, political deal-making meetings, and palace corridors to be foisted upon a people . . . [denied] the right to freely choose their own representatives."[24]

In Santo André, the first session of the câmara that followed the Inauguration Day clashes of 1 January 1948 demonstrated that at least one non-Communist politician was willing to gamble his future on the people. Full of righteous indignation, UDN vereador Anacleto Campanella urged the passage on 3 January of a resolution protesting the TSE's robbery of the votes of some 6,000 local residents. Although he was heatedly attacked by his fellow vereadores, the twenty-three-year-old accountant from São Caetano nonetheless went on to denounce the violence used against the crowd of protestors on 1 January. Refusing to support a motion in praise of the police at the following meeting, Campanella also attacked his colleagues for evicting from the inauguration a reporter from the Communist daily *Hoje*, which he called a "decent and honest newspaper."[25]

Only one other Santo André vereador, Syr Martins of the Partido Socialista Brasileiro (PSB), a dentist and a Protestant, chose to even moderately criticize the cassação of the PCB's elected officials in Santo André. The more traditional elements of the local political class were hostile to Campanella's demagogic pursuit of "Communist voters." Yet Anacleto Campanella was far from being a radical: a supporter of Brigadeiro Eduardo Gomes in 1945, he had also been a prominent backer of the PSD candidacies of industrialist Roberto Simonsen and São Caetano's Armando de Arruda Pereira in January 1947.[26]

The new electoral realities in ABC, it was clear, were fully capable of reshaping the urban-based politicians of even a preeminently antipopulist party. Indeed, this grass-roots UDN contribution to the emergence of populism has too often been overlooked because of an excessive emphasis on the UDN's anti-Getulista self-image. Historians have for too long associated populism exclusively with opponents of the UDN, like Getúlio Vargas and Adhemar de Barros. In urban industrial areas like Santo André, however, the followers of a traditionally elitist party that condemned populist strategies were forced to court working-class voters in order to avoid defeat. After Vargas, it was impossible to have a liberal democracy without working-class participation.

While many national UDN leaders cynically supported the cassação as "juridically possible and politically convenient," Santo André's UDN opposed it by invoking the liberal principles defended by Brigadeiro Gomes in 1945. This democratic juridical language of "eternal vigilance" and opposition to the Estado Novo provided a powerful rhetoric for Santo André's UDNistas in 1947, when the focus of attack had shifted from Getúlio Vargas to President Dutra.[27]

Dutra's effort to strip the Communist Party of its elected posts, a columnist wrote in the São Caetano UDN newspaper, *O Município*, was an attack upon the Constitution and the people that pleased only the "reactionary" and "totalitarian" currents of national life. The UDNista *Jornal de São Caetano* vigorously criticized the outlawing of the PCB, interventions in unions, and the proposed National Security Law as undemocratic methods of fighting extremism.[28] These militant UDNistas said they would not be deterred by opponents' charges that they were "crypto-Communists" or by the position taken by the UDN at the national level. The *Jornal* lamented that Gomes's party had, to date, capitulated to these "liberty-killing attacks." The São Caetano UDN also shared its aggressive rhetoric with the Santo André Socialist Party (PSB), the party of the other critical vereador Syr Martins. In July, a Socialist meeting to protest the repression of the PCB was banned by the local police delegado—the object of acerbic commentary in the *Jornal*.[29]

The stance adopted by Campanella and his followers in January 1948 reflected their confidence that the working-class vote could be used to overcome the public disapproval Campanella's behavior had earned among the conservative classes. His combativeness stemmed from the insurgent thrust introduced into ABC's politics since 1945. "The lessons of the present," as one Santo André populist journalist and politician had declared in April 1947, "have taught us to understand that it is our duty to struggle."[30]

A hotheaded orator, Campanella pioneered a nationalistic populist rhetoric with an openly anti-status-quo orientation. In August 1948, he was the founding president of São Caetano's Center for the Study and Defense of National Oil (Centro de Estudos e Defesa do Petróleo Nacional).[31] This push for a state monopoly of oil exploration, ownership, and refining was the single most visible and massive popular movement of the difficult years after 1948. Actively supported by Communists, it attracted the attention of the nation with a rhetoric and a program that recalled the Aliança Nacional Libertadora of 1935. Like the Aliança, the movement was led by non-workers, including many military men.

Despite virulent conservative opposition and police repression, the "oil is ours!" movement took hold early and deeply in urban areas like ABC. The first committees had been formed in Santo André and São Caetano in June 1948, and even the câmara municipal of Santo André officially endorsed the movement. Populist and Socialist politicians played crucial roles at all levels over the next six years—they included São Paulo PTB federal deputies Euzebio Rocha and Nelson Fernandes, and state deputies Jânio Quadros (PDC), Porfirio Paz, Vladimir de Toledo Piza, and ABC's own Tereza Delta (PSP). Even São Paulo's Governor Adhemar de Barros declared an "Oil Week" in October 1948, while continuing to authorize his police to attack the movement's public meetings and demonstrations.[32]

Campanella also helped build a popular cross-class movement in São Caetano between 1947 and 1948 to win the district's autonomy from neighboring Santo André. Fearful of losing São Caetano's tax revenues, Santo André's political leaders violently opposed independent municipal status for the neglected district. The lack of municipal autonomy had been a grievance of São Caetano's middle class since the 1920s, yet only in the late forties did the movement acquire a popular character. In their efforts to influence the state legislature, the *autonomistas* took to the streets in 1948 in the sort of emotional street agitation pioneered by São Caetano's ANL in 1935 and the PCB in the postwar years.[33]

The political energy being released in ABC's second-largest industrial district would soon become characteristic of electoral politics through the region. In São Caetano, elements of the politicized middle class thus stepped into the void that had been created by the state's intervention against the working-class Left. In barring the competition of the PCB, state repression gave the political class a second chance to establish its influence over local working-class voters.

Santo André's Antônio Flaquer, proclaimed prefeito over the Communist Armando Mazzo by TSE decision, had a clear notion of what politicians had to do in the wake of the heightened working-class mobilizations of 1945–47. Appearing in São Caetano in 1948, the substitute prefeito smugly told a Communist journalist that he knew precisely how to combat "your extremism": his administration would give "the people exactly what you are demanding." Another substitute vereador, the anticommunist pharmacist Benedito de Castro, said much the same in late January 1948: the challenge of the PCB would be dealt with by meeting the needs of the workers.[34]

The logic and direction of political change in ABC were clear. The workers of ABC in the late forties overwhelmingly rejected the repressive policies of the conservative parties, identified with the rich, who were allied with President Dutra. The urban popular vote, although still a minority of the national electorate, provided the mass base for a third force in national politics, opposed to both the PSD and the UDN.

The 1948 interparty accord between the PSD, the UDN, and the PR had aimed to control the presidential succession of 1950 by naming a common conservative candidate, thus excluding the urban-based populist forces of

Getúlio Vargas and Adhemar de Barros. Dutra's barring of the PTB and the PSP from such high-level discussions meant, as Vargas frequently complained, that the popular parties were to be accorded a strictly secondary role in the succession process. It was as if, one Adhemarista claimed, they were to be treated as political delinquents for "the crime of being of the streets."[35] In the end, however, the interparty accord could not resolve the conflicts generated by the hegemonic pretensions of the PSD and the minoritarian sensitivities of the UDN and the PR. Dutra's PSD nominated Cristiano Machado of Minas Gerais, while Brigadeiro Eduardo Gomes served, once again, as the candidate of the UDN and its supporters. The failure of the accord opened the way for the former dictator, Getúlio Vargas.[36]

Elite agreement between 1947 and 1950 had polarized the political atmosphere by dividing the country into two camps, the conservative and the populist. The popular prestige of Vargas, who had broken with Dutra in 1947, was also favored by economic difficulties and the lack of a sense of national direction during the last two years of Dutra's administration. To win, however, Vargas needed and got the support of São Paulo's formidable Governor Adhemar de Barros.[37] Running as the candidate of the populist alliance of the PTB and the PSP, Vargas appealed to the workers by attacking the government for its intervention in the unions, its refusal to increase the minimum wage, and its efforts to overturn the steps taken earlier to achieve social justice. "Help Getúlio to help you by voting for the PTB," ran the PTB slogan.[38]

In 1945, the polarization of the urban populace against the elites had benefited a tiny Communist Party, which at the time had only recently emerged from ten years of intense persecution. In 1950, however, a far larger Communist Party, recently the choice of 10 percent of the national electorate, was notable by its absence from the national political equation. Judging the fate of electoral democracy solely in terms of its own legality, the PCB after 1948 had quickly forsaken the combative if naive faith in democracy it had held between 1945 and 1947. Overnight, the PCB returned to the extremist voluntarism characteristic of the Aliança Nacional Libertadora of 1935.[39]

Denouncing the "Dutra dictatorship," Prestes urged the people in 1950 to boycott (*voto em branco*) all of the candidates of "the dominant classes" since they could expect nothing from such elections. At a moment when Getúlio and Adhemar offered working people hope for an alternative to Dutra, PCB militants were urged to concentrate their fire against "the tyrant Getúlio," the "hangman of the workers." Lumping together all "bourgeois parties" as part of the same "gang of thieves," the Communists denounced the PTB as the worst by far since Getúlio's demagoguery caused "dangerous illusions" among the laboring masses. Only revolution, they proclaimed, offered a solution to the people's problems.[40]

In their rhetoric and policies, Brazil's Communists of the late forties and early fifties expressed their frustration at the workers' betrayal of their self-proclaimed vanguard. Partisans of an all-embracing class politics, PCB leaders resented what they saw as a bourgeois invasion of a working-class political arena that they believed, were it not for repression, was theirs in both theory and reality. The activities of Getúlio, Adhemar, and their local populist counterparts represented a broadening of the competition for a popular working-class constituency in which the PCB had predominated, in part through default, between 1945 and 1947.

Ignoring the advice of Luis Carlos Prestes and the PCB, the workers of ABC struck back at their enemies with their votes on election day 1950. In the município of Santo André, Getúlio received an astonishing 84 percent of the total vote cast, while the PSP gubernatorial candidate Lucas Nogueira Garcez received 57 percent of the local vote.[41] Nationally, Getúlio's victory with 49 percent of the vote had its firmest foundation in urban areas, to which was added the support of important contingents of the PSD who broke with their party's candidate.

The return of the former dictator to the presidential office "in the arms of the people" was a devastating defeat for Dutra and his conservative allies who had sought, with little luck, to impose their will on a recalcitrant nation. The president of Santo André's PTB, vereador Benedito Rodolpho Serff, emphatically hailed the "categorical affirmation of the will of the people" in rejecting the illegitimate coup of 29 October 1945, which had ousted Vargas "against the will of the workers of Brazil."[42] The victory of Getúlio and Adhemar in 1950 allowed the consolidation of the Populist Republic that would last until the coup of 1964. Dutrismo and the interparty accord turned out, in the end, to be an isolated episode and not a portent of the future direction of the nation.

Conclusion • Workers and

Populists • The Terms of Alliance

The election of Getúlio Dornelles Vargas in 1950 was a setback for those who sought to turn back the tide of popular political participation unleashed in 1945. Vargas's return to the presidency guaranteed that certain essential popular gains of the immediate postwar years were preserved. Over the next fourteen years, the Left/Center labor movement slowly recovered its strength and became increasingly effective in exploiting the possibilities offered by the Populist Republic. Simultaneously, electoral participation by both organized and unorganized workers created the objective basis for the establishment of a populist electoral system in urban areas whose imperatives influenced *all* participants in the nation's politics.

"The most adequate image, if not concept, for understanding the relations between the urban masses" and populists, Francisco Weffort argued at one point, "is that of a (tacit) alliance between different social classes." Yet subsequent analysts have proved incapable of moving beyond images of corporatist domination, elite manipulation, or insidious co-optation in their efforts to come to terms with the populist conundrum.[1] While judging populism in light of a one-sided concept of class conflict, the corporatist consensus on Brazilian populism failed to understand that struggles between social classes can only play themselves out through a complicated web of alliances.

To conceptualize the relationship between workers and populists as an alliance is quite different from utilizing notions of co-optation. Unlike the latter term, "alliance" recognizes that each side plays a role, however unequal, in setting the terms of the bargain, and that neither achieves its total demands. In addition, alliances are never simply bilateral in nature but are part and parcel of each group's *system* of alliances, some of which even work at cross-purposes to each other.

Unlike narrower terms like "social pact" or "coalition," the concept of an alliance is fluid and dynamic in nature. Alliances can be established by express and formal agreements, or through unacknowledged but parallel actions. In addition, they are always subject to renegotiations that reflect shifts in power between the parties involved, the influence of their respective opponents, or the appearance of prospective new allies. And finally, alliances can be tactical or strategic, ephemeral or enduring, in nature— they can be betrayed, incompletely fulfilled, or even unfulfillable. In each case, we must understand the terms of alliance among the relevant actors at each level of the structure of power.

The Terms of Alliance at the Local Level

The overwhelming working-class predominance of the electorate in ABC— at least 50 percent of all voters—guaranteed that workers retained a central role in the region's new populist political system, but on very different terms than had obtained between 1945 and 1947. Political activities were no longer to be carried on *by* the workers themselves; indeed, workers were numerically insignificant in electoral politics over the next decades, whether in party leaderships, party slates, or among elected officials. Rather, ABC's politically active middle class would do things *for* the workers.

The transition after 1948 required a fundamental shift in the orientation of ABC's professional politicians and a redefinition of the nature of electoral politics. The political class of liberal professionals, white-collar employees, merchants, small industrialists, and businessmen would have to reshape its appeals to win workers' support.

Not all members of ABC's conservative middle class were willing, of course, to adjust to a transition that downgraded values they had cherished in the past. The *Borda do Campo* newspaper lamented that the day had passed when the câmara was filled with "upright and independent citizens . . . [renowned] for their knowledge, sedateness, and decorum." The UDN vereador Octaviano Gaiarsa, a medical doctor seated in place of a Communist in January 1948, openly registered his discontent with postwar developments that had undermined the foundations of the local social hierarchy: "We will never have peace and constructive labor," this son of a local textile industrialist declared, "as long as there is a division of humanity into classes or parties of different social classes."[2]

In other cases, older politicians proved unable to adjust to the demands of this new popular constituency and quickly lost their political relevance. Efforts to win working-class votes soon revealed that even style could be a barrier to success: personal fastidiousness and stuffiness were problematic in this new environment, and any appearance of social superiority was deadly to an aspiring politician. Not surprisingly, more and more politicians fit the socially egalitarian, free-wheeling style of Adhemar de Barros. For the first time, being of humble origin could be a useful attribute to those in politics.

Politicians who sought a continued electoral role also had to forsake the ideological conservatism that had served local politicians so well in the past. The sector of the middle class who persisted in openly adhering to conservative positions sacrificed their place in the front lines of local electoral politics. Yet even those politicians who sought to adjust to the new environment often found that it was difficult. Despite his control of the prefeitura, Santo André's Antônio Flaquer was elected in 1950 as PDC candidate for state deputy with fewer votes than had been received by the Communist candidates in 1945 and 1947. Analyzing the results, Santo André's *Fôlha do Povo* drew the conclusion that all that mattered now was "votes in the ballot box." The respectability and tradition represented by the Flaquer family were part of a past that was not to return.[3]

The postwar period also witnessed a decisive shift in the position of ABC politicians on the social question. The solidarity of ABC's political class with the employers and the government had been guaranteed in the past by a shared antiradicalism that led local politicians, as in 1935, to boycott any popular struggle with even a hint of the "subversive." Even in 1952 there were some individuals, Santo André vereador Fernando Figueroa complained, who still insisted that "we shouldn't protest . . . [and thus] provide communism with an opportunity." But opportunities for extremists, this Santo André merchant insisted, were created when non-Communists failed to involve themselves in popular struggles. "The social question among us," he concluded, "is purely and simply a question of the stomach."[4]

It was no longer possible for ABC politicians, whatever their personal inclinations, to openly support local employers against their workers. The politicians' response to strikes now ranged from an enthusiastic embrace of the "workers' just cause" to hostility concealed as neutrality. In 1957, for example, Santo André's câmara voted money for strike support over the objection of a first-term UDN vereador who hurried to rectify his mistake in the following meeting.[5] While strike movements still faced police repression during the populist republic, local prefeitos would insulate themselves from responsibility by blaming the state governor who continued to control the police, the state militia, and the DOPS.

The politicians of ABC did not become closely involved, on the whole, with local union affairs. The postwar experience had demonstrated the inherent difficulties of merging electoral and trade union activity. The example of the postwar PCB had revealed the danger of becoming identified as a partisan of strikes. At the same time, the experience of the Santo André PTB demonstrated the political drawbacks of involvement in the factional disputes of the local labor movement. For the most part, populist politicians restricted themselves to a support of labor in general, while seeking the endorsements of individual union leaders. There was common agreement on issues such as enforcement of the labor laws, or the upward revision of minimum wages; indeed, any increases in workers' salaries benefited many of the small merchants and entrepreneurs who served on the câmara. Yet the virtual unanimity of such a position on labor issues meant that candidates for office had to distinguish themselves from their competitors by specifically appealing to a particular group of workers.

Traditional patronage practices thus retained some importance, since the provision of services, jobs, and favors allowed a politician to build his personal clientele. A doctor who gave free care on occasion, or a pharmacist willing to extend credit for medicine to a family in need, could expect electoral dividends. Individuals of proven usefulness, especially those with a large family or circle of friends, could be hired to work at the prefeitura or in the enterprise of some politically connected employer. Yet such methods could not be as effective in a region with 30,000 voters as they had been in 1934 when there were only 5,000 voters.

As the new electoral system took root, local politicians realized that the key to becoming "good for votes" was in servicing working-class needs in the region's neighborhoods. Over the next decades, ABC's population would grow rapidly to meet the labor demands of the region's expanding industries, resulting in a haphazard urban sprawl. Tens of thousands of workers lived in wretched housing without water, sewers, streets, electricity, bus service, clinics, markets, libraries, recreational facilities, or other amenities. Politicians discovered that the neighborhood was a unit of mobilization that was smaller than the working class as a whole but larger than its individual members. For neighborhood mobilization to be an effective vote-getting venture, however, the politician needed to organize groups to win a particular demand and to assure that the victory was translated into votes for him on election day. Over the next decade, hundreds of Sociedades Amigos de Bairro (Friends of the Neighborhood Societies) would spring up throughout ABC.

The electoral utility of such neighborhood agitation, which quickly became the bread and butter of local politics, had first been demonstrated by the postwar Communist Party. Yet the PCB viewed such popular community organization as only a small part of a far more ambitious political agenda. In practice, the PCB bundled together the diverse elements that were combined and recombined in many other ways by the politicians who followed. For a brief moment after World War II, ABC's Communist Party had united both the workers' economic (trade union) and political (party) struggles. Bridging the gap between the workplace and the community, it had combined an intensely local agitation with an overarching project of societal reorganization on the national level.

The relative success of the Communist Party between 1945 and 1947 was made possible by an unprecedented unity of sentiment among local workers, whether sympathizers with the Communists or with the trabalhistas. For a brief moment, a class identity in the workplace was directly transferred into the electoral arena in the form of votes for the PTB or the PCB. The uniqueness of this phenomenon of class-based political expression serves to highlight the class content of the populist political system that emerged from the downturn of this movement of mass opinion.

The populist middle-class politics in ABC after 1950 helped to break up the unity of post–World War II working-class opinion. Driven by personal ambition, the region's political entrepreneurs competed vigorously for success in the electoral marketplace. As their penetration into working-class neighborhoods increased, these politicians emerged as leaders of popular agitation for urban improvements. While helping to bring a better life to tens of thousands of workers, their activities also fragmented the working-class vote into dozens of smaller units without broad class cohesion.

The requirements for political success under this system, and the very practical way in which political outputs were measured, acted to prevent workers from offering a serious challenge to the middle-class dominance of politics. Workers, with little free time to devote to political maneuver, had serious disadvantages in the political arena. They also lacked financial resources and município-wide connections that could catapult them into

office. Even those workers who did rise within the postwar political system, a more common phenomenon than in the past, did so for the most
part by rising from the working class into a local political class still largely
composed of nonworkers.

The opportunity to get workers' support also fostered the fragmentation
of middle-class politics, which became a highly individualistic free-for-all
once the key to success was no longer in the hands of those few who
already had power. Thus, the new alliance with the workers brought important material and even psychological benefits to ABC's politically active
middle class.

In the end, ABC's working-class Left had to adjust its goals and tactics to
these new realities. While the PCB was never again to experience its brief
postwar electoral success, it and the Left/Center labor movement of which
it was a part did regain a decisive position of leadership within local trade
unions by the late 1950s. The terms of the populist bargain, however,
would never satisfy this activist minority of radical workers whose dream of
total working-class liberation had persisted since the First Republic.

In 1945, the social isolation of ABC's industrial working class had reinforced the class appeals of Left/Center labor and the PCB. In fostering ties
with their working-class constituents, however, the populist politicians
who followed made the electoral expression of working-class consciousness far more difficult. In this way, the politically active middle class in
industrial regions like ABC made a decisive contribution to the stability of
Brazil's capitalist social and political order. In dividing the working-class
vote, they also lessened the workers' impact on national politics and eased
the pressure of working-class discontent.[6]

By blunting and absorbing such radical thrusts, the populist equilibrium that emerged after 1950 contributed to Brazilian stability, much as
Getúlio Vargas had believed it would. However, we must not confuse the
middle-class role after 1950 with the notion that these politicians were
merely "capitalist tools." The downward shift in their orientation and alliances, however logical in system-enhancing terms, was felt by the industrialists, quite correctly, to be a weakening of the formerly unassailable
power of the "conservative classes." Thus the populist political system that
emerged out of the struggles of the 1940s represented both a defeat and a
victory for workers. Through a reasonable and rational exchange of favors,
the workers were able to gain potentially important local allies in their
conflicts with their employers.

The Terms of Alliance at the State Level

By enhancing the workers' influence in local electoral politics, the new populist political system produced an analogous phenomenon at the level of state politics in São Paulo—the only state where half of the electorate was urban and fully a quarter were industrial workers. To play the electoral game under such conditions, opportunistic governors or would-be governors were forced to go the populist route in São Paulo despite their personal misgivings.

Adhemar in early 1947 pioneered the sort of studied opportunism in dealing with labor that would characterize all Paulista governors through 1963–64. How are we to judge this type of opportunism in larger social and historical terms? We must begin by realizing that the pursuit of principle in government and politics, so often invoked by labor leaders and industrialists alike, was not a value in and of itself for either party. In a strike or other labor conflict, concrete policy outputs, such as use of the police, were at stake. For labor, the weaker of the two parties, an opportunistic governmental stance that allowed labor an occasional victory was clearly preferable to the sort of principled antilabor stance that had been typical of all previous periods of Paulista government.

While later scholars have been infatuated with debates about the autonomy of the workers' movement, or the lack thereof, the real challenge for São Paulo's postwar labor movement was how to maximize their leverage within this inconsistently prolabor system. Of course, state governors, whatever their campaign rhetoric, had no more interest in creating or fostering labor militancy than had Adhemar after reaching office in 1947. Preferring expressions of verbal or symbolic support, they projected a vague message of "trust me," while emphasizing that they alone could resolve the workers' problems.

The irremediable clash of interests between workers and employers came to the fore in its most intractable form during strikes. In the manner of Adhemar, governors tried to avoid a clear-cut decision as long as possible. Yet a serious work stoppage could force them to take a stand, because under Brazil's highly centralized law enforcement system, the governor had direct control over the police, the state militia, and the DOPS. Generally the governors adopted a prolabor or antilabor position on a case-by-case basis, depending in part on the size of the conflict and the power or influence of the industrialists or union leaders in question. Often, as with

Adhemar in late 1947, the electoral calendar could play a decisive role in determining the position to be taken.

Under this system, the working class and the labor movement could expect little direct assistance from the governor in building their organizational strength. However, when they could gather their forces, they had the leverage to alter the calculus behind such political judgments—as long as elections remained the route to power. The most telling example can be found in the next major labor upsurge in the state after 1945–47: the famous "Strike of the 300,000" in metropolitan São Paulo in March and April 1953.

The significance of the broader political context of the latter movement has been overlooked by most commentators. Like the Rhodiaseta stoppage of March 1947, the strike began and spread in an atmosphere of working-class hope and empowerment, however illusory, generated by a political event: the unprecedented victory of Jânio Quadros as prefeito of São Paulo in the memorable populist campaign of "the penny against the million." Coming a year before the scheduled 1954 gubernatorial election, the 1953 events in the state capital were of fundamental importance for all political forces. Prefeito-elect Jânio Quadros, already contemplating running for governor, was vocal in support of the strike movement. Adhemar de Barros, having broken with the state governor who had been the PSP's candidate in 1950, also threw his party's support behind the strikers.[7]

Incumbent Governor Lucas Nogueira Garcez did not, of course, have the same range of options as Jânio and Adhemar.[8] The strike was marked by many dramatic clashes between strikers, the police, and the state militia that ended in arrests and beatings—a clear payoff to the employers. Nevertheless, the governor's behavior during the strike was also shaped by the political imperatives of the impending elections: he simply could not afford, in electoral terms, to openly embrace the industrialists' side of the dispute, and his dilemma led to some remarkably schizophrenic behavior. The same governor who allowed the police to attack picketing workers also made the state-owned Moóca Hippodromo stadium available for mass strike meetings. Moreover, the governor's representatives addressed such rallies on more than one occasion, and Nogueira Garcez himself publicly assured a delegation of strikers, "I understand your problems, because I too am of the people."[9]

The ultimate success of the Strike of the 300,000 also flowed from the actions of the federal government of the populist Getúlio Vargas. For one thing, the strike's organizational strength was due in good part to Getúlio's 1951 abolition of the hated *atestado de ideologia* (certificate of ideology) for candidates for union office. Supplied by the DOPS, the atestado had been the major mechanism used by the Dutra government to prevent the re-emergence of aggressive trade union leaderships, whether Communists or Getulistas.[10]

Moreover, the Strike of the 300,000, occurring in the state with the largest number of voters, could not help but have enormous political implications for the Vargas regime. Getúlio's presidential election in 1950, as candidate of Adhemar's PSP and the PTB, had depended on the overwhelming support received in the urban areas of São Paulo. Taking the strike as evidence of his own neglect of this labor constituency, Vargas sanctioned initiatives to bring about a settlement by São Paulo's Regional Labor Court favorable to the strikers.[11]

The self-seeking electoral calculations of each of these populist politicians decisively contributed to the success of the 1953 strike—which in turn was the key to the Paulista trade union movement's recovery from the repression of the late 1940s. Like the public discourse of the more radical of São Paulo's labor leaders in 1953, later commentators have tended to focus on the gap between the loose prolabor rhetoric of such politicians and government officials and their actual performance. Judging them solely in terms of the admitted absence of a consistently prolabor policy, many observers have been led into a contradiction of their own making, asking why workers let themselves be fooled by the "populist demagoguery" of these "capitalist politicians."[12]

For the hundreds of thousands of rank-and-file strikers, however, it was a reasonable political judgment to credit the populist politicians with being, in some sense, on their side in contributing to the strike's eventual victory. This roughest of judgments might not distinguish real from merely self-professed friends. However, since the late 1940s, Paulista workers had successfully used their votes to punish the individual politicians, of whatever party, who failed to meet an admittedly none-too-stringent test as to "which side are you on" (as workers had done in voting against the UDN and the PSD as parties during 1945–47).

We must also examine the populists' opportunism from the employers' point of view. In the aftermath of the 1953 strike, a Paulista industrialist could reasonably conclude that demagogic politicians, who had never met a payroll, had in fact contributed to a workers' victory. Despite the politicians' private talk and secret assurances, the industrialists could and did blame them for the increase in the costs of labor and the aggravation that ensued from the revival of trade unionism. Indeed, the antipopulist animus of Brazilian industrialists stemmed precisely from such a realistic judgment.

The 1973 memoirs of the Paulista textile industrialist Marcos Gasparian are remarkably frank in their discussion of politics, politicians, and labor after 1945. Recalling the horrors of 1945–47, Gasparian hailed Eurico Dutra as the best Brazilian president for having ruled "with order and authority." The late 1940s, he noted with nostalgia, had been marked by none of the "demagoguery" that returned following Vargas's 1950 election. He bitterly recalled what leftist critics have correctly labeled the demagogic social verbiage of postwar politicians. The "harangues" of candidates for even the lowest of elected posts, he remarked, had always included pledges to "do away with those exploiters of the misery of others, the industrialists, the sharks so often denounced by everyone." While having no choice but to do business with the populists once in power, industrialists found their only principled postwar allies among the military and the conservative politicians based in secure rural areas.[13]

Thus, it is no accident that São Paulo, the center of Brazil's industrial working class, should have generated three of the most enduring representatives of postwar populism: Hugo Borghi, Adhemar de Barros, and Jânio Quadros. Operating in the state where the social contradictions between capital and labor were most developed, these men were acutely aware of the social cleavages that had facilitated their postwar careers (Borghi—queremismo; Barros—Communist activism; Quadros—1953 strike). Yet this understanding had to be accompanied by a careful consideration of the strengths of the employers and the conservative classes. Hence, all three Paulista populists became masters of the tricky art of finding political advantage in moving back and forth among the contending parties without—and this is essential—being captured by either workers or employers.

Populism, as Mario Miranda Pacheco has written, has a mirrorlike quality in its relationship to the wider social world: the essence of the opportunism of an Adhemar de Barros can be found in the way in which his policies mirrored the state's profound social cleavages without altering them. Populism, Pacheco suggests in discussing Bolivia, "is a movement that maneuvers within but does not direct these contradictions."[14]

It has often been remarked that this two-sided, opportunistic maneuvering between conflicting social forces was also characteristic of the career of

Getúlio Vargas. Although this observation contains an element of truth, it fails to distinguish between what might be called postwar electoral populism (Borghi, Adhemar, and Jânio) and the reformist variant associated with Getúlio Vargas and some of his trabalhista inheritors like João Goulart.[15] While a thorough analysis is beyond the scope of this book, an examination of Vargas's career after 1930 suggests that for all his notorious flexibility, there was an underlying consistency in his objectives. His reformist project, which possessed an important ideological dimension, also had, as its final goal, a very different, if still capitalist, Brazil.[16]

Adhemar de Barros, by contrast, had no long-term goal or vision beyond his own career. He never combined his undoubted insight into the social bases of politics with any larger reformist impulse or desire to change the realities of power and wealth in Brazil. A leader like Adhemar was incapable of the sort of bold, reformist initiatives that characterized Getúlio Vargas's contribution to Brazilian life, whether in labor relations or in politics. As a politician, Adhemar's talent lay in his ability to exploit the new electoral realities created by the visionary statecraft of Vargas. Adhemar and his Paulista counterparts never emphasized, even in rhetoric, the need for or desirability of organization by the popular classes—a relatively constant feature of Vargas's political rhetoric. For all his working-class support, Adhemar was never comfortable with the notion of basing himself on any solid organizational foundation among working people.[17] A consistent tie to organized labor could only crimp and constrain a figure who, like Jânio Quadros, had built his career on a stance of social ambiguity combined with a fundamental loyalty to the status quo.[18]

Thus, it was natural enough that, in the crisis of the early 1960s, Adhemar would find himself on the opposite side from the reformist trabalhista variant of Brazilian populism. It was equally natural that the new military regime would decide in 1966 to cancel Adhemar's political rights. The elimination of the electoral route to power reduced Adhemar's usefulness to the conservative upper classes, which had, moreover, never forgiven him for his cynical inconsistencies and self-interested demagoguery. But in the final analysis the historical significance of Adhemarista populism never depended on the personal sincerity of its leader.

Whatever his motivations, Adhemar's defeat of São Paulo's political and economic establishment in 1947 opened the way to more favorable conditions for working-class struggle at both the state and local levels. Indeed, the consistency or coherence of any populist project, as Pacheco has written, flows precisely from the degree of consistency and coherence of the popular mobilizations that give populism its life and meaning. When workers and the popular classes are organized and powerful, the prevailing form of populism will mirror these realities; when they are weak and unorganized, there will be more leeway for populist inconsistency and maneuvering at workers' expense.[19]

Toward a Social History of Politics

The emergence of Brazilian populism and the growth of a powerful centralized state are inextricably bound up with the Brazilian transition from a society epitomized by the plantation to one symbolized by the factory. In the case of early twentieth-century Brazil, the social, economic, and political foundations of a predominantly rural and agrarian society based on export agriculture were being undermined as new social classes—such as workers, industrialists, and the middle sectors—sought to advance their interests within an oligarchical political system based on patronage.

For workers and employers alike, the most dramatic feature of the fifteen years that followed the Revolution of 1930 was the establishment of effective governmental intervention in employer-employee relations. For too long, this process was viewed simply as fulfilling the industrial bourgeoisie's need to control the working class. Collapsing industrial employers and the state into one category, this interpretation of legal unionism has led to a misguided emphasis solely on the drawbacks of the state-sponsored industrial relations system symbolized by the *CLT* labor code in 1943. Scholars have been content to cite the Mussolini-esque inspiration of Vargas's labor legislation and have naively assumed that the authoritarian intentions of its promulgators were achieved in practice. Failing to grasp the challenges facing workers before 1930, they have ignored the complex and ambiguous grassroots impact of such state intervention on relations between workers and employers.[20]

The Brazilian labor relations system that emerged after 1930 reflected a complicated triangular relationship between the conflicting interests and objectives of the state (itself divided), industrial employers, and workers. While making no apologies for the many negative features of the *CLT*, I have shown how this industrial relations system, at times against its own logic, actually facilitated labor mobilization, particular at key moments of political transition.

The new industrial relations framework established by the Vargas regime was combined, after 1945, with an emerging populist political system based upon mass enfranchisement and widespread popular participation. In my month-to-month exploration of the decisive years from 1945 to 1947, I have examined the explosive moment when electoral politics became, for the first time, a mass phenomenon in Brazil. Although far from adopting a celebratory stance toward populism, I have explained the very pragmatic and concrete ways in which middle- or upper-class politicians contributed, often against their own desires, to the workers' struggle to advance their interests.

Overall, this book has advanced a revisionist interpretation of the relationship between workers and populism while casting new light on the statecraft of Getúlio Vargas and Adhemar de Barros. By now, the reader should understand why "the study of the working class," as Paulo Sérgio Pinheiro hypothesized in 1975, does indeed hold "the key to understanding the [major political] transition in twentieth-century Brazilian history."[21]

We can now turn to what Paul Drake has defined as the central challenge of research on populism: the relationship between politics and socioeconomic development. Writing in 1982, Drake argued that the study of Latin American populism would achieve analytical vigor and comparative relevance only when it could relate the specifically political to the social and economic.[22] I have met this challenge by going beyond the mere detailing of the prerequisite socioeconomic or structural features and variables involved with populism.

Advancing a social historical approach to the study of politics, I have argued that an interactive model of social class provides the key to linking objective economic realities to political phenomena such as populism. In and of themselves, long-term social processes like industrialization and urbanization do not produce a particular political form such as populism. Nor can the explanation for populism be found by reference to the "social actors" model of class. Social class, after all, has long been viewed as central to twentieth-century Latin American politics, but scholars have been content, as a skeptical North American political scientist rightly observed in 1970, merely to manipulate the imputed political characteristics of social classes with little empirical research into class and politics.[23]

The ultimate explanation of the political outcome in postwar ABC can be found only by studying the radical transformation in the nature of all social classes brought about by the process of economic development since 1900.

In rejecting static notions of unilinear development or a single working class, this book has emphasized the reality of change within and between social classes throughout the fifty years covered by this study.

Industrial development in ABC gave rise to new industries, such as metalworking, and led to the eclipse of older industries and forms of semi-artisanal labor organization. Moreover, the internal composition of the working class was also changed as a result of such exogenous factors as foreign immigration, internal migration, and urbanization. Thus ABC's working class was never a static entity, but was constantly made and remade by objective economic trends in the workplace and by a process of internal composition and recomposition over time.

Knowledge of these transformations might be sufficient for a reasonable study of the evolution of the working class or its prospects for trade union militancy. However, changes among the workers are not sufficient in and of themselves to explain the political outcome of the 1900–1950 period. These same socioeconomic processes also changed the non-working-class social strata of ABC, and thus created new possibilities of alliances for the workers.

Marginalized by the growth of large-scale industry, ABC's changing middle class was deprived after 1945 of the certainties of its earlier alliance with the political and economic establishment. A shift in the outlook of the local middle class, although made possible by a growing separation from effective power and prestige, was very much dependent upon the specific political context of 1945. A continuation of dictatorship or the absence of effective working-class enfranchisement would have provided little incentive for ABC's refractory middle class to open itself to a possible alliance with workers. Once forced to court working-class voters, however, ABC's middle class would discover a solution, if still imperfect, to their own longtime grievances against a society based upon patronage. Their developing alliance with workers, however fragile or modest, had, in turn, an impact on the political outlook and behavior of ABC's industrialists and factory managers, who turned increasingly to alliances at the national level.

This complicated interweaving of cause and effect has further implications for our study of Latin American populism. For too long, scholars have dealt with *populist politics* or *populist ideology* as the fundamental unit of explanation, rather than emphasizing the transition to a *populist political system* that influenced the behavior of all participants. Indeed, scholarly dissatisfaction with the prevailing concept of populism has been motivated, in large part, by its use as a category to which a wide array of very different and even contradictory political phenomena are consigned. As this book suggests, there was not one populism but many, in addition to the populist elements incorporated into the political practices of all groups.[24]

Thus the populist phenomenon in postwar Brazil was shaped by the imperatives that flowed from the alteration of the basic rules and norms of electoral participation and competition. Once established, these democratic electoral forms provided the ideal environment for the most varied interactions between all social classes and strata. Yet an exclusive emphasis on interclass relations can grossly distort the analysis of electoral politics, which is decisively shaped by intraclass divisions, fractions, and substrata. The successful analysis of such a political system requires a further refinement of our understanding of the variety and complexity of alliances at all levels.

The restoration of democracy in Brazil and elsewhere on the continent in the 1980s highlights the importance of social and political alliances, placing the subject at the top of Latin Americanist research agendas. The current period has also seen the emergence of the industrial working class as a dynamic social and political force throughout the region, especially in Brazil. Thus the findings of this book are directly relevant to Brazilian developments since 1978 when a massive strike in the ABC region catapulted the president of São Bernardo's metalworkers' union, Luis Inácio ("Lula") da Silva, to national and international prominence. Lula, the embodiment of the self-styled "new" or "authentic" trade unionism, soon ventured into electoral politics through the socialist Workers' Party (PT) he helped found in 1979.[25] Ten years later, in the second round of the 1989 presidential elections, this former worker won 38 percent of the national vote in Brazil, compared to the 43 percent received by the winning candidate of the Center-Right.

Yet participants and scholarly observers continue to view the militant trade unionism and class-based electoral politics identified with Lula as totally without precedent in Brazilian working-class history. Viewing events in an ahistorical manner, as a complete novelty, they have failed to note the broad similarities between the political and trade union developments of 1977–82 and the popular upsurge of 1945–47 that gave birth to the Populist Republic. In both cases, explosions of labor militancy and working-class politics took place at moments of transition from dictatorial regimes—at the end of the Estado Novo in 1945, and at the beginnings of the "abertura" or political opening of the post-1964 military regime. Moreover, the key working-class leaders in each period emerged from within the structures of official trade unionism linked to the state. In both cases, the metalworkers were especially prominent; and in both cases, these leaderships gained credibility for their political options through mass strikes that encompassed 100,000 workers in metropolitan São Paulo in 1946 and 300,000–400,000 in the same area in 1978.

Despite differences in rhetoric, ambitious trade union leaders in both periods moved rapidly to construct explicitly class-based political parties—the PCB and the PT—that were designed to unify the workers' struggles in the trade union and community arenas. The two leftist labor-based parties also received the same share of the local vote in ABC: 28–33 percent for the Communist Party, and 26–33 percent for the Workers' Party. And finally, industrial workers in both cases embraced a form of class politics that stood for radical change but not for the revolutionary overthrow of capitalism.

The prominence and success of labor and the PT in the Nova República suggest the urgent need to deepen our understanding of workers, trade unionism, and electoral politics between 1945 and 1964, during the last extended period of democratic rule. The issues facing workers and unionists today, it should be clear, are not totally new; these challenges have in fact been faced by previous generations, at times with success.

Unfortunately, contemporary activists and sympathetic analysts have too often adopted a stance of alienation from past workers' struggles in Brazil. In dealing with the populist era, they have unwittingly accepted the claims advanced by the workers' enemies, the antipopulists of the pre-1964 period. Although meant to demonstrate confidence in the working class, the vigorous assertions that everything is radically new in fact suggest a strong fear that the workers' natural state, as defined by a defeatist vision of the past, is one of weakness and impotence.

My study remedies this severe case of historical amnesia and demonstrates that Paulista workers and their political and union organizations, in alliance with others, have been creating more favorable conditions for popular struggle, however slowly and unevenly, since 1900. In showing that labor's past is not one of unrelenting failure, I demonstrate that the conquests of prior generations are still helping to set the terms of today's struggles.

Whatever their politics, the forces of labor in Brazil today will need a great deal of inspiration to meet the challenges they face. Their struggles will be made a trifle easier if they can feel at ease with past progressive and working-class struggles; if they can feel the pride, accomplishments, and heroism of earlier generations; and if, after tasting the bitterness of past defeats, they can still understand the flawed and incomplete victories—but victories nonetheless—that followed.

Notes

Introduction

1. "Interview with Luis Inácio da Silva ("Lula"), President of the Sindicato dos Metalúrgicos de São Bernardo do Campo," translated from *Cara a Cara*, 1 no. 2 (1978), in *Latin American Perspectives* 6, no. 4 (1979): 90. Lula would reiterate these points over and over again in his interviews of the late 1970s; see João Guizzo, ed., *Lula, Discursos e Entrevistas*, 2d ed. (Guarulhos: *O Reporter de Guarulhos*, 1981), 28–29, 45, 56, 89, 94, 126, 139, 170.

2. The term "ABC" will be used throughout to refer to the entire region that is composed today of the municípios of Santo André, São Bernardo do Campo, São Caetano do Sul, Mauá, Ribeirão Pires, Diadema, and Rio Grande da Serra. The ABC region was one administrative unit until 1945. During the Empire, ABC was known as the parish of São Bernardo, attaining município status in 1889. The entire município of São Bernardo, with various district subdivisions, was rechristened Santo André in 1938. To avoid confusion, "Santo André" or "São Bernardo" will not be used to refer to the entire region of ABC. For a useful bibliography of studies of the region, see Grupo Independente de Pesquisadores da Memória do Grande ABC, *Levantamento Bibliográfico da Memória do Grande ABC* (São Bernardo: Prefeitura Municipal de São Bernardo do Campo [PMSBC], 1990).

3. "Interview with Luis Inácio da Silva," 93–94; quotation on 93. Elsewhere, Lula attacked the *CLT* as an antiquated fascist structure that lacked even originality; one dictator, Getúlio Vargas, had merely copied another, Benito Mussolini. This system, he argued, had tied Brazilian trade unionism to the government by an umbilical cord and bred union self-indulgence (*comodismo*). Indeed, Lula wavered between the argument that Brazilian unions had been asleep since their creation, and that they had been killed by the passivity of their leaders (see Guizzo, *Lula, Discursos*, 121, 185, 66, 102, 138, 104, 167).

4. "Interview with Luis Inácio da Silva," 90, 98, 91.

5. Ibid., 98.

6. Guizzo, *Lula, Discursos*, 16, 207.

7. José Álvaro Moisés, *Lições de Liberdade e de Opressão: Os Trabalhadores e a Luta pela Democracia* (Rio de Janeiro: Paz e Terra, 1982), 118; John Humphrey, *Capitalist Control and Workers' Struggle in the Brazilian Auto Industry* (Princeton: Princeton University Press, 1982), 26.

8. Alfred Stepan, "State Power and the Strength of Civil Society in the Southern Cone of Latin America," in *Bringing the State Back In*, ed. Peter Evans, Dietrich Rueschemeyer, and Theda Skockpol (Cambridge: Cambridge University Press, 1985), 332; Maria Helena Moreira Alves, "The PT and the New Republic," *Bulletin of Latin American Research* 4 (1985): 96.

9. Michael Löwy, "Un Parti de Type Nouveau: Le Parti des Travailleurs au Brésil," *Amérique Latine* (October–December 1985): 23; appeared in English as "A New Type of Party, The Brazilian PT," *Latin American Perspectives* 14 (1987): 453–64.

10. Margaret Keck, "From Movement to Politics: The Formation of the Workers' Party in Brazil" (Ph.D. diss., Columbia University, 1986), 1; quotation on 44–45. See also Moisés, *Lições*, 209, 216, 210–11.

11. See Torcuato Di Tella, "Populism and Reform in Latin America," in *Obstacles to Change in Latin America*, ed. Claudio Veliz (Oxford: Oxford University Press, 1965), 47–74; Kenneth Erickson, "Populism and Political Control of the Working Class in Brazil," *Proceedings of the Pacific Coast Council on Latin American Studies* 4 (1975): 117–44; Paul Drake, *Socialism and Populism in Chile, 1932–1952* (Urbana: University of Illinois Press, 1978), 7–9; Steve Stein, *Populism in Peru* (Madison: University of Wisconsin Press, 1980); David Collier, ed., *The New Authoritarianism in Latin America* (Princeton: Princeton University Press, 1979), 402; Michael Conniff, "Introduction: Toward a Comparative Definition of Populism," in *Latin American Populism in Comparative Perspective*, ed. Michael Conniff (Albuquerque: University of New Mexico Press, 1982), 13.

12. Ruth Collier, "Popular Sector Incorporation and Political Supremacy: Regime Evolution in Brazil and Mexico," in *Brazil and Mexico: Patterns in Late Development*, ed. Sylvia Ann Hewlett and Richard S. Weinert (Philadelphia: Institute for the Study of Human Issues, 1982), 73. See also Kenneth Paul Erickson, "Corporatism and Labor in Development," in *Contemporary Brazil: Issues in Economic and Political Development*, ed. H. Jon Rosenbaum and William G. Tyler (New York: Praeger, 1972), 139–66; Howard J. Wiarda, ed., *Politics and Social Change in Latin America: The Distinct Tradition* (Amherst: University of Massachusetts Press, 1974); Kenneth Paul Erickson and Kevin J. Middlebrook, "The State and Organized Labor in Brazil and Mexico," in Hewlett and Weinert, *Brazil and Mexico*, 213–63. The definition of corporatism is from Kenneth S. Mericle, "Corporatist Control of the Working Class: Authoritarian Brazil Since 1964," in *Authoritarianism and Corporatism in Latin America*, ed. James M. Malloy (Pittsburgh: University of Pittsburgh Press, 1977), 303.

13. Leôncio Martins Rodrigues, "Sindicalismo e Classe Operária (1930–1964)," in *História Geral da Civilização Brasileira*, ed. Boris Fausto, part 3, vol. 3 (São Paulo: DIFEL, 1981), 511, 530; Humphrey, *Capitalist Control*, 14, 16, 123, 23, 239; Moisés, *Lições*, 35, 83; José Pastore and Thomas Skidmore, "Brazilian Labor Relations: A New Era?," in *Industrial Relations in a Decade of Economic Change*, ed. Wilbur Daniels, Hervey Juris, and Mark Thompson (Madison: ILRA, 1985), 83–84.

14. Francisco Weffort, *O Populismo na Política Brasileira* (Rio de Janeiro: Paz e

Terra, 1978), 68; Leôncio Rodrigues, "Sindicalismo e Classe Operária," 516, 544; Humphrey, *Capitalist Control*, 22–23.

15. Leôncio Rodrigues, "Sindicalismo e Classe Operária," 542; Humphrey, *Capitalist Control*, 235, 20–21; Moisés, *Lições*, 84, 92.

16. Leôncio Rodrigues, "Sindicalismo e Classe Operária," 522; Moisés, *Lições*, 94; Pastore and Skidmore, "Brazilian Labor Relations," 74.

17. Humphrey, *Capitalist Control*, 24, 238; Moisés, *Lições*, 83–84, 118–20; Pastore and Skidmore, "Brazilian Labor Relations," 85.

18. When labor did engage in strikes, such as the famous "political strikes" of the early 1960s, it is argued, union leaders did so because such movements were not only tolerated by the state but stimulated by the factional struggles within the government. Such directed mobilization gained little for workers (see Moisés, *Lições*, 118, 83; Pastore and Skidmore, "Brazilian Labor Relations," 88; Weffort, *Populismo*, 21).

19. Weffort, *Populismo*, 21, 62; Moisés, *Lições*, 213, 176, 85.

20. Francisco Weffort, "Origens do Sindicalismo Populista no Brasil: A Conjuntura do Após-Guerra," *Estudos CEBRAP*, no. 4 (1973), 65–104.

21. Moisés, *Lições*, 118–19, 85, 120; Weffort, "Origens," 82–83; Francisco Weffort, "Democracia e Movimento Operário: Algumas Questões para a História do Período 1945/1964 [Part Two]," *Revista de Cultura Contemporânea* 2 (1979): 4; Humphrey, *Capitalist Control*, 19.

22. Weffort, "Origens," 33, 37, 39; Moisés, *Lições*, 215; Ronald Chilcote, *The Brazilian Communist Party: Conflict and Integration, 1922–1972* (New York: Oxford University Press, 1974), 299, 301.

23. For good examples, see Letícia Bicalho Canedo, *O Sindicalismo Bancário em São Paulo no Período de 1923–1944: Seu Significado Político* (São Paulo: Símbolo, 1978); Annez Andraus Troyano, *Estado e Sindicalismo* (São Paulo: Símbolo, 1978); Maria Andréa Loyola, *Os Sindicatos e o PTB: Estudo de um Caso em Minas Gerais* (Petrópolis: Vozes, 1980); Yonne de Souza Grossi, *Mina de Morro Velho: A Extração do Homen* (Rio de Janeiro: Paz e Terra, 1981); Dennis Linhares Barsted, *Medição de Forças: O Movimento Grevista de 1953 e a Época dos Operários Navais* (Rio de Janeiro: Zahar, 1981); Ingrid Sarti, *Porto Vermelho: Os Estivadores Santistas no Sindicato e na Política* (Rio de Janeiro: Paz e Terra, 1981).

24. Weffort, "Democracia," 4. Observers of all perspectives repeatedly emphasized this point. For Gino Germani, "the fact that President Goulart could not obtain the support of industrial workers [in March 1964] . . . can be considered another symptom of the lack of revolutionary potential of the urban lower class" (*Sociologia de la Modernización* [Buenos Aires: Paidos, 1969], 123). It would take a North American scholar twenty years later, however, to advance the absurd and undocumented claim that "the workers *favored* military intervention" in 1964 (Youssef Cohen, *The Manipulation of Consent: The State and Working-Class Consciousness in Brazil* [Pittsburgh: University of Pittsburgh Press, 1989], 3).

25. Di Tella, "Populism and Reform," 47, 71. In whole or in part, this influential essay was widely circulated in Latin America. See Torcuato Di Tella, "Populismo y Reforma en America Latina," *Desarrollo Económico* 4, no. 16 (1965); Fernando

Henrique Cardoso et al., *America Latina: Ensayos de Interpretacion Sociologico-Politica* (Santiago: Editorial Universitaria, 1970), 290–97; *Populismo y Contradicciones de Clase en Latinoamerica*, ed. Gino Germani, Octavio Ianni, and Torcuato Di Tella (Mexico: Ediciones Era, 1973 and 1977), 38–82.

26. Erickson, "Populism," 119, 117, 125; Florestan Fernandes, "Introdução," in Weffort, *Populismo*, 13. The elaboration of this new understanding of workers, labor militancy, and populism did not take place in an intellectual vacuum. In Brazil, as elsewhere, the late 1960s were not tranquil and uneventful years. In the face of apparent working-class weakness or quiescence, the oppositional impulse was carried forward through the lonely if heroic student struggles of 1968–69. Responding to imperatives that were very different from those that governed working-class life, the emerging student-based movement seemed to provide an example of a more principled, apparently resolute, and highly visible radical opposition that was capable of "settling accounts with the past" (Francisco Weffort, "Democracia e Movimento Operário: Algumas Questões Para a História do Período 1945/1964 [Part One]," *Revista de Cultura Contemporânea* 1 (1978): 7.

27. Hobart Spalding, *Organized Labor in Latin America* (New York: Harper and Row, 1977), 151; Erickson, "Populism," 119, 117. Steve Stein, for example, provided a wonderfully sensitive and nuanced portrayal of the Peruvian populist phenomenon in 1930; yet his introduction still presented populism primarily as a form of social control that served "to bolster an exploitative status quo, . . . [by reducing] pressures on established social structures, . . . [managing] potential and real conflict, and . . . [maintaining] passive, nonrevolutionary popular masses" (*Populism in Peru*, 15).

28. Weffort, *Populismo*, 43. See also Octavio Ianni, "Populismo y Relaciones de Clase," in Germani, Ianni, and Di Tella, *Populismo*, 132–34; Octavio Ianni, *Crisis in Brazil* (New York: Columbia University Press, 1970), 99, 111, 120, 199.

29. Citing the results of a survey of São Bernardo auto workers conducted in 1963, Erickson answered his own question by arguing that workers supported populists because they "had not yet developed a sense of class consciousness . . . [being bound together, at best, by] a vague sense of social solidarity" based on their similarity "as poor people" ("Populism," 127). For the survey in question, see Leôncio Martins Rodrigues, *Industrialização e Atitudes Operárias* (São Paulo: Brasiliense, 1970).

30. Weffort, *Populismo*, 34.

31. Ibid., 25. For examples, see the influential work of Argentine sociologist Gino Germani, *Política y Sociedad en una Época de Transición* (Buenos Aires: Editorial Paidos, 1962). On Brazil, see Alain Touraine, "Industrialisation et Conscience Ouvrière à São Paulo," *Sociologie du Travail* 3 no. 4 (1961): 77–95; Juarez Rubens Brandão Lopes, "O Ajustamento do Trabalhador a Indústria: Mobilidade Social e Motivação," in *Mobilidade e Trabalho: Um Estudo na Cidade de São Paulo*, ed. Bertram Hutchinson (Rio de Janeiro: INEP/NEC, 1960), 360–440; Brandão Lopes, *Sociedade Industrial no Brasil* (São Paulo: DIFEL, 1964); idem, *Crise do Brasil Arcaico* (São Paulo: DIFEL, 1967); Luis Pereira, *Trabalho e Desenvolvimento no Brasil* (São Paulo: DIFEL, 1965).

32. Weffort, *Populismo*, first and second quotations on 54–55; Francisco Weffort,

"Raízes Sociais do Populismo em São Paulo," *Revista Civilização Brasileira* 1 (1965): 39–60 (third quotation on 46–47); Weffort, *Populismo*, fourth quotation on 54.

33. Leôncio Rodrigues, "Sindicalismo e Classe Operária," 520; Spalding, *Organized Labor*, 183; Fernando Henrique Cardoso, "Le Proletariat Brésilien: Situation et Comportement Social," *Sociologie du Travail* 3, no. 4 (1961): 50–65 (Portuguese ed.: "Proletariado no Brasil: Situação e Comportamento," *Revista Brasiliense* 41 [1962]: 98–122); Leôncio Martins Rodrigues, *Sindicalismo e Conflito Industrial no Brasil* (São Paulo: DIFEL, 1966).

34. Leôncio Rodrigues, "Do Anarquismo ao Nacionalismo," in *Sindicalismo*, 101–211.

35. Azis Simão, *Sindicato e Estado* (1966; reprint, São Paulo: Ática, 1981); Paula Beiguelman, *Os Companheiros de São Paulo* (São Paulo: Símbolo, 1977); Sheldon Maram, *Anarquistas, Imigrantes e o Movimento Operário Brasileiro, 1890–1920* (Rio de Janeiro: Paz e Terra, 1979); Boris Fausto, *Trabalho Urbano e Conflito Social* (São Paulo: DIFEL, 1976); Michael Hall and Paulo Sérgio Pinheiro, *A Classe Operária no Brasil*, 2 vols. (São Paulo: Alfa-Omega, 1979; Brasiliense, 1981). Quotation from Paulo Sérgio Pinheiro, *Política e Trabalho no Brasil, dos Anos Vinte à 1930* (São Paulo: Paz e Terra, 1975), 9.

36. Sheldon Maram, "Labor and the Left in Brazil, 1890–1921: A Movement Aborted," *Hispanic American Historical Review* 57 (1977): 255; Sheldon Maram, "Anarcho-Syndicalism in Brazil," *Proceedings of the Pacific Coast Council on Latin American Studies* 4 (1975): 100. Quotations from Michael Hall, "Immigration and the Early São Paulo Working Class," *Jahrbuch für Geschichte* 12 (1975): 393, 407.

37. Leôncio Rodrigues, *Sindicalismo*; Hall, "Immigration," 407. See also Paulo Sérgio Pinheiro, "O Proletariado Industrial na Primeira República," in *História da Civilização Brasileira*, part 3, vol. 2, ed. Boris Fausto (São Paulo: DIFEL, 1977), 136–78; Fausto, *Trabalho Urbano*.

38. Miguel Murmis and Juan Carlos Portantiero, *Estudios sobre los Origens del Peronismo* (Buenos Aires: Siglo XXI, 1971).

39. Weffort, "Origens," 71; Francisco Weffort, "Sindicato e Política" (Ph.D. diss., Universidade de São Paulo, 1972).

40. Evaristo de Moraes Filho, *O Problema do Sindicato Único no Brasil* (1952; reprint São Paulo: Alfa-Omega, 1978); Weffort, "Sindicato," II.8

41. It is only in the 1980s that scholars, having abandoned an iconoclastic stance, have begun to grapple with popular mythologies about Getúlio Vargas. See Verena Stolcke, *Coffee Planters, Workers, and Wives: Class Conflict and Gender Relations on São Paulo Plantations, 1850–1980* (New York: St. Martin's Press, 1988), 193–96.

42. In his 1989 book, Youssef Cohen produced a particularly grotesque perversion of the revisionist critique popular in the early 1970s when he conducted his survey of workers' attitudes. Entirely eschewing the problematic that framed this debate, Cohen's thinly researched work simply ignores the issue of populism. Instead, he presents Brazilian history since 1930 entirely in terms of the success of "the frankly authoritarian [state] ideology" introduced by Brazilian elites in the 1930s. Beyond ignoring all subsequent research, Cohen does violence to the argu-

ments of the early advocates of the corporatist consensus. In his crude oversimpli-fication, for example, corporatist institutions enabled elites "to control the working class and secure its acquiescence" (and even consent) by "indoctrinating" the workers with authoritarian and antidemocratic beliefs and values that "served the interest of the elites far better than the interests of the working class" (Cohen, *Manipulation*, 5, 4, 9, 29, 33, 48, 50).

43. José Álvaro Moisés, *Greve de Massa e Crise Política (Estudo da Greve dos 300 Mil em São Paulo—1953–54)* (São Paulo: Polis, 1978), 111.

44. Carlos Estevan Martins and Maria Hermínia Tavares de Almeida criticized Weffort for ignoring the extent to which popular support for Getúlio Vargas repre-sented a barrier to alternative political projects for the working class: "Varguismo had succeeded in converting itself," they argued, "into a kind of mass political mentality within the heart of popular consciousness"; unable to ignore these real-ities, the Left had no choice in 1945 but to embrace a policy of "competition in alliance with Varguismo" ("Modus in Rebus: Partidos e Classes na Queda do Estado Novo" [Mimeograph, undated (1974)], 18–19). For additional critiques of Weffort's thesis, see Ricardo Maranhão, *Sindicatos e Democratização (Brasil 1945/1950)* (São Paulo: Brasiliense, 1979); Raimundo Santos, "Una Historia Obrera de Brasil: 1888–1979," in *Historia del Movimiento Obrero en America Latina*, ed. Pablo González Casanova (Mexico, D.F.: Instituto de Investigaciones Sociales de la UNAM, 1984), 4:9–72.

45. Maria Celia Paoli, Eder Sáder, and Vera da Silva Telles, "Pensando a Classe Operária: Os Trabalhadores Sujeitos ao Imaginário Acadêmico," *Revista Brasileira de História* 6 (1984): 129–49.

46. Francisco Weffort, "Participação e Conflito Industrial: Contagem e Osasco, 1968," *CEBRAP Caderno* no. 5 (1972).

47. As Christopher Abel and Colin Lewis noted in 1984, "the role of urban labor [in Latin America] is subject to conflicting interpretations," especially in terms of understanding the meaning of state-sponsorship of trade unionism after 1930; the whole field, they concluded, remains "fraught with problems of categorization and conceptualization" (*Latin America, Economic Imperialism, and the State* [London: Athlone Press, 1984], 24, 278).

48. John J. Johnson, "One Hundred Years of Historical Writing on Modern Latin America by United States Historians," *Hispanic American Historical Review* 65 (1985): 752–53, 760. Great progress has been made in the last decade in meeting this lacuna in studies on Latin American labor. For recent work, see the two bibliographies by John D. French ("Latin American Labor Studies: An Interim Bibliography of Non-English Publications (1989)" and "Latin American Labor Studies: A Bibliography of English Publications through 1989" [Miami: Center for Labor Research and Studies, Florida International University, 1989]). Among the English-language monographs, particularly excellent are Steve Stein, *Populism in Peru*; Daniel James, *Resistance and Integration: Peronism and the Argentine Working Class, 1946–1976* (Cambridge: Cambridge University Press, 1988); Peter Winn, *Weavers of Revolution: The Yarur Workers and Chile's Road to Socialism* (Oxford: Oxford University Press, 1986); and Jeffrey Gould, *To Lead as Equals:*

Rural Protest and Political Consciousness in Chinandega, Nicaragua, 1912–1979 (Chapel Hill: University of North Carolina Press, 1990).

Chapter One

1. See "Appendix I: The São Paulo Railway and the Evolution of ABC to 1900," in John D. French, "Industrial Workers and the Origin of Populist Politics in the ABC Region of Greater São Paulo, Brazil 1900–1950" (Ph.D. diss., Yale University, 1985), 577–93.

2. The figure of 1,000 industrial wage earners in ABC in 1907 is the most conservative estimate based on known employment levels at various factories. See "Appendix II: The Development of Industry in ABC to 1920," in French, "Industrial Workers," 594–601.

3. Founded in 1893 by Silva, Seabra & Cia., this textile plant had several different names and owners over the next seventy years but has been commonly known in Santo André as the "Ipiranguinha." See Maria Alice Rosa Ribeiro, *Condições de Trabalho na Indústria Têxtil Paulista (1870–1930)* (São Paulo: Hucitec/Unicamp, 1988), 39, 64, 194, 197; Juergen Richard Langenbuch, *A Estruturação da Grande São Paulo: Estudo de Geografia Urbana* (Rio de Janeiro: Fundação IBGE, 1981), 109.

4. Azis Simão, *Sindicato e Estado* (1966; reprint, São Paulo: Ática, 1981), 38.

5. Paula Beiguelman, *Os Companheiros de São Paulo* (São Paulo: Símbolo, 1977), 20–34.

6. "Os Presídios Industriais—Fábrica do Ipiranguinha," *A Terra Livre* (São Paulo), 24 March 1906, reprinted in Edgard Carone, ed., *Movimento Operário no Brasil*, 2 vols. (São Paulo: DIFEL, 1979–81), 1:51–53 (quotation on 52); Ademir Medici, "A Mais Antiga Greve e um Velho Livro de Atas," *Diário do Grande ABC (DGABC*, Santo André), 22 March 1981; Everardo Dias, *História das Lutas Sociais no Brasil* (1962; reprint, São Paulo: Alfa-Omega, 1977), 252; "Greve," *O Estado de São Paulo (ESP*, São Paulo), 21 March 1906. The *ESP* citation was originally mentioned in Barbara Weinstein's important article, "Impressões da Elite sobre os Movimentos da Classe Operária: A Cobertura da Greve em *O Estado de São Paulo*," in *O Bravo Matutino. Imprensa e Ideologia: O Estado de São Paulo*, ed. Maria H. Capelato and Maria L. Prado (São Paulo: Alfa-Omega, 1980), 135–76. Stanley J. Stein, *The Brazilian Cotton Manufacture: Textile Enterprise in an Underdeveloped Area, 1850–1950* (Cambridge: Harvard University Press, 1957), 64–65, reports that the earliest strikes at Rio's Petropolitana textile mill in 1891 and 1897 also originated in the weaving section alone.

7. Edgard Leuenroth, *Anarquismo, Roteiro da Libertação Social* (Rio de Janeiro: Mundo Livre, 1963). Paulo Sérgio Pinheiro and Michael Hall, eds., *A Classe Operária no Brasil, 1889–1930, Documentos*, 2 vols. (São Paulo: Alfa-Omega, 1979), 1:226.

8. Edgar Rodrigues, *Socialismo e Sindicalismo no Brasil* (Rio de Janeiro: Laemmert, 1969), 106.

9. Pinheiro and Hall, *Classe Operária*, 1:41–58. Four of the six FOSP delegates to the congress had visited Santo André during the Ipiranguinha strike.

10. As one early Paulista anarchist recalled, social differentiation within the immigrant community developed slowly at the turn of the century as the petty bourgeoisie or manufacturing employers gradually became distinct from the class of wage earners proper (Dias, *História das Lutas Sociais*, 239). See also Boris Koval, *História do Proletariado Brasileiro, 1857 a 1967* (São Paulo: Alfa-Omega, 1982), 101; Pinheiro and Hall, *Classe Operária*, 1:225; Edgar Rodrigues, *Nacionalismo e Cultura Social* (Rio de Janeiro: Laemmert, 1972), 80.

11. José de Souza Martins, *A Imigração e a Crise do Brasil Agrário* (São Paulo: Pioneira, 1973), 164. This is a superb study of turn-of-the-century São Caetano.

12. Edgar Rodrigues, *Alvorada Operária* (Rio de Janeiro: Mundo Livre, 1979), 20–27 (quotation on 23).

13. On the 1906 Paulista Railroad strike, see Beiguelman, *Companheiros*, 34–41; Dulce M. Pompeo C. Leme, *Trabalhadores Ferroviários em Greve* (Campinas: Editôra da UNICAMP, 1986).

14. Silvia Magnani, *O Movimento Anarquista em São Paulo (1906–1917)* (São Paulo: Brasiliense, 1982), 119.

15. Simão, *Sindicato*, 266–67; Pinheiro and Hall, *Classe Operária*, 1:78–79 (quotation on 82); Dias, *História das Lutas Sociais*, 267.

16. Pinheiro and Hall, *Classe Operária*, 2:157–58.

17. Magnani, *Movimento Anarquista*, 121–24.

18. Aureliano Leite, *História da Civilização Paulista (Subsídios)* (São Paulo: Saraiva, 1954), 268; Sheldon L. Maram, *Anarquistas, Imigrantes e o Movimento Operário Brasileiro, 1890–1920* (Rio de Janeiro: Paz e Terra, 1979), 53; Sheldon Maram, "The Immigrant and the Brazilian Labor Movement, 1890–1920," in *Essays Concerning the Socio-Economic History of Brazil and Portuguese India*, ed. Dauril Alden and Warren Dean (Gainesville: University of Florida Press, 1977), 197–99, 186.

19. Magnani, *Movimento Anarquista*, 126.

20. The Brazilian aphorism that "the social question is a police matter" is attributed to the Paulista Washington Luis, the Brazilian president ousted by Vargas in 1930. As a socialist opponent of Getúlio Vargas, Evaristo de Moraes Filho disputed this claim as erroneous (*O Problema do Sindicato Único no Brasil* [1952; reprint, São Paulo: Alfa-Omega, 1978], 210–11). José Albertino Rodrigues, however, cites passages from Washington Luis's campaign platforms in 1920 and 1926 that clearly state that "in São Paulo, at least, worker agitation is a question that concerns public order more than the social order" (*Sindicato e Desenvolvimento no Brasil* [1968; reprint, São Paulo: Símbolo, 1979], 68). Ironically, Rodrigues's source is Evaristo de Moraes Senior, a reformist social critic during the First Republic.

Washington Luis was also directly responsible for antilabor repression during the 1907 eight-hour strike, as the secretary of public security; and during the strikes of 1917 to 1919, as prefeito of São Paulo (Beiguelman, *Companheiros*, 46–48, 51–52, 80). Although the aphorism is inadequate to express the essence of public policy throughout the First Republic, as claimed by Hall and Garcia, it does capture São Paulo's especially hostile policy toward workers before 1930. See Michael M. Hall and Marco Aurélio Garcia, "Urban Labor," in *Modern Brazil: Elites and Masses in Historical Perspective*, ed. Michael Conniff and Frank McCann (Lincoln: University of Nebraska Press, 1989), 163; Maram, *Anarquistas*, 60.

21. Maram, *Anarquistas*, 104–13; Paulo Sérgio Pinheiro, "O Proletariado Industrial na Primeira República," in *História da Civilização Brasileira*, part 3, vol. 2, ed. Boris Fausto (São Paulo: DIFEL, 1977), 164; Michael Zaidan Filho, "Pão-e-Pau: Política de Governo e Sindicalismo Reformista no Rio de Janeiro (1923–1926)" (M.A. thesis, UNICAMP, 1981).

22. *A Terra Livre*, 10–13 June 1906, cited in Magnani, *Movimento Anarquista*, 93.

23. The term *anarchist* will be used as shorthand to characterize the dominant strain of radicalism in São Paulo (the term *anarcho-syndicalist* can also be used). Although distinct from the state's self-proclaimed Socialists, anarchists during the First Republic used the term in a way devoid of much of the ideological controversy and intellectual rigidity of their European or Argentine counterparts. Thus, an anarchist like Leuenroth also declared himself a Socialist, and Marx was cited without constraint along with more-properly-anarchist thinkers. Although some have distinguished various subgroupings within Brazilian anarchism, these finer distinctions are of doubtful utility for analyzing the practice of the state's labor movement (Pinheiro, "Proletariado Industrial," 149; Magnani, *Movimento Anarquista*).

24. For full minutes of the meeting, consult Pinheiro and Hall, *Classe Operária*, 1:74–106.

25. For an example, see José Ênio Casalecchi, *O Partido Republicano Paulista: Política e Poder (1889–1926)* (São Paulo: Brasiliense, 1987), 129–30.

26. Simão, *Sindicato*, 197. My description of the stonecutters' 1913 strike is drawn from the contemporary news articles quoted in Edgar Rodrigues, *Trabalho e Conflito: Pesquisa Histórica 1900–1935* (Rio de Janeiro: n.p., 1977), 194–95; and from the article "A Greve dos Canteiros de Ribeirão Pires," *DGABC*, 22 February 1981 (reprinted in Ademir Médici, *De Pilar a Mauá* [São Bernardo: Imprensa Metodista, 1986], 62–65), based on interviews with four retired stonecutters. The two sources coincide, and thus confirm each other. See also *A Voz do Trabalhador* (Rio de Janeiro), 1 September, 1 and 15 November 1913; 1 January, 1 February 1914.

27. On 1917, see Simão, *Sindicato*, 148; Boris Fausto, *Trabalho Urbano e Conflito Social* (São Paulo: DIFEL, 1976), 263. On 1918, see E. Rodrigues, *Trabalho e Conflito*, 203. On 1919, see E. Rodrigues, *Trabalho e Conflito*, 208, and Fausto, *Trabalho Urbano*, 263. On 1920, see Fausto, *Trabalho Urbano*, 265. On 1922, see E. Rodrigues, *Trabalho e Conflito*, 307–8. On 1923, see Edgar Rodrigues, *Novos Rumos (História do Movimento Operário e das Lutas Sociais no Brasil), 1922–1946* (Rio de Janeiro: Mundo Livre, 1978), 67.

28. E. Rodrigues, *Trabalho e Conflito*, 320.

29. Pinheiro and Hall, *Classe Operária*, 1:184; E. Rodrigues, *Alvorada Operária*, 184; *A Voz do Trabalhador*, 5 September 1914; 15 December 1913; 15 February, 1 April 1914; Leuenroth, *Anarquismo*, 128; Iara Aun Khoury, *A Greve de 1917 em São Paulo e o Processo de Organização Proletária* (São Paulo: Cortez, 1981), 172,

181, 189. The 1919 May Day rally was also attended by an anarchist group from Paranapiacaba (*ESP*, 3 May 1919).

30. São Paulo's *A Plebe* defined the anarchist goal as a "society without governments, without laws, constituted by federations of workers producing according to their capacities and consuming according to their needs . . . [a society] without money, . . . police, prisons, miseries, and dictatorships; a society where the individual could freely develop his personality through labor, science, and the arts" (cited in J. A. Rodrigues, *Sindicato*, 10). For a similar definition by Neno Vasco, see E. Rodrigues, *Trabalho e Conflito*, 194.

31. In 1981, retired Ribeirão Pires stonecutters recalled various leaders from this period, especially Alexandre Zanella, the main leader of the 1913 strike, who was finally deported to Italy in 1919; "Greve dos Canteiros," *DGABC*, 22 February 1981 (see also E. Rodrigues, *Nacionalismo*, 273; Fausto, *Trabalho Urbano*, 95; Edgar Rodrigues, *Os Anarquistas: Trabalhadores Italianos no Brasil* [São Paulo: Global, 1984], 178).

32. Maram, *Anarquistas*, 41–54. The radically different conditions faced by nonfactory artisans, skilled industrial workers, and the unskilled factory proletariat produced a differential logic of working-class organization that profoundly influenced the labor movement's strategies and tactics. Eliana de Freitas Dutra pursues an analogous analytical strategy in her rich and suggestive book on the labor movement in Minas Gerais during the First Republic (*Caminhos Operários nas Minas Gerais: Um Estudo das Práticas Operárias em Juiz de Fora e Belo Horizonte na Primeira República* [São Paulo: Hucitec–Editôra UFMG, 1988]). The practice and ideas of a given workers' movement, she argues, cannot be separated from the industrial structures that gave birth to the working class in question. Using systematic comparison, she provides convincing proof of her proposition that labor's "political and ideological activity is carried out within the limits of the possible. . . . Even though ideology and political practice have a certain weight in themselves," she concludes, their influence is always limited by the nature of the industrial structures in question (Dutra, *Caminhos Operários*, 26–27).

33. Simão, *Sindicato*, 137–45.

34. Pinheiro and Hall, *Classe Operária*, 1:51; Magnani, *Movimento Anarquista*, 106.

35. E. Rodrigues, *Alvorada Operária*, 108.

36. J. A. Rodrigues, *Sindicato*, 11.

37. Pinheiro and Hall, *Classe Operária*, 1:72–74.

38. Ibid., 98–101.

39. Ibid., 73.

40. Simão, *Sindicato*, 1–2.

41. It appears that activist weavers had given up their go-it-alone effort to sustain craft prerogatives by 1913, when a União dos Operários em Fábricas de Tecidos was briefly established in ABC (Simão, *Sindicato*, 197). Henceforth, weavers realized that the best defense of their own interests lay in spearheading the organization of the entire textile labor force.

42. Pinheiro and Hall, *Classe Operária*, 1:48; Maram, *Anarquistas*, 94; Khoury, *Greve de 1917*, 138.

43. Khoury, *Greve de 1917*, 133. For synthetic accounts of the 1917 strike, see Fausto, *Trabalho Urbano*, 192–200; Beiguelman, *Companheiros*, 83–91. For the reminiscences of the anarchist strike leader Edgard Leuenroth, see Pinheiro and Hall, *Classe Operária*, 1:226–37; Dias, *História das Lutas Sociais*, 291–304.

44. Simão, *Sindicato*, 147–48.

45. The committee's six-member leadership body included one Socialist and five anarchists, among them editor Edgard Leuenroth. See Maram, *Anarquistas*, 133–34; Khoury, *Greve de 1917*, 205; Francisco Foot and Victor Leonardi, *História da Indústria e do Trabalho no Brasil* (São Paulo: Global, 1982), 349; Magnani, *Movimento Anarquista*, 130; Pinheiro and Hall, *Classe Operária*, 1:236. Unaware of the contrast with the events of 1907, Leôncio Martins Rodrigues in his pioneering discussion of the 1917 strike (*Conflito Industrial e Sindicalismo no Brasil* [São Paulo: DIFEL, 1966], 146) emphasized the decentralization of the struggle and the ad hoc nature of the CDP.

46. Pinheiro and Hall, *Classe Operária*, 1:232–34.

47. Magnani, *Movimento Anarquista*, 182. Michael Hall and Marco Aurélio Garcia write that "in practice, leaders of anarcho-syndicalist unions negotiated with the state or otherwise violated movement doctrine on many occasions"; although noting this apparent contradiction, they appear to see it largely as a simple contrast between theory and practice and do not explain its social roots ("Urban Labor," 166).

48. Pinheiro and Hall, *Classe Operária*, 1:46.

49. Ibid., 1:52–54, 92–96. See also Emília Viotti da Costa, "Brazilian Workers Rediscovered," *International Labor and Working Class History* 22 (1982): 35.

50. Khoury, *Greve de 1917*, 140, 181, 189, 209, 212, 138.

51. Ibid., 148, 154, 166, 174.

52. Boris Fausto was the first to call attention to José Righetti's importance in the Paulista labor movement of the First Republic. In compiling information on anarchist labor leaders, Fausto found that all but one, Righetti, came from nonindustrial working-class backgrounds or occupations (*Trabalho Urbano*, 96–97).

53. Khoury, *Greve de 1917*, 157–64, 135, 137, 175.

54. Edgard Carone, *O P.C.B. Vol. 1: 1922–1943* (São Paulo: DIFEL, 1982), 336, 341, 344.

55. Discussing the Paulista labor movement in 1927–28, Leila Maria da Silva Blass has emphasized that "traces of anarchist or anarcho-syndicalist political-ideological orientations can be felt to a greater or lesser extent in the whole of the Paulista workers' and labor movement in this period" (*Imprimindo a Própria História: O Movimento dos Trabalhadores Gráficos de São Paulo no Final dos Anos 20* [São Paulo: Loyola, 1986], 19). For a concrete example, see the discussion in Chapter 2 (below) of the União Operária founded by three young Communists in Santo André in 1928.

56. Dias, *História das Lutas Sociais*, 184. For a brief account of strikes and other labor agitation between 1930 and 1934, see Edgard Carone, *A República Nova (1930–1937)* (São Paulo: DIFEL, 1974), 98–151.

57. Ricardo Antunes, *Classe Operária, Sindicatos, e Partido no Brasil da Revolução de 30 até a Aliança Nacional Libertadora* (São Paulo: Cortez, 1982), quota-

tions from Decree 19,770 on 76; Dias, *História das Lutas Sociais*, 179–83, 185 (second quotation on 180).

58. Dias, *História das Lutas Sociais*, 185; Antunes, *Classe Operária*, 89.

59. Antunes, *Classe Operária*, 97.

60. It is worth calling attention to a naive assumption that is commonly made about independent labor organizations in this and earlier periods. Too often, later commentators accept a proclamation of the existence of a given workers' organization at face value, as if the group in question can be assumed to "represent" the workers in some real sense. Often, these same observers will go on to berate the official legal unionism of later years for its *sindicatos de carimbo* ("rubber-stamp unions"—that is, unrepresentative unions that exist only on paper). Yet they fail to recognize that even independent and radical unions could be just as unrepresentative: the only difference might well be that in the latter case, five radical activists have proclaimed themselves a union rather than five "conservatives." Although one can grant the radicals more "authenticity" in recognition of their self-sacrifice, it makes them no more representative than the conservatives in terms of the tens of thousands of their fellow workers. This is especially true in the early 1930s, when there were likely to be two, three, or possibly even four such contending "unions," each claiming to represent the same unorganized group of workers.

61. The workers, the PCB warned in 1931, "can expect nothing . . . from a bourgeois government"—a conviction the Communists shared with the anarchist movement from which they had come (Carone, *PCB*, 1:319).

62. Letícia Bicalho Canedo, *O Sindicalismo Bancário em São Paulo* (São Paulo: Símbolo, 1978), 141–43.

63. Among the unions affiliated with the CSP was the São Paulo Sindicato de Gas, a moderate union organization, whose experiences in the early thirties are discussed in detail by Annez Andraus Troyano, *Estado e Sindicalismo* (São Paulo: Símbolo, 1978).

64. Simão, *Sindicato*, 160.

65. An affiliate of the anarchist International, the FOSP denounced the coalition's nonpolitical stance as merely a cover for its true position favoring the government. The FOSP, it declared, was the only workers' movement truly independent of any "political-party" or religious tendency—a claim based, however, on the arbitrary exclusion of anarchism from its definition of *political* tendencies (E. Rodrigues, *Alvorada Operária*, 349–55).

66. Edgard Carone, *A Segunda República (1930–1937)* (São Paulo: DIFEL, 1973), 412–15; Canedo, *Sindicalismo Bancário*, 145–46. The CSP had ties to São Paulo's Trotskyists and to the state's Brazilian Socialist Party led by the leftist tenentes Miguel Costa and João Cabanas. The CSP's Secretary-General Paulo Sesti ran unsuccessfully for office on the slate of the Coalition of the Left in 1934, and in 1945 he was elected alternate federal deputy for the São Paulo PTB.

67. Antunes, *Classe Operária*, 107, 97.

68. See the "Anarchist-Communist Manifesto," published in São Paulo's *A Plebe*, 16 September 1933; reprinted in E. Rodrigues, *Novos Rumos*, 362–67.

69. Carone, *PCB*, 1:346. Simão noted that anarchists rejected legal unionism per

se while the Communists were mainly opposed to harnessing the union to a *capitalist* state (*Sindicato*, 215–16).

Chapter Two

1. Iara Aun Khoury, *A Greve de 1917 em São Paulo e o Processo de Organização Proletária* (São Paulo: Cortez, 1981), 146, 144. For regional surveys of World War I and its aftermath, with a special emphasis on labor, see Bill Albert with Paul Henderson, *South America and the First World War: The Impact of the War on Brazil, Argentina, Peru and Chile* (Cambridge: Cambridge University Press, 1988); Thomas E. Skidmore, "Workers and Soldiers: Urban Labor Movements and Elite Responses in Twentieth-Century Latin America," in *Elites, Masses, and Modernization in Latin America, 1850–1930*, ed. E. Bradford Burns and Thomas E. Skidmore (Austin: University of Texas Press, 1979), 79–126, 141–56.

2. Khoury, *Greve de 1917*, 144–46.

3. My account of the Santo André Workers' Union is drawn from an untitled and undated manuscript by Marcos Andreotti (in my possession) and from my interviews with Andreotti, 20–22 and 27 September 1982, in Santo André. For evidence of labor activism in the districts of São Bernardo and São Caetano, see Azis Simão, *Sindicato e Estado* (1966; reprint, São Paulo: Ática, 1981), 197, 199, 200; Khoury, *Greve de 1917*, 172, 188.

4. The new wave of labor militancy in ABC in 1917 was concentrated in the districts of Santo André and São Caetano, which contained only half of ABC's population in 1920 but accounted for three-quarters of all ABC's workers and 80 percent of the capital invested in industry in the region. On the distribution of ABC's work force in 1920, see "Appendix II: The Development of Industry in ABC to 1920," in John D. French, "Industrial Workers and the Origin of Populist Politics in the ABC Region of Greater São Paulo, Brazil 1900–1950" (Ph.D. diss., Yale University, 1985), 594–601.

5. Sheldon Maram, *Anarquistas, Imigrantes, e o Movimento Operário Brasileiro, 1890–1920* (São Paulo: Paz e Terra, 1979), 137.

6. Untitled and undated manuscript by Marcos Andreotti; *Estado de São Paulo* (*ESP*), 3 and 6 May 1919.

7. My account draws on the Andreotti manuscript; *ESP*, 6 May 1919; "A Greve, A Passeata, O Tiro do Soldado e O Operário Castellani Cai Morto no Centro de Santo André . . . ," *Diário do Grande ABC* (*DGABC*), 2 May 1982, which includes further interviews and police information; an account by federal deputy Nicanor de Nascimento, who on 22 May 1919 denounced the killing in the *câmara de deputados* (Paulo Sérgio Pinheiro and Michael Hall, eds., *A Classe Operária no Brasil 1889–1930*, 2 vols. [São Paulo: Brasiliense, 1981], 2:288–89); and *A Vanguarda*, 2 June 1919, cited in Edgard Rodrigues, *Trabalho e Conflito* (Rio de Janeiro: n.p., 1977), 211.

8. Everardo Dias, *História das Lutas Sociais no Brasil* (1962; reprint, São Paulo: Alfa-Omega, 1977), 305.

9. Confident of victory, Antônio Pereira Ignacio responded to a strike at his factories in São Paulo and São Bernardo by declaring a "lockout" with the objective of purging the "bad elements, . . . malefactors and disorderly persons" in his employ. He had long urged the police to close the local Workers' Union in ABC and he had also infiltrated the group long before the strike to gather information on its members and plans (see Boris Fausto, *Trabalho Urbano e Conflito Social* [São Paulo: DIFEL, 1976], 221). Fausto did not identify the plant that Pereira Ignacio owned in São Bernardo (a designation at that time for both the município and a district within it). I formerly assumed, apparently incorrectly, that the enterprise in question was the Ipiranguinha (French, "Industrial Workers," 55).

10. Cristina Hebling Campos, *O Sonhar Libertário (Movimento Operário nos Anos de 1917 a 1921)* (Campinas: Editôra da UNICAMP, 1988), 95; *DGABC*, 2 May 1982.

11. Pinheiro and Hall, *Classe Operária*, 2:202–3; Warren Dean, *The Industrialization of São Paulo, 1880–1945* (Austin: University of Texas Press, 1969), 164.

12. Pinheiro and Hall, *Classe Operária*, 2:202–3.

13. On the 1917–19 strikes and their impact on the elite "public opinion" of the day, see Evaristo de Moraes Filho, *O Problema do Sindicato Único no Brasil* (1952; 2d ed. São Paulo: Alfa-Omega, 1978), 197–208. Brazil's foremost liberal statesman, Rui Barbosa, was moved to give a famous speech, "The Social and Political Question in Brazil," but did not endorse trade unionism. Evaristo de Moraes Filho has produced the definitive annotated text of the speech, along with a useful introduction (Rui Barbosa, *A Questão Social e Política no Brasil* [São Paulo: LTR Editôra, 1983]).

14. See French, "Industrial Workers," 65–68, 94–103, and 108–12 for a discussion of labor-tenentista contacts and an analysis of each group's discourse.

15. Edgard Leuenroth, *Anarquismo: Roteiro da Libertação Social. Antologia de Doutrina, Crítica, História, Informações* (Rio de Janeiro: Mundo Livre, 1963), 119. For the text of the motion, see Edgar Rodrigues, *Alvorada Operária* (Rio de Janeiro: Mundo Livre, 1979), 331–34. On the São Paulo revolt itself, see the excellent book by Anna Maria Martinez Corrêa, *A Rebellião de 1924 em São Paulo* (São Paulo: Hucitec, 1976), 158–59.

Despite the impression of later observers, anarchist support for just rebellions was not necessarily in contradiction with anarchist theory or practice. The Paulista workers' movement in 1924, as one anarchist shoemaker recalled, was eager to participate in this "political struggle" in 1924, but sought to do so without "compromising their ideals" (Edgar Rodrigues, *Novos Rumos: Pesquisa Social, 1922–1946* [Rio de Janeiro: Mundo Livre, 1978], 218). The problem for anarchist leaders was that this new "revolutionary" politics, originating with non-working-class groups, had the potential to undermine the integrity of *their* revolutionary project. Moreover, the drawing together of working-class radicals and the middle-class tenentistas necessarily involved the creation of a common platform of struggle that no longer expressed purely anarchist or working-class ideals.

16. José Albertino Rodrigues, *Sindicato e Desenvolvimento no Brasil* (1968; reprint, São Paulo: Símbolo, 1979), 16.

17. Constantly harassed, Righetti was arbitrarily deported to Rio Grande do Sul by the police in January 1920 and arrested yet again when he finally made his way back. On 1 January 1920 he signed a joint letter with other militants reaffirming their anarchist beliefs. Later that year, he attended the national labor congress and saw the UOFT destroyed (Edgar Rodrigues, *Nacionalismo e Cultura Social* [Rio de Janeiro: Laemmert, 1972], 309, 381; E. Rodrigues, *Trabalho e Conflito*, 236, 237). For an account of the strike of 1920, see Campos, *Sonhar Libertário*, 77–110. Although Righetti remained active among São Paulo textile workers into the early 1930s, he moved away from anarchism in the 1920s and allied himself with the progressive tenente Miguel Costa (Fausto, *Trabalho Urbano*, 96–97; Leôncio Basbaum, *Uma Vida em Seis Tempos [Memórias]* [São Paulo: Alfa-Omega, 1976], 122–23, 127–28).

18. Leuenroth, *Anarquismo*, 120. For a discussion of the state of siege and relevant documents, see Herman G. James, *The Constitutional System of Brazil* (Washington, D.C.: Carnegie Institution, 1923), 155–73, 257–59.

19. The DOPS was created by Decree Law 2,034 of 30 December 1924 (Polícia do Estado de São Paulo, *Gabinete de Investigações [Esboço Histórico]* [São Paulo: Garraux, 1927], 17). Reference to the DOPS factory census is made by the U.S. consul in São Paulo (General Correspondence, U.S. Consulate in São Paulo, Brazil, 1927, vol. 11, Record Group 84, U.S. Department of State [USDS], United States National Archives [USNA]).

20. Museu de Santo André (MUSA), letter from São Bernardo (ABC) police delegado to Prefeito Saladino Cardoso Franco, 1927. In that same year, the U.S. consul in São Paulo reported that a brief "half-hearted" stoppage had been attempted at the new General Motors plant in São Caetano in protest against the Sacco and Vanzetti frame-up in the United States (letter from Cameron to Edwin Morgan, U.S. Ambassador, 9 September 1927, General Correspondence, U.S. Consulate in São Paulo, vol. 10, RG 84, USDS, USNA). A worker-militant in ABC was also arrested in 1927 and surreptitiously transferred by the police to jail in Santos in order to frustrate efforts to file a writ of habeas corpus on his behalf (E. Rodrigues, *Nacionalismo*, 289).

21. Biographical background on Andreotti and the early history of the Workers' Union is drawn from the Andreotti manuscript as well as from interviews by the author with Marcos Andreotti in Santo André on 20–22 and 27 September 1982. Andreotti's trade union career will be explored in my forthcoming book *The Metalworkers of ABC*.

22. The Praça da Sé played an unusually important role in working-class life and politics even in the 1930s. See the memoirs of the Spanish-born worker militant Eduardo Dias, *Um Imigrante e a Revolução* (São Paulo: Brasiliense, 1983), 29. For a fine evocation of the feel of working-class life in the city of São Paulo in these years, see Maria Celia Paoli, "Working-Class São Paulo and Its Representations, 1900–1940," *Latin American Perspectives* 14 (Spring 1987): 204–25.

23. Simão, *Sindicato*, 84–92.

24. The *outorga* thesis was definitively articulated in 1939 by Oliveira Vianna, the ideologue of the government's corporatist labor legislation (*Direito do Trabalho*

e Democracia Social [O Problema da Incorporação do Trabalhador no Estado] [Rio de Janeiro: José Olympio, 1951], quotation on 65). For a full analysis of this historiographical controversy, see John D. French, "The Origin of Corporatist State Intervention in Brazilian Industrial Relations, 1930–1934: A Critique of the Literature," *Luso-Brazilian Review* 28 (1991): 13–26.

25. The imposition thesis was well articulated by Ricardo Antunes in 1982. The fundamental traits of state-labor relations between 1930 and 1935, he wrote, were "the exclusion of the popular classes from any effective participation," the "political and ideological repression [of workers] unleashed by the State," and the establishment of a manipulative labor legislation designed to control and demobilize the labor movement (*Classe Operária, Sindicatos, e Partido no Brasil: Da Revolução de 1930 até a Aliança Nacional Libertadora* [São Paulo: Cortez, 1982], 73).

26. In her unpublished dissertation, Maria Hermínia Tavares de Almeida correctly emphasized the weakness of the Paulista labor movement in the early 1930s ("Estado e Classes Trabalhadores no Brasil 1930–1935" [Tese de doutoramento, Universidade de São Paulo, 1978]).

27. Interview with Marcos Andreotti, Santo André, 22 September 1982; Fátima Murad, "Marcos Andreotti," *DGABC*, 19 September 1982.

28. For references to labor activity in ABC, see Antunes, *Classe Operária*, 104; E. Rodrigues, *Novos Rumos*, 324. On industrial trends, see Annibal V. Villela and Wilson Suzigan, *Política do Governo e Crescimento da Economia Brasileira, 1889–1945* (Rio de Janeiro: IPEA/INPES, 1973), 179. Figures are from Table C3, "Industrial Employment in ABC by Branch of Industry, 1930," in French, "Industrial Workers," 622.

29. *O Imparcial* (Santo André), 25 October 1947.

30. *O Imparcial*, 3 May 1934.

31. Andreotti manuscript; interviews by author with Andreotti, 21–22 and 27 September 1982.

32. As far back as 1917, radical Paulista labor leaders objected to the narrow *corporativismo* of some union organizations that concerned themselves only with the fate of their group and divorced themselves from labor as a whole and its emancipatory goal. This particularism was no doubt even more common among unorganized workers solely concerned with their own situation (Khoury, *Greve de 1917*, 135–36).

33. Angela de Castro Gomes recently argued a similar point. Working-class participation in the legal unions, she wrote, did not represent "an adhesion to the corporativist unionism proposed by the state"; the legal labor movement between 1933 and 1935, she went on, was in fact marked by the prominence of "diverse political tendencies [which were] not submissive to the Labor Ministry" (*A Invenção do Trabalhismo* [São Paulo: Vértice/IUPERJ, 1988], 181).

34. For an example of joint meetings of textile workers and metalworkers and the publication of separate minutes for each union, see *A Platéia* (São Paulo), 26 August and 9 September 1934.

35. Information on Palmieri from Andreotti interviews; *A Platéia*, 9, 21, and 22 September 1934. Palmieri's case was also mentioned in the constituent assembly, *Annaes da Assembléia Nacional Constituinte*, 14:475. The persecution of labor

militants in São Paulo between 1930 and 1934 was, in fact, more a private than a governmental enterprise, with vigorous employer pressure against known union members and labor leaders, regardless of political outlook. Indeed, the repression was so unremitting that only one set of candidates was nominated for union office in 1934, since most had already lost their jobs, including the reelected president Andreotti ("Sindicalismo no ABC," *DGABC*, 30 September 1979).

36. *O São Bernardo* (Santo André), 4 November 1934.

37. Clovis de Oliveira, *A Indústria e o Movimento Constitucionalista de 1932* (São Paulo: CIESP/FIESP, 1956).

38. See the 1934 speech by former industrialist Jorge Street in *Idéias Sociais de Jorge Street*, ed. Evaristo de Moraes Filho (Brasília: Senado Federal/Fundação Casa Rui Barbosa, 1980), 429–30.

39. Almeida, "Estado e Classes Trabalhadores," 225. Judging from the frustrated remarks of Communist leaders, many working-class activists must have adopted a pragmatic attitude like Andreotti's. In 1931, the São Paulo PCB leadership was vocally critical of labor leaders who participated in "fascist" legal unions. The union-ists who did so, it reported, claimed to be organizing the workers now in order to later set them against the government; Communist leaders, however, were con-vinced that such "naiveté" could have only "disastrous results" ("Aos Trabalhadores em Fábricas de Tecidos de São Paulo," a 1931 PCB pamphlet reprinted in Edgard Carone, *O P.C.B. Vol. 1: 1922–1943*) [São Paulo: DIFEL, 1982], 319). In December 1931, the PCB's National Union Commission also complained about the "grave opportunism" of many comrades who were saying that "the masses want a union opened so that they can organize; therefore we will open a union somehow, chang-ing the name, subjecting ourselves to the demands . . . of the government, feeding the illusions of the masses" (Manoel Luiz Lima Salgado Guimarães, ed., *A Revo-lução de 30: Texto e Documentos* [Brasília: Editôra Universidade de Brasília, 1982], 2:288–89).

40. A month before the foundation of the CSP, the federal government had moved to please the Paulista industrialists by delegating the Labor Ministry's respon-sibilities over labor relations in the state to the more pliable São Paulo Labor Depart-ment (Letícia Bicalho Canedo, *O Sindicalismo Bancário em São Paulo* [São Paulo: Símbolo, 1978], 141–43). In June 1932, by contrast, Labor Minister Salgado Filho had rejected a FIESP request to suspend temporarily the implementation of the federal government's social and labor legislation in São Paulo (Edgard Carone, *A Segunda República, 1930–1937* [São Paulo: DIFEL, 1973], 230–31).

41. *O Imparcial*, 3 May 1934; *A Platéia*, 26 August, 3 and 9 September 1934.

42. Departamento Estadual Estatística (DEE), *Estatística Industrial do Estado de São Paulo, 1930* (São Paulo: DEE, 1931).

43. *O São Bernardo*, 26 August 1934; *Fôlha do Povo* (Santo André), 26 August 1934; *A Platéia*, 11 September 1934.

44. *O São Bernardo*, 26 August 1934; *A Platéia*, 31 August 1934.

45. *Fôlha do Povo*, 23 September 1934.

46. *A Platéia*, 7 September 1934; *O Imparcial*, 13 September 1934.

47. *O São Bernardo*, 26 August 1934; *Fôlha do Povo*, 26 and 30 September 1934; *O Imparcial*, 4 October 1934. The ABC delegado Abelardo Larangeira handled

other strikes with a heavier hand, although he always stopped short of direct strike-breaking. On 20 September 1934 Larangeira and a sizable contingent of police responded quickly to a strike by workers on the foreign-owned Light utility company construction project in the Capivary neighborhood. The police prevented disturbances and brought the strike to an end in two days, with company agreement to dismiss only ten rather than the planned sixty employees. In the same month, the delegado also claimed credit for ending, in one day, a strike against the Ipiranguinha textile factory in Santo André owned by Boyes S.A. (*O Imparcial*, 27 September 1934; *Fôlha do Povo*, 30 September 1934).

48. *A Platéia*, 11 September 1934; *O Imparcial*, 13 September 1934.

49. *O Imparcial*, 13, 20, and 27 September 1934; *A Platéia*, 22 September 1934; *Fôlha do Povo*, 23 and 30 September 1934.

50. *O Imparcial*, 13 September 1934.

51. *O Imparcial*, 1 November 1934; interviews by the author with Marcos Andreotti, 21 and 22 September 1982, Santo André, provided much supplementary information on this strike.

52. *O Imparcial*, 1 and 8 November 1934.

53. Ibid.; *O São Bernardo*, 18 November 1934; interviews by the author with Marcos Andreotti, 21 and 22 September 1982, Santo André.

54. *O Imparcial*, 1 November 1934.

55. *O São Bernardo*, 18 November 1934; *O Imparcial*, 8 November 1934; interviews by the author with Marcos Andreotti, 21 and 22 September 1982, Santo André.

56. *O São Bernardo*, 18 November 1934.

57. *O Imparcial*, 8 March and 1 November 1934.

58. *O Imparcial*, 8 November 1934.

59. Many later observers freely speculate about the advantages of militant and autonomous working-class organizations free from any taint of collaboration with the government. They forget that, even if all of Brazil's metalworkers had been class conscious, organized, and eager to fight, the exercise of the workers' organized economic pressure on a nationwide scale through an independent "state-free" strategy would have required formidable political prerequisites if labor were to neutralize the employers' access to state coercion against the workers.

60. Adolf Sturmthal and David Felix, "Latin American Labor Unions," *Monthly Labor Review* 73 (June 1960): 616.

61. Based on an account by a labor ministry official in the early 1930s, Angela Maria de Castro Gomes has suggested that the ministry's inspection service helped win support for the government from labor leaders in Rio de Janeiro by enforcing labor laws. As far as can be ascertained, there was little such enforcement activity in ABC during this period. Indeed, even the Rio inspections that are mentioned by Gomes involved enforcing the law against small entrepreneurs who owned barber shops, restaurants, and bakeries—not against large-scale industrial manufacturing (*Invenção do Trabalhismo*, 178–79).

62. See Angela Maria de Castro Gomes, *Burguesia e Trabalho. Política e Legislação Social no Brasil, 1917–1937* (Rio de Janeiro: Editôra Campus, 1979); Rosa

Maria Barbosa de Araujó, *O Batismo do Trabalho: A Experiência de Lindolfo Collor* (Rio de Janeiro: Civilização Brasileira, 1981); Marisa Saenz Leme, *A Ideologia dos Industriais Brasileiros* (Petrópolis: Vozes, 1978).

Most analysts of Brazilian labor describe this process of union legalization in sui generis terms as the harnessing (*atrelamento*) of the trade unions to the state. When viewed in comparative perspective, however, the Brazilian case is clearly a variant of a process that is common to all capitalist societies but whose mechanisms vary from country to country. Regardless of whether the laws are more or less favorable to labor, the winning of legal status for workers' institutions always involves a trade-off that simultaneously restricts and enhances working-class power. Whether dealing with a corporatist or a pluralist state, labor loses a degree of freedom of action (which is often only theoretical) while gaining certain legal guarantees that, in part at least, facilitate trade union organization.

63. Even though they ran a few token candidates at the state level, the Paulista Communists in 1934 remained true to their anarchist roots and adopted an openly antiparliamentary and antielectoral line, unlike their socialist opponents led by the state's leftist tenentes, such as Miguel Costa and João Cabanas (Tribunal Regional Eleitoral de São Paulo [TRE SP], *Livro de Registro de Candidatos de 1933 a 1936*; Canedo, *Sindicalismo Bancário*, 147). For further background on the Socialist Party in São Paulo, see the memoirs of the exiled Italian socialist Francisco Frola (*Recuerdos de un Antifascista, 1925–1938* [Mexico, D.F.: Editorial México Nuevo, 1939]).

64. On anarchist support for the Aliança, see "O Comício Antiintegralista no São Paulo-Rink," *A Plebe*, 22 June 1935, reprinted in Edgard Carone, *Movimento Operário no Brasil (1877–1944)*, 2 vols. (São Paulo: DIFEL, 1979–81), 1:134–37; John W. F. Dulles, *Anarchists and Communists, 1900–1935* (Austin: University of Texas Press, 1973), 519.

65. We still lack a first-rate scholarly biography of this fascinating figure. On Prestes, see Abguar Bastos, *Prestes e a Revolução Social* (Rio de Janeiro: Calvino, 1946); Jorge Amado, *O Cavalheiro da Esperança* (Rio de Janeiro: Vitória, 1945); Dênis de Moraes and Francisco Viana, eds., *Prestes: Lutas e Autocríticas* (Petrópolis: Vozes, 1982).

66. For the São Paulo state ANL diretório, see *A Platéia*, 20 May 1935.

67. For the text, see Bastos, *Prestes*, 304–15; Carone, *PCB*, 1:172–81.

68. The most complete accounts of the 1935 gathering and its platform can be found in Boris Koval, *História do Proletariado Brasileiro (1857–1967)* (São Paulo: Alfa-Omega, 1982), 294–95; and Canedo, *Sindicalismo Bancário*, 146–47. For examples of the PCB's overly optimistic assessments, see Koval, *História do Proletariado*, 288; Carone, *PCB*, 1:182–86.

69. For the ANL diretórios in Santo André (six people) and São Caetano (ten people), see *O Imparcial*, 30 May and 5 July 1935.

70. For examples of ANL appeals on labor issues in ABC, see *O Imparcial*, 13 June and 11 July 1935; *A Platéia*, 8 June and 27 May 1935.

71. Interview by the author with Marcos Andreotti, Santo André, 27 September 1982.

72. *A Platéia*, 13, 16, and 17 July 1935.
73. *O São Bernardo*, 18 August and 1 September 1935; *A Platéia*, 7, 14, 19, and 31 August, 4 October, 22 July, and 6 November 1935.
74. *O Imparcial*, 12 September 1935; F. de A. Souza Netto, *Legislação Trabalhista* (São Paulo: Livraria Acadêmica, 1939), 224.
75. *A Platéia*, 30 July 1935.
76. *A Platéia*, 7 and 16 September 1935; *O Imparcial*, 19 September 1935.
77. *O Imparcial*, 12 September 1935; *A Platéia*, 25 September 1935.
78. *A Platéia*, 20 July 1935; *O Imparcial*, 19 September 1935.
79. *A Platéia*, 15 October 1935; *O Imparcial*, 3 October 1935.
80. *A Platéia*, 22 July 1935.
81. Sindicato dos Metalúrgicos de Santo André, Mauá, Ribeirão Pires, e Rio Grande da Serra, *50 Anos de Luta (1933–1983)* (Santo André: Sindicato dos Metalúrgicos de Santo André, Mauá, Ribeirão Pires, e Rio Grande da Serra, 1983), 37.

Chapter Three

1. Plínio de Abreu Ramos, *Os Partidos Paulistas e o Estado Novo* (Petrópolis: Vozes, 1980), 174–84.
2. Angela de Castro Gomes, *A Invenção do Trabalhismo* (São Paulo: Vértice/ IUPERJ, 1988), 191; Reynaldo Pompeu de Campos, *Repressão Judicial no Estado Novo. Esquerda e Direita no Banco dos Réus* (Rio de Janeiro: Achiamé, 1982), 48–50.
3. See Delegacia de Polícia de São Bernardo, "Autos de Inquérito, Motivos de Ordem Social, 1936," enclosed in Tribunal de Segurança Nacional (TSN) Processo 705 (1939), 4:316–61.
4. TSN Processo 705 (1939). The records include material from a police raid on the home of Andreotti's wife in São Paulo. Although Andreotti was not captured, the police did confiscate subversive material—some in his handwriting—which was included in the *processo*. My account also draws on my detailed interviews of 28 September 1982 and 1 October 1982 with Marcos Andreotti, Santo André.
5. See John D. French, "Industrial Workers and the Origin of Populist Politics in the ABC Region of Greater São Paulo, Brazil 1900–1950" (Ph.D. diss., Yale University, 1985), 198–99, 207, for examples of the use of such family metaphors by Armando de Arruda Pereira, manager of Roberto Simonsen's Cerâmica São Caetano, in the mid-1930s.
6. Jorge Street, "O Reconhecimento dos Sindicatos Operários," *Jornal do Comércio*, 13 June 1919, reprinted in *Idéias Sociais de Jorge Street*, ed. Evaristo de Moraes Filho (Brasília/Rio de Janeiro: Senado Federal/Fundação Casa Rui Barbosa, 1980), 405–10 (quotations on 406–8).
7. Heitor Ferreira Lima, *Tres Industrialistas Brasileiros* (São Paulo: Alfa-Omega, 1976), 158–59.
8. Ibid., 158.
9. In 1969, a skeptical Warren Dean scoffed at Street's reputation as "an industrialist with an exceptionally well developed social conscience" (*The Industrializa-

tion of São Paulo, 1880–1945 [Austin: University of Texas Press, 1969], 156). For a more convincing and sympathetic portrait, see the biographical sketch offered by Evaristo de Moraes Filho (*Idéias Sociais*, 15–118) and the recent book by Palmeira Petratti Teixeira, *A Fábrica do Sonho: Trajetória do Industrial Jorge Street* (Rio de Janeiro: Paz e Terra, 1990).

10. Moraes Filho, *Idéias Sociais*, 122–23.

11. In 1924, ABC prefeito Saladino Cardoso Franco specifically praised Roberto Simonsen's Companhia Nacional de Artigos de Cobre (CONAC), the Belgian-French Companhia Brasileira de Construção Fichet Schwartz-Hautmont, and the English Atlantis Brasil for constructing new factories in the region that met the highest standards of hygiene and industrial safety (Prefeitura Municipal de São Bernardo [PMSB], *Relatório Apresentado a Câmara Municipal de São Bernardo pelo Prefeito Saladino Cardozo Franco, 1924* [Santos: Typografia São José, 1925], 27–28).

12. The term "welfare capitalism," coined in the United States, should not be confused with the later provision of social services and benefits by the government, as in the welfare state. On the U.S. example, see Stuart Brandes, *American Welfare Capitalism, 1880–1940* (Chicago: University of Chicago Press, 1970). This is by no means identical to "Fordism," an expansive but vague term used by some Brazilian scholars. In fact, I see little to be gained from adopting a secondhand term about U.S. industrial development based on clearly speculative comments made by the Italian Marxist Antonio Gramsci. On "Fordism" and "Fordist liberalism," see Luiz Werneck Vianna, *Liberalismo e Sindicato no Brasil* (Rio de Janeiro: Paz e Terra, 1976), 65–71.

13. Prefeitura Municipal de Santo André (PMSA), unpublished "Estatística Industrial 1938," in possession of the author.

14. Attuned to the U.S. example in 1918, Simonsen criticized his fellow industrialists for paying less attention to their work forces than they did to the purchase of raw materials, the mounting of machinery, or the organization of their financial affairs. By failing to individualize their treatment of workers, employers also failed to make "efficient use of their work force" or to "intelligently" promote cooperation with their employees (Ferreira Lima, *Tres Industrialistas*, 158–59).

15. João Netto Caldeira, *Album de São Bernardo* (São Paulo: Bentivegna, 1937); *O São Bernardo* (Santo André), 29 October 1944; 6 May 1937; 3 March 1938; 24 June 1934.

16. *O Município* (Santo André), 30 May 1937; *O Imparcial* (Santo André), 26 September and 18 July 1935; *O São Bernardo*, 24 June 1934.

17. *O Município*, 30 May 1937; *O São Bernardo*, 2 March 1938, 6 May 1937, 24 June 1934; Caldeira, *Album*; *O Imparcial*, 26 September 1935.

18. Teixeira emphasizes that industrialists such as Jorge Street sought to prevent the state from providing social benefits to workers because of their "desire to maintain control of the labor force" (*Fábrica*, 121, 152).

19. Ferreira Lima, *Tres Industrialistas*, 158–59.

20. Barbara Weinstein, "The Industrialists, the State, and the Issues of Worker Training and Social Services in Brazil, 1930–50," *Hispanic American Historical Review* 70 (1990): 383–84.

21. For a more detailed discussion of the labor issues in state and local politics in the 1930s in São Paulo, see French, "Industrial Workers," 201–9.

22. Hélio Silva, *1937: Todos os Golpes se Parecem* (Rio de Janeiro: Civilização Brasileira, 1970); Hélio Silva, *1938: Terrorismo em Campo Verde* (Rio de Janeiro: Civilização Brasileira, 1971); Nelson J. O. Garcia, *O Estado Novo: Ideologia e Propaganda Política* (São Paulo: Loyola, 1982).

23. Dean, *Industrialization*, 209, 220–21; *O São Bernardo*, 28 November 1943.

24. Werneck Vianna, *Liberalismo*, 210–11, 213, 223–26 (quotations on 213, 223, 226). Unlike many proponents of the corporatist consensus, Vianna does not assume such an identity of interests between the industrial bourgeoisie and Vargas's social and labor legislation going back to 1930; rather, he sees an evolution of attitudes that finally leads industrialists to fully identify with the state's social legislation and the corporatist union structure after 1937 (*Liberalismo*, 63).

25. Weinstein, "Industrialists," 63.

26. Dean, *Industrialization*, 225; Azis Simão, *Sindicato e Estado* (1966; reprint, São Paulo: Ática, 1981), 78, 82.

27. The categorization of the unionization law was made by the famous banker and entrepreneur Eugênio Gudin, in Fabio Sodré, "As Necessidades dos Operários Brasileiros," *Estudos Brasileiros* 1 (1938): 79, 70; Boris Fausto, "Estado, Trabalhadores, e Burguesia [1920–1945]," *Novos Estudos CEBRAP*, no. 20 (March 1988), 31. Gudin was an ideological opponent of the sort of state economic interventionism advocated by Simonsen. I believe, however, that his open hostility to state-sponsored unionism more broadly reflected the viewpoint of the industrial bourgeoisie than the more politically attuned progressive rhetoric of Simonsen during this period. Although we disagree on this point, Barbara Weinstein notes that "most of the major industrial figures [in São Paulo] continued to be hostile" to governmental intrusion into capital/labor relations. As she says, the prominent industrialist leader Otávio Pupo Nogueira continued to advance a "strikingly reactionary" argument against social legislation well into the 1930s. She also notes the industrialists' "almost pathological aversion [in the mid-1930s] to intervention into the factory routine, however mild, whether by government officials or union leaders." While not denying a diversity of voices among industrialists, I do not believe that such gut reactions evaporated as a result of the post-1937 rapprochement between Paulista industrialists and the Vargas regime (Weinstein, "Industrialists," 381–83).

28. The talented Brazilian historian Angela de Castro Gomes has recently suggested a periodization of the years between 1930 and 1945 that parallels my own. Sharing my argument about 1930–35, she argues that 1935 marked the beginning of a phase of labor silence that endured until 1942, when the political imperatives of the postwar transition created a political opening toward labor that lasted until 1945. Yet she overlooks the existence of two distinct subperiods between 1935 and 1942. Indeed, the regime's opening toward labor after 1942 could not have succeeded had it not been for fundamental governmental decisions made in 1938 and 1939, initiatives whose possibilities were fully exploited by grass-roots working-class activists (Gomes, *Invenção do Trabalhismo*, 191–92).

29. Edgard Carone, *O Pensamento Industrial no Brasil (1880–1945)* (São Paulo:

DIFEL, 1977), 276. In the 1920s, Jorge Street made similar criticisms of state policy makers and their proposed social and labor legislation (Teixeira, *Fábrica*, 106, 111, 113–14, 116, 122).

30. Jorge Street, "A Legislação Social-Trabalhista no Brasil," in Moraes Filho, *Ideias Sociais*, 433. Opposed to unionization, a hostile Paulista businessman, deputy Horácio Lafer, argued in 1934 that Brazil must make a choice: either the nation recognizes the right to strike and does not need a labor justice system, or it should do away with the right to strike and replace it with labor courts (*A Acção da Bancada Paulista "Por São Paulo Unido" na Assembléia* [São Paulo: Imprensa Oficial, 1935], 366–67).

31. Antônio Carlos Bernardo, *Tutela e Autonomia Sindical: Brasil, 1930–1945* (São Paulo: T. A. Queiroz, 1982), 168–69; interview with Miguel Guillen, "Sindicalismo no ABC," *DGABC*, 7 October 1979; Robert Alexander, *Organized Labor in Latin America* (New York: Free Press, 1965), 73.

32. Interview by author with Filadelfo Braz, 10 September 1982, Santo André; Sindicato dos Metalúrgicos de Santo André, Mauá, Ribeirão Pires, e Rio Grande da Serra, *50 Anos de Luta (1933–1983)* (Santo André: Sindicato dos Metalúrgicos de Santo André, Mauá, Ribeirão Pires, e Rio Grande da Serra, 1983), 41; Armando Mazzo, *Memórias de um Militante Político e Sindical no ABC* (São Bernardo do Campo: PMSBC, 1991), 86–87, 91–92.

33. *O São Bernardo*, 10 May 1942.

34. Michael Hall and Marco Aurélio Garcia argue, for example, that while the essential features of state labor control were already visible in 1931, the system only achieved its final form during the Estado Novo ("Urban Labor," in Michael Conniff and Frank McCann, *Modern Brazil: Elites and Masses in Historical Perspective* [Lincoln: University of Nebraska Press, 1989], 171). See also Leôncio Martins Rodrigues, "Sindicalismo e Classe Operária (1930–1964)," in *História Geral da Civilização Brasileira*, ed. Boris Fausto, part 3, vol. 3 (São Paulo: DIFEL, 1981), 511, 513, 518; Werneck Vianna, *Liberalismo*, 222.

35. Bernardo, *Tutela*, 172. See also Hall and Garcia, "Urban Labor," 173.

36. Vania Malheiros Barbosa Alves, *Vanguarda Operária: Elite de Classe?* (Rio de Janeiro: Paz e Terra, 1984), 83; Robert Alexander, "Brazil, Argentina and Chile," in *Labor in Developing Economics*, ed. Walter Galenson (Berkeley: University of California Press, 1962), 158; Michael Löwy, "Do Movimento Operário Independente ao Sindicalismo de Estado (1930–1964)," in *Introdução a uma História do Movimento Operário Brasileiro no Século XX* (Belo Horizonte: Editôra Vega, 1980), 24–51; Bernardo, *Tutela*, 191. Quotation from Karl Loewenstein, *Brazil under Vargas* (New York: Macmillan, 1942), 344.

37. Bernardo, *Tutela*, 155–59.

38. Ibid., 156, 161, 172. In a one-sided assessment, anarchist Edgard Leuenroth wrote that clandestine anarchist activism after 1937 "could not impede the emergence of unions entirely subject to the influence and direct and ongoing control of the government, that made them the object of its demagoguery in the maneuvers of *politicagem* [corrupt petty politics]. Since then, the Brazilian working class has been entirely subject to governmental action, through the Labor Ministry, and to

the corrupting action of the union bureaucracy" (*Anarquismo: Roteiro da Libertação Social. Antologia de Doutrina, Crítica, História, Informações* [Rio de Janeiro: Mundo Livre, 1963], 108–9).

39. Bernardo, *Tutela*, 169.

40. Löwy, "Movimento Operário," 46; Barbosa Alves, *Vanguarda*, 80; Bernardo, *Tutela*, 169. Werneck Vianna has written that after 1936 the unions were "emptied" of their content (*Liberalismo*, 229). Yet one must be careful in discussing the Estado Novo, as Edgard Carone warns, not to confuse reality with "the image of total [working-class] subordination" projected by such "regimes of force, based upon propaganda and coercion" (*O Estado Novo (1937–1945)* [São Paulo: DIFEL, 1977], 126).

41. Oliveira Vianna, *Direito do Trabalho e Democracia Social (O Problema da Incorporação do Trabalhador no Estado)* (Rio de Janeiro: José Olympio, 1951), 34–35, 291–92, 43–44; Loewenstein, *Brazil under Vargas*, 339.

42. See Table A2, "Population of ABC, 1872–1970," and Table A4, "Industrial Employment in ABC, 1900–1960," in French, "Industrial Workers," 608, 610.

43. Angela Maria de Castro Gomes, *Burguesia e Trabalho* (Rio de Janeiro: Campus, 1979), 214; Timothy Harding, "The Political History of Organized Labor in Brazil" (Ph.D. diss., Stanford University, 1973), 128.

44. Untitled and undated manuscript by Marcos Andreotti (in my possession); *O Imparcial*, 28 January 1939; interview with Augusto Savietto, "Sindicalismo no Grande ABC," *DGABC*, 11 November 1979.

45. Interview with Augusto Savietto, *DGABC*; *Hoje* (São Paulo), 21 November 1945.

46. *O Imparcial*, 10 December 1938; Sindicato dos Metalúrgicos, *50 Anos*, 39; Andreotti manuscript.

47. Interview with Augusto Savietto, *DGABC*; Sindicato dos Metalúrgicos, *50 Anos*, 38–39; *O Imparcial*, 12 August 1939.

48. Interview with Augusto Savietto, *DGABC*; Mazzo, *Memórias*, 79–80, 89.

49. Sindicato dos Metalúrgicos, *Estatutos do Sindicato dos Trabalhadores nas Indústrias Metalúrgicas, Mecânicas, e de Material Elétrico de Santo André* (Santo André: n.p., n.d.).

50. On identification cards, see *O Imparcial*, 27 August 1939 and 3 February 1939. On housing, see Sindicato dos Metalúrgicos, *50 Anos*, 40; *O São Bernardo*, 16 June 1940. See Mazzo, *Memórias*, 89, 92–93, for examples of how both were used later to build the union. For a brief description of Santo André's five unions in this period, see Raul de Andrada e Silva, "A Cidade de Santo André e sua Função Industrial," *Revista do Arquivo Municipal* (São Paulo), 79 (1941): 202–16.

51. Gomes, *Burguesia e Trabalho*, 214, 235.

52. Loewenstein, *Brazil under Vargas*, 346.

53. Most studies of the minimum wage by labor economists deal only with the 1950s or later. See Roberto Santos, *Leis Sociais e Custo da Mão-de-Obra no Brasil* (São Paulo: Editôra da USP, 1973); Russell E. Smith, "Wage Indexation and Money Wages in Brazilian Manufacturing, 1964–1978" (Ph.D. diss., University of Illinois, Urbana-Champaign, 1985). To date, there has been little effort to empirically test the Brazilian government's own contemporary estimates that one-and-a-third mil-

lion workers benefited in 1940 (Carone, *Estado Novo*, 137–38). Werneck Vianna (*Liberalismo*, 239) ends an inconclusive discussion of the impact of the minimum wage in São Paulo by arguing that it hurt industrial workers but aided urban workers in other sectors of the urban economy—itself a doubtful proposition. Bernardo (*Tutela*, 179) suggests that the minimum wage favored the industrial bourgeoisie while creating the illusion among workers that their wages had improved.

We need more studies like that of José Sérgio Leite Lopes, who found that the enormous Paulista textile company in Pernambuco carried out sustained resistance to the minimum wage; over the course of this long public controversy, the company resisted the government's efforts by deliberately obfuscating its payment system (*A Tecelagem dos Conflitos de Classe na Cidade das Chaminés* [São Paulo: Editôra Marco Zero e Editôra Universidade de Brasília, 1988], 301–11).

54. Francisco de Oliveira, "A Economia Brasileira: Crítica a Razão Dualista," *Estudos CEBRAP*, no. 2 (1972), 11. For critiques, see Leôncio Rodrigues, "Sindicalismo e Classe Operária," 525; Sonia Draibe, *Rumos e Metamorfoses: Um Estudo sobre a Constituição do Estado e as Alternativas da Industrialização no Brasil 1930–1960* (Rio de Janeiro: Paz e Terra, 1985), 97–98.

55. Interview with Augusto Savietto, *DGABC*; *O Imparcial*, 4 May 1940. For the employer and employee statements and the text of the decree containing the new minimum wage scales, see Edgard Carone, *A Terceira República (1937–1945)* (São Paulo: DIFEL, 1976), 545–55. For FIESP's public objections in 1939, see Carone, *Pensamento Industrial*, 497–501. See also the discussion in Robert William Howes, "Progressive Conservatism in Brazil: Oliveira Vianna, Roberto Simonsen, and the Social Legislation of the Vargas Regime, 1930–1945" (Ph.D. diss., Cambridge University, 1975), 179–94.

56. Loewenstein, *Brazil under Vargas*, 346–47.

57. For surveys, see José Albertino Rodrigues, *Sindicato e Desenvolvimento no Brasil* (1968; reprint, São Paulo: Símbolo, 1979), 111–13; Alexander, *Organized Labor*, 90–98.

58. Barbosa Alves, *Vanguarda*, 79. Robert Rowland has argued that the labor courts "took away the unions' initiative regarding the conditions of labor and impeded the outbreak of conflicts at the only level—that of the enterprise—favorable to the development of a strong rank-and-file [labor] movement" ("Classe Operária e Estado de Compromisso [Origens Estruturais da Legislação Trabalhista e Sindical]," *Estudos CEBRAP*, no. 8 [1974], 32). Beyond the overly optimistic assessment of the potential of industrial workers for direct action, it is important to realize that institutionalized shop-floor organization had never existed in São Paulo before 1937, or even 1930. As Leôncio Rodrigues has written, the regime's action was more "a bureaucratic incorporation than a union and political demobilization of previously participating masses" ("Sindicalismo e Classe Operária," 530).

59. Interview with Augusto Savietto, *DGABC*. For an example of a labor court ruling that restricted management's right to hire and fire, see the 1942 ruling involving the General Motors plant in São Caetano (Elmano Cruz, *Direitos e Deveres dos Súditos do Eixo* [Rio de Janeiro: Editôra Nacional de Direito, 1944], 194–95).

We know far too little about the operation of the labor courts and even less about

310 Notes to Page 87

the institution's impact on workers' consciousness. After all, the labor courts provided workers for the first time with "the right to present grievances and hope to receive just consideration" (Neuma Aguiar Walker, "The Mobilization and Bureaucratization of the Brazilian Working Class, 1930–1964" [Ph.D. diss., Washington University, 1969], 129). As Francisco Weffort pointed out, the social and labor legislation so benevolently bestowed upon the workers by the government is then transformed into a legal right; and when a worker demands that it be met, "the original relationship of 'donation' (and thus of dependency) disappears. What counts now is that the citizen is demanding fulfillment of the law, that he demands 'his rights' as a free man" (O Populismo na Política Brasileira [Rio de Janeiro: Paz e Terra, 1978], 75).

Based on extensive oral interviews, José Sérgio Leite Lopes presents a persuasive argument for the empowering impact of the labor courts in developing a philosophy of rights among rank-and-file textile workers in Pernambuco (Tecelagem, 359–68). Sonia de Avelar provides the only systematic study of labor court grievances filed by textile workers, with union assistance, in São José dos Campos between 1946 and 1964. Her superb analysis demonstrates patterns of working-class behavior shaped by internal workplace conditions, the collapse of employer paternalism, and the growth of union militancy. In an appendix, she includes the individual case data as well ("The Social Basis of Workers' Solidarity: A Case Study of Textile Workers in São José dos Campos, Brazil" [Ph.D. diss., University of Michigan, 1985], 197–244, 375–416).

60. If we are to understand the labor courts, it is important to realize that they did impose some restrictions on the industrialists' freedom of action, however small. As a result, the labor courts were "never regarded by employers as entirely legitimate," despite the many legal loopholes the law afforded employers (Walker, "Mobilization," 129). Yet most scholars continue to downplay management's ambivalence toward the labor courts. Barbara Weinstein recently argued, for example, that Paulista industrialists found the labor courts "a highly attractive alternative to open class conflict, especially since the [tripartite] composition of the boards gave the manufacturers an obvious edge in the negotiations" ("Industrialists," 385). Yet it is doubtful that employers at this time so feared outright conflict with their workers that they sought a legal intermediary. Moreover, they could only expect routinely favorable treatment if they believed that the state's representative could always be trusted to vote management's way.

61. Carone, Pensamento Industrial, 276–77.

62. In 1941, ABC's former prefeito Décio Toledo Leite was appointed judge of the fifth labor court junta in neighboring São Paulo, and Prefeito José de Carvalho Sobrinho was appointed to head the state Comissão Técnica de Orientação Sindical in 1944 (O Imparcial, 3 May 1941; O São Bernardo, 9 April 1944). Howes, "Progressive Conservatism," 81, notes that the Labor Ministry's monthly bulletin contained "a far greater number of articles justifying the new social legislation as a branch of Law than, for example, suggesting practical ways of enforcing it."

63. Robert Alexander kindly made available a typescript document containing statistical data on the national and regional labor courts between 1944 and 1954. Tables are included that report the outcome of the 131,092 complaints (recla-

mações) handled by courts at this level between 1941 and 1945. Workers are reported to have won 18 percent of the cases, employers won 9 percent, and conciliations were reached in another 40 percent. The remaining 33 percent was accounted for by a murky and undefined category, "other decisions" (Secção de Estatística, "Poder Judiciário, Justiça do Trabalho, Produção Verificada nos Diversos Orgãos" [Rio de Janeiro: 1955]). We badly need serious empirical studies of the operation of this crucial institution, the outlook of its members, and how it changed over time.

64. Loewenstein, *Brazil under Vargas*, 344; Harding, "Political History," 141–42.

65. Teixeira, *Fábrica*, 143. Edgard Carone was rightly skeptical about Roberto Simonsen's claims that São Paulo's industrialists not only did not object to social and labor legislation but had supported all such just measures; this progressive-sounding rhetoric, he concluded, was verbiage designed to conceal the employers' actual policy of combating such legislation and avoiding its implementation by the Labor Ministry (*Estado Novo*, 118–19).

66. Peter Winn reports a similar pattern of employer behavior vis-à-vis the state in the Chilean case. In the 1930s and 1940s, he says, "Juan Yarur was using his wealth to secure 'the collaboration' of venal state labor inspectors and his political influence to block governmental enforcement of the workers' rights under Chile's labor laws" (*Weavers of Revolution* [New York: Oxford University Press, 1986], 41).

67. Street, "Legislação," 429.

68. Weinstein, "Industrialists," 404.

69. John Humphrey, *Capitalist Control and Workers' Struggle in the Brazilian Auto Industry* (Princeton: Princeton University Press, 1982), 15.

70. Löwy, "Movimento Operário," 47.

71. Interview with Augusto Savietto, *DGABC*.

72. *O Imparcial*, 12 August 1939.

73. Howard Wiarda, *The Brazilian Catholic Labor Movement: The Dilemmas of National Development* (Amherst: Labor Relations and Research Center, University of Massachusetts, 1969).

74. *O Imparcial*, 9 March and 12 October 1940; "Notas sobre uma Organização Operária de Santo André," *São Paulo de Ontem, Hoje e de Amanhã* 2 (April–September 1942): 30–31.

75. Gomes, *Invenção do Trabalho*, 192; PMSA Processo 7024/45.

76. Sindicato dos Metalúrgicos, *Estatutos*. Sonia de Avelar reminds us that such mundane and frustrating realities are part and parcel of union life even after the Estado Novo: "From a reading of [union] meeting minutes," she writes, "it is apparent that the workers [in São José dos Campos] had difficulties in dealing with the unfamiliar task of creating a collective association and in becoming acquainted with the gap between conceived projects and constraints of all sorts in their implementation" ("Social Basis," 148).

77. Alexander, "Brazil," 156; Barbosa Alves, *Vanguarda*, 82; Löwy, "Movimento Operário," 46. For further details on the PCB's fate, see the problematic book by John W. F. Dulles, *Brazilian Communism, 1935–1945: Repression during World Upheaval* (Austin: University of Texas Press, 1983). However, the best single portrait of clandestine Communist activity in São Paulo during these years remains

Jorge Amado's three-volume *Os Subterrâneos da Liberdade* (Rio de Janeiro: Record, 1980).

78. See the biography of Euclides Savietto in *Hoje*, 21 November 1945.

79. Mazzo, *Memórias*, 71. Guillen's family had been involved with rural union activities during the late twenties in Jaú, São Paulo. See Sindicato dos Metalúrgicos, *50 Anos*, 37; interview with Miguel Guillen, "Sindicalismo no Grande ABC," *DGABC*, 7 October 1979.

80. Sindicato dos Metalúrgicos, *50 Anos*, 42–43; *O São Bernardo*, 19 and 26 July, 1 March 1942.

81. Andreotti manuscript; Sindicato dos Metalúrgicos, *50 Anos*, 42. See Mazzo, *Memórias*, 90–91, for a striking first-person account of a meeting between local trade unionists and Getúlio Vargas.

82. One suspects that Gomes shied away from the use of the more apt term "populist" because of the pejorative connotations attached to it in much of the existing literature. Werneck Vianna, by contrast, has no difficulty with the use of the label "populist" for Vargas's 1944 initiatives (*Liberalismo*, 250).

83. Gomes, *Invenção do Trabalhismo*, 199–203, 229–54. We are far from grasping the intricacies of internal regime factionalism and how such groups were articulated with social forces outside the state. Despite his crucial role, for example, we have a very unsatisfactory understanding of Marcondes Filho, a Paulista lawyer who, in earlier periods at least, had good ties to the state's industrialists (Weinstein, "Industrialists," 385–86).

84. Alexandre Marcondes Filho, *Trabalhadores do Brasil!* (Rio de Janeiro: Edição da Revista Judiciária, 1943), reprints some of the labor minister's radio talks, which are analyzed in Gomes, *Invenção do Trabalhismo*, 238–46.

85. Maria Helena Moreira Alves, *State and Opposition in Military Brazil* (Austin: University of Texas Press, 1985), 45.

86. Evaristo de Moraes Filho, *O Problema do Sindicato Único no Brasil* (1952; 2d ed., São Paulo: Alfa-Omega, 1978), 243–44; J. A. Rodrigues, *Sindicato*, 97.

87. Gomes, *Invenção do Trabalhismo*, 202.

88. Ibid., 201. Approaching these developments primarily from the point of view of the government, Gomes tends to underestimate the importance of grass-roots initiatives in laying the groundwork for this emerging alliance between labor and elements of the regime.

89. Records of the U.S. Consulate in São Paulo, reports dated 22 March, 21 August, and 3 November 1944, Record Group 84, U.S. Department of State (USDS), U.S. National Archives (USNA).

90. Ibid., report of 10 January 1945, 6, 13; reports of 8 October and 7 November 1945.

91. Ibid., reports of 23 December 1943, 24 May, 12 August, 20 September, and 29 November 1944.

92. The refusal to include in-plant organization in the unionization law of 1931 was not enough to still the employers' apprehensions regarding legal unionism. In 1931, the Centro Industrial do Rio de Janeiro criticized the unionization law for providing guarantees to union leaders against employer reprisals. If such a law had to be passed, they argued, it should include a specific provision "expressly prohibit-

ing the naming of union agents or representatives to function within commercial and factory establishments" (Edgard Carone, *O Centro Industrial do Rio de Janeiro* [Rio de Janeiro: Cátedra, 1978], 127). Given employers' adamant opposition to shop-floor representation, it is remarkable that Segadas Vianna, who helped draft the *CLT*, would favorably discuss the utility of having union delegates in large enterprises in a book published in 1943 (*Organização Sindical Brasileira* [Rio de Janeiro: O Cruzeiro, 1943], 88). For employers, the unwillingness of such top-level government bureaucrats and lawyers to understand the realities of factory life was a source of constant frustration; their only consolation was that Segadas Vianna was not serious about implementing such a system.

93. Street, "Legislação," 405.

94. Records of the U.S. Consulate in São Paulo, report of 21 January 1944, RG 84, USDS, USNA.

95. Ibid., report of 19 June 1944. Ricardo Maranhão makes reference to the repression at the Laminação Nacional de Metais, which he claims also involved the military (*Sindicatos e Democratização (Brasil 1945/1950)* [São Paulo: Brasiliense, 1979], 41). See also Mazzo, *Memórias*, 72, 81–83, 86–87, for accounts that confirm the growing restiveness and incipient militancy of the workers in the late Estado Novo.

96. Records of the U.S. Consulate in São Paulo, report of 22 March 1944, RG 84, USDS, USNA.

97. Ibid., report of 23 December 1943; Werneck Vianna, *Liberalismo*, 245.

98. Records of the U.S. Consulate in São Paulo, reports of 19 November 1943 and 17 January 1944, RG 84, USDS, USNA.

99. An interesting description of Getúlio's wartime relationship to workers is provided by the then-Trotskyist intellectual Hilcar Leite, who emphasized the positive popular response to Getúlio's wartime initiatives: Getúlio aimed, he said, "to have the masses of the laborers—the masses, he didn't want the working class [as such]—on his side in order to be able to manipulate and pressure all the social segments that were against him" (Angelo de Castro Gomes, ed., *Velhos Militantes* [Rio de Janeiro: Zahar, 1988], 189).

100. J. A. Rodrigues, *Sindicato*, 124, 130.

101. For a description of the rally and Getúlio's speech, see *São Paulo de Ontem, Hoje e de Amanhã* 2 (June 1944): 1–14.

Chapter Four

1. Thomas Skidmore has noted this characteristic of the anti-Getulista opposition in *Politics in Brazil, 1930–1964* (New York: Oxford University Press, 1967), 58–59.

2. Armando de Salles Oliveira, *Diagrama de uma Situação Política, Manifestos, Políticos do Exílio* (São Paulo: Editôra Renascença, 1945), 95–96.

3. Hélio Silva, *1945: Por que Depuseram Vargas* (Rio de Janeiro: Civilização Brasileira, 1976), 15–24, provides a basic chronology for the years from 1942 to 1949.

4. The conspiracies that brought forth the candidacy of Eduardo Gomes in 1945 started within the military itself and, while claiming a "democratic" mantle, involved many of the more right-wing figures within the world of military and civilian politics. General Góes Monteiro publicly attacked the Vargas government on 1 March 1945. Góes Monteiro, one of two dominant figures in the 1937 coup, had been so closely identified with fascist models from Europe that Armando de Salles Oliveira attacked him as an advocate of "reactionary theories" in a 1939 letter to Minister of War General Dutra (Silva, *1945*, 113–16, 260–63; Salles, *Diagrama*, 23). The author of the Estado Novo constitution of 1937, the "corporatist" jurist Francisco Campos, joined in the attack on the Vargas regime on 2 March 1945 (Silva, *1945*, 113).

5. Osvaldo Trigueiro do Vale, *O General Dutra e a Redemocratização de 1945* (Rio de Janeiro: Civilização Brasileira, 1978), 40–42; Silva, *1945*, 138. John W. F. Dulles refers to a conspiracy between Góes Monteiro and Dutra in late 1944 (*Vargas of Brazil* [Austin: University of Texas Press, 1967], 255).

6. Earlier interpretations of the coup that overthrew Getúlio Vargas in October 1945 were largely shaped by a UDN-influenced mythology that portrayed Vargas and Gomes as the principal actors in an "epic struggle" over the Estado Novo dictatorship. This perspective distorted the real relationship between Vargas and the two military candidates, and between Gomes and Dutra. In this interpretation, Dutra was the forlorn orphan candidate loyal to and badly used by his president. Two North American historians, for example, have written that Dutra was known, above all else, for his personal loyalty to Vargas (Dulles, *Vargas*, 261; Richard Bourne, *Getúlio Vargas of Brazil, 1883–1954: Sphinx of the Pampas* [London: Charles Knight, 1954], 118).

For revisionist research that has dethroned such explanations, see Trigueiro, *General Dutra*; and Stanley Hilton, "The Overthrow of Getúlio Vargas in 1945: Intervention, Defense of Democracy, or Political Retribution?," *Hispanic American Historical Review* 67 (February 1987): 1–37. However, neither author has fully grasped the nature of Getúlio Vargas's strategy in 1945 and its undoubted success. Indeed, Michael Conniff has incorrectly argued that Vargas rejected a populist strategy in December 1944, and that Getúlio's "continuing lack of nerve and grasp of populist strategy" led to failure in 1945 (*Urban Politics in Brazil: The Rise of Populism, 1925–1945* [Pittsburgh: University of Pittsburgh Press, 1982], 169–70).

7. Trigueiro, *General Dutra*, 86, 94, 65–69.

8. Ibid., 76.

9. Silva, *1945*, 136; Trigueiro, *General Dutra*, 39, 43.

10. Eduardo Gomes, *Campanha da Libertação* (São Paulo: Livraria Martins Editôra, n.d.), 331–35.

11. Maria Victoria de Mesquita Benevides, *A UDN e o Udenismo: Ambigüidades do Liberalismo Brasileiro (1945–1965)* (Rio de Janeiro: Paz e Terra, 1981), 28–32, 44–45. Peter Flynn has correctly emphasized that the UDN was fearful of the organized working class and opposed to "any substantially enlarged popular participation" (*Brazil, A Political Analysis* [Boulder: Westview Press, 1978], 118). His analysis of the politics of 1945 parallels my own, although his characterization of

the UDN as "a party of class solidarity" is inexact, and the granting of a progressive character to the PSD overdrawn.

12. Gláucio Soares has written that politics before 1945 was "fundamentally a game for the elites and for the upper middle class" and that even large sections of the lower middle classes did not vote (*Sociedade e Política no Brasil* [São Paulo: DIFEL, 1973], 58).

13. The conservative local paper in Santo André reported that the meeting was representative of what it called the state's "political milieu and the productive classes" (*Borda do Campo*, 18 and 25 March 1945). The PSD, as one scholar has remarked, was built "from within to outside the state, from the top to the bottom" (Maria do Carmo Campello de Souza, *Estado e Partidos Políticos no Brasil [1930–1964]* [São Paulo: Alfa-Omega, 1976], 109).

14. *Borda do Campo*, 25 March 1945. For the list of members of the diretórios of the PSD in São Bernardo and Santo André, see *Borda do Campo*, 12 August and 28 October 1945.

15. *Diário de São Paulo* (*DSP*), 11, 14, 24 November 1945.

16. After declaring that democratic majorities must be "real in quantity and consciously willed," the Santo André paper rejected the validity of majorities won through "demagogic means" among the "popular classes with deficient instruction" (*Borda do Campo*, 10 June 1945).

17. *O São Bernardo*, 22 April 1945.

18. Azis Simão, *Sindicato e Estado (Suas Relações na Formação do Proletariado de São Paulo)* (1966; reprint, São Paulo: Ática, 1981), 40.

19. Brazil's foremost political sociologist had described the PSD and the UDN in 1945 as parties of the oligarchical elite that simply built upon the already existing organizational structures of coronelismo (Soares, *Sociedade e Política*, 41, 70). David V. Fleischer has shown that the UDN's and the PSD's federal deputies in 1945 shared similar occupational characteristics ("Dimensões do Recrutamento Partidário," in *Os Partidos Políticos no Brasil*, ed. Fleischer [Brasília: Universidade de Brasília, 1981], 1:59–60).

20. Getúlio Vargas, *A Nova Política do Brasil*, vol. 11, *O Brasil na Guerra* (Rio de Janeiro: José Olympio, 1947), 38, 27, 58, 56. See John D. Wirth, *The Politics of Brazilian Development, 1930–1954* (Stanford: Stanford University Press, 1970), 71–132, for a discussion of the complicated maneuvering by Vargas that resulted in the building of the Volta Redonda steel complex.

21. Vargas, *Nova Política*, 11:37, 123–25.

22. Vargas did not hold a rigidly autarchical economic position, but his vision of national development was based upon Brazilian efforts rather than primarily foreign investment. In 1945, he warned that Brazil was coveted by others: "it is not by invasion *manu militari* alone that a nation can lose its independence and suffer threats to its sovereignty. This can also happen through the transfer of ownership of key industries, by ceding strategic materials, or if capital factors of national defense are put in foreign hands" (*Nova Política*, 11:40).

23. Russell Landstrom, *The Associated Press News Annual: 1945* (New York: Rinehart, 1946), 280.

24. The quotations from Vargas's speech in the following five paragraphs come from Vargas, *Nova Política*, 11:141–51.

25. Ibid., 11:19.

26. Ibid., 11:125, 18.

27. Edgard Carone, *A Terceira República (1937–1945)* (São Paulo: DIFEL, 1976), 453.

28. See Angela de Castro Gomes, *A Invenção do Trabalhismo* (São Paulo: Vértice/IUPERJ, 1988), 305, for more on the final drafting of *Lei Eleitoral (Decreto Lei No. 7586—28-5-45)* (Rio de Janeiro: Imprensa Nacional, 1954). For the text of Constitutional Amendment no. 9 of February 1945, see Carone, *Terceira República*; or Silva, *1945*, 480–88. For the features of the pre-1930 legislation, consult Manoel Rodrigues Ferreira, *História dos Sistemas Eleitorais Brasileiros* (São Paulo: Livraria Nobel, 1976); for the 1932 code and modifications, consult Octávio Kelly, ed., *Código Eleitoral Anotado* (Rio de Janeiro: A Coelho Branco Filho, 1933); and Ministério da Justica, *Lei N. 48, de 4 de Maio de 1935, Modifica o Código Eleitoral* (São Paulo: Imprensa Oficial do Estado, 1937).

29. Vargas, *Nova Política*, 11:103; Gomes, *Invenção do Trabalhismo*, 296–97.

30. The Brazilian Left opposed the literacy requirement as a restriction of popular participation since it barred half of the adult population from voting. The measure's practical impact, however, was to favor the urban areas that had a lower rate of illiteracy and that tended to vote Left. See Boris Fausto, ed., *História Geral da Civilização Brasileira*, part 3, vol. 4 (São Paulo: DIFEL, 1984), 236; Levi Carneiro, *Voto dos Analfabetos* (Petrópolis: Vozes, 1964).

31. For a discussion of female electoral, political, and trade union activity in postwar ABC, see John D. French with Mary Lynn Pedersen, "Women and Working Class Mobilization in Postwar São Paulo, Brazil 1945–1948," *Latin American Research Review* 24 (Fall 1989): 99–125.

32. As Gomes has documented, this type of ex officio voter registration procedure was being proposed in the secret "Plano B" drawn up for Vargas in December 1943. Contemplating the impending postwar transition, the document was quite explicit about the aim of such a measure which was part of the shift in Getulista policy after 1942 that was overseen by Labor Minister Marcondes Filho (*Invenção do Trabalhismo*, 297–300).

33. Vargas, *Nova Política*, 11:103. The little-studied ex officio voter registration has most often been depicted, as it was by Getúlio's opponents, as a form of "officialized fraud" (Campello de Souza, *Estado e Partidos*, 121; Maria D'Alva Gil Kinzo, *Representação Política e Sistema Eleitoral no Brasil* [São Paulo: Símbolo, 1980], 81–82). In fact, the bulk of ex officio voter registration probably came from factory payroll enrollments. The appropriate company official was required to submit a list of employees to an electoral judge, who returned the electoral identification cards for distribution within the factory. For examples, see TRE SP, "Consultas," 1945.

34. Eduardo Gomes set forth his central theme in a 17 April 1945 interview after the announcement of planned elections and other concessions by Vargas. The only way to guarantee that "the government would not interfere in the electoral process," he went on, was for Vargas to resign immediately. He raised the stakes further when

he invoked the sacrifices of the Brazilian soldiers fighting in Europe "for the freedom of oppressed countries" while their homeland was still "dominated by an identical regime" (Gomes, *Campanha*, 331–35). Vargas responded to such charges by mocking the "strange mentality of the enemies of the government! They demand democracy, the vote, elections; but when they are given the opportunity" by his action, their only response is to call for his overthrow (Vargas, *Nova Política*, 11:148).

35. Trigueiro, *General Dutra*, 86, 110.

36. "The problem of political institutions," Gomes insisted, "lay at the root of all other" problems, including the economic difficulties of the nation. The Brigadeiro's 3 May 1945 interview provides evidence of his preference for the terrain of political and juridical debate: he spent the entire interview reiterating his "juridical theses" that the illegitimate regime of Vargas must be ended by passing power to the judiciary, the only institution surviving from the country's last and only valid constitution, that of 1934. The UDN candidate assured his readers that this position had been sustained by the "most trustworthy specialists" of the legal profession— an argument unlikely to convince a non-middle-class audience (Gomes, *Campanha*, 115, 336–44).

37. Ibid., 342, 35–36. As one scholar has noted, the Brigadeiro's rhetoric in 1945 presented the question of democracy as a restoration, a reestablishment, and a return to the past that he himself had helped destroy (João Almino, *Os Democratas Autoritários: Liberdades Individuais de Associação Política e Sindical na Constituição de 1946* [São Paulo: Brasiliense, 1980], 39).

38. Warren Dean credits the UDN's hostility to "the creation of domestic industry" as an expression of the interests of the "liberal middle class of the cities," who lost the elections to "the party of the rural bosses," the PSD, supported by the industrialists (*The Industrialization of São Paulo, 1880–1945* [Austin: University of Texas Press, 1969], 235).

39. For Gomes, the rural majority was homogeneous and was not divided between employers and employees, since all "feel themselves united by the same luck, employers, and employees." Discussing the misery and abandonment of the rural workers, he argued that increases in their wages did not represent a solution since it would lead them "to reduce their weekly labor by some days to the detriment of the tasks which, by the pressure of time, cannot be put off" (*Campanha*, 48, 46).

40. Ibid., 46, 101, 40, 50.

41. Vargas, for example, was explicit in his assurances that an "agrarian reform" in Brazil would "not imply redistribution" of land in the hands of its present owners (*Nova Política*, 11:39). Yet this did not mean that Vargas and his followers completely excluded rural labor from their reformist project of popular inclusion in national life. Clifford Welch in his fine recent dissertation presents a revisionist interpretation that counters the dominant view that populist initiatives were directed exclusively toward urban workers and excluded the rural majority ("Rural Labor and the Brazilian Revolution in São Paulo, 1930–1964" [Ph.D. diss., Duke University, 1990]).

42. Gomes, *Campanha*, 278, 46, 278.

43. Ibid., 278, 48, 266.

44. Ibid., 20–21.

45. Ibid., 46, 30–33, 45, 51–52.

46. Gomes dismissed the president's "flattery" of the people as a "demagogic appeal" of a man who sought at all costs to avoid an electoral contest. In his nine-page interview of 3 May 1945, Gomes devoted only three sentences to the "misery and hunger" of the "poorer classes." After qualifying even that statement, the UDN candidate blamed the problem on the disorganization of "public finances" in Brazil and proposed no concrete steps to remedy the problem (ibid., 336, 342).

47. The workers' almost instinctive hostility to the UDN's candidate in 1945 has too often been attributed to the dishonest if skillful demagoguery of Getúlio's supporters, whose smears were allegedly accepted as truth by an uninformed working class. Popular opposition to the Brigadeiro is often credited to the rumor started by São Paulo PTB leader Hugo Borghi that the UDN's candidate disdained the vote of *marmiteiros* (a derogatory term for unskilled workers derived from the metal pail in which they carried their lunches); see Benevides, *UDN*, 45; Trigueiro, *General Dutra*, 179. For Borghi's account, see *Fôlha da Manhã*, 12 December 1945; Gomes, *Invenção do Trabalhismo*, 317; Valentina da Rocha Lima, ed., *Getúlio: Uma História Oral* (Rio de Janeiro: Record, 1986), 160. While candidate Gomes was unlikely to disdain votes from any source, the rumor quite accurately captured the disdain for the masses among UDNistas.

48. The quotations from Gomes's speech in the two following paragraphs come from Gomes, *Campanha*, 13, 16–17.

49. For the position of the Brazilian socialists as they began to organize in 1945, see the two manifestos in Edgard Carone, ed., *Movimento Operário no Brasil*, 2 vols. (São Paulo: DIFEL, 1979–81), 2:3–16. The Democratic Left (Esquerda Democrática) was founded in August 1945 and supported Gomes for president while running its own candidates for other posts—with minimal success. Almino, *Democratas Autoritários*, 27, cites a socialist student activist in São Paulo, Germinal Feijó, on the social question.

50. For the text of the Sorocaba speech, see Gomes, *Campanha*, 280–85; and see 294–97 for his later disavowal of these positions.

51. In his Sorocaba speech, the Brigadeiro also lectured his listeners that private property corresponded to "human nature" and warned of the horrors of the "exclusively proletarian solution" attempted in Russia (ibid., 280–85).

52. The labor problem, Gomes argued, was ultimately spiritual in nature. It would be resolved when both parties realized that they needed and depended upon each other, as the Catholic Church had so long argued (ibid., 282–83).

53. Even if Gomes had been sincere in São Paulo when he pledged support for the "right to strike," it is important to remember that he offered no guarantee that a particular group of workers could successfully strike or that he would support them if they did.

54. Gomes, *Invenção do Trabalhismo*, 322–23; Trigueiro, *General Dutra*, 103–6.

55. Almino, *Democratas Autoritários*, 36–37.

56. Trigueiro, *General Dutra*, 105.

57. Ibid.; Dean, *Industrialization*, 235–36.

58. For the text of the May 1945 Vasco da Gama speech by Prestes, see Edgard

Carone, *O P.C.B. Vol. 2: 1943–1964* (São Paulo: DIFEL, 1982), 25–40. Unlike the followers of the UDN, the Communist leader detected phases and turning points within the Estado Novo, distinguishing between Vargas and other reactionary groups that made up the regime.

59. For a dramatic rendering of the life and fate of Olga Benario Prestes, see the bestseller by Fernando Morais, *Olga*, 14th ed. (São Paulo: Alfa-Omega, 1987).

60. Carone, *PCB*, 2:36–37.

61. Vargas, *Nova Política*, 11:172–73. Prestes's informal comment about the idols of the people in 1945 is recounted by an informant in Juiz de Fora, Minas Gerais (Maria Andréa Loyola, *Os Sindicatos e o PTB* [Petrópolis: Vozes/CEBRAP, 1980], 60). Robert Alexander interviewed Senator Prestes on 27 August 1946; his notes paraphrase the Communist leader as saying that the "PTB has some workers, not so advanced, who still believe in the legend of Vargas. They are mainly in São Paulo and the Federal District but [the] party doesn't have many deep roots, and most workers who adhere to it are followers of Vargas personally" (interview by Robert Alexander with Luis Carlos Prestes, 27 August 1946, Rio de Janeiro; in the private archive of Robert Alexander).

62. Carone, *PCB*, 2:40–57. After his release from prison for Communist activities in 1944, former metalworkers' president Marcos Andreotti began to frequent the union in Santo André once again despite apprehension by some of its leaders that his presence would precipitate repression. He recalls disagreeing with even the Communists in the union over their excessively uncritical attitude toward Vargas. Having just come from a term in prison with many of the leading Communists, Andreotti was aware of the Party's evolution—on the leadership if not the rank-and-file level—toward a more assertive and independent policy by 1944. This recalls the comments of Prestes in August 1945 when he criticized the earlier one-sided interpretation that had been given to the slogan of "unconditional support" for the war effort of the Vargas regime (Carone, *PCB*, 2:50–52).

63. Silva, *1945*, 195–96; Carone, *PCB*, 2:56.

64. An examination of the Communist press and reports confirms Prestes's insistence that "We want a Constituent Assembly with Getúlio" was never an official party slogan in 1945 (Dênis de Moraes and Francisco Viana, eds., *Prestes: Lutas e Autocríticas* [Petrópolis: Vozes, 1982], 106).

65. Trigueiro, *General Dutra*, 79. Prestes said, "It would be difficult to find two candidates as similar" as Dutra and Gomes (Moraes and Viana, *Prestes*, 104–5).

66. Adolph A. Berle, *Navigating the Rapids, 1918–1971* (New York: Harcourt Brace Jovanovich, 1973), 551, regarding a 1 October 1945 interview with Vargas.

67. Ibid., 529–30.

68. In his August 1946 interview with Alexander, Prestes denied meeting with or entering any formal agreement with Vargas in 1945. "The policies of Vargas and the CP," he explained, simply "ran along parallel lines" during late 1945 in much the same way that the PCB and the UDN had worked together for amnesty earlier that year. "Vargas was against [a] military golpe because it would overthrow him," he went on, and the "CP [was] against [it] since it would probably be aimed first at them since the Army was primarily in the hands of fascist elements that hated the PCB" (interview by Alexander with Prestes, 27 August 1946, Rio de Janeiro; in the

private archive of Robert Alexander). Hugo de Faria, one of Vargas's associates, also refers to the pragmatic nature of the PCB's decision to come to terms with Vargas (Lima, *Getúlio*, 157).

69. Even at the height of the PCB's much-discussed alliance with Vargas later in 1945, the Communists enjoyed an ambiguous status in which they were publicly tolerated and enjoyed a de facto but not yet de jure status as a legal political party. Indeed, the PCB was only finally given legal status by the Tribunal Superior Eleitoral (TSE) on 27 October 1945, two days before Vargas was ousted. The PCB's application had earlier been put on hold pending clarifications related to the provision of the May 1945 electoral legislation that banned parties "whose programs violate the democratic principles, or the fundamental rights of man defined in the constitution" (*Lei Eleitoral [Decreto Lei No. 7586]*, 25). Thus the initiative in mid-1945 was firmly in the hands of Vargas, who could influence whether the PCB would be legalized or not.

70. Lima, *Getúlio*, 155–56. For a sketchy and unsatisfactory discussion of queremismo, see Arnaldo Spindel, *O Partido Comunista na Gênese do Populismo* (São Paulo: Símbolo, 1980), 59–67.

71. Silva, *1945*, 136–37. The discourse of Getúlio Vargas and Brigadeiro Gomes offered strikingly different visions of the social composition of Brazilian society. Vargas addressed an audience he defined as those who "labor and produce in the fields and cities, in the workshops, offices, factories, and on the railroads, on board ships, on sea and on earth, behind the counters of banks, and in the establishments where public functionaries work" (*Nova Política*, 11:136). When Brigadeiro Gomes discussed the effect of inflation on the "great majority of the population," he identified the following groups: "the class of magistrates, public functionaries, the military men, the middle class, small commerce, the employees in all branches of activities, teachers, retired persons, salaried persons in general, and manual workers" (Gomes, *Campanha*, 40).

72. Vargas, *Nova Política*, 11:103.

73. Gomes, *Invenção do Trabalhismo*, 308–14.

74. John D. French, "The Communications Revolution: Radio and Working Class Life and Culture in Postwar São Paulo, Brazil" (Working Paper, Third Latin American Labor History Conference, Yale University, 18–19 April 1978); Elysabeth Carmona and Geraldo Leite, "Radio, Povo e Poder: Subserviência e Paternalismo," in *Populismo e Communicação*, ed. José Marques de Melo (São Paulo: Cortez, 1981), 125–34. By contrast, the UDN's efforts to use radio were woefully inadequate compared to their opponents' aggressive campaigning (Silva, *1945*, 302; Trigueiro, *General Dutra*, 178).

75. The recollections of the PSD's Amaral Peixoto still capture this sense of discomfort and ill feeling (Lima, *Getúlio*, 157).

76. Almino, *Democratas Autoritários*, 57; Berle, *Navigating the Rapids*, 548. The queremista agitation also alarmed the military establishment. The army's chief of staff, General Barcelos, made clear that the military would "oppose any action of the extremisms of creed or ambition that would bring us to anarchy" (Trigueiro, *General Dutra*, 115, 145).

77. Gomes, *Campanha*, 57.

78. Trigueiro, *General Dutra*, 120–22. The São Paulo UDN used the term "comuno-queremismo" in its campaign advertisements (*DSP*, 25 November 1945).

79. *Borda do Campo*, 12 August 1945; Prefeitura Municipal de São Bernardo do Campo, Processo 606–45.

80. *Borda do Campo*, 15 July and 2 September 1945.

81. Ibid., 5 August, 16 September, 21 October 1945. One article complained that some workers could now be heard in local bars and cinemas joking "that the factory and its owner's home will soon be ours" (ibid., 10 September 1945).

82. Gomes, *Campanha*, 81, 108–10. The Brigadeiro's anticommunist theme, coming less than a month after Japan's surrender, well preceded the deterioration of U.S.-Soviet relations with the onset of the cold war. The UDN leader thus broke with that large body of public opinion, in Brazil and worldwide, that viewed the Soviet Union with sympathy for its contribution, at the cost of twenty million lives, to the defeat of Hitlerism.

83. To stand silent in the face of the reorganization of communism in Brazil, Brigadeiro Gomes told a group of graduating military officers, was to evade one's "unavoidable responsibilities," whether from naiveté or cowardice. Having defined communism as "an economic theory that proposes a reconstruction of society, based on the suppression of private property," he denounced its philosophy of "radical materialism" that denied God and sought to implant, "concealed from the eyes of the distracted multitudes," a Marxist-Leninist regime based on propaganda, compulsion, and coercion (ibid., 148–50).

84. Vargas's survival for fifteen years attested to his grasp of the importance of the military. As his secretary wrote in 1944, without "the army, no one in this country can think of revolt" (Luiz Vergara, *Fui Secretário de Getúlio Vargas: Memórias dos Anos de 1926–1954* [Rio de Janeiro: Globo, 1960], 158).

85. General Góes Monteiro tells a story about Getúlio's reaction to the triumph of Argentina's Major Juan Perón on 17 October 1945 when he was taken from prison to power in the arms of the people. Vargas is said to have commented that it showed "the power of the masses," to which his minister of war, Góes Monteiro, claims to have replied that it wasn't the masses, but the pro-Perón military who had brought him back to power. After so many years in power, Getúlio was aware of such realities. Góes Monteiro, on the other hand, shows that mistaken narrowness, so common to his caste in 1945, that would dismiss the "people" as a factor of any real importance (Lourival Coutinho, ed., *O General Góes Depõe* [Rio de Janeiro: Coelho Branco, 1956], 438–39).

86. Trigueiro, *General Dutra*, 107–14; Coutinho, *General Góes*, 415, 417–18.

87. Trigueiro, *General Dutra*, 123, 144–45.

88. Berle's strongly expressed opinions about Brazil's internal political affairs caused a diplomatic incident (Silva, *1945*, 214–23; Berle, *Navigating the Rapids*, 553). Bryce Wood in his 1985 book examines the U.S. State Department background to this incident and concludes that it was, despite public denials, a conscious U.S. intervention in Brazilian domestic affairs (*The Dismantling of the Good Neighbor Policy* [Austin: University of Texas Press, 1985], 122–25).

89. Trigueiro, *General Dutra*, 148–49.

90. Vargas, *Nova Política*, 11:185–92; Trigueiro, *General Dutra*, 151.

91. Coutinho, *General Góes*, 437; Trigueiro, *General Dutra*, 151–54.

92. Trigueiro, *General Dutra*, 154–64.

93. *Borda do Campo*, 4 November 1945.

94. Trigueiro, *General Dutra*, 166–69.

95. Moraes and Viana, *Prestes*, 109.

96. Trigueiro, *General Dutra*, 94.

97. Vergara, *Fui Secretário*, 183; Skidmore, *Politics*, 59.

98. Silva, *1945*, 292–93, 204, 309.

99. Ibid., 305–6. See Gomes, *Invenção do Trabalhismo*, 315–18, for more on the PTB's internal divisions at this time.

100. Carone, *PCB*, 2:60–61.

101. Moraes and Viana, *Prestes*, 111.

102. Silva, *1945*, 297, 308.

103. Ibid., 312, 317–18; Trigueiro, *General Dutra*, 177–78, 180.

104. Trigueiro, *General Dutra*, 181–84; Silva, *1945*, 318–19.

105. Kenneth Erickson, "Populism and Political Control of the Working Class in Brazil," *Proceedings of the Pacific Coast Council on Latin American Studies* 4 (1975): 126; Soares, *Sociedade e Política*, 41.

106. TSE, *Dados Estatísticos* (Rio de Janeiro: Imprensa Nacional, 1950), 1:8.

107. TRE SP Serviço Informática, "1945: Resultado Final do Numero de Eleitores Devidamente Inscritos . . ." (unpublished document).

108. TSE, *Dados Estatísticos*, 1:11.

109. Gomes's supporters remained stubbornly self-righteous in the aftermath of defeat. For example, UDN Secretary General Virgilio de Melo Franco asked: "The UDN was not populist? We would have been much more popular if we had acted in another manner, they say. But if we had . . . the people would have been left without elections" (*ESP*, 14 February 1946). For even more rancorous views, see the interview with the UDN's Prado Kelly in Lourenço Dantas Mota, ed., *A História Vivida* (São Paulo: Estado de São Paulo, n.d.), 1:159.

110. Dutra's victory, as Gomes remarks, was viewed by contemporary observers as unequivocal proof of the overwhelming force of Getúlio Vargas's personal appeal (*Invenção do Trabalhismo*, 318). At the same time, the surprisingly strong vote for the Communists served as a disincentive to those conservative elements of the army and Dutra's new administration who thought seriously about stripping Vargas of his political rights. To do so, they realized, would drive the workers into the hands of an even more dangerous enemy, the Communists of Luis Carlos Prestes (Almino, *Democratas Autoritários*, 68–69).

111. Silva, *1945*, 286–87.

112. Moraes and Viana, *Prestes*, 112.

113. See Table G4, "Presidential Election Results for Industrial Zones and State of São Paulo, December 2, 1945," and Table G5, "Presidential Election Results in Santo André, December 2, 1945," in John D. French, "Industrial Workers and the Origin of Populist Politics in the ABC Region of Greater São Paulo, Brazil 1900–1950" (Ph.D. diss., Yale University, 1985), 660–61.

114. TRE SP Serviço Informática, "Quadro Demonstrativo da Votação Obtido no

Estado de São Paulo, pelos Candidatos a Presidência da República 1945" (unpublished document).

115. TSE, *Dados Estatísticos*, 1:43; *Fôlha da Manha*, 12 December 1945.

116. I use the results for federal deputy to estimate party support rather than the vote for president, since the latter was not broken down by party. For Santo André results, see Table G7, "Câmara Federal Election Results in Santo André and State of São Paulo, December 2, 1945," in French, "Industrial Workers," 663–64.

117. Whether Dutristas or UDNistas, contemporary observers also saw the election results as proof of the forceful and irreversible entrance of working people into national political life (Gomes, *Invenção do Trabalhismo*, 318–21). In a book published in 1945, the distinguished anti-Getulista jurist and socialist politician Hermes Lima underscored the significance of Getúlio's opening to the people. Throughout Brazilian history, he observed, politics had been reserved "to elements of the 'educated classes'. . . [and] viewed as a privilege and result of their culture." Whether under the monarchy or the republic, he went on, there was always a "fear of the active participation of the people in public life." The Brazilian upper class was convinced, he stressed, that the great mass of the populace lacked the education needed to exercise their rights and to prevent them from falling "into the camp of demagoguery, or as they prefer to say, of anarchy." Elected a Socialist Party federal deputy in 1945, Lima stressed that Brazilian politicians to date had "shown themselves doubtful of the capacity of the people, suspicious . . . [and] convinced that the people was a species of sleeping volcano" (Hermes Lima, *Notas da Vida Brasileira* [São Paulo: Brasiliense, 1945], reprinted in *Antologia do Pensamento Social e Político no Brasil*, ed. Luis Washington Vital [São Paulo: Grijalbo, 1968], 407–8).

Chapter Five

1. In his study of the Constituent Assembly, for example, Evaristo Giovanetti Netto reflects the existing historiography when he places primary emphasis on the state's and the elites' success in controlling the transition of 1945–46. Thus he arrives at the excessively pessimistic conclusion that the postwar redemocratization "did not imply a significant enlargement of the margins of participation or a significant increase in the degree of freedom" in Brazilian society (*O PCB na Assembléia Constituinte de 1946* [São Paulo: Novos Rumos, 1986], 14, 23). For an influential formulation of the continuity hypothesis, see Maria do Carmo Campello de Souza, *Estado e Partidos Políticos no Brasil (1930 a 1964)* (São Paulo: Alfa-Omega, 1983), 105.

2. Vicente U. de Almeida and Octávio T. Mendes report that 1940–46 was the period of greatest sustained migration to the city of São Paulo from the interior (*Migração Rural-Urbana* [São Paulo: Secretariado da Agricultura, 1951], 16). This population movement was spurred by the high demand for labor and the manifest advantages of life in the metropolis.

3. U.S. Bureau of Labor Statistics (USBLS), *Labor Conditions in Latin America,*

nos. 14 and 15 (1943); Octaviano A. Gaiarsa, *A Cidade que Dormiu Três Séculos* (Santo André: Bandeirante, 1968), 141–42.

4. USBLS, *Labor Conditions*, no. 20 (1944).

5. USBLS, *Labor Conditions*, nos. 14 and 15 (1943). Although a downward trend is clear, there are conflicting estimates of how much purchasing power was lost during World War II. See Pedro Alim, *O Seguro Social, a Indústria Brasileira, e o Instituto dos Industriários* (Rio de Janeiro: IAPI, 1950), 140–41; Francisco de Oliveira, "A Economia Brasileira: Crítica a Razão Dualista," *Seleções CEBRAP*, no. 1 (São Paulo: Brasiliense, 1977), 41; or the minimum wage calculations done by Departamento Intersindical de Estatística e Estudos Socio-Econômicos that are reprinted in Vania Malheiros Barbosa Alves, *Vanguarda Operária: Elite de Classe?* (Rio de Janeiro: Paz e Terra, 1984), 133.

Determining the trend of real industrial wages, even in the long term, involves difficult empirical and technical issues. The significance of the real value of the minimum wage, for example, depends upon what percentage of the industrial work force falls under its coverage. On this question between 1945 and 1951, see Edmar Bacha, Milton da Mata, and Rui Lyrio Modenesi, *Encargos Trabalhista e Absorção de Mão-de-Obra* (Rio de Janeiro: IPEA/INPES, 1972), 92–93. To arrive at a firm judgment, we need detailed studies of wages by industry and enterprise carried out by labor economists. Only then will we be able to tackle the even more difficult question of calculating the standard of living of working-class families in São Paulo. For an introduction to the complexities involved, see the superb two-part series by John Wells, "Industrial Accumulation and Living-Standards in the Long-Run: The São Paulo Industrial Working Class, 1930–75 (Parts I & 2)," *Journal of Development Studies* 19 (January and April 1983), 145–69, 297–328. For a Peruvian example, see Wilma Derpich, José Luis Huiza, and Cecília Israel, *Lima Años 30: Salários y Costo de Vida de la Clase Trabajadora* (Lima: Fundaçiõn Friedrich Ebert, 1985).

While essential, such data still will not tell us how people perceived their economic circumstances. In a 19 September 1946 interview with Robert Alexander, a Porto Alegre professor suggested that the "popularity of Vargas [during World War II was] due to the fact that inflation which has now reached its apogee started under Vargas but then appeared to be only prosperity and not inflation. Now Dutra has to take responsibility for the logical results of Vargas's policy" (interview by Robert Alexander with Otto Alcides, 19 September 1946, Porto Alegre).

6. Gaiarsa, *Cidade*, 158; USBLS, *Labor Conditions*, no. 15 (1943).

7. Albert H. Berman, *Industrial Labor in Brazil* (Washington, D.C.: U.S. Office of Inter-American Affairs, Research Division, 1944), 29.

8. Gaiarsa, *Cidade*, 49.

9. Prefeitura Municipal de Santo André (PMSA), Processo 6567 (1946).

10. PMSA, Processos 1369, 1397, 1171 (1945).

11. "Santo André," *Economia* (undated clipping in possession of the author).

12. USBLS, *Labor Conditions*, no. 19 (1944), 1–2.

13. USBLS, *Labor Conditions*, no. 13 (1942).

14. USBLS, *Labor Conditions*, no. 19 (1944), 1–2.

15. "O Sr. Getúlio Vargas em Visita a Laminação Nacional de Metais," *São Paulo de Ontem, Hoje e de Amanhã* 2, no. 49 (January 1944): 33.

16. Osvaldo Trigueiro do Vale, *O General Dutra e a Redemocratização de 45* (Rio de Janeiro: Civilização Brasileira, 1978), 103–4.

17. See, for example, Hélio Silva, *1945: Por que Depuseram Vargas* (Rio de Janeiro: Civilização Brasileira, 1976); Thomas Skidmore, *Politics in Brazil, 1930–1964* (New York: Oxford University Press, 1967); Richard Bourne, *Getúlio Vargas of Brazil, 1883–1954: Sphinx of the Pampas* (London: Charles Knight, 1974); John W. F. Dulles, *Vargas of Brazil* (Austin: University of Texas Press, 1967); Ronald Chilcote, *The Brazilian Communist Party: Conflict and Integration, 1922–1972* (New York: Oxford University Press, 1974); Peter Flynn, *Brazil, A Political Analysis* (Boulder: Westview Press, 1978); Antônio Mendes de Almeida Júnior, "Do Declínio do Estado Novo ao Suicídio de Getúlio Vargas," in *História Geral da Civilização Brasileira*, ed. Boris Fausto, part 3, vol. 3 (São Paulo: DIFEL, 1981), 225–94; Leôncio Martins Rodrigues, "Sindicalismo e Classe Operária (1930–1964)," in ibid., 507–55.

18. Yonne de Souza Grossi, *Mina de Morro Velho: A Extração do Homen* (Rio de Janeiro: Paz e Terra, 1982); Maria Andréa Loyola, *Os Sindicatos e o PTB: Estudo de um Caso em Minas Gerais* (Petrópolis: Vozes, 1980).

19. Francisco Weffort, "Origenes do Sindicalismo Populista no Brasil," *Estudos CEBRAP*, no. 4 (April–June 1973), 65–106.

20. Associação Comercial e Industrial de Santo André (ACISA), *Atas*, 2:186, notes the "profound internal revolt caused by the barbarous attitude of Nazi submarines" that sank Brazilian merchant vessels in August 1942. A local movie theater organized fund-raising showings for the Brazilian victims of the sinking. Ibid., 192, notes the rubber drive overseen by the ACISA. Also see undated and untitled manuscript by Marcos Andreotti (in my possession).

21. Gaiarsa notes the "participation of all social classes in these demonstrations of happiness" at the news of the victory in Europe, "a true harmonization of the entire population" (*Cidade*, 158). This memory by local resident Gaiarsa takes on greater weight given his UDNista affiliations.

22. David Brody, *Steelworkers in America: The Non-Union Era* (New York: Harper and Row, 1969).

23. *Hoje*, 28 October 1945.

24. Neuema Aguiar Walker, "The Organization and Ideology of Brazilian Labor," in *Revolution in Brazil*, ed. Irving Louis Horowitz (New York: Dutton, 1964), 254–55. As Luiz Werneck Vianna pointed out, the social meaning of Vargas's terminology and rhetoric changes depending upon the political context; thus, his aggressive courtship of workers in 1944–45 served to deflate Vargas's earlier "discourse of harmony and organic integration of social classes" (*Liberalismo e Sindicato* [Rio de Janeiro: Paz e Terra, 1976], 249).

25. Carlos Estevan Martins and Maria Hermínia Tavares de Almeida, "Modus in Rebus, Partidos e Classes na Queda do Estado Novo" (Mimeograph, undated [1974]).

26. Addressing a festive rally in the district of Mauá in ABC, the political secre-

tary of the São Paulo PCB, Mario Scott, chided the many "comrades who allowed themselves to be taken in by *politiqueiros* and demagogues" (*Hoje*, 6 October 1945).

27. This standard view derived from a misinterpretation of a famous article by Azis Simão. Acknowledging rural migrant support for both the PCB and the PTB, Simão actually made far finer distinctions among rural migrants: between those who came to the capital before the war, and the newcomers of the years between 1940 and 1946 ("O Voto Operário em São Paulo," *Revista Brasileira de Estudos Políticos* 1 [1956]: 130–41).

28. Attorney José Artur da Frota Moreira, for example, a key postwar PTB leader and future federal deputy in São Paulo, was head of the loosely organized Centro de Estudos Políticos Econômicos e Sociais set up by Segadas Vianna within the labor ministry in 1942 (Angela de Castro Gomes, *A Invenção do Trabalhismo* [Rio de Janeiro: IUPERJ/Vértice, 1988], 293). A *procurador* in the labor court system, Frota Moreira served as delegate of the national PTB in São Paulo during 1945 (TRE SP, Processo 7 [1945]). Frota Moreira was repeatedly attacked by the Communists as a "ministerialist agent" for his supposed inefficiency in handling the dissídio of Laminação Nacional de Metais (*Hoje*, 11 March 1946; 1 January 1946).

29. In the all-important capital city of São Paulo, the PTB's diretório was headed by Luiz Fiuz Cardia, a delegate of the state clothing workers' federation. Fiuz Cardia's stationery listed both his union and political posts with the PTB. Other unionists also played roles of some prominence, including José Sanches Duran, the head of São Paulo's metalworkers' federation, and Deocleciano Hollanda de Cavalcanti, head of the Union of Employees in the Drink Industry and future president of the powerful National Confederation of Industrial Workers (Confederação Nacional dos Trabalhadores na Indústria, or CNTI) (TRE SP, Processo 7A [1945]; Consulta 238 [1945]). These leaders had attained their greatest prominence during the Estado Novo (*São Paulo* 2, no. 49 [January 1944]).

30. TRE SP, *Livros de Diretórios Municipais*, 2:54.

31. Ricardo Maranhão, *Sindicatos e Democratização (Brasil 1945/1950)* (São Paulo: Brasiliense, 1979). Gomes has noted that, although "the PTB existed at the ballot box, [it] was almost a fiction in organizational terms" in 1946 (*Invenção do Trabalhismo*, 320).

32. These neighborhood Democratic Committees (CDPs) were to be nonparty organizations open to all "democrats" regardless of class, party or belief. In the less socially diverse environment of ABC, they consisted almost exclusively of members of the working class. The CDPs were to fight to improve the conditions of the local populace by struggling for immediate, practical, and realizable popular goals such as better public transportation, clinics, schools, markets, and day-care centers. The committees were also to create schools to ι. ach literacy and to conduct classes, debates, and discussions about the larger issues of the redemocratization of the country. The PCB's guidelines for the CDPs, dated 21 July 1945, are reprinted in Edgard Carone, *O P.C.B. Vol. 2: 1943–1964* (São Paulo: DIFEL, 1982), 57–59.

33. *Hoje*, 10 December 1945; 23 January 1946; 28 December 1945; 18 March 1946; 20 February 1946. In particular, see the detailed twelve-point program laid

out in the founding manifesto of the Comitê Democrático Progressista de Santo André (*O Imparcial*, 26 January 1946).

34. *Hoje*, 28 October 1945; 2 February 1946; 23 and 27 February 1946; 1 and 11 March 1946; 28 October 1945.

35. *Hoje*, 6 October 1945. The PCB organization in Paranapiacaba was a "sub-cell" of São Paulo Railway workers, linked to a similar occupational cell in the port city of Santos; *Hoje*, 21 and 22 February 1946.

36. Andreotti manuscript; *Hoje*, 28 March 1946; 9 February 1946.

37. An emphasis on the political importance of the trade union after World War II runs against the grain of earlier commentary. In his classic work, José Albertino Rodrigues argued that unions in the immediate postwar years did not participate in politics in an "active" and "organic" manner. He contrasted the postwar period, said to be characterized by individual party recruitment of union leaders, with the developments of the 1950s (*Sindicato e Desenvolvimento no Brasil* [1968; reprint, São Paulo: Símbolo, 1979], 159). The evidence, from ABC at least, suggests that unions were more important to political mobilization between 1945 and 1947 than they were at any later point in the Populist Republic.

38. Drawing from a 1952 anti-Getulista critique of the *Consolidação das Leis do Trabalho* (*CLT*) of 1943, Francisco Weffort highlighted the postwar survival of the fascist-inspired corporatist *CLT*, which he believed fundamentally compromised the new liberal democratic era of 1946–64 ("Democracia e Movimento Operário: Algumas Questões para a História do Período 1945–1964 [Part One]," *Revista de Cultura Contemporânea* 1 [1978]: 10). That the survival of the *CLT* remained for so long the fulcrum of our discussion of labor demonstrates Weffort's extraordinary ability to set the intellectual agenda of his generation. At the same time, it has meant that excessive attention has been directed toward a question that has little to do with working-class behavior and practice or the actual politics of the Brazilian labor relations system. Rather than proving its centrality, the survival of the *CLT* since 1943 could be taken to suggest that the importance of institutional and legal structures has been grossly exaggerated by most analysts of Brazilian industrial and labor relations.

39. Edgard Carone, for example, divides the labor movement in 1945 into two camps. He sees "'peleguismo' and the absence of a free working-class conscious-ness that persists in various strata of the [working] class" as being pitted against the actions of "the more conscious and revolutionary vanguards" who undertook action against the Estado Novo (*O Estado Novo (1937–1945)* [São Paulo: DIFEL, 1977], 129).

40. Loyola, *Sindicatos*, 65–77. See also José Sérgio Leite Lopes's observations about the non-Communist leadership of the Pernambuco textile workers' union between 1941 and 1947 (*A Tecelagem dos Conflitos de Classe na Cidade das Chaminés* [São Paulo: Marco Zero/Editôra Universidade de Brasília, 1988], 300–301, 306, 319–21).

41. *Borda do Campo*, 3 February 1946.

42. Robert Alexander, *Organized Labor in Latin America* (New York: Free Press, 1965), 73, 75–76; Robert Alexander, *Communism in Latin America* (New Bruns-

wick, N.J.: Rutgers University Press, 1957), 119; Skidmore, *Politics*, 62; Arnaldo Spindel, *O Partido Comunista na Gênese do Populismo* (São Paulo: Símbolo, 1980), 55.

43. Maranhão, *Sindicatos*, 79.

44. *Hoje*, 4 February 1946; 27 October 1945; 28 October 1945; 5 February 1946; 27 October 1945; 18 December 1945; 22 January 1946.

45. *Hoje*, 27 October 1945; 22 January and 9 March 1946. Officially registered with the Ministry of Labor, these "professional associations" were the first step toward the establishment of legally recognized unions for these occupations in ABC.

46. Maranhão, *Sindicatos*, 61–66; Jover Telles, *O Movimento Sindical no Brasil* (1962; reprint, São Paulo: Ciencias Humanas, 1981), 23–24; Carone, *Estado Novo*, 248–49; *Hoje*, 13 November 1945; 6 March 1946. The importance of and form taken by the MUT varied from place to place. Although MUT sections for individual unions or factories existed in São Paulo, the MUT in ABC was organized only on a district level and participated actively in the street agitation and campaigns organized by the PCB and the CDPs (*Hoje*, 23 October 1945; 23 and 27 February 1946). Yet the MUT, in ABC at least, quickly disappeared when the locus of labor activism shifted entirely to within the structures of the revitalized trade unions.

47. Weffort, "Origens," 81–88.

48. *Hoje*, 23 October 1945.

49. *Hoje*, 7 January 1946.

50. *O Estado de São Paulo* (*ESP*), 10 January 1946.

51. *ESP*, 12 and 15 January 1946; *Diário de São Paulo* (*DSP*), 18 January 1946; *ESP*, 16 January 1946 (reprinted in *Movimento Operário no Brasil*, 2 vols., ed. Edgard Carone [São Paulo: DIFEL, 1979–81], 2:186–88).

52. *Hoje*, 23 January 1946.

53. *DSP*, 17 January 1946; *ESP*, 9 January 1946.

54. *DSP*, 17 January 1946.

55. An understanding of the tripartite political division within labor's leadership has very practical applications for those interested in studying union politics. The political complexion of the postwar Brazilian labor movement, as Robert Alexander expressed it in a private letter in 1953, was "rather complicated," with three broad groupings he labeled as Communists, Independents, and pelegos (letter from Alexander to Jay Lovestone, 23 June 1953; in the personal archive of Robert Alexander). In addition to the opinionated terminology, the use of these labels does not accurately reflect the political orientations of all or even most members of each current.

An even more finely grained analysis can be reached by recognizing that the labor Center itself contained a spectrum of views, or, as Alexander put it, that there was an "infinite modulation within these categories" (ibid.). It is possible in ABC to distinguish between the more cautious Center forces who, although allied with a weaker Left within their unions, still sought to straddle Left and Right, and those Center unionists who enthusiastically embraced unity with the Left. Thus, we can distinguish between *Center/Left* trade unions in ABC, such as the rubber and furniture workers, and *Left/Center* organizations, such as the local chemical workers' and metalworkers' unions, where the Left was the leading force in the leadership.

56. *Hoje*, 27 October 1945.

Chapter Six

1. "Political circumstances," Michele Perrot reminds us, "weigh very heavily and provide the key both to the quiet periods and to the major upsurges of [strike] activity. If fear serves to repress desire, the hope raised by improved political perspectives fuels a very active ferment of demands" among workers that encourages strikes (*Workers on Strike: France 1871–1890* [New Haven: Yale University Press, 1987], 314). Too often neglected in favor of simplistic economic explanations, this truism of working-class life is ably illustrated in Peter Winn's study of Chilean textile workers. With just one exception, the workers of Yarur mobilized only after presidential elections that led to governments that "were expected to be pro-labor and sympathetic to popular movements. . . . The [state's] central role in labor relations," Winn explained, "meant that workers had to believe that their efforts would enjoy state support" before they acted on their own behalf (*Weavers of Revolution: The Yarur Workers and Chile's Road to Socialism* [New York: Oxford University Press, 1986], 40).

2. *Hoje*, 27 October 1945.

3. Whatever the total, the absolute levels of union membership in ABC had undoubtedly increased since 1941 when even the exaggerated estimate of total union membership in Santo André was given as only 4,000, approximately 20 percent of ABC's work force at that time (Raul de Andrada e Silva, "A Cidade de Santo André e sua Função Industrial," *Revista do Arquivo Municipal* 79 [1941]: 215).

4. The estimate of 2,000–3,000 union members would mean that between 4 and 6 ½ percent of ABC's workers had joined a union by 1945. See Joel Wolfe, "The Rise of Brazil's Industrial Working Class: Community, Work, and Politics in São Paulo, 1900–1955" (Ph.D. diss., University of Wisconsin-Madison, 1990), 167, 177, for membership figures for the textile workers' and metalworkers' unions in the município of São Paulo in the early Estado Novo, which varied from 2 to 3 percent of all workers in textiles and from 4 to 5 percent for the metalworkers. Sonia de Avelar, who has carried out the only comprehensive analysis of a trade union's membership before 1964, found that 11 percent of all textile workers in São José dos Campos belonged to the textile workers' association (later union) formed in 1946 in that small city in the interior of São Paulo ("The Social Basis of Workers' Solidarity: A Case Study of Textile Workers in São José dos Campos, Brazil" [Ph.D. diss., University of Michigan, 1985], 152–59).

Even membership figures, however, do not reflect the even more limited dimensions of the actual activist core of the grass-roots labor movement. In late 1946, for example, there were still fewer than 700 members of the Cooperative of Unionized Workers of Santo André, despite the overall increase in union membership that year ("Lista dos Trabalhadores Sindicalisados Inscritos na 'Cooperativa de Consumo dos

Trabalhadores Sindicalisados de Santo André, Limitada,'" dated 4 September 1946, in Prefeitura Municipal de Santo André (PMSA), Processo 6567 [1946]).

5. In the aftermath of the December elections, for example, the PCB's Mario Scott had warned of the danger of reactionaries "forging new Cohen plans," a reference to the anticommunist, anti-Semitic fabrication that provided the pretext for the coup of 1937 (*Hoje*, 11 December 1945).

6. *Hoje*, 21 February 1946.

7. *Hoje*, 5 January 1946; *ESP*, 11 January 1946. The Communists and allied unionists had not, however, categorically rejected the strike as a means of working-class struggle, as even Francisco Weffort admits. After all, the superbly organized dockers of Santos who signed the antistrike manifesto had struck in May 1945 when such actions were not common elsewhere in the state (Ricardo Maranhão, *Sindicatos e Democratização (Brasil 1945/1950)* [São Paulo: Brasiliense, 1979], 42).

8. Francisco Weffort, "Origens do Sindicalismo Populista no Brasil (A Conjuntura do Após-Guerra," *Estudos CEBRAP*, no. 4 (1973), 82, 86, 88–91. For the Left/Center leaders of São Paulo's militant bankworkers' union, Letícia Canedo demonstrates, "to advise against strikes for salary increases [in 1945] did not stem just from a policy of support for the government . . . but also represented an attempt to mobilize the bankworkers to achieve a more solid and all-embracing goal, the reconstruction [and strengthening] of the bankworkers' movement itself'"; as in ABC, the leaders' desire for a gradual buildup of organizational strength did not prevent them from endorsing strike action in January 1946 (*Bancários: Movimento Sindical e Participação Política* [Campinas: Editôra da UNICAMP, 1986], 48, 57–60).

9. *Hoje*, 5 February 1946.

10. *DSP*, 7 February 1946; *Hoje*, 8 February 1946; *DSP*, 15 February 1946; *Hoje*, 24 January 1946.

11. *DSP*, 30 January and 7 February 1946; *Hoje*, 2 and 8 February 1946. Figures on the number of workers on strike at any given factory are drawn, for the most part, from the 1945 statistics on individual factory work forces (Departamento Estadual de Estatística, *Catálogo das Indústrias do Estado de São Paulo [Exclusive o Município da Capital]* [São Paulo: DEE, 1947]). The numbers given in newspaper articles are usual higher, which most likely reflects either a tendency toward exaggeration or, less likely, an increase in the number of employees between 1945 and early 1946. In a few cases, I have had to use the individual factory employment figures for 1947 when figures for 1945 were missing or questionable (PMSA, unpublished "Estatística Industrial [1947]").

12. *DSP*, 7 February 1946; *O Imparcial* (Santo André), 26 January 1946.

13. *O Imparcial*, 2 February 1946.

14. See *O Imparcial*, 2 February 1946, for coverage of the Firestone meeting, as discussed and quoted in the following paragraphs.

15. On the prospects for a legally mandated Christmas bonus, the union's attorney proved prophetic. The "thirteenth month wage," as it came to be known, was finally enacted in 1962 under Getúlio Vargas's trabalhista protégé, President João "Jango" Goulart.

16. *O Imparcial*, 2 February 1946.

17. When interviewed by a reporter, the local representative of the union of mestres and contramestres presented the strike against the Ipiranguinha as having its origin in the "ill will" of the company, which refused, he said, to obey the labor laws (*O Imparcial*, 2 February 1946).

18. Unlike the rightist labor leaders, the Left/Center leaders of unions such as the bankworkers in São Paulo fought "to avoid direct control by the Labor Ministry" and to defend "the workers' organizational autonomy" as part of a drive "for the gradual transformation of the union structure"; however, this did not mean, as Letícia Canedo has noted, that they repudiated "state protection for labor's demands" or called for the "destruction of the [existing] union structure" (*Bancários*, 35).

19. *DSP*, 7 February 1946; *Hoje*, 4 and 8 February 1946. Indeed, rubber workers at the Goodyear factory in São Paulo were organized to provide financial aid to their colleagues at Firestone (*DSP*, 3 February 1946).

20. *Hoje*, 8 February 1946.

21. In the case of Rhodia Química, the strike occurred in a union whose alignment with the Left/Center camp was far less firm than in the case of the rubber workers' union. Following the strike, the union membership ousted all but one of the members of the diretório of the chemical workers' union for allegedly "betraying" the strike. This takeover by Left/Center forces was not, however, legally recognized by the government, which would intervene in the union the following year to restore the ousted leadership (*Hoje*, 3 March 1947).

22. Weffort, "Origens," 87, 89; Francisco Weffort, "Democracia e Movimento Operário: Algumas Questões para a História do Período 1945–1964 [Part One]," *Revista de Cultura Contemporânea* 1 (1978): 13. In analyzing strikes, scholars must subject their own abstractions to a process of deconstruction. It is best to avoid, for example, the use of overly dramatic metaphors to describe mass strikes. The 1946 movement was hardly an "explosion" in ABC, given that 80 percent of the workers in the immediate vicinity did not participate in the strike; moreover, those who did join did not strike simultaneously but in a staggered fashion over a six-week period. As long as one discounts the damage it implies, "eruption" may be a somewhat more appropriate term, since volcanic activity can last for a considerable period of time.

23. Weffort's economic explanation for the strikes was one of the weak points of his pioneering article. Timothy Harding suggested in his 1973 dissertation that the strikes might have been a response to inflation, but that the timing was dictated by political factors: they struck only in early 1946, he noted, but inflation had been going on for a long time ("The Political History of the Organized Labor Movement in Brazil" [Ph.D. diss., Stanford University, 1973], 180–81). Six years later, Ricardo Maranhão also pointed out that economics offered only a partial explanation for the 1946 strikes; the workers' economic situation would radically worsen later in the 1940s without prompting similar episodes of mass militancy (Maranhão, *Sindicatos*, 118).

24. Maranhão, *Sindicatos*, 43; Wolfe, "Rise," 277, 241. Wolfe incorrectly claims

that Maranhão and French "argued the PCB actually led these strikes" ("Rise," 272).

25. Harding, "Political History," 182–83; Maranhão, *Sindicatos*, 44; Wolfe, "Rise," 267–73. Ricardo Maranhão was the first to call our attention to these forms of rank-and-file organization, which he called "factory commissions, [that is] para-union or extra-union mechanisms within the workplace" (*Sindicatos*, 44). Yet the term itself may be misleading, since it implies a degree of formal organization and continuity that did not in fact characterize these groups, which were, as Maranhão suggested, fluid, semiclandestine, and unstable in nature.

26. In some cases, the failure to analyze the strike phenomenon in depth stems from a paucity of documentation. The lacuna in existing studies of 1946, however, is explained by the fact that earlier analysts were primarily interested in using the strikes to address broader questions about trade union policy, working-class political strategy, and the state. Thus, they tended to use strikes interchangeably as illustrations of this or that general truth. Peter Winn, by contrast, has suggested that even the periodic workers' movements that occur in a single factory have "different origins, politics, and characters, as well as differing dynamics, plots, and dramatics" (Winn, *Weavers of Revolution*, 40). As Michele Perrot suggests, "the nature, objectives and style of a strike" vary, as do their temperaments and language. "The strike," she suggests, "is not an empty form. As a social process, it has its own life, its rules, its custom and practice to which everyone bends, its overall movement and its specific course" (*Workers on Strike*, 312–13).

To read a strike with nuance and sensitivity requires that the phenomenon be disaggregated in order to reveal the diversity and complexity that exist at the factory level. Close attention must be paid to chronology, to the actions and rhetoric of employers, trade unionists, and workers, and to the variety of behaviors and motivations found at the mass level. Strikes, it must be remembered, are specific to a given historical moment; in other words, a strike is not a strike is not a strike.

The analysis in this chapter is based on a systematic examination of eighty-eight newspaper articles, from five sources, that covered strikes and dissídios in Santo André and São Caetano between 23 January and 15 March 1946. Unfortunately, even these abundant sources are biased, since they do not answer the question of why workers at so many other plants did *not* strike—which would be crucial to a total understanding of the strike phenomenon.

27. Yet there is little evidence to suggest that such "commissions" or "committees" were independent bodies with a long existence and an established place within factory life—especially given the rigorous employer and governmental repression before 1946. Rather, these ad hoc "commissions" are best understood as the outcome of a process by which small groups of workers came together and were moved to action under the impact of the euphoria of 1945. Thus the use of the term "delegation" better captures the nature of the phenomenon than the term "factory commission" or "committee," although the latter is appropriate in certain cases. For example, a factory committee composed of thirty-three individuals at the Cerâmica São Caetano reported in April 1946 that most workers, despite some dissension, had supported the group's efforts. As proof, they cited the success of their drive to get

workers to donate money to make up the salaries lost by committee members who took days off to oversee the factory's dissídio coletivo (*Hoje*, 15 April 1946).

28. Going well beyond the carefully qualified claims of Ricardo Maranhão, Joel Wolfe's 1990 dissertation argues for the centrality of such factory commissions in the município of São Paulo, their continuity with the past, and their independence from unions, the state, and working-class radicals such as the Communists or, earlier in the century, the anarchists. It is true that small groups of activists, since the earliest days of Paulista industrialization, have tried to organize their fellow workers in the shops. While not to be belittled, the success and even representativeness of such "activist minorities" or "vanguards" should not be exaggerated. Wolfe admits at one point that these activists were a minority, but he too often equates them with their less courageous fellow workers. Moreover, he insists upon using the term "factory commission" to characterize all of their activities. One of his informants, Gloria Salviano, by contrast, distinguishes between the levels of formal and informal organizing that he conflates (Wolfe, "Rise," 267–73).

29. Based on his interviews with workers, Wolfe rightly emphasizes the importance of the workers' sense of confidence in understanding their behavior in 1945–46 ("Rise," 256, 268, 270).

30. United States of Brazil, *The Consolidation of Brazilian Labor Laws* (Rio de Janeiro: Imprensa Nacional, 1944), 197–200.

31. Edgard Carone, *O Estado Novo (1937–1945)* (São Paulo: DIFEL, 1977), 136–37.

32. After peaking in 1946 (420), dissídios coletivos nationwide declined to 295 in 1947, 183 in 1948, 143 in 1949, and 134 in 1950. As late as 1955 they still had not regained the level of 1946 (Robert Alexander, *Labor Relations in Argentina, Brazil and Chile* [New York: McGraw Hill, 1962], 93).

33. Idealizing aggressive and antistatist trade union militancy, Edgard Carone argues that use of the dissídio procedure—even in conjunction with a strike—is proof that "the workers' movement [in this period] had not yet totally freed itself from government paternalism" because victories were gained through the Ministry of Labor (*Estado Novo*, 129). For those familiar with collective bargaining elsewhere, Carone's notion of a totally government-free labor relations system seems a bit naive, while the ideal he upholds is anachronistic for the mid-1940s.

34. For the text of the textile acôrdo of February 1946, see *O Imparcial*, 5 May 1946.

35. *Hoje*, 8 and 14 January 1946; *ESP*, 24 and 27 February 1946; *DSP*, 30 January 1946; *ESP*, 14 February 1946.

36. *Hoje*, 7 February 1946; Pedro Pomar, "Greve Não é Desordem," *Tribuna Popular*, 24 January 1946 (reprinted in Edgard Carone, *O P.C.B. Vol. 2: 1943–1964* [São Paulo: DIFEL, 1982], 2:277–78); quotation in *Hoje*, 11 February 1946. Prior to this January 1946 statement, the Communist Party's official attitude toward strikes was "ambivalent" or "hesitant," in the words of Timothy Harding; yet this was far less true, he argued, at the grass-roots level, and the PCB, once the strikes began, sought to enhance its power by leading them successfully ("Political History," 182–83). The party's shift in position reflected the negative grass-roots re-

sponse reported by a multitude of local PCB leaders. For example, Rolando Frati, one of the top Communists in Santo André, recalled in the 1970s that some Communists counseling restraint to striking workers were booed, and in a few cases even stoned (Rolando Frati, "Contribuição ao Estado do Movimento Operário IV," *Debate* [Paris], no. 22 [1976]: 21; see also Elias Chaves Neto, *Minha Vida e as Lutas de Meu Tempo: Memórias* [São Paulo: Alfa-Omega, 1977], 89). For a version of Weffort's original critique of the PCB's stance, see Arnaldo Spindel, *O Partido Comunista na Gênese do Populismo* (São Paulo: Símbolo, 1980), 76–83.

37. *Hoje*, 11 February 1946.

38. *DSP*, 7 February 1946; *O Imparcial*, 9 February 1946.

39. *Hoje*, 8 and 9 February 1946.

40. *Hoje*, 9 February 1946.

41. *Hoje*, 14 and 16 February 1946; *ESP*, 20 February 1946. Similar journalistic estimates of 100,000 strikers are given in the *Fôlha da Manhã* of 20 February 1946 (cited in Maranhão, *Sindicatos*, 43) and in an editorial in São Paulo's *Digesto Econômico* (2, no. 16 [March 1946]). Such contemporary figures, which usually tend toward exaggeration, are inadequate for serious analysis. Credible estimates can be established only by identifying and researching the enterprises that were struck in order to establish the branch of industry and the number and composition of the work force. For examples of incomplete and idiosyncratic strike lists that do not meet these criteria, see Francisco Weffort, "Sindicatos e Política" (Ph.D. diss., Universidade de São Paulo, 1972), pp. A-2 to A-9 [reproduced in Spindel, *Partido Comunista*, 95–102]; Maranhão, *Sindicatos*, 43–44.

Despite the importance of mass strike waves in Brazil, scholars have until recently neglected the necessity of quantifying participation in order to establish patterns of collective behavior over time. This should shift with the pioneering work being done by Salvador Antonio Mireles Sandoval ("Strikes in Brazil 1945–1980" [Ph.D. diss., University of Michigan, 1984], and "General Strikes in Brazil, 1980–1989," *Latin American Labor News* nos. 2–3 [1990], 11–13).

42. *Hoje*, 8 February 1946. The strikes created an atmosphere that led even the rightist PTB president of the textile workers to join the new central labor body in ABC. Prior to the strikes, Poleto had consistently boycotted local union events in protest against Left domination (*Hoje*, 23 October 1945).

43. *Hoje*, 9 February 1946; *O Imparcial*, 2 March 1946.

44. *Hoje*, 9 and 13 February 1946.

45. *DSP*, 15 February 1946; *Hoje*, 18 February 1946.

46. In recognition of preexisting services, the Serviço Social de Indústria (SESI) could reduce the monthly payment owed by a given employer to this industrialists' social service agency. In an effort to qualify, Pirelli invited a SESI team to inspect its Santo André operations in March 1948. Despite the company's good connections and the generally favorable nature of the unpublished report, it is noteworthy that Pirelli received a reduction of only 14 out of a possible 50 percent in what it owed SESI (private communication from Barbara Weinstein, 1 November 1991).

47. *DSP*, 15 February 1946. At least one local newspaper, sympathetic to the strikers, had expected Pirelli to avoid a strike because of its efforts to arrive at an understanding with the metalworkers' union (*O Imparcial*, 9 February 1945).

48. *Hoje*, 16 and 19 February 1946; *DSP*, 17 February 1946.

49. *DSP*, 15 February 1946; *Hoje*, 15 February 1946; *O Imparcial*, 16 February 1946.

50. *ESP*, 9 February 1946; *Hoje*, 19 February 1946; *DSP*, 17 February 1946.

51. *DSP*, 19 and 15 February 1946.

52. *DSP*, 14 and 16 February 1946.

53. For examples, see *Hoje*, 2 February 1946; *DSP*, 15 February 1946.

54. *DSP*, 23 February 1946; *Hoje*, 19 February 1946.

55. *Hoje*, 20 and 21 February 1946; *DSP*, 21 February 1946.

56. *DSP*, 21 February 1946; *Hoje*, 21 February 1946. Of the twenty-six employees listed as fired (*DSP*, 23 February 1946), twenty-two could be positively identified from a list of employees submitted by the Laminação Nacional de Metais to the electoral justice system in 1945 (TRE SP, Consulta 207 [1945]). The group includes a mix of skilled and unskilled occupations and, curiously enough, nine white-collar or office employees. Unfortunately, it is unclear whether these workers were leaders of the strike or whether the strike was merely being used as a pretext to fire them, as the union charged. In any case, only one of the twenty-six names turns up in a trade union context, either then or later.

57. *Hoje*, 22 February 1946.

58. In repeated meetings with various employers' associations, rightist labor leaders accepted the industrialists' argument that workers were misinformed as to the causes of and solutions to the high cost of living (*carestia*). The Right's Union Coalition attacked "sectarian groups" and infiltrators and urged the workers to adopt a "pacific attitude" and place their confidence "in the patriotism of the government and the loyalty of the employers" (*DSP*, 20 February 1946). On 21 February, the state union federations and Santo André's textile union openly appealed to the workers to respect authority and return to work. The paid advertisements of the FIESP found such statements helpful: one union federation president in the capital openly supported the employers' "no negotiations" stance against the striking members of his own union (*DSP*, 14 February 1946; *ESP*, 16 February 1946; *DSP*, 20 and 21 February 1946; *ESP*, 2, 21, 15, 22 February 1946).

59. *DSP*, 15 February 1946; *Hoje*, 16 February 1946.

60. *Hoje*, 16 February 1946.

61. Ibid.; *DSP*, 19 February 1946.

62. *Hoje*, 11 and 21 February 1946.

63. *Hoje*, 26 February 1946.

64. *Hoje*, 22, 23, 25 February 1946. Saad's affiliation with the DOPS is noted in PMSA, Processo 6817 (1946).

65. *Hoje*, 28, 19, 23 February 1946.

66. *Hoje*, 26 and 27 February 1946.

67. *DSP*, 22 February 1946.

68. *Hoje*, 22 February 1946.

69. *Hoje*, first quotation in 23 February 1946; second quotation in 27 February 1946.

70. *ESP*, 31 January 1946.

71. *DSP*, 7, 19, 20 February 1946.

72. *Hoje*, 19 February 1946; João Almino, *Os Democratas Autoritários: Liberdades Individuais de Associação Política e Sindical na Constituição de 1946* (São Paulo: Brasiliense, 1980), 82.

73. *DSP*, 19 and 20 February 1946; *ESP*, 31 January 1946.

74. *Hoje*, 27 February; 9, 23, 27 March; 9 April 1946.

75. *Hoje*, 12 December 1946.

76. *Hoje*, 15 and 9 April 1946; 4, 8, 12 March 1946 (quotation in 15 April 1946).

77. For an example, see Joel Silveira, *Grã-Finos em São Paulo e Outras Notícias do Brasil* (São Paulo: Cruzeiro, 1945), which contains articles that both criticize the rich in São Paulo and sympathize with working people, in São Paulo and elsewhere.

78. *Hoje*, 28 February; 1, 2, 4 March 1946.

79. *Hoje*, 26 February 1946; 1, 4 March 1946; 27 February 1946.

80. *Hoje*, 4, 7, 8 March 1946. "Unlike the strikes during the First Republic (1889–1930)," a study of female participation in the postwar strike wave concluded, "no laments were heard about the abject behavior of women in refusing to strike. Nor was the likelihood of a work stoppage tied to the percentage of women employed in a given factory" (John D. French with Mary Lynn Pedersen, "Women and Working Class Mobilization in Postwar São Paulo, 1945–1948," *Latin American Research Review* 24 [1989]: 114).

81. *Hoje*, 2, 8 March 1946.

82. *ESP*, 2 March 1946.

83. Almino, *Democratas Autoritários*, 186–93; Hans Füchtner, *Os Sindicatos Brasileiros: Organização e Função Política* (Rio de Janeiro: Graal, 1980), 64–65. For a further sense of employer discourse in response to the strikes, see the editorials "As Greves," *O Observador Econômico e Financeiro* 11, no. 125 (June 1946), 23–24; and "Regulamentação do Direito de Greve," *Digesto Econômico* 2, no. 16 (March 1946). In the latter editorial, the Paulista businessmen's magazine criticized the spread of *both* strikes *and* dissídios coletivos in 1946 as evidence of a national pathology that required urgent governmental action. For local editorial opinion in ABC critical of the strikes, see *Borda do Campo*, 3 March 1946; *O Imparcial*, 23 March 1946.

84. Harding discusses the Dutra antistrike decree, although he claims, incorrectly, that "neither the PTB nor the PCB strongly protested the new law" ("Political History," 186–93). See also *Hoje*, 18 March 1946; Almino, *Democratas Autoritários*, 159.

85. *Hoje*, 15 March 1946. For the background of the Louças Adelinas situation, see *Hoje*, 27 February and 8 March 1946.

86. Starting his career in the early 1930s, Albino da Rocha became an important figure within the higher levels of the Paulista union bureaucracy with special prominence during the Estado Novo. An unsuccessful PTB candidate in 1945, he would be one of the signatories of the telegram that requested the labor minister to close the national union congress of September 1946 (*ESP*, 21 September 1946).

87. *Hoje*, 9 March 1946.

88. While calling the PTB "reactionary in its leadership and program," the national PCB in January 1946 had still accepted the possibility of formal collaboration with the trabalhistas ("Informe Político da Comissão Executiva ao Comité Nacional, em 4 de

Janeiro de 1946," in Moisés Vinhas, *O Partidão* [São Paulo: Hucitec, 1982], 121). As the PCB gained strength over the following months, however, Communist attitudes hardened—reflecting, in part, the tensions that flowed from the PTB's status at the time as an ally of the PSD. In the Constituent Assembly, for example, the trabalhistas voted for the continued validity of the Estado Novo's 1937 Constitution—a measure opposed by the PCB (ibid.; see also the *Hoje* editorials, "Desmascarando os 'Trabalhistas,'" 9 February 1946, and "Trabalhismo sem Máscaras," 13 March 1946).

89. *Hoje*, 9 April 1946; 12 and 14 February 1946 (quotation in 12 February 1946). Unlike the PCB, the local PTB was virtually moribund during the dramatic months of the postwar strike wave. In April 1946, a Santo André PTB advertisement admitted that the party had been "resting on its laurels" and promised an end to its "apparent inactivity" (*Borda do Campo*, 14 April 1946).

90. *Hoje*, 5 and 18 April 1946.

91. *O Imparcial*, 2 March 1946.

92. On the rural origin of the local populace and the factory work force, see Table H6, "Comparison of Places of Birth, Santo André, 1940–1950," in John D. French, "Industrial Workers and the Origin of Populist Politics in the ABC Region of Greater São Paulo, Brazil 1900–1950" (Ph.D. diss., Yale University, 1985), 678.

93. Nationwide, the mobilizational initiatives of local labor leaderships laid the groundwork for a spectacular increase of total union membership: Brazilian trade unions gained 322,748 new members between 1945 (474,943) and 1946 (797,691). Using the government's own statistics, one can see that only 123,369 workers had joined trade unions in Brazil between 1939 and 1945, despite the government-sponsored unionization drives after 1942 (José Albertino Rodrigues, *Sindicato e Desenvolvimento no Brasil* [1968; reprint, São Paulo: Símbolo, 1979], 124, 129–30). The impetus for the unprecedented postwar increase, by contrast, came from below and reflected the ability of labor's local leaders to exploit the opportunities created in 1945–46.

94. By the end of 1946, Communist Party cells were active in the Laminação Nacional de Metais, the Ipiranguinha plant (Moinho Santista), and Firestone, among others (*Hoje*, 10 September 1946). The Pirelli plant already had a party cell prior to the strikes.

95. *O Imparcial*, 2 March 1946. This conclusion was reinforced by the experience of several of the nonstriking enterprises whose dissídios were still unresolved as late as August 1946 (*Hoje*, 24 May and 1 August 1946).

96. *Hoje*, 23 February, 1 and 4 March 1946; 16 February 1946.

97. *Hoje*, 20 March 1946; for the text of this protest, see also Almino, *Democratas Autoritários*, 86.

Chapter Seven

1. *Hoje*, 3 April 1946.

2. In part, the PSD enjoyed an absolute majority of deputies and senators as the result of the *sobras* mechanism contained in the 1945 electoral law (Maria do

Carmo Campello de Souza, *Estado e Partidos Políticos no Brasil (1930 a 1964)* [São Paulo: Alfa-Omega, 1983], 119–20, 123). See also Maria Victoria de Mesquita Benevides, *A UDN e o Udenismo: Ambigüidades do Liberalismo Brasileiro (1945–1965)* (Rio de Janeiro: Paz e Terra, 1981), 69–73.

3. Ricardo Maranhão, *Sindicatos e Democratização* (São Paulo: Brasiliense, 1979), 86–87. For a detailed description of the case against the PCB presented by the DOPS, see *PCB, Processo de Cassaçã do Registro (1947)* [Belo Horizonte: Aldeia Global, 1980], 4–10.

4. *Borda do Campo*, 24 March and 12 May 1946. The Catholic Church gave a high priority to the anticommunist struggle in the postwar period; see Antônio Flávio de Oliveira Pierucci et al., "Igreja Catolica: 1945–1970," in *História Geral da Civilização Brasileira*, ed. Boris Fausto, part 3, vol. 4 (São Paulo: DIFEL, 1984), 347, 351–52.

5. Such veteran Communists in ABC in 1946 included Marcos Andreotti, Graciano Fernandes, and Iguatemy Lopes de Oliveira—all of whom had been tried and imprisoned by the Tribunal de Segurança Nacional during the Estado Novo.

6. *Hoje*, 29 March, 8 July, 22 August, 2 October 1946.

7. *Hoje*, 1, 9, 20, 27 March 1946.

8. While Andreotti was prevented from working in the metalworking industry, as he would have preferred, his public notoriety did not prevent a local textile company from hiring him. Francisco Claro Dias Lopes was a welder at Companhia Brasileira de Construção Fichet Schwartz-Hautmont who ran as a Communist candidate for *vereador* (councilman) in Santo André in 1947; his employers did not fire him despite their knowledge of his political affiliation, but they did try to keep him isolated from contact with his fellow workers (Sindicato dos Metalúrgicos de Santo André, Mauá, Ribeirão Pires, e Rio Grande da Serra, *50 Anos de Luta (1933–1983)* [Santo André: 1983], 41).

9. When skilled Communist and leftist workers did suffer from employer reprisals, their skills provided them with at least some protection from unemployment. This was shown in an August 1946 "Voice of the Factory" column in *Hoje*, which discussed the numerous textile-plant foremen (*contramestres*) in São Caetano who had been fired for their Communist and union militancy. Masters of their skills, they quickly found new employment in the industry but feared a concerted blacklisting effort against them in the future. The labor law, these workers proposed, should be amended to ban firings for political reasons (*Hoje*, 22 August 1946).

10. João Almino, *Os Democratas Autoritários: Liberdades Individuais de Associação Política e Sindical na Constituição de 1946* (São Paulo: Brasiliense, 1980), 88–89.

11. *Hoje*, 2 August 1946.

12. *Hoje*, 22, 23, 25 February 1946. The transition to democracy was not well accepted by the police. A member of Rio's elite Polícia Especial captured these feelings in his descriptions of the popular turbulence of the postwar era: the "public order," he reported, was "profoundly sacrificed" by the Communist "contractors of disorder" whose "aggressiveness . . . [and] unrestrained political demagoguery . . . instigated the people to go on sprees" (Olyntho V. Scaramuzzi, *Memórias de um Ex-*

Polícia Especial [Obsessão ao Poder] [Rio de Janeiro: Revista Continente Editorial, 1981], 20–21).

13. The labor movement in ABC protested vigorously, and a delegation of fifteen local women visited the imprisoned Santos union leaders in late June (*Hoje*, 4, 13, 29 May; 17 and 27 June 1946). "The result of the conflict now in progress in Santos," the U.S. consul in São Paulo observed, "will largely determine the trend of labor demands in the state" (Cecil Cross to Paul C. Daniel, 15 May 1946, Record Group 84, U.S. Department of State [USDS], U.S. National Archives [USNA]).

14. *Borda do Campo*, 23 June 1946; *Hoje*, 25 May 1946; Edgard Carone, *A Quarta República* (São Paulo: DIFEL, 1979), 10–19.

15. The impassioned antiradicalism of many Brazilian politicians was already clear during the meetings of the national Constituent Assembly. In February 1946, PCB demonstrators in Rio booed those deputies who had supported the maintenance of the 1937 Constitution as they left the Congress building. As one reporter recalls, the PSD chair of the Assembly responded with great indignation: "I myself," Fernando de Mello Viana declared, "with my authority as a judge, would order the militia to fire on the people if that were necessary" (Yvonne R. de Miranda, *Homens e Fatos da Constituinte de 1946 [Memórias de uma Reporter Política]* [Rio de Janeiro: Editôra Argus, 1982], 43).

16. PMSA, Processo 6817 (1946).

17. On the arrests, see *Hoje*, 8, 9, 10, 11, 12 July 1946.

18. *Hoje*, 17, 12, 23, 27 May; 8, 10, 19, 24 July; 1 August 1946.

19. *Hoje*, 19, 22 July; 1 August 1946 (quotation in 10 July 1946).

20. *Hoje*, 10, 19, 24 July; 1 August 1946.

21. *Hoje*, 11, 12, 31 July 1946.

22. The Communists were quick to exploit the radicalization that ensued from the repressive activities of the government. *Hoje*, 9 April 1946, details the case of an unemployed worker in São Caetano who was arrested by then-subdelegado Saad while selling the PCB paper outside the Companhia Brasileira de Mineração e Metalúrgica in São Caetano. A voter for Dutra, Vargas, and Marcondes Filho in December 1945, the vendor reported that he was only selling *Hoje* because the Communist paper was the most popular at the plant. The PCB used the incident to attack the government while falsely trying to tie the PTB to Saad's actions.

23. *Hoje*, 1 August 1946; *ESP*, 7 August 1946.

24. *ESP*, 8 August 1946; *Hoje*, 8 August 1946. It is doubtful that Negrão de Lima was ever a PTB party minister, as opposed to a Dutra appointee with a convenient PTB affiliation. In 1937, Negrão de Lima played an important role in the preparatory work that established the Estado Novo dictatorship (Hélio Silva, *1937: Todos os Golpes se Parecem* [Rio de Janeiro: Civilização Brasileira, 1970], 445–545).

25. The minister of justice, for example, ordered a two-week suspension of Rio de Janeiro's Communist daily newspaper, *Tribuna Popular* (*Hoje*, 16, 17, 23 August 1946; *ESP*, 8 August 1946).

26. *Hoje*, 10 July 1946; 2 April 1946; 22 July 1946. The Communists criticized the new Constitution for failing to "meet the needs of the working masses," but they still hailed it as "a great step toward democracy" and a "victory for the people" (*Hoje*, 24 September 1946).

27. *Hoje*, 23 and 24 September 1946. The behavior of Santo André's PCB during this incident followed the recommendations of the draft resolution of the PCB's third national conference. The PCB's policy of respecting the government's orders did not, the document said, mean "passive submission to the arbitrary orders of the police" or "opportunistically conforming [to them] without protest." Communists were told to use "all legal means and appeals before accepting such orders" and, on each occasion, to use "higher and more vigorous forms of struggle" (*Hoje*, 15 July 1946).

28. The DOPS officer leading the raid on Santo André's PCB that day had been the commandant of the Maria Zélia prison, site of the killing of four Aliancista and PCB prisoners in 1938 (*Hoje*, 23 September 1946). The Maria Zélia "massacre" was a live memory for the PCB in 1946, and one of the party's cells in Santo André was named after one of its victims, the youthful bankworker Augusto Pinto.

29. This popular feeling of rights was well captured in the memoirs of a member of a Rio elite police unit. Dispatched to patrol the streets during the return of the Brazilian expeditionary force in 1945, the police were warned by their chief João Alberto Lins de Barros to take care. "We perceived what he was trying to say. The times had changed. The atmosphere no longer allowed police authoritarianism" (Scaramuzzi, *Memórias*, 47–48).

30. The new legal strictures meant that even Eduardo Gabriel Saad could not make his official arbitrariness supreme. In August 1946, for example, he raided the meeting of the Union of Democratic Women of Santo André, yet he was unable, once at the police station, to legally book those he had arrested (*Hoje*, 13 August 1946).

31. Almino, *Democratas Autoritárias*, 90–91. Procurador Geral Temístocles Brandão Cavalcanti advised the TSE on 23 April 1946 to rule against the challenge of the PCB's legal registry. Voted down, the case was turned over to a young sub-procurador, Alceu Barbedo, who was to make the case against the PCB (Alceu Barbedo, *O Fechamento do Partido Comunista do Brasil [Os Pareceres Barbedo]* [Rio de Janeiro: Imprensa Nacional, 1948], 115).

32. *Hoje*, 5, 13, 14 August 1946. The political underpinnings of this military court decision in São Paulo are unclear, but it was consistent with the stance taken later by General Renato Piquet toward a possible PCB/Adhemar victory in January 1947. "We, of the Army," the commandant of the São Paulo military region declared, "have nothing to do with party competitions, and our mission does not involve preferences of a political sort" (João Batista Berardo, *O Político Cândido Torquato Portinari* [São Paulo: Edições Populares, 1983], 78).

33. *Hoje*, 13 and 14 August 1946. Almino, *Democratas Autoritárias*, 88, cites a governmental Decree 9,502 of 26 March 1946 that suspended elections for one year.

34. *Hoje*, 31 July 1946. In principle, the labor Center and Left rejected the government's decree because they opposed governmental intervention in internal union affairs. In practice, however, they welcomed the test of mass influence that would result from holding union elections. The president of the rubber workers' union of São Paulo and Santo André, for example, argued that this "reactionary" decree could be used to oust the "enemies of the working class" who had installed

themselves in the unions during the Estado Novo (*Hoje*, 5 August 1946). Another union president, Alberto Zamignani of ABC, proposed that rank-and-file workplace commissions select, finance, and conduct the campaigns of candidates for union office; in this way, he argued, workers could guarantee that the union officers, once elected, would serve the members and not their own personal interests (*Hoje*, 14 August 1946).

35. *Hoje*, 13, 14, 28, 29 August 1946.

36. *Hoje*, 25 July; 7 and 19 August 1946.

37. A U.S. functionary, William Wheeler, blamed the founding of the CGTB on "general political confusion" and the "hood-winking of an ingenuous Minister, Negrão de Lima," who was outmaneuvered by the Communists ("Repression of Communism-Labor," memorandum for the U.S. Ambassador from William M. Wheeler, Junior, 31 July 1947, RG 84, USDS, USNA).

We still lack a thorough, well-documented study of this important national meeting. Indeed, even the number of delegates reported in different sources varies, with claims of 1,752 in one instance and 2,400 in another (José Albertino Rodrigues, *Sindicato e Desenvolvimento no Brasil* [1968; reprint, São Paulo: Símbolo, 1979], 162; *ESP*, 12 September 1946). A short discussion of some of the congress resolutions is provided by Luiz Werneck Vianna, *Liberalismo e Sindicato no Brasil* (Rio de Janeiro: Paz e Terra, 1976), 257–60.

38. *Hoje*, 13, 14, 28, 29 August; 28 September 1946. In an interview with the *Estado de São Paulo*, the delegate from the São Paulo Journalists' Union, Plínio Gomes Melo, admitted that there were "a large number of Communists among the delegates" but emphasized the political diversity of the congress. The majority of those attending, this member of the Esquerda Democratica and self-identified onetime Trotskyist said, were "trabalhistas, Socialists, democrats, liberals, and even anarcho-syndicalists" (*ESP*, 22 September 1946).

39. Indeed, the resolutions would have reduced the state to a powerless position even in such matters as the founding of unions, the drafting of statutes, and the oversight of union financial affairs. For texts and summaries of congress resolutions, see *Hoje*, 16 September, 2 October 1946; *ESP*, 15, 17, 18, 19 September 1946. See also the "Monthly Labor Report" by Edward J. Rowell, 13 January 1947, RG 84, USDS, USNA).

40. "Monthly Labor Report" by Edward J. Rowell, 13 May 1947 (first quotation); "Monthly Labor Report" by Edward J. Rowell, 8 April 1947 (second and third quotations), RG 84, USDS, USNA.

41. *Hoje*, 24 September 1946. Santo André's civil construction union proposed that all of the union tax be used for the benefit of the workers. The 20 percent kept by the Labor Ministry, they argued, should be turned over to the unions (*Hoje*, 22 June 1946).

42. The draft resolution of the Third National Conference of the PCB argued that "to be efficient, union work must be based, above all else, on life in the factories." It cited the experience of São Paulo's union commissions in this regard (*Hoje*, 15 July 1946).

43. *Hoje*, 30 August, 29 November 1946.

44. *Hoje*, 21, 23, 24 September 1946; *ESP*, 21 and 22 September 1946. The

creation of the CNTI had been authorized under Article 535 of the 1943 *CLT* Labor Code but had never before been implemented. The new organ, composed of existing federations, was grafted onto the existing system in order to frustrate leftist infiltration. Through control over credentials, the CNTI's president, Deocleciano Hollanda de Cavalcanti, would retain power until 1961. By law, this higher-level association was a bureaucratic organ of "coordination" and was denied the role of "representing" the interests of its affiliate organisms (United States of Brazil, *The Consolidation of Brazilian Labor Laws* [Rio de Janeiro: Imprensa Nacional, 1944], 120). On the defeat of Hollanda de Cavalcanti in 1961, see Lucília de Almeida Neves, *CGT no Brasil, 1961–1964* (Belo Horizonte: Vega, 1981), 36–37.

45. *Hoje*, 30 September 1946. See Jover Telles, *O Movimento Sindical no Brasil* (1962; reprint, São Paulo: Ciências Humanas, 1981), 243–59, for a heated contemporary debate over the results of the congress in the state assembly in Rio Grande do Sul.

46. *ESP*, 12 September 1946.

47. "In theory," Rowell also noted, the Labor Ministry "should rely on these [*ministerialista*] leaders for guidance in its labor program but in fact does so only to a very limited extent and not on questions related to the form and scope of the labor movement" ("Monthly Labor Report" by Edward J. Rowell, 13 May 1947, RG 84, USDS, USNA).

Having arrived in Brazil in 1944, labor attaché Rowell was a foreign service professional who would later serve as U.S. consul general in Recife in 1966. Interviewed by Robert Alexander in 1946, Rowell said that the PCB "gives no evidence of being controlled by Russia, or even of being primarily interested in Russia. . . . It is dangerous, perhaps, and might be in a crisis," he went on, but there was "little evidence" to indicate that they were "foreign agents in any sense." His fair-minded judgments on labor and the PCB carry special weight precisely because they do not reflect any left-wing political agenda. Even the staunchly anticommunist Alexander concluded that Rowell, despite his opinions, was "not particularly a commie symp" (interview by Robert Alexander with Edward Rowell, 26 August 1946, Rio de Janeiro; in the private archive of Robert Alexander).

48. "Monthly Labor Report" by Edward J. Rowell, 13 May 1947, RG 84, USDS, USNA; unpublished letter by Robert Alexander to Jay Lovestone, 23 June 1953, in the private archive of Robert Alexander.

49. *Jornal de São Caetano*, 10 November 1946. Morvan Dias de Figueiredo's appointment to head the federal Labor Ministry came as no surprise to Paulista unionists. As early as 1 August 1946, *Hoje* had reported rumors that Morvan Dias was under consideration to head the newly empowered State Labor Department in São Paulo.

Chapter Eight

1. Cecil M. Cross to Paul C. Daniels, 6 November and 2 December 1946, U.S. Consulate in São Paulo, Brazil, Record Group 84, U.S. Department of State (USDS), U.S. National Archives (USNA).

2. Tribunal Regional Eleitoral de São Paulo (TRE SP), Processo 8b (1946).

3. *Diário de São Paulo*, 14 January 1947; *Borda do Campo*, 12 and 19 May; 11 August 1946.

4. *Hoje*, 15 July; 28 August; 3 and 14 September 1946; *O Imparcial*, 13 July 1946; *Jornal de São Caetano*, 18 August 1946; *Borda do Campo*, 25 August 1946.

5. *Borda do Campo*, 22 September; 20 October; 10 and 24 November; 22 December 1946; *Hoje*, 10 September 1946; 20 February 1947.

6. *Jornal de São Caetano*, 12 January 1947. See also *Fôlha da Manhã*, 15 January 1947; *Diário de São Paulo*, 3 January 1947. In 1954, a Paulista sociologist described these efforts by the PSD's men of industry to win urban votes in the postwar period: like rural coronéis, "the great industrialist has around him a court of dependents who support him; not the workers, but all of the interests that have come to depend on him through his multiple business affairs" (Maria Isaura Pereira de Queiroz, "Contribuição para o Estudo da Sociologia Política no Brasil," in *Anais do I Congresso Brasileiro de Sociologia* [São Paulo: 1955], 227).

7. *Jornal de São Caetano*, 22 December 1946; 12 January 1947; quotation in *Fôlha da Manhã*, 18 January 1947.

8. Antônio de Almeida Prado, *Jornada de Democracia: Discursos Pronunciados na Campanha Eleitoral como Candidato ao Cargo de Governador do Estado de São Paulo* (São Paulo: Livraria Martins, 1948), 6.

9. Ibid., 86, 90.

10. Aureliano Leite, *Páginas de uma Longa Vida* (São Paulo: Livraria Martins, n.d.), 367–68; *Diário de São Paulo*, 5 and 11 January 1947; Almeida Prado, *Jornada*, 81–82; Herbert Levy, *Problemas Básicos da Nação* (São Paulo: n.p., 1950), 36.

11. Almeida Prado, *Jornada*, 33.

12. Ibid., 90–92. Sergio Miceli has explored the historical background of this Paulista "fraction [whose members] specialized in political, technical, and cultural work" (*Intelectuais e Classe Dirigente no Brasil [1920–1945]* [São Paulo: DIFEL, 1979], 2, 6).

13. Almeida Prado, *Jornada*, 81–82.

14. Ibid., 86–87, 126.

15. On Borghi, see Gastão Pereira da Silva, *Constituintes de 1946: Dados Biográficos* (Rio de Janeiro: Spinoza, 1947), 227–28. For a summary of Borghi's views as expressed to U.S. diplomatic representatives, see Cecil M. Cross to Paul C. Daniels, 16 October 1946, U.S. Consulate in São Paulo, RG 84, USDS, USNA. For further biographical details on Adhemar, see Mario Beni, *Adhemar* (São Paulo: Grafikor, n.d.); Regina Sampaio, *Adhemar de Barros e o PSP* (São Paulo: Global, 1982); Israel Beloch and Alzira Alves de Abreu, eds., *Dicionário Histórico-Biográfico Brasileiro, 1930–1983* (Rio de Janeiro: Forense Universitário and FGV-CPDOC, 1984), 1:316–24.

16. While denying that Borghi's monetary support for the PTB was as extensive as claimed, national PTB leader Paulo Baeta Neves admitted in 1947 that some funds had been received from companies controlled by Borghi in 1945 ("Weekly Labor Notes" by Edward J. Rowell, 11 April 1947, U.S. Embassy in Rio de Janeiro, RG 84, USDS, USNA).

17. Pereira da Silva, *Constituintes*, 228; *Fôlha do Povo*, 19 June 1953; Prefeitura Municipal de Santo André (PMSA), Processo 8746/46.

18. Sampaio, *Adhemar*, 53; *Hoje*, 28 November 1946; *O Estado de São Paulo* (*ESP*), 10 January 1947.

19. Sampaio, *Adhemar*, 49–51.

20. TRE SP, Processos 4, 6, 9 (1945).

21. *Hoje*, 4 November 1945; 27 February and 27 September 1946.

22. "Dados Biográficos dos Prefeitos de São Bernardo do Campo," Banco de Dados, Prefeitura Municipal de São Bernardo do Campo; Attílio Pessotti, *Vila de São Bernardo* (São Bernardo: Prefeitura Municipal de São Bernardo do Campo, 1981), 108–9.

23. *Hoje*, 6 and 7 August 1946.

24. Ademir Médici, *São Bernardo, Seus Bairros, Sua Gente* (São Bernardo: PMSBC, 1981), 84–90; interview by the author with Raymundo Nonato da Silva, 19 July 1982, São Bernardo do Campo.

25. *Hoje*, 22 August 1946; 3 March 1947.

26. *Hoje*, 7 August 1946.

27. *Hoje*, 6 August 1946.

28. *Hoje*, 7 August 1946.

29. *Diário de São Paulo*, 25 November 1945; quotation in Edmundo Soares de Souza, "Gênese da Hora que Passa," *O Imparcial*, 16 February 1946.

30. *Hoje*, 9 January 1946.

31. Ibid. Braga's rejection of charity's unequal exchange was of recent origin. In 1941, he had served as the head of an ACISA committee charged with organizing "The First Great Christmas for the Children of the Workers of Santo André" (*O Imparcial*, 6 December 1941).

32. *Diário de São Paulo*, 5 January 1947; Beni, *Adhemar*, 180–81.

33. *Diário de São Paulo*, 7 and 8 January 1947; *Hoje*, 7 and 8 January 1947; *ESP*, 10 and 14 January 1947; Carlos Laranjeira, *Histórias de Adhemar* (São Paulo: Edição do autor, 1988), 37, 40.

34. Aureliano Leite, *Subsídios para a História da Civilização Paulista* (São Paulo: Saraiva, 1954), 374. U.S. Embassy sources reported that PSD candidate Tavares was the "consensus victor, largely on the grounds that his party controls the state political machinery" ("Monthly Labor Report" by Edward Rowell, 13 January 1947, U.S. Embassy in Rio de Janeiro, RG 84, USDS, USNA).

35. TRE SP, *Boletim Eleitoral* 1, no. 8 (1947): 94.

36. Clovis Leite Ribeiro, "A Classe Média e as Eleições de 19 de Janeiro," *Digesto Econômico* 3, no. 29 (1947): 73.

37. Table G8 in John D. French, "Industrial Workers and the Origin of Populist Politics in the ABC Region of Greater São Paulo, Brazil 1900–1950" (Ph.D. diss., Yale University, 1985), 655–66.

38. See Armando Mazzo, *Memórias de um Militante Político e Sindical no ABC* (São Bernardo do Campo: PMSBC, 1991).

39. Table G9, ibid.; TRE SP, unpublished "Votação dos Candidatos a Assembléia Estadual . . ."; TRE SP, *Boletim Eleitoral* 1, no. 24 (1948): 269, 285. The rightist state labor leaders who ran on the PTB ticket did especially badly in the voting. Artur

Albino da Rocha, for example, received only 51 votes in all of ABC. The new president of the government's National Confederation of Industrial Workers (CNTI), Deocleciano Hollanda de Cavalcanti, did even worse, with only 23 votes in the whole of greater São Paulo.

40. Table G10, in French, "Industrial Workers," 667. In the senatorial race, Roberto Simonsen beat the Communist candidate, the world-famous painter Cândido Torquato Portinari, by only 3,708 votes out of almost half a million cast for both candidates. In fact, Portinari led in the first weeks of the count until later results from the interior came in. The PCB filed a challenge of the count alleging fraud (TRE SP, Processo 3708 [1948][326/TSE]; João Batista Berardo, *O Político Cândido Torquato Portinari* [São Paulo: Edições Populares, 1983], 102–3).

41. See Francisco Iglesias, ed., *Caio Prado Júnior: História* (São Paulo: Ática, 1982), for a brief biography and a selection of writings by Brazil's foremost historian at mid-century. See also Maria Angela D'Incão, ed., *História e Ideal: Ensaios sobre Caio Prado Júnior* (São Paulo: Editôra UNESP and Editôra Brasiliense, 1989).

42. TSE, *Dados Estatísticos* (Rio de Janeiro: Imprensa Nacional, 1950), 1:63.

43. Ribeiro, "Classe Média," 73.

44. The PSD's loss in the cities, however understandable, was accompanied by an electoral disaster in the interior, where both the PTB and the PSP/PCB alliance outpolled it—a political revolution that deserves fuller study.

45. The unusually high degree of interpenetration between the holders of political and economic power in São Paulo between 1889 and 1937 is carefully documented in Joseph L. Love and Bert J. Barickman, "Rulers and Owners: A Brazilian Case Study in Comparative Perspective," *Hispanic American Historical Review* 66 (1986): 743–65.

46. UDNista Aureliano Leite recalls that many members of the middle and upper classes embraced the extralegal argument that Adhemar should not be allowed to take office because he was a minority candidate with only 35 percent of the vote (*Subsídios*, 374). Paulista newspapers such as *O Jornal*, owned by the Diários Associados chain of Assis Chateaubriand, openly called on Dutra, the military, and the conservative classes to bar Adhemar de Barros, a mere "puppet of Prestes," from office (*O Jornal*, 1 February 1947). The "official position" of the PSD state administration, a "generally reliable source" reported to the U.S. Embassy in late January 1947, was that "regardless of the election results, . . . the state administration . . . should under no circumstances be handed over to Barros and the Communists" (Memorandum from São Paulo, 28 January 1947, U.S. Embassy in Rio de Janeiro, RG 84, USDS, USNA).

47. U.S. Embassy sources reported in mid-March that "it now appears that he [Adhemar] has been successful in obtaining the support of most of the conservative parties . . . and that he will give little recognition to the communists for their support. . . . According to reports from São Paulo, business interests are quite reconciled to de Barros as governor" ("Election Results in the State of São Paulo, 13 March 1947," U.S. Embassy in Rio de Janeiro, RG 84, USDS, USNA).

48. *ESP*, 15 March 1947; *Hoje*, 27 February; 10, 11, and 18 March 1947; "Monthly Labor Report" by Edward J. Rowell, 30 April 1947, U.S. Embassy in Rio de Janeiro, RG 84, USDS, USNA.

49. *Hoje*, 19 March and 7 May 1947.

50. These "ideological weaknesses" and "dangerous illusions" among Paulista Communists, the PCB's Secretary General Luis Carlos Prestes argued, reflected their close links to "the working-class masses" of the state whose "reformist tendencies" persisted despite their display of "the greatest class consciousness" (*Hoje*, 27 February 1947).

51. *Hoje*, 9 and 18 March 1947.

52. This account draws on *Hoje*, 22 and 25 March 1947.

53. For more on the gender dynamics of postwar strikes in ABC, see John D. French with Mary Lynn Pedersen, "Women and Working Class Mobilization in Postwar São Paulo, 1945–1947," *Latin American Research Review* 24 (1989): 99–125.

54. The opposition within the textile workers' union praised Poleto's decision to support the strike, and their comments reveal their notions of what a union and its leaders should be. They hoped that Poleto would, "once and for all, understand that conditions have changed and that it is necessary to maintain a position as a true union president, faithful to the interests of the organization he directs and loyal to the union members who elected him" (*Hoje*, 22 March 1947).

55. TRE SP, *Diretórios Municipais*, 7:94. The ouster of Hugo Borghi by the national PTB had led to an internal party upheaval in São Paulo. With the advice of labor *procurador* José Artur da Frota Moreira, the new state leadership sought to appoint trade unionists to replace the non-working-class elements who, they said, had "parachuted" themselves into the party under Borghi's leadership (*Noite de São Paulo*, 26 February 1947).

56. *Hoje*, 19 March 1947. A similar nationalist theme was stressed by CGTB head Roberto Morena (*Hoje*, 18 March 1947).

57. As in Argentina, there was general agreement in Brazil that industrialization was important for the nation's future. "The real issue at stake in the 1940s," as Daniel James has written about Peronism, "was not therefore so much industrialization *versus* agrarian development, or state intervention *versus* laissez-faire. Rather it was the issue of the different potential meanings of industrialism, the social and political parameters within which it should take place which were at stake" (*Resistance and Integration: Peronism and the Argentine Working Class, 1946–1976* [Cambridge: Cambridge University Press, 1988], 20).

58. *Hoje*, 22 March 1947.

59. *Hoje*, 20 March 1947. On Morvan's avowedly antilabor views, see also the "Weekly Labor Report" by Edward J. Rowell, 29 May 1947, U.S. Embassy in Rio de Janeiro, RG 84, USDS, USNA.

60. *Hoje*, 19 March and 7 April 1947.

61. *Hoje*, 25 March 1947.

62. *Hoje*, 19 and 22 March; 2 April 1947; "Monthly Labor Report" by Edward J. Rowell, 30 April 1947, U.S. Embassy in Rio de Janeiro, RG 84, USDS, USNA. A fascinating first-person account of the bitter São Paulo–Goiás railroad strike can be found in Eduardo Dias, *Um Imigrante e a Revolução (Memórias de um Militante Operário, 1934–1951)* (São Paulo: Brasiliense, 1983), 89–103. In shouldering its new responsibilities as a governing party, the PCB made efforts to moderate some

strike struggles. This led to anger and disillusionment among some party leaders involved with the railroad strike, especially since Adhemar failed, in the end, to help resolve the stoppage in the workers' interests (ibid., 100–101).

63. *ESP*, 15 March 1947; *Hoje*, 21 March 1947.

64. *Hoje*, 22 and 25 March; 8 and 10 April 1947; quotations in 25 March 1947.

65. *Hoje*, 27 March 1947.

66. Session of 30 April 1947, *Anais de Assembléia Legislativa de São Paulo*, 1:903–6.

67. Labor's political dilemma was exacerbated by the dissipation of the pro-Vargas queremista coalition of the PCB and the PTB in 1945. The influence of working-class voters in São Paulo would have been strengthened if the two popular parties had remained united in postwar politics.

68. Leite, *Subsídios*, 347; Paulo Nogueira Filho, *Regime de Liberdade Social* (Rio de Janeiro: José Olympio, 1951); Beni, *Adhemar*, 186–88; *ESP*, 7 May 1946.

69. *Hoje*, 18 April 1947.

70. *ESP*, 1 May 1947; *Hoje*, 6 May 1947. Typically, on 1 May Adhemar also appeared at the First Workers' Sports Games organized by the employers' Social Service of Industry (SESI), headed by São Caetano's Armando de Arruda Pereira. One hundred and fifty sports teams competed, including ABC's Rhodia Brasileira and Indústrias Reunidas Francisco Matarazzo (*ESP*, 3 May 1947).

71. *ESP*, 1 May 1947.

72. *ESP*, 1 and 3 May 1947.

73. A derisive treatment of the PCB's alliance with Adhemar goes back to the contemporary polemical literature. The North American cold warrior journalist Edward Tomlinson argued, for example, that by supporting Adhemar, the "arch-prototype of [the] grabbing capitalist," the Communists had revealed themselves as "the cynical opportunists they are" (*Battle of the Hemisphere: Democracy vs. Totalitarianism in the Other America* [New York: Scribners, 1947], 66–67). A more recent history of the PCB fails to go much beyond this, merely citing the pact with Adhemar as an example of "the party's traditional opportunism" (Ronald Chilcote, *The Brazilian Communist Party: Conflict and Integration, 1922–1972* [New York: Oxford University Press, 1974], 299, 301).

74. A Communist intellectual recalls Adhemar's subsequent behavior in these bitter terms: "When the winds changed, Adhemar de Barros, perhaps to make clear the difference between himself and the Communists who had supported him, unleashed against them a terrible police repression during his whole term in office" (Elias Chaves Neto, *Minha Vida e as Lutas de Meu Tempo: Memórias* [São Paulo: Alfa-Omega, 1977], 92). Events such as the killing of three Communists at Tupã in 1949, repeated raids on the offices of the PCB newspaper, and wholesale violence against demonstrations did indeed characterize much of Adhemar's administration in the late 1940s (José Antônio Segatto et al., *PCB: Memória Fotográfica* [São Paulo: Brasiliense, 1982], 96–97).

75. The *Diário de São Paulo*, 19 October 1947, was vocally critical of the Communists' ability to open electoral headquarters without interference. The DOPS, they reported, claimed it was unable to act unless the hammer and sickle of the PCB was openly displayed.

76. *O Município*, 13 September 1947; session of 11 October 1947, *Anais da Assembléia Legislativa*, 5:167.

77. *Hoje*, 19 June and 23 September 1947.

78. Memorandum from São Paulo, 18 January 1947, U.S. Embassy in Rio de Janeiro, RG 84, USDS, USNA.

79. In a career spanning four decades, the pragmatic Adhemar gained a reputation for unprincipled flexibility. Having backed Getúlio Vargas in 1950, he nonetheless campaigned actively against the presidential candidates of the national coalition that expressed the Vargas legacy in 1955 and 1960. Yet his 1958 gubernatorial campaign led him to solicit and win trabalhista (PTB) and Communist support. This feint to the left was followed in 1962 by Adhemar's return to the governorship of the state as the candidate of the anticommunist "forces of order."

In the years that followed, this prime beneficiary of the Populist Republic became a key actor in the conspiracies that brought an end to competitive electoral politics in March 1964. However, within two years Adhemar himself would fall victim to the military's distrust and antipopulist animus. His political rights were canceled in 1966 and he died in exile in Paris in 1969 (Beloch and Alves de Abreu, *Dicionário*, 1:324; Alfred Stepan, *The Military in Politics: Changing Patterns in Brazil* [Princeton: Princeton University Press, 1971], 220; Peter Flynn, *Brazil: A Political Analysis* [Boulder: Westview, 1979], 341). For a review of the historiography and mythology surrounding the figure of Adhemar, see John D. French, "Workers and the Rise of Adhemarista Populism in São Paulo, Brazil 1945–1947," *Hispanic American Historical Review* 68 (1988): 1–4.

Chapter Nine

1. *Hoje*, 18 March 1947.

2. *Hoje*, 10 (first quotation) and 18 March 1947; 22 February 1947 (second quotation).

3. *Hoje*, 18 March 1947.

4. *Hoje*, 2 April 1947.

5. *Hoje*, 27 February and 4 March 1947.

6. *Hoje*, 26 February; 3 March; 22 April 1947.

7. *Hoje*, 3, 7, 13, 19 March 1947.

8. *Hoje*, 7 March 1947.

9. The Communists were by no means exuberant in their evaluation of the 1946 Constitution. Communist labor lawyer Lázaro Maria da Silva told São Caetano workers that the new charter did not "meet the needs of the working masses" but should nonetheless "be respected . . . [as] a great step toward democracy" (*Hoje*, 24 September 1946).

10. Brazil, *Constituição dos Estados Unidos do Brasil, 1946* (Rio de Janeiro: Imprensa Nacional, 1946), 43–44.

11. Article 157 of the new Constitution became the chief battleground between employers and employees in 1946 and 1947. The trade unions moved immediately to demand that this provision for a day of paid weekly rest be automatically enforced

and that this should be incorporated into all labor dissídios—an interpretation shared by some local labor courts. The metalworkers of Lidgerwood in Santo André received such a ruling in November 1946 despite the protests of the employers. Industrialists and the higher levels of the labor justice system were equally adamant in insisting that this clause could be activated only through the issuance of official regulations—a position shared, not surprisingly, by the Paulista industrialist Morvan Dias de Figueiredo, the head of the Ministry of Labor, Industry, and Commerce (*Jornal de São Caetano*, 8 December 1946; 2 March 1947; *Hoje*, 29 November 1946; 4, 22, 24, 27 February 1947).

12. Under conditions of illegality, estimates of Communist Party membership are likely to be exaggerated by both supporters of the PCB and its elite opponents. Edgard Carone, for example, cites without comment Leôncio Basbaum's incredible claim that there were 2,000 to 3,000 active PCB members in 1942; at the same time, he offers another informant's far lower and undoubtedly more realistic estimate that the PCB had only 100 active members in 1940 (*O Estado Novo (1937–1945)* [São Paulo: DIFEL, 1977], 241).

It is striking, nonetheless, that there has been little effort to document or estimate the legal PCB's membership after World War II. The widely accepted estimates for PCB membership by 1947 range from 150,000 to 200,000. The figure of 180,000 was given by São Paulo PCB deputy Jorge Amado in a speech before the Câmara Federal on the eve of the cassação of the PCB in May 1947 (Alfredo Wagner Berno de Almeida, *Jorge Amado: Política e Literatura* [Rio de Janeiro: Campus, 1979], 204). The figure of 60,000 members in São Paulo is provided in a book by a former PCB Central Committee member (Moisés Vinhas, *O Partidão: A Luta por um Partido de Massas* [São Paulo: Editôra Hucitec, 1982], 89).

13. Multiple interviews by the author with Marcos Andreotti in 1982, Santo André; for the names of the local PCB cells, see *Hoje*, 22 February; 10, 16, 19 September 1946.

14. As the personification of all virtues, Prestes was the focus of unabashed adulation among Communists and their supporters. For examples from ABC, see *Hoje*, 4 January, 17 May, 24 April 1946. The attractiveness of the figure of Prestes is attested to in the interviews with PTB leader Ivete Vargas (Centro de Pesquisa e Documentação de História Contemporânea do Brasil [CPDOC], Fundação Getúlio Vargas). In his memoirs, the socialist deputy Hermes Lima also displays great respect for Prestes in 1946 despite his own clashes with Communists on numerous occasions (Hermes Lima, *Travessia (Memórias)* [Rio de Janeiro: José Olympio, 1974], 213).

15. As the U.S. labor attaché observed in January 1947, the growth in support for the two popular parties in industrial areas was "an expression by masses of industrial workers of a growing awareness of their political force and dignity" and of their "resentment against the apparent indifference" of other parties ("Monthly Labor Report" by Edward J. Rowell, 13 January 1947, U.S. Embassy in Rio de Janeiro, Record Group 84, U.S. Department of State [USDS], U.S. National Archives [USNA]).

16. *Hoje*, 18 March 1947. The 1947 Communist electoral platform in the município of Santo André drew directly from the platform adopted by the Santo André

Comité Democrático Progressista in January 1946 (*O Imparcial*, 26 January 1947).

17. *Hoje*, 27 February 1947.

18. As a state deputy, Armando Mazzo did not ignore constituency service such as expediting the request of a newly established butcher for a quota of meat (Prefeitura Municipal de Santo André [PMSA], Processo 5460/47).

19. Sessions of 30 July, 29 August, and 5 September 1947, *Anais da Assembléia Constituinte do Estado de São Paulo*, 1:588–90; 2:871–73; 3:205–23. U.S. diplomatic records on labor are full of references to the economic difficulties afflicting important industrial sectors in São Paulo between 1946 and 1947 ("São Paulo Weekly Labor Notes," 24 April 1947; "Rio Weekly Labor Notes" by Edward J. Rowell, 8 May 1947; "Monthly Labor Reports" by Edward J. Rowell, 30 September 1947, 26 November 1947, RG 84, USDS, USNA).

20. On 22 August 1947 and again on 2 September, ABC's deputy called for a massive public campaign to establish a state monopoly of oil in order to bar Brazil's "national enslavement" at the hands of Standard Oil. Mazzo's interventions followed on the heels of the famous speeches by General Horta Barbosa; see sessions of 22 August and 2 September 1947, *Anais da Assembléia*, 2:577, 3:53–54. For a thorough account of this famous nationalist campaign, see Maria Augusta Tibiriça Miranda, *O Petróleo É Nosso: A Luta Contra o "Entreguismo" pelo Monopólio Estatal* (Petrópolis: Vozes, 1983).

21. TRE SP, Processo 8 (1945); session of 28 April 1947, *Anais da Assembléia*, 1:842–44. See also "O Imperialismo Matará a Nossa Indústria," *Hoje*, 9 April 1947; "Quarterly Labor Report" by Edward J. Rowell, 10 April 1947, U.S. Embassy in Rio de Janeiro, RG 84, USDS, USNA.

22. See "O Proletariado da 'Electro-Aço' Luta Contra o Imperialismo," *Hoje*, 26 July 1946. See also *Hoje*, 15 July and 2 August 1946. In 1947, Electro-Aço workers sought an interview with the new governor Adhemar de Barros to request his help in securing the pay, indemnification, and vacation time still owed them by the bankrupt company (*Hoje*, 27 March 1947).

23. *Hoje*, 26 July 1946. See Anapio Gomes, *Radiografia do Brasil* (Rio de Janeiro: Irmãos Pongeti, 1960).

24. The confusion over how to treat foreign-owned industrial enterprises is suggested by the activities of one local cell in Santo André. While mentioning the city as "a focus of imperialist enterprises," the group's list of projected activities contained no concrete suggestions as to what was to be done about this reality (*Hoje*, 7 April 1947).

25. Session of 28 April 1947, *Anais da Assembléia*, 1:843; Armando Mazzo, *Memórias de um Militante Político e Sindical no ABC* (São Bernardo do Campo: PMSBC, 1991), 113. See also Luis Carlos Prestes, *Os Comunistas e o Monopólio da Terra* (Rio de Janeiro: Horizonte, 1945).

26. The decision to legalize the PCB in 1945, Nogueira wrote, flowed from "a literalistic legalism . . . completely divorced from real life"; this mixture of "Pangloss [and] Alice in Wonderland," he suggested, was not entirely absent from the Brazilian parliament, which had its share of "crypto-Communists and sympathizers" (*PCB Processo de Cassação do Registro [1947]* [Belo Horizonte: Aldeia Global, 1980], 77, 80–81, 93).

27. Ibid., 133; *ESP*, 6 and 9 May 1947. The U.S. government no doubt encouraged the Brazilian government to outlaw the PCB. Hélio Silva, *1945: Por que Depuseram Vargas* (Rio de Janeiro: Civilizaçao Brasileira, 1976), 376–82, discusses the contemporary evidence adduced by the PCB to prove this charge. A recent, carefully researched piece on Chile suggests that U.S. economic and diplomatic pressure played a significant role in the 1947 decision by Chilean President González Videla to oust the Communists from his government (Andrew Barnard, "Chilean Communists, Radical Presidents and Chilean Relations with the United States, 1940–1947," *Journal of Latin American Studies* 13 [1981]: 373).

28. Assured that the decision provided no precedent for action against other parties, the initial non-Communist opposition began to fade. Whatever their opinion of the decision, argued the PTB, the UDN, and others, it had been properly made by the appropriate judicial authority and hence deserved respect (*ESP*, 6 and 9 May 1945).

29. The PCB's optimistic interpretation was based, in part, on assurances they had received from Dutra's minister of justice on the day of the decision. Communist federal deputy Jorge Amado, for example, was told that the government had no intention of stripping the PCB of the posts it had won in the elections of 1945 and 1947—but that was precisely what the government proceeded to do (*ESP*, 10 May 1947; *Hoje*, 8 May 1947). Indeed, a total lack of good faith characterized Dutra's PSD in all of its dealings with the Communists—a behavior that contrasts with Adhemar's willingness to deliver on any promises to the PCB, for however long. In September 1946, for example, a formal agreement was reached between the PSD and the PCB over the election of officials of the new *câmara federal*. After voting for all of the PSD's candidates, the Communists failed to receive the promised PSD votes to elect São Paulo PCB deputy Milton Caires de Brito as fourth secretary, even in a second vote. "There are many accords that fall apart," a contemporary journalist later recalled, "but for one party to fulfill everything that was agreed to and the other, after having received all the benefits, to cut the cord at the last moment; this was the first time this had happened" (Yvonne Miranda, *Homens e Fatos da Constituinte de 1946* [Rio de Janeiro: Nórdica, 1982], 185–86).

30. *ESP*, 10 May 1947; *Hoje*, 10 May 1947; Polícia do Estado de São Paulo, Delegacia de Santo André, "Termo de Arrolamento (Santo André)," in TRE SP, Processos Soltos. John D. French and Kent Jensen are preparing a publication that will make this statewide collection of police documentation available for general access by scholars ("Outlawing 'Subversion': Police Repression of Leftist Activities in São Paulo, Brazil, in 1947," forthcoming). For some preliminary thoughts on the police in São Paulo, see John D. French, "Legal Coercion in Twentieth-Century São Paulo, Brazil: Police Self-Definitions, Mentality, and Practice" (unpublished paper presented at the December 1990 meeting of the Conference on Latin American History, New York City).

31. Polícia do Estado de São Paulo, Delegacia de Santo André, "Termo de Arrolamento (São Bernardo do Campo, Utinga, Vila Camilópolis, São Caetano)," in TRE SP, Processos Soltos.

32. *PCB Processo de Cassação*, 7–8 (quotation on 120). Interestingly enough, the Labor Ministry report to the TSE said that it could "not find concrete, material, and

irrefutable proof of the responsibility" of the Communist Party for postwar strikes. More attuned to the valid grievances of the working class, officials of the Labor Ministry were less inclined to the simple-minded conclusions about "outside agitators" offered by the DOPS and those judges who supported the cassação (ibid., 14). The same logic applies to the strongly anticommunist PTB federal deputy Edmundo Barreto Pinto, who argued, in May 1946, that in truth the PCB "was even containing strikes because if they really wished to encourage them, we would have neither light nor gas nor transportation" (Miranda, *Homens e Fatos*, 66).

33. In discussing Decree 23,046, the U.S. labor attaché noted that the elimination of "units of rank and file representation—such as the shop committees" was one of the labor ministry's five top objectives ("Monthly Labor Report" by Edward J. Rowell, 1 July 1947, U.S. Embassy in Rio de Janeiro, RG 84, USDS, USNA).

34. *ESP*, 8 May 1947. Although he could provide no direct evidence of PCB-ordered stoppages, Morvan Dias de Figueiredo cited several strike leaders who appeared on the candidate lists of the PCB such as Roque Trevisan and Vitorio Martorelli in his home state of São Paulo. The elimination of such agitators, he suggested, would reestablish "the [natural] harmony of producing classes" and restore the "most friendly relations" that had hitherto prevailed between labor and capital. After all, he pointed out, "all good workers are animated by a desire to collaborate [with employers] for the reconstruction of our economy" (ibid.; see also "Monthly Labor Report" by Edward J. Rowell, 1 July 1947, RG 84, USDS, USNA).

35. Morvan Dias de Figueiredo's remarks to the press also demonstrated that he still viewed the government's labor relations bureaucracy with hostility. Asked about purging the "700 Communist functionaries," Morvan Dias thought the numbers "exaggerated, even counting the Labor Ministry employees with extremist ideas who are not affiliated with the PCB." His willingness to consider trabalhistas and Socialists as "extremists" suggests a considerable suspicion of the ministry's labor specialists (*ESP*, 8 May 1947).

36. "Monthly Labor Report," 26 August 1947, and "Labor Comment Summary on Selected Local and International Subjects," 9 December 1947, by Edward J. Rowell, U.S. Embassy in Rio de Janeiro, RG 84, USDS, USNA.

37. There are two conflicting sources on the number and geographic distribution of trade union interventions in São Paulo in 1947. Thirty-six interventions are reported in *ESP* (8, 9, 10 May 1947), while twenty-two are listed in "Repression of Communism-Labor" (Memorandum to the U.S. Ambassador from William W. Wheeler, Jr., 31 July 1947, U.S. Embassy in Rio de Janeiro, RG 84, USDS, USNA). Thus, interventions affected at least 15 percent and perhaps as many as 25 percent of the 152 legally recognized unions in the state of São Paulo in mid-1946 ("Relação das Federações e Sindicatos Existentes no Estado de São Paulo em 31 de Julho, de 1946," typed manuscript on stationery from "Cunha Lima Sociedade Anônima, Técnicos em Contabilidade," from the private archive of Robert Alexander). In both sources, however, almost no interventions are listed in the interior of the state, and the rank order of interventions—both in absolute number and as a percentage of trade union entities in each area—parallels areas of trade union strength and membership: Santos, the município of São Paulo, and the ABC region.

38. Robert Alexander, "Brazil, Argentina and Chile," in *Labor in Developing*

Economies, ed. Walter Galenson (Berkeley: University of California Press, 1962), 159. The 300,000 figure was provided by unnamed Labor Ministry sources to the U.S. labor attaché in Rio ("Monthly Labor Report" by Edward J. Rowell, 26 August 1947, U.S. Embassy in Rio de Janeiro, RG 84, USDS, USNA). Total claimed union membership stood at 797,691 nationwide in 1946 (José Albertino Rodrigues, *Sindicato e Desenvolvimento* [1968; reprint, São Paulo: Símbolo, 1979], 130).

39. *Hoje*, 24 May 1947; "Repression of Communism-Labor," by Wheeler, RG 84, USDS, USNA.

40. *Hoje*, 19 June 1947. On Miguéis, see *Borda do Campo*, 27 November 1949; *O News Seller* [title later changed to *Diário do Grande ABC*], 21 June and 12 July 1959; 7 May 1961; *Diário do Grande ABC*, 19 December 1981. On the intervention in the civil construction union, see PMSA, Processo 3814/47.

41. *Hoje*, 2 June 1947. For the founding manifesto of the Agremiação Paulista de Trabalhadores, see *Anais da Assembléia*, 4:156–57; see also "Monthly Labor Report" by Edward J. Rowell, 27 October 1947, U.S. Embassy in Rio de Janeiro, RG 84, USDS, USNA.

42. "The Brazilian working classes," the U.S. labor attaché noted, "are not apt to be too impressed by the menace of communism *per se*" ("Monthly Labor Report" by Edward J. Rowell, 1 July 1947, RG 84, USDS, USNA).

43. Hélio Silva, *1945: Por que Depuseram Vargas* (Rio de Janeiro: Civilização Brasileira, 1976), 403; *Jornal de São Caetano*, 10 August 1947.

44. The protest against the cassação de mandatos was signed by Santo André representatives of the PSB, UDN, PTB, PSP, PPP, and PDC (Session of 7 August 1947, *Anais da Assembléia*, quotation on 1:935–36). Other than the PSD, the only Santo André parties that did not sign the protest against the cassação were the PRP and the PTN, both with 1 percent of the vote in the elections of January 1947. The PRP's position reflected the party's ideological roots in the right-wing Integralist movement of the thirties, while the absence of Borghi's PTN reflected the party's lack of local organization in Santo André.

45. *Hoje*, 23 September 1947.

46. Founded as the Proletarian Party of Brazil in 1946, the São Paulo PST received legal recognition in September 1947. With little prospect of electoral success, the PST state diretório was open to making deals with candidates in search of a legal registry, including the PCB. Within a month, the PCB, in its strongholds such as São Paulo and Santo André, had registered its own slates under the PST label (TRE SP, Processo 17 [1946]; *Diário de São Paulo*, 17, 19, 26 October 1947). The São Paulo PST had endorsed Adhemar de Barros in January 1947 (*Diário de São Paulo*, 12 January 1947).

47. *O Município*, 25 October 1947. In mid-1947, the national PST was taken over by Maranhão's conservative senator Vitorino Freire de Brito as a party label under which to group dissidents from the established elite parties. For biographical data on the well-connected senator, see Sergio Miceli, "Carne e Osso da Elite Política Brasileira Pos-1930," in *História da Civilização Brasileira*, ed. Boris Fausto, part 3, vol. 3 (São Paulo: DIFEL, 1981), 578–79.

48. TRE SP, Processo 17A (1947); PST (PCB) leaflet, "Santo André e Seus Problemas," of 8 November 1947, in TRE SP, Processo 6254/174 (1947).

49. PMSA, Processo 8768/47; *O Município*, 1 November 1947; *Hoje*, 4 November 1947.

50. TRE SP, *Diretórios Municipais*, 7:94.

51. TRE SP, Processo 11R (1947). The *Jornal de São Caetano*, 2 November 1947, reported that the nomination of Ícaro Sydow, a resident of São Paulo, was imposed by the state PTB head, Deputy Nelson Fernandes. Silva, *1945*, 309, reports that Sydow was serving as the PTB's acting vice-president in November 1945.

52. After all, control of municipal patronage had not led to a PSD victory in December 1945 in Santo André, and Adhemar's appointed prefeito, Alfredo Maluf, would discover in late 1947 that he could not even control his own Partido Social Progressista (PSP). This intense factionalism led to campaign advertisements that listed individuals as "candidates of the UDN and dissidents of the PSP and PTN" (*O Município*, 18 October 1947; *Borda do Campo*, 8 October 1947; *O Imparcial*, 25 October 1947).

53. *ESP*, 6 November 1947; *Hoje*, 8 November 1947. President Dutra and the PSD were publicly critical of those in the PSD who were backing Carlos Cyrillo, Jr. (*Diário de São Paulo*, 31 October and 4 November 1947). Cyrillo, a former member of the Partido Republicano Paulista, had distinguished himself as an enemy of Vargas and the PCB over the previous years (*Borda do Campo*, 29 September and 8 December 1947; Silva, *1945*, 428–31).

54. *Borda do Campo*, 2 November 1947; *ESP*, 5 November 1947; quotation in *Hoje*, 5 November 1947; *Diário de São Paulo*, 5 November 1947.

55. Carlos Alberto Balista, "Comunistas na Prefeitura de Santo André," *DGABC*, 3 October 1982; *Hoje*, 21 October 1947.

56. *Diário de São Paulo*, 22 October 1947. On 27 October 1947 President Dutra declared both the state capital of São Paulo and the port of Santos to be "military bases or ports of exceptional importance" and stripped them of the right to elect their prefeito (TRE SP, *Atas das Sessões*, vol. 2).

The conciliatory tone of the non-Communist parties is suggested by the local press. *O Imparcial*, 25 October 1947, called the Communist candidate for prefeito, Armando Mazzo, a "studious, intelligent, and hard-working youth" but predicted that the irregularities in his registry would bar him. The *Jornal de São Caetano*, 2 November 1947, called Mazzo "a bold candidate, hard-working and intelligent." Citing the problem of his registry, it phrased its criticisms in mild terms. Santo André needed, it went on, a man with solid administrative experience. While in the state assembly, it asked, "what did he [Mazzo] do besides reading petitions" of workers?

57. *Diário de São Paulo*, 26 October and 8 November 1947; *ESP*, 8 November 1947; TRE SP, *Atas das Sessões*, vol. 2, 12 November 1947; TRE SP, Processos 6253/174 (1947) and 6253/729 (1947).

58. TRE SP, Processos 6253/174 (1947) and 6253/729 (1947); *Hoje*, 8 November 1947.

59. TRE SP, Processos Soltos 7R, 10R, 6R, 11R, 12R, and 8R (1947).

60. These occupational data were compiled by local electoral notaries from the records they were required to maintain on the 30,000 registered voters in the município of Santo André. One-third of the electorate were women, and 16 percent

of *all* those registered listed their occupation as housewives, who were not required by law to vote (for the complete breakdown, see Tables F8 to F12, in John D. French, "Industrial Workers and the Origin of Populist Politics in the ABC Region of Greater São Paulo, Brazil 1900–1950" [Ph.D. diss., Yale University, 1985], 652–56). John D. French and Mary Lynn Pedersen have created a statewide data base using this 1948 breakdown of the São Paulo electorate; for the preliminary findings, see "Once Women Vote: The Politics of Female Enfranchisement in São Paulo, Brazil" (unpublished paper presented to the June 1990 Berkshire Conference on the History of Women, New Brunswick, N.J.).

61. Table I1, "Municipal Candidates by Occupational Category, Santo André, November 9, 1947," in French, "Industrial Workers," 679. The percentages used in this comparison of the occupations of the electorate and local party candidates were derived from an "adjusted electorate." While including working women, the adjusted electorate leaves out housewives (16 percent of the total local registration), who cannot reasonably be apportioned to the different social categories used here. As might be expected, politics in ABC was extremely male-dominated; only 4 women were included among the 221 municipal candidates presented by Santo André's eight political parties.

62. *Diário de São Paulo*, 8 October 1947. The PTB labor nominees included textile union president Henrique Poleto, São Paulo ceramics confederation leader Artur Albino da Rocha, and an activist in the Santo André furniture workers' union, Cristovam Vaz. However, the intervenor in the chemical workers' union, Gervasto Elizeu Maschio, was not nominated despite being a member of the local PTB diretório; the reasons for this are unclear.

63. TRE SP, Processo 6253/173 (1947); Processo 8A (1945); *Hoje*, 21 November 1945.

64. Carmen Edwiges Savietto was the preeminent female activist in the local PCB and was heavily involved with organizing the postwar leftist women's movement. For a profile of Savietto, see John D. French with Mary Lynn Pedersen, "Women and Working Class Mobilization in Postwar São Paulo, 1945–1948," *Latin American Research Review* 24 (1989): 115–18.

65. See Table I5, "Communist Candidates by Occupational Category in São Paulo and Santo André, 1945–1947," in French, "Industrial Workers," 683.

66. Ibid. Ten of the fifteen founders of the PST diretório in Santo André were workers (TRE SP, Processo 17A [1947]).

67. The 33 percent of local voters who were salaried employees felt most comfortable in the more orthodox and less radical parties without, at this time, the disproportionate representation in the PTB that one might expect.

68. *Hoje*, 5 November 1947.

69. See Table I2, "Municipal Candidates by Place of Birth, Santo André, November 9, 1947," in French, "Industrial Workers," 680. The decisively rural origin of ABC's industrial working class can be documented in the payroll records for three local factories in 1945. Data for the 1,232 Brazilian employees of the Laminação Nacional de Metais and for 322 workers of a Santo André textile factory show that 57 percent of the metalworkers and textile workers were from the "true non/industrial interior," so defined to exclude the major cities in the interior of the state. Fully

91 percent of the 98 employees of ABC's Companhia Brasileira de Indústrias Químicas were from the true interior (Table H6, "Comparison of Places of Birth, Santo André, 1940–1950," in ibid., 678).

70. "Santo André e Seus Problemas," in TRE SP, Processo 6254/174 (1947).

71. In his report on the January 1947 election campaign, PCB leader Diógenes de Arruda harshly criticized the functioning of the party's local cells (*Hoje*, 26 February 1947).

72. Electoral participation had suffered a cumulative decline of 17 percent since December 1945 in Santo André, and 8 percent fewer voters turned out in November 1947 than ten months earlier in January 1947—but both declines were below the state average.

73. TRE SP, unpublished results for vice-governor, "Eleição para Vice-Governador Realizada em 9 de Novembro de 1947, Votos Computados pela Comissão Designada pelo Tribunal Regional Eleitoral." Aureliano Leite, *Páginas de uma Longa Vida* (São Paulo: Livraria Martins, 1967), 402, notes the relief with which the conservative classes met the defeat of the seemingly unbeatable PTB/PCB combination, even if by Adhemar.

74. Table G12, "Municipal Election Results in Santo André by Party, November 9, 1947," in French, "Industrial Workers," 669; TRE SP, "Actas e Resultados da Comissão Apuradora das Eleições Municipais de Santo André, 9 de Novembro de 1947" (found in an uncatalogued folder).

75. Session of 22 November 1947, *Anais da Assembléia Legislativa*, 7:244.

76. The PCB's absolute support in November 1947 was only a bit below that received by the PCB in 1945, when its candidates for federal deputy received 6,819 votes in Santo André and its presidential candidate, Yedo Fiuza, received 7,059.

77. "Manifesto aos Trabalhadores e ao Povo de Santo André," in TRE SP, Processo 6254/174 (1947).

78. Ibid.

Chapter Ten

1. *Hoje*, 18 November 1947; TRE SP, Processos 6253/173 (1947), 6254/174 (1947), 17A (1947); session of 24 November 1947, *Anais da Assembléia Legislativa do Estado de São Paulo*, 7:301–2.

2. TRE SP, Processo 6254/174 (1947), 8.

3. Ibid.

4. The São Paulo PSD, PSB, PR (Partido Republicano), and UDN all objected to this procedure in a 1948 appeal to the TSE (TRE SP, Processo 26,752 [1948] [7784/TSE]).

5. Interview with Miguel Guillen in Carlos Alberto Balista, "Comunistas na Prefeitura de Santo André," *Diário do Grande ABC* (*DGABC*), 3 October 1982; Ademir Medici, "A Vitória dos Candidatos de Prestes" (unpublished manuscript, PMSA, 1990), 78–81; Armando Mazzo, *Memórias de um Militante Político e Sindical no ABC* (São Bernardo do Campo: PMSBC, 1991), 116.

6. Session of 3 January 1948, *Anais da Câmara Municipal de Santo André*, 1:11–12; Balista, "Comunistas na Prefeitura."

7. For an account of the raid by *Hoje* editor Elias Chaves Neto, see *Minha Vida e as Lutas de Meu Tempo* (São Paulo: Alfa-Omega, 1977), 93–94. On the final cassação de mandatos, see Hélio Silva, *1945: Por que Depuseram Vargas* (Rio de Janeiro: Civilização Brasileira, 1976), 449–57; session of 12 January 1948, *Anais da Assembléia Legislativa*, 9:753–54.

8. Silva, *1945*, 39. Zampol remained one of ABC's outstanding politicians until his death in 1977. For biographical detail, see *DGABC*, 29 and 30 September; 19 November 1977.

9. *Jornal de São Caetano*, 2 November 1947 (first quotation); session of 23 October 1948, *Anais da CMSA*, vol. 14; *Borda do Campo*, 11 December 1949 (second quotation); 17 July 1949.

10. Data drawn from Table 11, "Municipal Candidates by Occupational Category, Santo André, November 9, 1947," in John D. French, "Industrial Workers and the Origin of Populist Politics in the ABC Region of Greater São Paulo, Brazil 1900–1950" (Ph.D. diss., Yale University, 1985), 679.

11. Poleto criticized the Tribunal Regional do Trabalho for "its slowness of action" resulting in the "workers losing patience, since the time passes and the cost of living continues to rise astonishingly"; the result was "to encourage strikes among the workers," despite his efforts to dissuade them (session of 15 July 1948, *Anais da CMSA*, vol. 9). Santo André's câmara became involved in the efforts to resolve the strike (Ricardo Maranhão, *Sindicatos e Democratização [Brasil 1945/1950]* [São Paulo: Brasiliense, 1979], 107).

12. For a discussion of the workers' economic situation, see Maranhão, *Sindicatos*, 115–19.

13. Interview by author with Marcos Andreotti, 28 October 1982, Santo André; Balista, "Comunistas na Prefeitura"; Chaves Neto, *Minha Vida*, 106–7; *Voz Operária*, 2 November 1949; Medici, "Vitória," 85–86; Mazzo, *Memórias*, 121.

14. Interview by author with Marcos Andreotti, 28 October 1982, Santo André; *Fôlha do Povo*, 29 March 1953. Like its affiliates, the national CGTB in 1953 was, in the words of its chief, more a movement than a trade union confederation (interview by Robert Alexander with Roberto Morena, 6 October 1953, Rio de Janeiro, in the private archive of Robert Alexander).

15. See Table A4, "Industrial Employment in ABC, 1900–1960," in French, "Industrial Workers," 610.

16. Karl Loewenstein, *Brazil under Vargas* (New York: Macmillan, 1942), 343. Fabio Sodré argued that "the absence of union organization and the difficulty of establishing it" had been "the greatest obstacle to revolutionary action in Brazil" ("As Necessidades dos Operários Brasileiros," *Estudos Brasileiros* 1 [1938]: 772).

17. Clovis Leite Ribeiro, "A Classe Média e as Eleições de 19 de Janeiro," *Digesto Econômico* 3, no. 29 (April 1947): 74. In his memoirs, Aureliano Leite, a conservative UDN federal deputy from São Paulo, emphasized how shocked the state's "upper classes" were by the results of the 1945 elections. The results, he suggested, were a strong warning "to the Brazilian bourgeoisie that the so-called humble

classes were gaining consciousness of their great social force" (Aureliano Leite, *História da Civilização Brasileira* [São Paulo: Livraria Martins, 1946], 231).

18. Ribeiro, "Classe Média," 71.

19. By mid-1948, Adhemar's relations with the state's conservative parties and Dutra had once again deteriorated to the point where federal intervention was threatened. At mass rallies, a rotund Adhemar highlighted his predicament in 1948 with self-deprecating humor: "They want to depose me? It's easy. Five men are sufficient: one to fire and four to carry my body" (Mario Beni, *Adhemar* [São Paulo: Grafikor, n.d], 64).

Under these circumstances, Adhemar again accepted the support of the PCB, whose state leaders soon found themselves under indictment as a result of their manifesto against the continuing threat of federal intervention in São Paulo. On this short flirtation with the PCB, see Israel Beloch and Alzira Alves de Abreu, eds., *Dicionário Histórico-Biográfico Brasileiro* (Rio de Janeiro: Forense Universitária and FGV-CPDOC, 1984), 1:319; Chaves Neto, *Minha Vida*, 106.

20. Maria do Carmo Campello de Souza, *Estado e Partidos Políticos no Brasil (1930–1964)* (São Paulo: Alfa-Omega, 1976), 118. Despite its anticommunism, the PTB opposed the cassação of the PCB officeholders at both the state and national levels (session of 22 November 1947, *Anais da Assembléia Legislativa*, 7:245).

21. These parliamentary fears could not be stilled by the verbal pledges of the Dutra administration. The crucial test came in the case of Pedro Pomar and Diógenes de Arruda, two Communist federal deputies, who had been elected in January 1947 as candidates of Adhemar's PSP. Ignoring the appeals of the PSD, the parliament and courts both ruled that the electoral mandates of these top PCB leaders were inviolable, despite the cassação of the PCB. Thus two top Communist leaders remained in the federal parliament even after the ouster of Prestes and the PCB group. See TRE SP, Processo 3698 (1947) (325/TSE).

22. "Código Eleitoral (Lei no. 1164 de 24 de Julho de 1950)," *Boletim Eleitoral* (São Paulo) 3 (July 1950): 983.

23. A charge made by an opponent in the session of 23 April 1947, *Anais da Assembléia Legislativa*, vol. 1.

24. Session of 20 November 1947, *Anais da Assembléia Legislativa*, 7:96–97.

25. Sessions of 3 and 6 January 1948, *Anais da CMSA*, 1:11–15, 21, 29, 30.

26. Over the following decades, Campanella would serve as state and federal deputy and twice as prefeito of São Caetano. After the 1964 coup that ended the populist republic, he was elected federal deputy by the opposition Movimento Democrático Brasileiro (MDB) until he himself was cassado and lost his political rights through the military regime's Ato Institucional No. 5 (Beloch and Alves de Abreu, *Dicionário*, 1:565–66; Nicola Perrella, *Roteiro da Vida de um Homem Público, Anacleto Campanella* [São Paulo: Edições Alarico, 1962]). On Campanella's support for Simonsen and Arruda Pereira, see *Fôlha da Manhã*, 15 January 1947. For a striking example of his later prolabor rhetoric, see his scathing denunciation of the treatment of workers at São Caetano's Indústrias Reunidas Francisco Matarazzo (*News Seller* [later *Diário do Grande ABC*], 11 December 1960).

27. Maria Victoria de Mesquita Benevides, *A UDN e o Udenismo: Ambigüidades do Liberalismo Brasileiro (1945–1965)* (Rio de Janeiro: Paz e Terra, 1981), 66.

28. *O Município*, 16 August 1947; *Jornal de São Caetano*, 8 and 22 June, 10 August 1947. These two UDN newspapers in São Caetano refashioned the rhetoric of the 1945 "campaign of white handkerchiefs" in a popular direction. For more on these newspapers, see Valdenizio Petrolli, "História da Imprensa no ABC Paulista," 2 vols. (M.A. thesis, Instituto Metodista de Ensino Superior [Santo André], 1983), 2:40–46, 48–56.

29. *Jornal de São Caetano*, 22 June 1947 (first quotation); 10 August 1947 (second quotation); 6 July 1947.

30. *O Imparcial*, 9 April 1947.

31. For the São Caetano diretório, see *Anais da CMSA*, 1948, 10:3.

32. Maria Augusta Tibiriçá Miranda, *O Petróleo É Nosso: A Luta Contra o "Entreguismo" pelo Monopólio Estatal* (Petrópolis: Vozes, 1983), 49, 70, 72, 109, 148, 255, 257, 368. On Adhemar's action, see session of 2 October 1948, *Anais da CMSA*, vol. 13. For an example of conservative polemics against the movement, see São Paulo Departamento de Ordem Política Social, *Atividades Comunistas Junto à Campanha do Petróleo* (São Paulo: DOPS, 1949).

33. See *Anais da CMSA*, 1948, passim. For a brief account, see José de Souza Martins, *São Caetano em Quatro Seculos* (São Paulo: Saraiva, 1957), 127–43.

34. *Borda do Campo*, 17 November 1948; session of 31 January 1948, *Anais da CMSA*, 2:26. Although it is often overlooked today, few urban politicians during the Populist Republic failed to recognize that the working-class Left had pioneered what became the tactics and organizational forms of their trade. Interviewed in the late 1970s, the former president of the metropolitan São Paulo Women's Commission of Adhemar's PSP recalled the popular agitation she had participated in so actively: "Even in the most distant neighborhoods, you would find women talking of the PSP and calling upon the people to struggle. Before the PSP developed," Dulce Borges Barreiro observed, "only the Communists did this sort of politics" (Regina Sampaio, *Adhemar de Barros e o PSP* [São Paulo: Global, 1982], 142).

35. For the text of the interparty accord, see Hélio Silva, *1954: Um Tiro no Coração* (Rio de Janeiro: Civilização Brasileira, 1978), 301–2. For a fuller treatment, see Benevides, *UDN*, 69–76. The complaint that the interparty accord was directed against the PTB and the PSP was often made by Getúlio Vargas (*A Campanha Presidencial* [Rio de Janeiro: José Olympio, 1951]), as well as by Lopes Rodrigues in *Adhemar de Barros Perante a Nação* (São Paulo: Editôra Piratininga, 1954), 143.

36. Maria Celina Soares d'Araújo, *O Segundo Governo Vargas: Democracia, Partidos, e Crise Política* (Rio de Janeiro: Zahar, 1982), 41–63, examines the political maneuvers leading up to this outcome.

37. Erlindo Salzano, *A Campanha de 50: Aliança Adhemar e Getúlio* (São Paulo: Edameris, n.d.).

38. Vargas, *Campanha Presidencial*, 69–70, 88. The campaign slogan is cited in *Hoje*, 7 October 1950. D'Araújo, *Segundo Governo Vargas*, 86–92, also examines Getúlio's rhetoric on workers and trade unions in 1950.

39. In late 1947, the PCB's newspaper headlined the dramatic but unrealistic slogan of Central Committee member Diógenes de Arruda Câmara, "No one can govern São Paulo against the Communists or without the Communists" (*Hoje*, 26 October 1947). For the evolution of national PCB policy, see Edgard Carone, *O*

P.C.B. Vol. 1: 1922–1943 (São Paulo: DIFEL, 1982), 72–112. The extremist position taken by the PCB's top leadership can best be seen in the "Manifesto de Agôsto de 1950," reprinted, with illustrations, in Moisés Vinhas, *O Partidão* (São Paulo: Hucitec, 1982), 140–58.

40. On the electoral tactics of 1950, see *Voz Operária*, 23 September 1950. For further examples of anti-Getulista rhetoric, see *Hoje*, 7 October 1951. At least one careless but widely read observer has made the glaring error of claiming that "the PCB involved itself resolutely" in favor of Vargas in the presidential elections of 1950 (Frei Betto, *Batismo do Sangue* [Rio de Janeiro: Civilização Brasileira, 1982], 13–14).

41. See Table G15, "Presidential and Gubernatorial Election Results in Santo André (Official but Incomplete), October 3, 1950," in French, "Industrial Workers," 672. Before the final results were published, contemporary observers had been uncertain whether Santo André's workers would heed the PCB's call for a boycott against Vargas (*Fôlha do Povo*, 6 October 1950).

42. *Fôlha do Povo*, 24 November 1950.

Conclusion

1. Francisco Weffort, *O Populismo na Política Brasileira* (Rio de Janeiro: Paz e Terra, 1978), 75. Most approaches to the study of populism, as Daniel James observes, have emphasized the "aberrant quality of working class participation . . . [which] has been treated as something of an historical conundrum requiring explanation, most usually in terms of notions such as manipulation, passivity, cooptation, and not uncommonly, irrationality" (*Resistance and Integration: Peronism and the Argentine Working Class, 1946–1976* [Cambridge: Cambridge University Press, 1988], 2).

2. *Borda do Campo*, 11 December 1949; *O Município*, 1 November 1947.

3. *Fôlha do Povo*, 3 November 1950.

4. Session of 15 February 1952, *Anais da Câmara Municipal de Santo André*, 2:18.

5. Sessions of 18 and 22 October 1957, *Anais da CMSA*, vol. 6 passim.

6. Clovis Leite Ribeiro advocated precisely this innovative role for the middle class in 1947: instead of continuing its traditional "servile conservatism," he said, the middle class should serve as the means of "overcoming class conflicts through the broadest and most fraternal union of all classes. . . . Freeing itself from subjection to capitalist reaction," he argued, the middle class could fulfill its "historic mission" of providing the "leadership of a broad movement for national unity" that would redeem the workers from "misery, ignorance and hatred" ("A Classe Média e as Eleições de 19 de Janeiro," *Digesto Econômico* 3, no. 29 [April 1947]: 72).

7. Adhemar de Barros, Regina Sampaio notes, encouraged support for the 1953 strike by top PSP politicians despite his party's ostensible neutrality and its denunciations of Communist infiltration (*Adhemar de Barros e o PSP* [São Paulo: Global, 1982], 144). According to a newspaper article, PSP Deputy Juvenal Lino de Matos,

a member of Adhemar's inner circle, was even beaten up by the police in the Praça da Sé during the strike (undated and unidentified newspaper article, "A Greve dos Teçelões," from the private archive of Robert Alexander). The same article includes references to prostrike activities by politicians from the Partido Democrata Cristão and even the Partido Republicano in São Paulo.

8. Interviewed shortly after the 1953 strike, the president of the striking São Paulo metalworkers' union, Remo Forli, reported that "all political parties in the city [of São Paulo] tried to profit from the strike. Virtually all proclaimed their support of it," with the Communist Party, the PSP of Adhemar de Barros, and the PTB playing the most active roles. Jânio Quadros, he went on, "also supported the walkout. [And] Lucas [Nogueira] Garcez, the governor of the state, was responsible for the final settlement. However his police were rough on the strikers while the walkout was on" (interview by Robert Alexander with Remo Forli, 16 June 1953, São Paulo). The vice-president of Forli's union was even more revealing in his comments. Declaring his support for Adhemar over Governor Lucas Nogueira Garcez, Santo Rizzo explained that Adhemar "is a more hard-working man, though he is crooked while Garcez is honest. [However,] Ademar [sic] has more interest in the workers and he is very ambitious, so is likely to do more for them so as to gain their support. However, Garcez has no ambition and is rather cold" (interview by Robert Alexander with Santo Rizzo, 16 June 1953, São Paulo).

9. José Álvaro Moisés, Greve de Massa e Crise Política (Estudo da Greve dos 300 Mil em São Paulo—1953–54) (São Paulo: Polis, 1978), 84, 86, 88, and photos (quotation on 84).

10. During the 1950 campaign, Vargas openly criticized the "bureaucratic machine" of the labor ministry and those who commanded it. Union elections, he said, should be "freely and effectively carried out" and their results accepted by the government. "True leaders of the laboring classes," he went on, "dedicated and full of abnegation, are at times unjustly accused of being Communists in order to remove them from electoral competitions in the unions. I receive your complaints," he told trade unionists, "and I recognize that these accusations are unjust. I have confidence in the workers and they should have confidence in me" (Hélio Silva and Maria Cecília Ribas Carneiro, Getúlio Vargas: A Segunda Deposição [São Paulo: Grupo de Comunicação Três, 1983], 51).

11. The recollections of Segadas Vianna, Vargas's labor minister during the 1953 strike, reveal a great deal about the approach to labor taken by Getúlio Vargas. First, it is significant that Getúlio had appointed Vianna and his predecessor even though neither was as actively prolabor as the first poststrike labor minister, the controversial future trabalhista president João "Jango" Goulart.

In his comments, Vianna makes clear his disapproval of the "Strike of the 300,000," which he viewed, then and later, as an illegal and Communist-infiltrated movement. It was for precisely this reason, he recalls, that he refused to meet with a delegation of strike leaders when his airplane stopped in São Paulo on its way back to the capital. Having made his point, however, he then told strike leaders that they could meet with him in Rio de Janeiro but only in their capacity as union officials. Satisfied with such symbolic niceties, he ends his account by referring to his own initiatives through the Delegacia Regional do Trabalho in São Paulo to reach a settlement of the strike (Valentina da Rocha Lima, ed., *Getúlio: Uma História Oral* [Rio de Janeiro: Record, 1986], 179–80; "Greve dos Teçelões").

Left to his own devices, Vianna hints, he might have favored more drastic action against the strike in São Paulo. Indeed, shortly thereafter, on the eve of leaving the Labor Ministry, he proposed to draft maritime workers into the navy in order to halt a planned strike—an action prevented by Goulart, who viewed it as "impolitic." Yet in explaining his contrary course of action vis-à-vis the São Paulo movement, Vianna directly referred to *Vargas's* preferred approach to labor issues. When faced with a serious labor problem, he recalls, Vargas always recommended that care be taken "not to hurt the country's economy, but [at the same time he also recommended] that one should not react solely to meet the demands of the Simonsens, the industrialists of São Paulo." This careful balancing act was quite distinct from the partisan antilabor stance adopted by Dutra (Lima, *Getúlio*, 180).

12. In a well-known essay, Kenneth Erickson asked: "Why did workers succumb to the blandishments of populist politicians if the latter did not move the locus of political power down the social pyramid?" Simply restated, he implicitly asked "Why don't workers vote right (left)?" The answer, he believed, stemmed from their lack of "class consciousness," which led them to only "dimly" perceive class relations ("Populism and Political Control of the Working Class in Brazil," *Proceedings of the Pacific Coast Council on Latin American Studies* 4 [1975]: 127, 129). An examination of mass working-class voting from the perspective of "revolution," however, distorts the broad, very practical rationality behind workers' choices at the ballot box.

13. Marcos Gasparian, *O Industrial* (São Paulo: Martins, 1973), 55, 78.

14. Mario Miranda Pacheco, "El Populismo en Bolivia," in *El Populismo en América Latina*, ed. Werner Altman et al. (Mexico, D.F.: UNAM, 1983), 123, 130.

15. Drawing on his personal experience as an aide to Goulart in the early 1960s, Darcy Ribeiro provides a wonderful cutting vignette of the populist politicians of Adhemar's sort; observing that the populist label has often been applied with little attention to the differences among those so classified, he insists upon distinguishing "populists" like Adhemar from "reformists" like Vargas (*O Dilemma da América Latina: Estruturas de Poder e Forças Insurgentes* [Petrópolis: Vozes, 1978], 154–62). I prefer nonetheless to continue using the term "populist" to discuss both groups "as part of the same populist universe" (Octavio Ianni, *Crisis in Brazil* [New York: Columbia University Press, 1970], 94). Ribeiro's distinction can be reformulated as the difference between a more purely electoral populism and a more purely reformist populism.

Those populist leaders who sought to implement social reforms faced a dilemma. To overcome the resistance of those who held economic power, they had no choice but to tolerate, if not support, the large-scale mobilization of workers. Thus, in the end, reformist populists like Getúlio Vargas encouraged the social conflict they abhorred. In thus facilitating popular mobilization, later trabalhista leaders like Jango Goulart aroused the enmity of the powerful economic and political forces who would have their day after the coup of 1964 that ended the Populist Republic.

16. In an interesting essay, Werner Altman demonstrates that there was indeed

an ideological dimension to classic populist discourse in the 1930s and 1940s ("Cárdenas, Vargas y Peron: Una Confluencia Populista," in Altman et al., *Populismo*, 43–96).

17. E. Bradford Burns emphasizes the parallels between Getúlio Vargas and Adhemar de Barros; citing their common "mass popular following," he suggests incorrectly that both "appealed directly and openly to workers, informing them of their power and advising them how to use it" (*A History of Brazil*, 2d ed. [New York: Columbia University Press, 1980], 451). While correctly characterizing trabalhismo, the emphasis on organized popular support is associated with reformist populists and not with electoral populists such as Adhemar.

18. Populist politicians, a trabalhista labor minister under Goulart recalled in 1968, "were at the same time supporters essentially of the status quo and fomentors of actions by the masses" (interview by Robert Alexander with Almino Affonso, 16 July 1968, Santiago, Chile; in private archive of Robert Alexander).

19. Mario Miranda Pacheco, "El Populismo en Bolivia," in Altman et al., *Populismo*, 130.

20. As legal analyst Tamara Lothian has recently suggested, the corporatist model of labor relations, although pioneered by right-wing authoritarian regimes, has often proved in practice to contribute to the emergence of a vigorous, independent, and politicized labor movement ("The Political Consequences of Labor Law Regimes: The Contractualist and Corporatist Models Compared," *Cardozo Law Review* 7 [1986]: 1003). See also the revisionist essay by Leôncio Martins Rodrigues, "O Sindicalismo Corporativo no Brasil," in idem, *Partidos e Sindicatos* (São Paulo: Ática, 1990), 46–76.

21. Paulo Sérgio Pinheiro, *Política e Trabalho no Brasil, dos Anos Vinte à 1930* (São Paulo: Paz e Terra, 1975), 10.

22. Paul Drake, "Populism in South America," *Latin American Research Review* 17 (1982): 190–99.

23. Charles W. Anderson, "The Concepts of Race and Class and the Explanation of Latin American Politics," in *Race and Class in Latin America*, ed. Magnus Mörner (New York: Columbia University Press, 1970), 235–36, 250–51.

24. The failure to grasp this transformation explains the "terminological inexactitude" that has drawn comment by all students of populism. Discussing efforts at definition, Margaret Canovan points out that the "common features of 'populist' movements [that are identified] are really common features of modern political movements in general," including socialist and labor parties. The result, she notes, is a "nebulous and distended concept of populism" ("Two Strategies for the Study of Populism," *Political Studies* 30 [1982]: 547).

25. See my forthcoming book, *The Metalworkers of ABC*.

Index

60, 263–64, 266–67, 270, 274–75, 277–78, 358 (n. 19), 360–61 (n. 7); biography, 203, 348 (n. 79); search for urban allies in ABC, 204–9; alliance with the PCB, 209–10, 340 (n. 32), 347 (n. 73); 1947 election results, 210–13; relationship with labor movement as governor, 213–20, 345 (nn. 46, 47); break with the PCB, 220–24, 347 (n. 74)

Barros-Loureiro ceramics factory, 95. *See also* Louças Adelinas

Berle, Adolph A., Jr., 115, 121–22, 124–25, 321 (n. 88)

Bezerra, Gregorio, 239–40

Bittencourt, Abelcio, 148

Blacklisting, 43–44, 59, 178. *See also* Repression, employer or government

Borda do Campo, 107, 123, 126, 182, 249, 269

Borghi, Hugo, 176, 200, 203–4, 209–12, 214, 239, 258, 277, 318 (n. 47), 343 (n. 16), 346 (n. 55)

Botani, Olivério, 48

Braga, Antônio, 208–9, 245, 344 (n. 31)

Cabrera, Antônio, 227

Caires de Brito, Milton, 237, 351 (n. 29)

Callejon, Maria, 70

Calzolari, Pedro, 185

Câmara de deputados (chamber of deputies, federal congress), 68, 77, 181, 249, 260, 351 (n. 29)

Câmara Municipal de Santo André (CMSA; Municipal Council of Santo André), 244–50, 264, 269, 270

Camargo, Agenor de, 20

Campanella, Anacleto, 263–64, 358 (n. 26)

Cardia, Luis Fiuz, 326 (n. 29)

Cardoso Franco, Saladino, 47, 185

Carestia (high cost of living), 31, 94–95, 133–34, 137–38, 153, 167, 172, 201, 203, 205–6, 217, 229–30

Carteiras profissionais (worker identification cards that serve as working papers), 42, 49, 52, 84

Carvalho Sobrinho, José de, 106, 169, 182, 201, 208

Cassação (cancellation): *de registro* (of a party's electoral registry) 182, 189, 221–22, 232–33, 236, 259, 261, 264, 340 (n. 31), 351–52 (n. 32); *de mandatos* (of electoral mandates), 223, 237–38, 248–49, 260, 262–63, 351 (n. 28), 353 (n. 44). *See also* Anticommunism; Partido Comunista do Brasil

Castellani, Constantino, 42–43, 48, 233, 250

Castro, Benedito de, 265

Castro Gomes, Angela de, 70, 93–94

Cavalcanti, Deocleciano Hollanda de, 150, 167, 190, 326 (n. 29), 341–42 (n. 44), 344–45 (n. 39)

Centro de Estudos e Defesa do Petróleo Nacional (Center for the Study and Defense of National Oil), 115, 264, 350 (n. 20). *See also* Nationalism

Centro de Indústrias do Estado de São Paulo (CIESP; Center of Industries of the State of São Paulo). *See* Federação das Indústrias do Estado de São Paulo

Centro dos Industriais de Fiação e Tecelagem de São Paulo (CIFTSP; Center of Weaving and Spinning Industrialists of São Paulo), 23–24, 44, 164, 172

Cerâmica São Caetano, 75–76, 78, 106, 134, 168, 201, 211–12, 227

Ceramics industry, workers, and unions, 75–76, 78, 146, 148, 174, 177, 242. *See also* Albino da Rocha, Artur; Cerâmica São Caetano; Civil construction and industrial ceramics union of Santo André

Chemical industry, workers, and union: 48, 50, 52, 67, 84, 146, 148,

Immigration, 11–12, 19, 22, 47, 251–
52, 280, 292 (n. 10)
Imparcial, 165, 208
Imposition thesis, 49, 300 (n. 25). *See
also* Outorga thesis
Impôsto sindical (union tax), 5, 82,
88–89, 148–49, 174, 217–18
Indirect action. *See* Struggle, working-
class, forms of: direct and indirect
action
Industrial health and safety, 58, 60,
62, 71–72, 135, 147, 228, 305
(n. 11)
Industrialists, labor, and government,
23–24, 43–44, 53–55, 60, 72–78,
96, 117, 144, 155–56, 164–65, 168,
170–74, 184, 208, 234, 250, 253,
255, 258–59, 273, 276–77, 279,
311 (n. 65), 343 (n. 6). *See also* Arruda Pereira, Armando de;
Federação das Indústrias do Estado
de São Paulo; Simonsen, Roberto;
Street, Jorge; Welfare capitalism
Industrialization, 78, 114, 109, 117–
18, 216, 230–31, 251–53, 279–81,
346 (n. 57)
Industrial proletariat, 27–30, 32–33,
41–42, 49–52, 56–57, 67, 73–74,
251–53, 257, 282, 294 (n. 32)
Indústrias Aliberti, 134
Indústrias Reunidas Francisco
Matarazzo, 177, 358 (n. 26)
Instituto de Aposentadorias e Pensões
dos Industriários (IAPI; Industrial
Employees' Pension and Retirement
Institute), 84, 136, 138
Integralists, 77, 90, 123, 137
Interparty accord of 1948, 260, 265–67
Ipiranguinha, 19–23, 42, 48, 70–73,
96, 156–58, 162, 291 (n. 3), 301–2
(n. 47)
Irmãos Corazza, 65–66

Jogo de bicho (numbers game), 207
Jornal de São Caetano, 201, 264
Jundiaí, 43, 165

Kowarick, 23, 90

Labor and electoral politics, 5, 38, 40,
57–59, 62, 112–13, 130, 181, 192–
93, 195, 199–200, 209, 225, 236–
46 passim, 254, 257–59, 327
(n. 37). *See also* Electoral participation; Ex officio voter registration;
Partido Comunista do Brasil; Partido
Trabalhista Brasileiro
Labor and the state, 4–5, 6–7, 13,
23–25, 28, 31–32, 37, 39–40, 49,
51–52, 59–61, 65–66, 76–77, 79–
80, 82–88, 95–97, 112, 116–17,
136–37, 146–49, 171–72, 180,
186–87, 191–94, 228, 279, 290
(n. 47), 329 (n. 1), 341 (n. 39). *See
also* Labor courts; Trade unions: legalization of
Labor courts (labor justice system),
49, 79, 82, 85–88, 110, 147–49,
157–58, 171–72, 178, 192, 208,
216, 255, 276 309–10 (nn. 58, 59,
60, 63), 348–49 (n. 11), 357
(n. 11). *See also Dissídios coletivos;
Dissídios individuais*
Labor discourse, 59, 96, 148–49, 179,
181, 228, 245–46
Labor law enforcement, 55–56, 59–
62, 65–66, 68, 79, 85, 96, 135, 168,
192, 255, 271, 310 (n. 62), 311
(n. 66), 331 (n. 17). See also *Dissídios individuais*; Labor courts
Labor markets, 44, 47, 49, 61, 95,
133, 135, 137
Labor Ministry. *See* Ministério do Trabalho, Indústria, e Comércio
Lagoa, Francisco de Paula da Rocha,
221
Laminação Nacional de Metais, 95–
97, 166–68, 171–72, 178, 183, 227,
335 (n. 56), 355 (n. 69)
Leather products and tanning workers, 146, 148
Lei de Segurança Nacional (LSN; National Security Law), 237, 264